About Island Press

Since 1984, the nonprofit organization Island Press has been stimulating, shaping, and communicating ideas that are essential for solving environmental problems worldwide. With more than 800 titles in print and some 40 new releases each year, we are the nation's leading publisher on environmental issues. We identify innovative thinkers and emerging trends in the environmental field. We work with world-renowned experts and authors to develop cross-disciplinary solutions to environmental challenges.

Island Press designs and executes educational campaigns in conjunction with our authors to communicate their critical messages in print, in person, and online using the latest technologies, innovative programs, and the media. Our goal is to reach targeted audiences—scientists, policymakers, environmental advocates, urban planners, the media, and concerned citizens— with information that can be used to create the framework for long-term ecological health and human well-being.

Island Press gratefully acknowledges major support of our work by The Agua Fund, The Andrew W. Mellon Foundation, Betsy & Jesse Fink Foundation, The Bobolink Foundation, The Curtis and Edith Munson Foundation, Forrest C. and Frances H. Lattner Foundation, G.O. Forward Fund of the Saint Paul Foundation, Gordon and Betty Moore Foundation, The JPB Foundation, The Kresge Foundation, The Margaret A. Cargill Foundation, New Mexico Water Initiative, a project of Hanuman Foundation, The Overbrook Foundation, The S.D. Bechtel, Jr. Foundation, The Summit Charitable Foundation, Inc., V. Kann Rasmussen Foundation, The Wallace Alexander Gerbode Foundation, and other generous supporters.

The opinions expressed in this book are those of the author(s) and do not necessarily reflect the views of our supporters.

The End of Automobile Dependence

The End of Automobile Dependence

How Cities Are Moving Beyond Car-Based Planning

Peter Newman and Jeffrey Kenworthy

Washington | Covelo | London

Island Press is a trademark of The Center for Resource Economics.

   Library of Congress Control Number: 2014958512

✹ Printed on recycled, acid-free paper

Manufactured in the United States of America
10 9 8 7 6 5 4 3 2 1

Keywords: Automobile city, climate change, decoupling theory, Global Cities Database, light rail, heavy rail, high-speed rail, Marchetti's constant, metro rail, sustainability and cities, transit city, transportation modeling, transportation planning, urban density, urban fabrics, walking city

To my family—Jan, Christy, Renee, and Sam—who have come along with me on this 40-year journey to understand cities and their transport . . . and helped beyond their imagining. And to our grandchildren—Josie, Lilah, and Arish—who will be in their forties in 2050.

—*Peter Newman*

This book is dedicated to my mother, Roma Marjorie Hayward (nee Walker), whose strong emphasis on education, hard work, and conscientiousness has allowed me to focus on what is important in the world and hopefully to contribute something to it. Thank you for your undying support, self-sacrifice, and belief in me. And thank you especially for giving me the opportunity to have the education and the life that, as an intelligent and talented young girl growing up in Australia in the 1930s and '40s, you were never able to have. Whatever good a book such as this may do, you are part of that.

—*Jeff Kenworthy*

Contents

Preface: The Trilogy

In 1989, we published *Cities and Automobile Dependence*, which was based on a decade of data collection and a short lifetime of urban experiences. We had both lived in a city based upon the car, and we had glimpsed that perhaps it was not as edifying as cities could be. Twenty-five years later we are convinced. But now we have an army of supporters, and cities everywhere are showing that it is a mistake to give over cities to the car. We all know that cars are useful, but when cities are built to depend on them it becomes clear that cars are good servants but bad masters.

Perhaps more importantly, in 1989 we also published "Gasoline Consumption and Cities" in the *Journal of the American Planning Association* (Newman & Kenworthy 1989a). This had been rejected when it was first submitted, but a new editor had found it in the files and she was immediately intrigued by the data showing the large differences among the world's cities in their degree of automobile dependence. The publication released a storm of outrage. How could we attack the American shibboleth of a car-based culture? We suggested that cities were not so much automobile dependent because they were wealthy and could afford it, but because they had prioritized the car in every aspect of their physical development, in particular through urban sprawl, the development of urban freeways, and ignoring walking, cycling, and urban transit. They therefore needed to reorient their transportation priorities and to "re-urbanize" rather than suburbanize.

The emotional reaction was something to behold when, in the next issue of *JAPA*, we were rocked by the rhetoric of Gordon and Richardson (1989):

The idea of planners turning our world upside down in pursuit of a single-minded goal is as horrible as it is alien. NK's world is the Kafkaesque nightmare that Hayek (1945) always dreaded, a world in which consumers have no voice, relative prices have no rule, and planners are tyrants. . . . NK have written a troubling paper. Their distortions are not innocent, because the uninformed may use them as ammunition to support expensive plans for central-city revitalization and rail-transit projects or stringent land-use controls in a futile attempt to enforce urban compactness. . . . Perhaps Newman and Kenworthy would be well advised to seek out another planet, preferably unpopulated, where they can build their compact cities from scratch with solar-powered transit. (p. 342, 344, 345)

Although we were severely taken aback by such responses, we slowly realized that underlying the critique there was a lot at stake in the politics of land development and transportation priorities. Indeed, the horrible nightmare future they railed against seemed pretty good to us—and to an increasing group of urban dwellers worldwide. Wherever we went in automobile-dependent cities there were NGOs and local governments using our book and papers to show why and how they must build rail projects and revitalize central cities. The talks we gave to the people we met throughout North America, Australia, Asia, and Europe revealed a mounting tsunami of dissatisfaction with the shortcomings of cities built predominantly around the automobile. It gradually became clearer that the vision we had put forward was not as alien as Gordon and Richardson had attempted to cast it, not even in the United States. Thus we continued to gather data, life experiences, and a lot of telling visual evidence about how cities could deal with automobile dependence.

This second stage in our work culminated in 1999 with the publication of *Sustainability and Cities: Overcoming Automobile Dependence*, which was launched at the White House (Newman and Kenworthy 1999a). There were many stories of hope from cities around the world seeking to modify their automobile dependence. The book has helped to set the agenda for city planning ever since (Banister 2006).

A lot of changes took place in automobile-dependent cities in Australia and Canada as we began to look more to Europe than the United States for our urban models. The United States also began to change, however; for example, New Urbanism, Smart Growth, and the Intermodal Surface Transportation Efficiency Act of 1991 (ISTEA) all came to the fore as part of a major urban reform movement designed to produce the more compact, transit-oriented development patterns and provide funding for the more extensive rail-based transit systems that we had spoken about in our original book and article. Nations and cities everywhere began competing to reduce their automobile-dependence in central-city revitalization, new transit projects, and associated transit-oriented developments (TODs). The transition away from automobile dependence was under way

This book, *The End of Automobile Dependence*, is now the third stage in the trilogy.

We are witnessing a new phenomenon where cities are showing "peak car use," urban rail is thriving, suburban sprawl is reversing, and central cities have revitalized and are attracting young people to live, work, and play. Many cities (including Vancouver, Los Angeles, and Washington) have become more polycentric, with significant sub-centers based around rail-transit systems built in the last 30 years or so. Cities such as San Francisco, Paris, and Seoul are even studying how urban rail, in conjunction with the tearing down of major freeway infrastructure, can help to revitalize urban environments. Walking and cycling are again on the increase in many cities, as are ubiquitous bike-sharing schemes, which have led to central cities like Melbourne, Seattle, Chicago, and New York having new investment and vitality. Electrically assisted bicycles (pedelecs), which greatly extend the comfortable range of a normal pushbike, are growing in popularity among both private owners and, increasingly, in bike-sharing schemes. Smart-city technology is enabling sustainable transport modes to become more competitive.

We are thus in a new era that has come much faster than we had predicted: the end of automobile dependence. The planning paradigm that enabled cities to be built around the car is now virtually dead; a different kind of city can now be envisaged and each day sees more evidence of its reality being implemented for economic, environmental, and social reasons. Perhaps the only horror from Gordon and Richardson not to happen is the "stringent land-use controls in a futile attempt to enforce urban compactness"; instead it is the opposite, as well-located suburbs enforce low-density controls in a desperate fight to stop market forces from redeveloping at higher densities. There isn't much "solar-powered transit" either (yet), just a few examples like Calgary, with its light-rail system running on wind energy (Ride the Wind), and several Indian rail projects that are to be solar powered.

So this is the third book in the Trilogy on Automobile Dependence. As in all good trilogies, we have seen the rise of an empire (in this case, that of the automobile) and the peak of its power, and now we are seeing the decline of that empire.

We have called this the "end" of automobile dependence rather than just the "decline" for several reasons. We should emphasize that we are not claiming the end of the "automobile," only the elimination of *dependence* on it. This is a very big difference. Most developed cities are showing a decline in vehicle–kilometers traveled (VKT) per capita and even total automobile travel, but they are still dominated by the car; in these cities there is still no real option other than a car in most parts of the city. We believe that all cities, if they are to be competitive, viable, and sustainable, will need to go beyond automobile dependence to a future where the vast majority of urban areas have options by which people will not have to use a car for all journeys. In other words, they will no longer be *dependent* on the car. When this happens in a city there are still a lot of cars around—but the character of the city has changed.

Already we are seeing that some parts of cities—the old walking and transit city areas—are having a revival as they have become the site of all the knowledge-economy jobs that require highly efficient land use and highly intensive modes servicing them: rail, bikes, and walking. Those areas of the city where cars predominate tend to have an economy that is mostly oriented to consumption rather than to creative, innovative jobs and services; it is to the latter realm that young people are flocking to live, work, and play. With such economic drivers in place, the end of automobile dependence is not likely to reverse.

It will take considerable analysis to show what we mean, but most people can tell when they go to a city where automobile dependence is not built into its very fabric. It is different in quality. Although there will likely still be a lot of cars in all future cities, they are likely to be carbon-free and, in our view, they will be part of a mobility system that enables freedom and connection—not dependence. This is the end of automobile dependence, and most of all it means an end to the twentieth-century planning paradigm that assumes car dependence in all of its rules, planning tools, and visions for urban development. This book will therefore set out to show how cities are rapidly moving beyond automobile-dependent planning, and it will present a few ideas on how we can keep the momentum going.

Acknowledgments

The authors wish to thank many people who have directly and indirectly assisted in making this book possible. First of all, we would not have been able to write this book without the quantitative data that underpins our analyses of cities around the world. The basis of this work dates back a few years and especially to the indispensible and timely support given by the Helen and William Mazer Foundation in New Jersey, which kindly provided two grants to help provide needed research assistance to ensure that the collection of data for 2005 could continue. In particular, we are very grateful to Steve Bercu from the Foundation for his support and his commitment to sustainable transportation.

Ms. Monika Brunetti provided invaluable research assistance over six years, helping to collect the cities data and managing all the data records for the research. This is a large task and we have many meters of tall bookshelves full of thick files documenting all the data collected. We also owe a great debt to our research assistant Phil Webster for his tireless attention to detail. Phil has been a rock of support in helping us to prepare the graphic material in the book, managing the referencing system for us, and generally being on call to attend to many details.

There are many friends who have provided insight and literature to keep us going in our quest to understand automobile dependence. These include: John Whitelegg, Mike Day, Robert Cervero, Jan Gehl, Tim Beatley, Annie Matan, Jeb Brugman, Mike Mouritz, Matthew Bradley, Preston Schiller, Eric Bruun, and many others too numerous to name.

There are literally hundreds of people worldwide without whose generous support the data collection for this book would not have been possible. There are simply too many to name here. But in general, without the willing help of government people located in planning, transportation, environmental, statistical, and other departments worldwide it is simply impossible to assemble the data we have put together for this book. This is because so many of the items are just not available on websites or in standard publications, but must be sought from those whose day-to-day work revolves around, for example, running and managing traffic models in cities. To these countless people we say thank you for your patience and goodwill, and we hope that in some small way your efforts are rewarded by the value we hope we have added to your data in bringing so many cities together in one place and in a standardized way.

This book also draws on the original work of others, which we have referenced in this book. But in particular we want to acknowledge: the true comaraderie of Curtin University Sustainability Policy (CUSP) Institute, for its wonderful support for our research, especially Christine Finlay; Dr. James MacIntosh and Dr. Roman Trubka from CUSP, for their work on transit-oriented development, value capture, and the modeling of trends in car-vehicle-kilometers of travel; and Mr. Leo Kosonen from Kuopio in Finland, for his original work on the theory of urban fabrics, which we have developed together and have used in this book.

Finally, we want to sincerely thank our editor, Heather Boyer of Island Press, without whose help this book would not have been possible. Thank you for your tireless and insightful guidance in developing and focusing our key messages and in shaping the book's structure.

1

The Rise and Fall of Automobile Dependence

In the early twentieth century, automobiles began to be used in cities as a convenient replacement for horse-drawn carriages. Henry Ford's mass-produced Model T, the most influential automobile in history, was sold between 1908 and 1927. With the assistance of a rapidly growing and ever more powerful consortium of automobile interests such as General Motors and Firestone Tires, American cities as early as the 1920s began to tear out their streetcar (tram) systems, thus sowing the seeds for the automobile's usurping of local transportation. Through this process, New York had lost most of its extensive surface streetcar system by 1926 (Klein & Olson 1996). However, car usage was never really central to city shaping in any urban area until after the 1940s, when major freeway and parking infrastructure began to be built entirely for the automobile. In American cities this process accelerated after 1956 with the establishment of the Highway Trust Fund, which used a dedicated gasoline tax to accumulate prodigious sums of money for freeway building in order to facilitate their vast car-dependent suburbs. A similar process occurred in those Australian cities that, in our data, have developed most closely to the American model.

For the previous hundred years in all cities of the now "developed world," trains and trams were the dominant city-shaping transport system, and before that it was walking. During World War II, urban tram systems in particular were still overwhelmingly popular (due, in part, to gasoline rationing), but they fell into a rapid decline thereafter as more and more systems were torn up throughout the world. (See chapter 4 for an expansion of this as the theory of urban fabrics.)

The development of automobile dependence in cities is a complex process, enacted over decades of land-use and infrastructure development linked to the dominant economic waves of innovation (Freeman 1996; Hargroves & Smith 2005; Newman et al. 2009). Over many years much has been written on this by the big thinkers on cities, such as Mumford (1961), Jacobs (1961), and Schneider (1979), who have all traced these processes in different ways and have all shown the problems that result from reshaping cities totally around cars. Thomson (1977) developed typologies for cities based on their dominant urban form and transportation systems; one such type was the automobile city, which he termed "full motorization." No matter how they are described, cities built around the car have many serious problems related to the costs of sprawl and to the costs of transport, including the oil vulnerability issues that seem to have been a major factor in causing the global financial crisis, or GFC (Newman & Kenworthy 1999a, 2011a).

The environmental and social impacts from automobile dependence have been the major focus of twentieth-century urban transport writing, with an assumption that economic outcomes were favored by the car but these externalities should be considered. However, the twenty-first century is showing a very different perspective, with the environmental and social impacts worsening (congestion and carbon emissions as well as a growing list of health impacts, including obesity and depression in sprawling suburbs), and the economic aspects of automobile dependence are now tipping toward redevelopment and sustainable transport modes (Newman & Matan 2012b; Trubka et al. 2010a, 2010b; Glaeser 2011). New data will be used in this book to address these matters, especially the economic perspective, as cities are now competing on how quickly they can reduce their automobile dependence.

Although they did attempt to bring a little data to support their ideas about the way cities evolve and function from a transportation perspective, mid-twentieth-century contributions from urban scholars remained largely conceptual on issues related to car-based planning. There remained a need for sound and systematic data on cities to provide an adequate perspective on the evolution of their transportation systems. In fact, such data are rare until around 1960, when transportation engineers in urban governments began to collect data for the "science" of transportation planning and modeling.

Our own data-collection work commenced in the late 1970s, when we attempted to collect systematic data back to 1960 on transportation, land use, infrastructure, and energy (see Kenworthy et al. 1999 and Newman & Kenworthy 1999a for a complete perspective on our Global Cities Database). Using a highly standardized

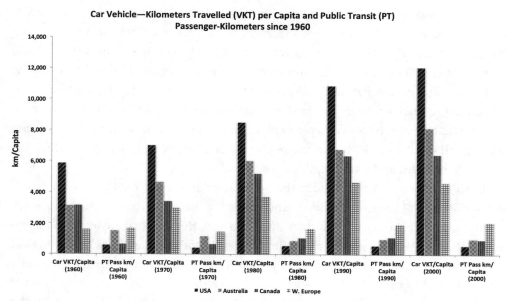

Figure 1-1. Trends in car vehicle kilometers-traveled and public transit passenger-kilometers per capita in 26 cities, by region, from 1960 to 2000. Source: Authors' own data

process, we have continued to collect data on a wide variety of global cities, though in many cities and regions the data-gathering process continues to be too difficult. For that reason, there are, for example, no Latin American, African, or low-income Asian cities included in our comparison of world cities in this book, although some new data on Sao Paulo and Taipei are presented in chapter 3.

Using the Global Cities Database, we have now pieced together the most comprehensive data set possible from 1960 to 2000 on 26 cities across the world.[1] The data, set out in the table in the appendix, are provided to show how universal was the growth in vehicle-kilometers-traveled (VKT) across different cities and regions. The first signs of a plateau appear in the last decade of the twentieth century (see figure 1-1 for this perspective from our urban data, and figure 1-3 for this in the USA as a whole). Canadian and European cities plateaued, Australian and US cities slowed. US cities grew 2,200 kilometers 1980 to 1990, but only 1,000 kilometers 1990 to 2000, with San Francisco, Los Angeles, and Phoenix showing no growth. (The peak was starting.)

We examined this 40 year trend of growth in VKT to determine the factors that best explain why it occurred.[2] In the transportation planning community there is some disagreement about the causes of VKT growth, and analysis of this unique database provides a chance to resolve the matter. There is no doubt that cultural changes and motoring costs are contributors, but the biggest points of contention seem to be whether transit services or density are significant factors, and how the provision of road space contributes to the trends (Kirwan 1992; Breheny 1995; Boarnet & Crane 2001; Mindali et al. 2004; Coevering & Schwanen 2006; Gordon & Richardson 2007; Mees 2009a, 2009b). The explanatory data we have assembled across this 40-year period to explain automobile VKT per capita cover population size, centralization (percentage of metropolitan jobs in the central business district, or CBD), urban density, public transit service levels per capita and the proportion of that service representing rail modes, public transit use per capita, parking availability in the CBD, cars per 1,000 persons, and road length per capita.

In this chapter and throughout the book we examine the data on recent trends in car use and rail use in the world's cities, as well as density changes. However, these trends are chosen from each country's own data and, though they are likely to be reliable in themselves, they are not all on the same scale and comparable as in our original Global Cities Database (Newman & Kenworthy 1999a). Thus in chapter 2 we look at a smaller sample of cities that have been carefully placed on the same data scales in order to achieve a more scientifically correct understanding of the trends, as shown in the 1960–2000 data analysis above and below.

The Causes of the Twentieth-Century Rise and Plateau in Automobile Dependence

The data in the table in the appendix address the question of the underlying causes of automobile dependence (for details see McIntosh et al. 2014). Findings suggest that the two most significant indicators of levels of car use are urban density and transit service levels, with a minor role played by road length per capita (see figure 1-2). In chapter 6 we provide a further discussion of the issue of urban density versus transit service levels in trying to understand transportation patterns, as this is a major debate in the literature that needs to be resolved (for example, see Mees 2009a, 2009b; Newman & Kenworthy 2011c).

The data also very clearly demonstrate that rail-based transit services are the most strikingly linked to reduction in car VKT per capita. Thus, cities seeking to limit car dependence should be investing in quality rail systems and building up urban densities around them, rather than increasing road capacity—just as Gordon and Richardson (1989) suspected but found abhorrent. The data suggest that growth in car use occurred in the midcentury period because transit services and density were allowed to drop, but by the end of the century car use began to plateau as transit services and density began growing again. These two factors continue to be critical to our story on car dependence, as they have been for the past 30 years.

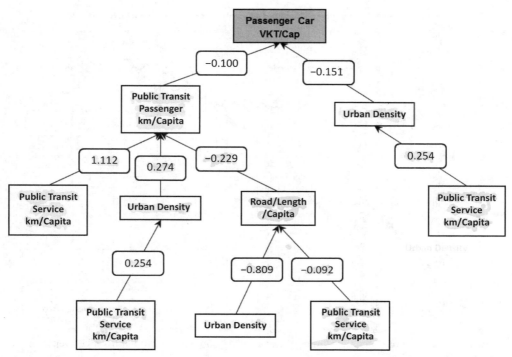

Figure 1-2. Determinants of car VKT per capita in cities based on an analysis of urban data from 1960 to 2000, showing the significance of public transit services and density. Source: McIntosh et al. (2014).

The Fall of Automobile Dependence in the Twenty-First Century

In 2009, the Brookings Institution in Washington, D.C., was the first to recognize a new phenomenon in the world's developed cities: declines in car use (Puentes & Tomer 2009). "Peak car use" suggests that we have reached the peak of growth in car use and the end of building cities around cars as the primary goal of planning—at least in the developed world. The twenty-first century is witnessing the end of automobile dependence in the same countries and cities that gave birth to it.

Puentes and Tomer (2009) showed that between 2004 and 2010 an absolute decline in car use was evident. Figure 1-3 shows this peaking in the US vehicle–miles of travel. Sivak (2015) found that these trends continued into 2013.

Stanley and Barrett (2010) found a similar trend in Australian cities at a similar time: car use peaked in 2004. We have since mapped this in all Australian cities, including small ones (Canberra) where congestion is no issue (figure 1-4). Car use per capita continued to trend down (Newman & Kenworthy 2011b).

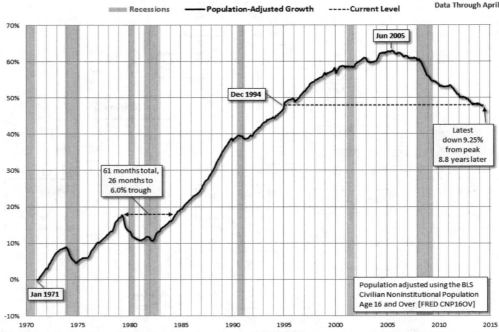

Figure 1-3. Peaking of US vehicle–miles of travel (VMT). Source: Compiled from US Department of Transportation data.

Millard-Ball and Schipper (2010) examined the trends in eight industrialized countries that demonstrate what they call "peak travel." Figure 1-5 shows this for six of the countries.

Millard-Ball and Schipper conclude:

> Despite the substantial cross-national differences, one striking commonality emerges: travel activity has reached a plateau in all eight countries in this analysis. The plateau is even more pronounced when considering only private vehicle use, which has declined in recent years in most of the eight countries. . . . Most aggregate energy forecasts and many regional travel demand models are based on the core assumption that travel demand will continue to rise in line with income. As we have shown in the paper, this assumption is one that planners and policy makers should treat with extreme caution. (p. 372)

It is possible to see similar data on many countries worldwide. Gargett (2012) provides a comprehensive examination of a time series of car-use data, which shows a similar peaking of car use in a number of nations. This has become accepted by some economists, who see it as a part of decoupling GDP from car use

Figure 1-4. Peaking of car use in Australian cities. Source: Newman and Kenworthy (2011).

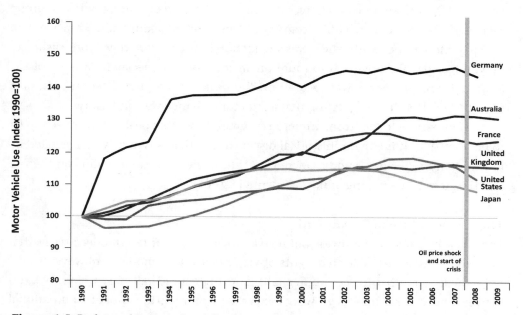

Figure 1-5. Peak travel in six industrialized nations. Source: Millard-Ball and Schipper (2010).

in more-developed nations; certainly it is obvious in the very wealthy centers of big cities like New York and London. The *Times* reported that in Central London traffic fell by 19 percent between 2000 and 2009, and further noted: "Supporters of 'Peak-Car' theory see a future in which the inner cities are given over to pedestrians, cyclists, and public transport, and café culture replaces car culture. . . ."[3] A PricewaterhouseCoopers real estate report suggests that there has been a structural change in Canadian cities: Canadians are moving back into cities in growing numbers in search of a live/work/play urban environment rather than car-based commutes stuck in traffic.[4] In Toronto, the central city has added 300,000 people to the population and has 150 high-rise towers about to be built.[5]

In chapter 3 we will show evidence that the peak in car use is not necessarily occurring just in wealthy cities; indeed, where policies to improve transit services and increase densities are made, then cities change quite rapidly in their car dependence, even in the emerging cities of the world. In the United States there have been many newspaper articles and websites discussing the peak car-use phenomenon and especially the cultural issues associated with it. The PIRG Report (Davis et al. 2012) that interviewed young people from across America found that they valued their mobile phones more than cars. An article titled "Cars Are So Yesterday: Young and Rich Leave Guzzlers Behind" showed that "from 2001 to 2009, car use by 16- to 34-year-olds decreased from 10,300 miles to 7,900 miles per capita—a drop of 23 percent."[6] Modal share (the choice of transportation type) among this age group increased 100 percent in public transit, 122 percent in biking, and 37 percent in walking. More importantly, there was a reduction in the need to travel long distances by younger people moving into more urban locations. A special 2013 issue of the journal *Transport Reviews* was focused on the peak car-use phenomenon with data from the world's cities suggesting that a structural change was underway.

In summary, evidence from numerous sources shows that peak car use does appear to be occurring. It is a major historical discontinuity that was largely unpredicted by most urban professionals and academics. At the same time, urban rail is on the rise and this, too, is happening at unprecedented rates.

The Rise and Rise of Urban Rail
There is now a major worldwide rail revival, including light rail (modern trams that can run on streets or dedicated rights-of-way), metro rail (modern subways), heavy rail (usually suburban or commuter rail), and high-speed rail (fast trains that run between cities). This reflects growing concerns by municipal, regional, and national governments about the need to make their transportation systems more sustainable,

their cities more livable, and their economies more resilient to future shocks from oil vulnerability and from the need to reduce CO_2 emissions in the face of global warming (Newman et al. 2009).

The multiple advantages of modern urban rail are clearly attractive to policy makers. Hass-Klau et al. (2003, 2004), Litman (2004), and Kenworthy (2008) have summarized the major advantages of rail, especially its ability to use much less space than car-based infrastructure (a rail line can carry up to 20 times as many people as a freeway lane), its comparatively low impact (if well designed), and its potential to generate funding opportunities through land-value capture (covered in detail in chapter 6) and hence ease its cost.[7]

Many of these advantages have been known for some time, but rail systems in the twentieth century did not grow anything like they have in the twenty-first century. So the surprise is how dramatically successful these urban rail systems now appear to be, with their patronage growth far exceeding expectations, in most cases. The rise of urban rail parallels the phenomenon of peak car use and is therefore linked in a very real way to the end of automobile dependence.

The following section of this chapter presents a wide range of data that collectively demonstrate that urban rail is experiencing a surge of popularity that is perhaps unparalleled since its golden age in the nineteenth century and the first half of the twentieth century. The data are presented first for the more traditionally rail-oriented dense cities of Europe, Asia, and the Middle East (a special analysis of Sao Paulo is provided in chapter 3), and then for the traditionally automobile-oriented cities of North America and Australia.

Emerging Rail Trends in Dense Cities of Europe, Asia, and the Middle East
The form of the data presented in this section varies. Although some data are raw and unadjusted for the effects of population growth, system expansion, and increases in rail-service levels, such increases in the availability of rail systems are themselves part of the current ascendency of rail and are therefore integral to the argument presented here. In short, rail systems are being expanded, they are increasing their service levels, and they are being better utilized.

1. Europe
In Europe, most cities were built around suburban rail systems that have been retained, though many European cities, especially in the United Kingdom, removed their urban tram systems in the 1950s and '60s. So the revival of light rail has been a major addition to rail in the majority of European cities. No fewer than 65 cities built new or

Table 1-1. Selected European countries with light-rail systems (2007).

Country	Cities	Total Light Rail Network Length (km)	Country	Cities	Net (km)
Austria	6	313	Poland	14	1,445
Belgium	5	332	Portugal	2	65
Croatia	2	57	Romania	14	461
Czech Republic	7	333	Sweden	3	186
France	11	202	Switzerland	2	112
Germany	56	2,768	Slovakia	3	68
Hungary	4	188	Spain	4	206
Italy	7	209	Turkey	5	66
The Netherlands	5	280	United Kingdom	7	156
Norway	2	47			

Source: Konig & Heipp (2012).

expanded light-rail systems between 1980 and 2007, bringing the total number of European cities with light rail at that time to over 160 (see table 1-1).[8] Further growth in light rail has continued since then, particularly in France, Spain, and Portugal.

New and expanded metro rail systems have also been added or are under construction in many of the larger European cities, including Paris, Madrid, Athens, London, Vienna, Stockholm, Munich, and Frankfurt. For example, since 2009 London has been building Crossrail, a new 118-kilometer rail system linking key parts of the city—Europe's largest construction project—scheduled to open in 2018, as well as the London Overground to provide a ring rail network around the city. Meanwhile Paris (the Ile-de-France) is completing an orbital metro to complement the extensive upgrades made to the radial metro and RER suburban rail networks.

Europe has also rapidly expanded its network of high-speed rail lines for intercity travel, with extensive networks in France, Germany, Spain, and Italy, and new lines planned or under construction in the United Kingdom, France, Turkey,

Sweden, and other countries. There are ongoing plans for a direct service from Frankfurt to London on a German ICE (Intercity Express), which will take less total time than it would to make the journey by air, allowing for travel to and from airports and waiting time in terminals. (Indeed, travel time has been a major factor in determining travel choices for centuries, and we'll return to this topic later, with further data on the continuing importance of the travel time budget.) Increasingly in this century, Europe has shown that rail has a future both within its cities and between them.

2. Middle East

A large expansion of rail systems is underway in the Middle East (Middle East Rail Market Report, 2012). For example:

- In Doha, Qatar, a four-line, 212-kilometer metro network is under construction, with the first section to be completed by 2019 and finished by 2026. Additional rail projects include an LRT line, the West Bay People Mover system, and a planned high-speed rail network linking Doha airport, Doha town center, and Bahrain.
- In Saudi Arabia, contracts were awarded in July 2013 for construction of a metro network for Riyadh, eventually planned to include six lines totaling 176 kilometers, with construction commencing in 2014. The Haramain high-speed rail line will be the region's first when it opens in 2014. Approval has also been given recently for a major metro system for Makkah (Mecca), with a planned length of 182 kilometers.
- In Dubai, a 75-kilometer metro is currently open with a plan for 108 kilometers, and an integrated light-rail and bus system is partly completed. The first LRT line opened in 2014 and more is under construction, with buses integrated at many stations.
- Other metros are planned for Kuwait, where a 160-kilometer, 69-station system with three lines is due for completion by 2020.
- Contracts will be awarded for a 131-kilometer metro system in Abu Dhabi in 2015, with the first phase to be completed in 2017.
- A pan–Gulf Cooperation Council (GCC) interlinking rail system is planned, with a current projected cost of about $30 billion. This network will include the first rail line linking all the GCC member states.[9] Congestion on road systems joining the individual Emirates is now legendary (e.g., from Dubai to Sharjah) and is one reason why Abu Dhabi has introduced a new law requiring every worker in Abu Dhabi to be a resident. Dubai is set to do the same. The pan-GCC rail system is also meant to help address the problem.

3. Asia

Asian cities have been urbanizing at a rapid pace. Coupled with rising incomes, this urbanization has led to an explosive growth in the number of cars and motorcycles and a decline in the use of bicycles and small vehicles. The densities of most Asian cities mean that mass-transit systems will need to handle an increasing share of traffic in response to congestion levels. The rationale for building new systems usually specifies the multiple advantages of rail, both environmental and social, but in particular the economic advantages. A large number of Asian cities have responded with what is the biggest rail boom since the original railway age in the late nineteenth century in Europe and America. For example:

- Singapore has built a highly efficient mass-transit system encompassing metros and automated light-rail feeders, complemented by buses, and carefully integrated with land-use planning for major developments to be concentrated at stations on the rail network.
- Hong Kong has also built a major, modern high-capacity metro network that includes a high-speed metro line to the new airport. It has also built a successful LRT system in the New Territories.
- Kuala Lumpur, Bangkok, Manila, Delhi, Kolkata, Mumbai, Seoul, Taipei, and other major Asian cities have added a variety of rail-based systems, including above-ground metros or monorails, underground metros, and light-rail systems.
- India opened its first metro in Kolkata in 1984 and now has five cities with metro systems; there were plans or actual construction work in a further 22 cities up to 2021 (based on a population cut-off of 2 million and above), but then in 2014 the new prime minister, Narendra Modi, lowered the population cut-off to 1 million so now there are 46 Indian cities building metros. This means that, with rapid growth in their smaller cities, India could have 87 cities with metros by 2031.
- China has seen the largest expansion. In 1969, China had only one metro, in Beijing, which was expanded in 2008 for the Olympics and became a model for other Chinese cities. Shanghai was the second city to open a metro, in 1993, and expanded their system rapidly in recent years; it has built some 14 metro lines in the last two decades. Beijing and Shanghai now have two of the world's largest systems, with 9 million and 8 million passengers a day, respectively. These two cities set the example; between 1997 and 2013, only a 16-year period, China opened metros in 17 additional cities. As of 2014, there were a further 20 metros under construction, while an additional 23 cities have approved, planned, or proposed metro construction projects.[10] Overall, between 1993 and 2014 China has installed or planned metro systems at the rate of about three per year. Dozens

of cities have added light rail. China has also built the world's largest high-speed rail network in the last 15 years (with over 11,500 km), adding to the networks in countries such as Japan, Korea, and Taiwan.

What is clear from the trends discussed above is that denser cities in Europe, the Middle East, and Asia appear to be drawn to the multiple advantages of developing rail systems. Megacities are building metros because of their ability to manage high-capacity mobility in narrow spaces, and small cities are building light-rail systems at city sizes that previously were not thought to be viable (see below). All of them are significantly faster than the traffic-congested streets of these rapidly growing cities.

Emerging Rail Trends in Traditionally Car-Dependent Cities

The trend back to rail is perhaps to be expected in the relatively dense cities and countries in Europe, the Middle East, and Asia that have traditionally been less car-dependent and where rail rather than roads can be rationalized simply in terms of spatial limits. Perhaps the more surprising trends have been in the United States, Canada, and Australia, where traditionally car-dependent cities, once considered suitable only for bus transit in their suburbs, are now seeing a future based around rail.

In particular, light rail is emerging as the core of the mass-transit system in medium-size but relatively low-density cities such as Portland (Oregon, USA), Edmonton and Calgary (Alberta, Canada), and the Gold Coast (Queensland, Australia). Ottawa, a traditionally bus-only city using busways as the main spine of its system, is moving more toward rail due to capacity problems. It has one 8-kilometer light-rail line (opened in 2001) but is currently constructing a further 12.5-kilometer light-rail metro with 13 stations. In larger and higher-density cities such as San Francisco, Toronto, or Sydney, light rail is emerging as a secondary system to support heavy-rail/metro systems and is particularly suited to shorter-distance radial corridors in inner suburbs, to circumferential or ring routes, or to radial corridors to secondary centers.

1. United States

There has been a significant resurgence in mass transit in the United States, with patronage as estimated by APTA (the American Public Transportation Association) now 23 percent higher than in 1993 and growing faster than car usage. The growth has been particularly strong since about 2003, and it has continued since 2008 despite the significant economic downturn in the United States due to the global financial crisis, which resulted in declining economic growth, increasing unemployment, and significant financial pressures on urban transit systems, as well as a reduced ability for individuals to buy and use cars.

However, it is interesting that all of the growth in patronage since 1993 has been on rail-based modes (heavy rail, commuter rail, light rail). In contrast, total patronage on bus-based modes (bus, trolleybus, demand-responsive transit[11]) has been essentially static in terms of overall patronage (see figure 1-6).

As shown in figure 1-7, light rail has had the fastest growth rate of any mode, almost tripling patronage between 1993 and 2011, though from a low base.

As a result of the differential in growth rates, rail modes have increased their shares of total patronage, particularly heavy rail (from about 25 percent to 35 percent of the total), while the bus share has significantly declined, from 65 percent to 50 percent. Bradley and Kenworthy (2012) address in detail the issue of bus failure in terms of the lack of congestion pricing, but the data are also discussed in this book in terms of the lower spatial efficiencies of buses and cars compared with rail, cycling, and walking.

Unlike bus patronage, the patronage on light rail has increased rapidly from a relatively small base of 168 million to 481 million over the same period, passing the patronage on commuter rail (which has also increased relatively rapidly). The number of light-rail systems in the United States has grown from 15 in 1995 to 29 in 2014. This increase in LRT patronage has occurred despite the fact that not all LRT lines are on dedicated rights-of-way. Some lines or sections of lines operate in mixed traffic and thus suffer the same problems as most bus systems, but they still seem to be more popular.

Figure 1-8 breaks the above data into three groups:
- *"Legacy" systems.* These are in cities that kept at least part of their original tram/light-rail systems, and subsequently built on these (they include cities such as Baltimore, Boston, New Orleans, Philadelphia, Cleveland, and Buffalo).
- *"Early wave" systems.* These are in cities that opened their first light-rail lines by 1990 (this includes cities such as San Diego, Portland, Oregon, Pittsburgh, San Jose, Sacramento, and Los Angeles).
- *"Post-1990" systems.* These are cities that opened their first light-rail lines after 1990. This group includes cities such as St. Louis, Denver, Dallas, Seattle, and Salt Lake City.

As can be seen, the cities with "legacy" systems had roughly static patronage until 2004, but patronage has grown around 25 percent since then. The "early wave" cities saw more than a doubling of patronage, while further growth has come from the "post-1990" systems in the increasing number of cities with light rail in the last 25 years, as well as from expansion of already established LRT networks.

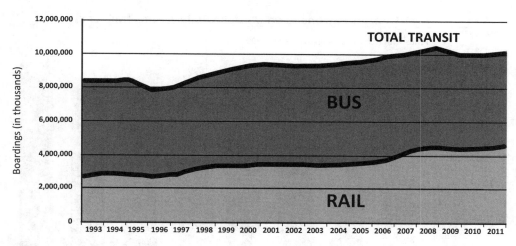

Figure 1-6. Annual patronage by bus-based and rail-based transit systems in the United States, 1993–2011. Source: Compiled from APTA data.

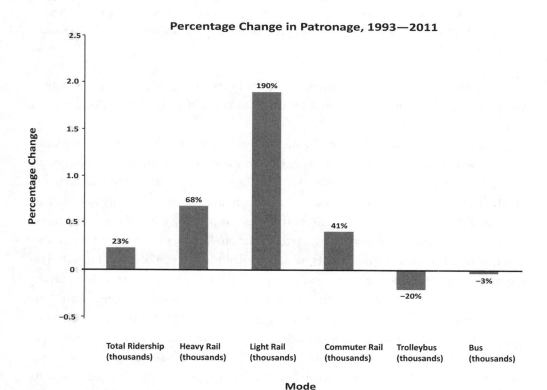

Figure 1-7. Percentage changes in patronage of public transit modes in the United States, 1993–2011. Source: Compiled from APTA data.

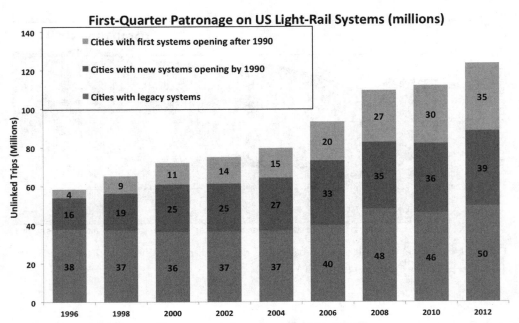

Figure 1-8. Different types of US light-rail systems and their patronage, 1996–2012. Source: Compiled from APTA data.

The cities with the fastest growth in light-rail patronage are Portland, Oregon, Los Angeles, and Newark, with first-quarter patronage from 1996 to 2012 shown in Figure 1-9.

Separating trends in patronage by mode, figure 1-10 shows trends for Portland, Oregon, which is one of the cities with the fastest growth in overall public transit use in US cities. As is apparent, essentially all the growth in patronage has occurred on light rail, with bus volumes static. The implementation of LRT in Portland in 1986 and the later addition of a streetcar system, especially through the revitalized Pearl District, were accompanied by dramatic improvements in the downtown area and nearby city-street environments, which contributed to the boost in rail use. The improvements include the conversion of parking lots to city squares, the tearing down of the Harbor Freeway along the waterfront and its replacement with Tom McCall Park, new farmers' markets, the widening of footpaths, the introduction of high-quality street furniture and artwork, and a revival of downtown residential development. People rediscovered their central city and pre-automobile inner areas by using a convenient public transit option. The experience of Portland has thus shown another important qualitative aspect of LRT: it gives the opportunity to radically change the dynamics of street use in favor of pedestrians and cyclists, and it can

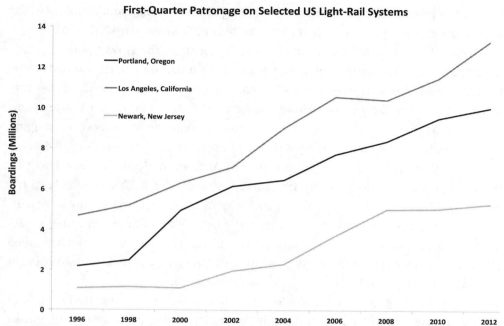

Figure 1-9. Patronage of LRT in Portland, Oregon, Los Angeles and Newark, 1996–2012. Source: Compiled from APTA data.

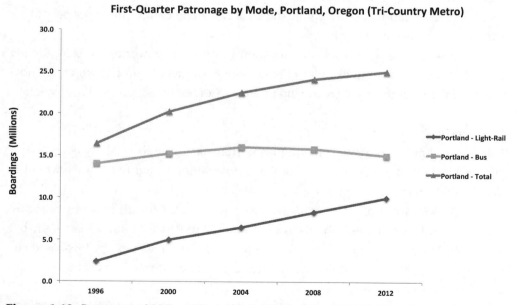

Figure 1-10. Patronage of LRT and buses in Portland, Oregon, 1996–2012. Source: Compiled from APTA data.

be part of a process involving a major upgrading of urban design and livability in the neighborhoods it serves (Gehl 2010; Schiller, Bruun, & Kenworthy 2010).

Overall, the patronage data from US cities demonstrate the growing role of public transit, especially rail-based modes, in handling the urban transportation task in the United States, although overall travel remains heavily car dominated. It also suggests that there is likely to be further strong growth in public transit patronage in the future, as there are still significant investments occurring in many cities, ranging from upgrades to the metros in New York and Chicago, to significant expansions of light rail and other systems in cities from Los Angeles to Houston. Even Phoenix, one of the lowest-density cities in the United States, opened a 32-kilometer light-rail line in 2008 and has plans to expand it. Many of these expanding transit systems continue to gain voter support, notwithstanding the difficult financial situation facing many city and state governments; however, there are also some projects killed off by state governors in Florida, Wisconsin, and New Jersey. The important topic of funding rail systems is returned to in detail in chapter 6.

The American Public Transportation Association (APTA) has reported that 2013 saw the greatest use of public transit by Americans since 1956, with total transit use of 10.7 billion trips nationwide, up a further 5 percent from the 10.2 billion in 2011.[12] The same article, from the president of APTA, states that: "There is a fundamental shift going on in the way we move about our communities. People in record numbers are demanding more public transit services and communities are benefiting with strong economic growth."[13]

Similar patronage trends are also apparent in other "new world" cities in Canada and Australia, which have historically been heavily car-dependent but which are now investing significantly in rail-based (and in some cases bus-based) public transit systems.

2. Australia

Patronage of public transit is growing faster than car usage in virtually every major city in Australia, and car usage per capita is now falling in many cities (Newman & Kenworthy 2011b; see figure 1-4).

The growth in public transit patronage has occurred for all modes (see figure 1-11), but with the highest growth in suburban rail in Perth, suburban and light-rail growth in Melbourne, and suburban rail and bus use in Brisbane. The bus-based cities of Canberra, Hobart, and Darwin did not grow in public transit patronage despite also showing peak car use.

The contrast in the growth in rail use between Perth and Adelaide is striking (see figure 1-12). Perth opened the 74-kilometer Southern Rail line (to Mandurah) in

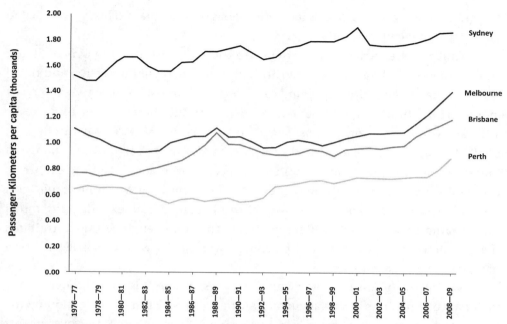

Figure 1-11. Per capita public transit travel (passenger-kilometers) in Australian cities, 1976–2008. Source: Compiled from BITRE (2011) data.

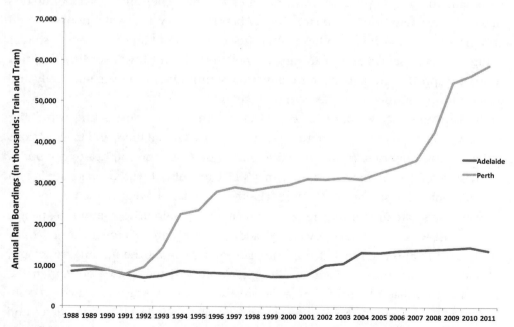

Figure 1-12. Annual rail boardings in Perth and Adelaide, 1988–2011. Source: Compiled from data provided in the annual reports of Perth and Adelaide rail operators.

December 2007, while Adelaide's rail network has been stagnant. This is examined in more detail in chapters 4 and 5.

Australian cities reflect similar trends to those occurring in the United States, where urban sprawl has slowed, densities in inner areas are increasing, and travel behavior has begun shifting from cars to public transit and active transport modes. The future for automobile-dependent cities is therefore not likely to be a linear extrapolation of the postwar period, which for 50 years saw declines in public transit patronage and rapid rises in car use. Another sign of the change in Australia has been the financial failure of recent toll roads, including the Cross City and Lane Cove Tunnels in Sydney, and the Clem 7 tunnel in Brisbane, with early signs that the Airport Road Tunnel in Brisbane is also experiencing much lower traffic than forecast (Goldberg 2012). The traffic-engineering consultants that predicted the growth in toll patronage were so far wrong that legal action has been taken against them.

Governments in Australia are beginning to respond to this shift through moves to enhance public transit. Infrastructure Australia, in a historic intervention by the Federal Government, provided over half of its funds to urban rail. State governments have generally hedged their bets with plans for major new railways and new freeways, but this is a big change from previous decades where highways dominated funding. The new prime minister, Tony Abbott, has reversed this, however, and announced a series of multi-billion-dollar freeways without any cost-benefit studies being done and said that "urban rail was not in their knitting." Nevertheless, this has not stopped some state governments from continuing to pursue politically and economically sensible rail projects in their cities:

• In Sydney, the New South Wales (NSW) government is constructing two major heavy-rail extensions, the South West and North West Rail links, and to extensions of the small light-rail system into the inner west, CBD, and southeastern suburbs. In March 2014, an extension of Sydney's LRT to Dulwich Hill opened, adding an additional nine stations to the line. The resulting patronage increase was so overwhelming that announcements had to be made by train drivers imploring people to please wait for the next service.[14] In addition, a second rail crossing over Sydney harbor has also been included in the plan, though as yet the funding, timetable, and design are unclear. Light-rail lines in Western Sydney, based on Parramatta, and in the adjacent city of Newcastle, are also under investigation based on committed funds from the NSW government. The heavy-rail fleet is being updated and expanded, and a new approach promises much closer integration among rail, bus, ferry, and light-rail modes.

- In Melbourne, there have been incremental extensions to the heavy- and light-rail systems, some additional trains and buses, and improved bus services in the outer suburbs. However, despite rapid increases in patronage the improvements have not kept up with the rapid growth in demand, and there have been significant complaints regarding the reliability and quality of services. Planning is continuing for a new heavy-rail line through the CBD to provide additional capacity, and work is under way on the first stages. The state government will share the AUD$4-billion price tag with the federal government.

- In Perth, the rail system has been significantly expanded with the 74-kilometer Mandurah rail line to the south, which opened in 2007, as well as extensions to the Joondalup line to the north, which opened initially in 1993, and increased rolling stock to cope with much higher demand than was expected. The original system (three lines) was electrified in 1991, thus increasing its operating speed significantly. However, rolling stock has only just kept pace with the very rapid growth in demand, which has seen rail patronage increase tenfold, as shown in figure 1-12. The Western Australian state government has, however, announced its intention to build a AUD$1-billion airport rail and a further AUD$1-billion light-rail network for the CBD and inner suburbs, which will help to handle demand from these areas and support more sustainable land-use patterns. Figure 1-12 also shows how rail can stagnate when it is based on a slow diesel service with no expansion, as has been the case in Adelaide for the past decade—though Adelaide's heavy-rail system south, newly electrified and extended, reopened in late 2014, and its light rail has also now been successfully extended.

- In Brisbane, there have been some extensions to the rail network (the Gold Coast line and the Springfield line) with more extensions planned (to Redcliff and potentially the Sunshine Coast). There has also been significant expenditure on a busway network, including an underground link through the CBD for buses, necessitated by the volumes of buses entering the city on surface streets and causing major congestion. Planning for a major new rail line through the CBD—the Cross River Rail link—has been finalized, but as in Sydney, no funding or timetable has been announced.

- In the Gold Coast, a $1-billion light-rail line was completed in 2014 and has shown very high patronage levels. The project was a Public Private Partnership (PPP) based on a local transport levy.

- In Canberra, plans for light rail are progressing; funding has been resolved, and construction will begin in 2016. Similar concept plans are under discussion in Hobart, Darwin, Bendigo, Cairns, and other smaller regional cities.

The overall global picture suggests an increased focus on rail. Governments are generally recognizing the crucial need to further upgrade, expand, and extend urban rail systems. There seems to be a global shift in the new urban paradigm that is consistent with the trends in car use and the new economy of cities.

The End of Automobile Dependence: Why?

The century-long growth in the use of the automobile in cities appears to have plateaued and is now beginning to decline across the world's developed cities (Goodwin & Melia 2011; Goodwin & Van Dender 2013; Gargett 2012; Newman & Kenworthy 2011b). At the same time, public transit, cycling, and walking have all rapidly increased—and most importantly—people have begun to move back into the city in areas that are not car-dependent. These new trends set in before the global financial crisis (GFC) and are approaching a decade with little sign of reversing. Why?

1. The Price of Fuel

The decline in car use occurred simultaneously in 2004 across many cities when oil reached $80 per barrel. From a plateau, car use then dropped significantly when oil reached $140 per barrel in 2008 and propelled the world's cities into the global financial crisis (GFC), especially the vulnerable car-dependent outer suburbs (Leinberger 2011). Australian cities were buffered from much of the GFC due to a combination of quick capital infusion by the government, well-regulated banks, and China's continuing demand for resources. Nevertheless, a significant decline in Australian car use per capita continued from 2004 to the present, and rail use in most cities grew from that period (although it mostly grew where new rail investment had coincided with this period of car-use decline and high fuel prices). Such data suggest that the supply of rail options and also demand reductions in car use due to fuel prices are likely to be part of the explanation for peak car use, consistent with the analysis from the Global Cities Database outlined at the start of this chapter.

The vulnerability of outer suburbs to increasing fuel prices was noted in the first fuel crisis in 1973–74 and in all subsequent fuel-crisis periods when fuel price volatility was clearly reflected in real estate values, with outer suburbs losing value compared to inner areas (Fels & Munson 1974; Romanos 1978). Despite the global recession, the twenty-first century has been faced by a consolidation of fuel prices at the upper end of those experienced in the last 50 years of automobile city growth. Oil commentators, including oil companies, now admit that the era of cheap oil may have ended, even if they do not fully accept the peak-oil phenomenon (Newman, Beatley, & Boyer 2009). The elasticities associated with fuel price are obviously going to contribute to reducing car use, though few economists would have suggested that these price increases were enough to cause peak car use, which set in well before the 2008 peak of $140 a barrel. As fuel prices dropped dramatically in early 2015, it will be of interest to see whether the peak-car phenomenon continues or whether the structural issues outlined here will continue to end automobile dependence (see chapter 8 for more on this).

2. Hitting the Traffic Wall

Cesare Marchetti was the first to recognize that residents in all cities have a similar average daily travel time budget of around one hour (Marchetti 1994). This seems to be biologically based in humans: they don't like to take more out of their day than around an hour just to get to their workplaces and back home. Thus, we have applied this understanding to the technology of city building (Newman & Kenworthy 1999a, 1999b) to show that people always "hit the wall" (that is, exhaust their tolerance) when cities are more than 50 kilometers or "one hour wide." Pedestrians hit the wall after 3–4 kilometers; mass-transit riders hit the wall after 20–30 kilometers (though fast rail can go much farther); and drivers hit the wall after about 50 kilometers. Beyond 50 kilometers, traffic becomes a major issue. As cities have filled with cars, the limit to the spread of the city has become more and more apparent, with the politics of road rage becoming a bigger part of everyday life and many people choosing to live closer to amenities. Fast trains have been the only technology to break this car-based limit, though they are restricted in their origins and destinations in cities built around cars and soon hit the wall also.

The travel-time budget limit is observable in most automobile-dependent cities where the politics of transportation have been based on the inability of getting sufficient road capacity to keep automobile travel under one hour to meet the average daily travel-time budget. The automobile-based city seems to have hit the traffic wall. There has been a shift to providing faster and higher-capacity public transit based on the growing demand to go around traffic-congested corridors or to service the growing inner-city districts. At the same time, the politics of planning in the past decade have turned irrevocably to enabling greater redevelopment and regeneration of suburbs at higher densities. This approach will be expanded into a more general theory in chapter 4.

3. The Exponential Link between Public Transit and Automobile Use

The extraordinary revival of public transit outlined above is obviously going to play a part in the decline of car use and vice versa. But how are they linked?

Our data has always shown that transit and car use are linked exponentially, as shown in figure 1-13. Items are "exponentially related" if they grow or decline more dramatically than in a simple one-to-one relationship. Thus when one passenger leaves a rail service and starts driving, they increase their travel kilometers by a lot more than what they had previously used on the train. Transportation planners always saw the growth in public transit as a small part of the overall transportation task and believed that car-use growth would continue unabated. However, the exponential relationship between car use and public transit use, as shown in figure 1-13, indicates how significant the impact of public transit can be. By increasing public transit use per capita, the use of cars per capita is predicted to go down exponentially. This is the so-called transit leverage effect (Neff 1996; Newman et al. 2008), in which people walking to and from public transit complete other trips such as shopping or child-care collection, enabling one transit trip to replace a range of car trips. In transportation, this is called "trip-chaining." This drives other changes, such as selling a second car or moving closer to public transit or amenities. Thus, even small increases in public transit use can begin to put a large dent in car-use growth and eventually will cause it to peak and decline.

4. The Exponential Link between Density and Automobile Use
If density increases then car use will decrease exponentially, according to the graph we have popularized over many decades. Figure 1-14 shows this relationship between density and car use through the energy used per capita for private-passenger transportation. Thus, as cities begin to regenerate and to redevelop existing areas faster than they are opening up new areas further out, a range of car-use-reduction mechanisms begin to kick in: distances become shorter; walking, cycling, and public transit all become more viable due to time savings, and businesses begin to locate nearer to the people who have shifted. This is density leverage.

But is density increasing in global cities? Chris Leinberger has studied the historic population shift back into US cities—a twenty-first-century phenomenon that has been accelerated by the oil-price generated GFC:

> In the late 1990s, high-end outer suburbs contained most of the expensive housing in the United States, as measured by price per square foot. Today, the most expensive housing is in the high-density, pedestrian-friendly neighborhoods of the center city and inner suburbs. Simply put, there has been a profound structural shift—a reversal of what took place in the 1950s, when drivable suburbs boomed and flourished as center cities emptied and withered. (Leinberger 2011)

This reinvestment in cities has led to increases in density, reversing the declines that characterized the growth phase of automobile-dependent cities in the past 50

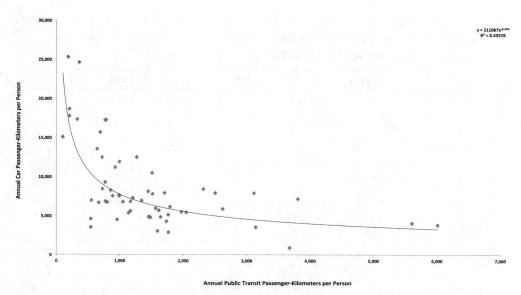

Figure 1-13. The exponential link between car use and public transit showing the "transit leverage" effect in developed cities, 1995. Source: Authors' own data.

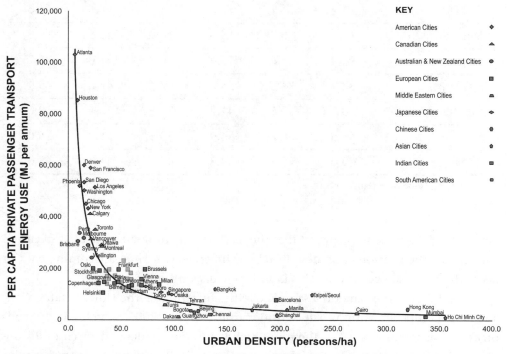

Figure 1-14. Rapid decline in car use per capita with increasing urban density, as reflected through energy use, 1995. Source: Authors' own data.

Table 1-2. Trends in urban density (persons per hectare) in some US, Canadian, Australian, and European cities, 1960–2005.

Cities	1960	1970	1980	1990	1995	2005
Brisbane	21.0	11.3	10.2	9.8	9.6	9.7
Melbourne	20.3	18.1	16.4	14.9	13.7	15.6
Perth	15.6	12.2	10.8	10.6	10.9	11.3
Sydney	21.3	19.2	17.6	16.8	18.9	19.5
Chicago	24.0	20.3	17.5	16.6	16.8	16.9
Denver	18.6	13.8	11.9	12.8	15.1	14.7
Houston	10.2	12.0	8.9	9.5	8.8	9.6
Los Angeles	22.3	25.0	24.4	23.9	24.1	27.6
New York	22.5	22.6	19.8	19.2	18.0	19.2
Phoenix	8.6	8.6	8.5	10.5	10.4	10.9
San Diego	11.7	12.1	10.8	13.1	14.5	14.6
San Francisco	16.5	16.9	15.5	16.0	20.5	19.8
Vancouver	24.9	21.6	18.4	20.8	21.6	25.2
Frankfurt	87.2	74.6	54.0	47.6	47.6	45.9
Hamburg	68.3	57.5	41.7	39.8	38.4	38.0
Munich	56.6	68.2	56.9	53.6	55.7	55.0
Zurich	60.0	58.3	53.7	47.1	44.3	43.0

Source: Authors' own data.

years. Our data on density suggest that the nadir in declining urban density occurred even before the phenomenon described by Leinberger. Our cities are coming back in faster than they are going out. This is a historic discontinuity.

Table 1-2 contains data on a sample of cities in Australia, the United States, Canada, and Europe showing urban densities from 1960 to 2005, which clearly demonstrate this turning point in the more highly automobile-dependent cities. In the small sample of European cities, densities are still declining due to "shrinkage" or absolute reductions in population, as well as increases in peri-urban development

(Nilsson et al. 2014). In general, the European data show the rate of decline in urban density slowing down and almost stabilizing as re-urbanization occurs.

In Sydney in the twenty-first century, a dramatic reversal has occurred in where population is being accommodated. After 100 years of urban sprawl, the city is turning back inward (see table 1-3).

Table 1-3. Population change in Sydney, 2001–2011.

	Population (in thousands)			% Change
	2001	2011	Change	
Inner Sydney	991	1,144	+153	+15.4%
Middle Sydney	2,289	2,559	+270	+11.8%
Far outer Sydney	848	903	+55	+6.5%

Source: Compiled from ABS (2001 and 2011) census data.

The relationship between density and car use / energy use is an exponential function, as shown in figure 1-14. If a city begins to slowly increase its density, then the impact can be more extensive on car use than expected. Density not only reduces travel distances and times, but is also a multiplier on the use of transit and walking/cycling. Increases in density can result in greater mixing of land uses to meet peoples' needs nearby. This is seen, for example, in the return of small supermarkets to the central business districts of cities as residential populations increase and demand local shopping opportunities within an easy walk. Overall, this reversal of urban sprawl will undermine the growth in car use.

5. The Aging of Cities

The average age of people living in the cities of the developed world has been increasing. People who are older tend to drive less, with people in their seventies driving about half as much as those in their twenties to fifties (see Davis et al. 2012). Therefore, cities that are aging are likely to show lower car use. But the fact that car use in all American and Australian cities began declining around 2004 suggests there were other factors at work, as not all cities in these places are aging at similar rates. The younger cities of Brisbane and Perth in Australia peaked in 2004, at the same time as the older cities.

6. The Growth of a Culture of Urbanism

One of the reasons that older-aged city populations drive less is that older people move back into cities from the suburbs: the so-called empty-nester syndrome. This was largely not predicted at the height of the automobile-dependence growth phase, nor was it seen that the children growing up in the suburbs would begin flocking back into the cities rather than continuing the life of car dependence (Leinberger 2007; Florida 2010). This has now been underway for over a decade, and the data presented by the Brookings Institution suggest that it is a major contributor to the peak-car-use phenomenon (Puentes & Tomer 2009).

Leinberger quotes a National Association of Realtors survey showing that presently only 12 percent of future home buyers in the United States want to buy car-dependent suburban houses (Leinberger 2011). The market behind this trend is a combination of baby boomers and millennials, according to Leinberger: "The shift is durable and lasting because of a major demographic event: the convergence of the two largest generations in American history, the baby boomers (born between 1946 and 1964) and the millennials (born between 1979 and 1996), which today represent half of the total population" (2011). This trend reveals the end of car dependence in a far more direct way than any travel survey, as it obviates the need for a car.[15]

Urban commentators suggest that this return to the city is not just a passing fashion but a structural change based on the opportunities that are provided by greater urbanism (Glaeser 2010; Florida 2010; Hardesty 2013; also, see figure 1-15). The need for closer creative connections in a services / knowledge-oriented economy is driving the need for this change. The cultural change associated with this urbanism is reflected in the *Friends* TV series, not the *Father Knows Best* series of the earlier suburban generation. The shift in attitudes to car dependence is also apparent in Australia (Newman & Newman 2006). The underlying economic drivers are affecting cities around the world and are expressed in spatial and transportation patterns that will be elaborated further in this book.

Interdependencies in Six Factors

It is not hard to see that the six factors involved in understanding peak car use are all interwoven and interdependent and can result in multiplicative effects that are greater than the sum of the individual parts. For example:

1. The growing price of oil may have been a substantive factor in pushing the trend to reduce cars, though the other structural factors around the culture and economics of urbanism were also pulling the trend along.
2. The re-urbanization of car-based cities and the reorientation of transport priorities

Figure 1-15. The growing culture of urbanism for all ages in Portland's Pearl District redevelopment. Source: Jeff Kenworthy.

around transit, walking, and cycling are policies that feed on each other; once one begins the other tends to follow, and together they can set in motion exponential declines in car use.

3. The motivation to move to a more urban location with less car dependence can stem from a combination of time saved in the travel-time budget, fuel saved, a preference for urbanism, and even getting older.

Underneath all these is an economic driver that reflects the spatial efficiencies of non-car modes and associated land uses. Intensive urban economic activity requiring close human interactions (now called the knowledge economy) require intensive land uses, and such accessibility requires intensive modes (rail, walking, and biking) that enable large numbers of people to be brought together and that themselves take up minimal urban space.

For the reasons discussed above, in the past few decades the urban planning

profession has been developing alternative plans for automobile cities with the rationale of reducing car dependence involving all of the above factors; few would have
thought they would be quite so successful, perhaps because each of the factors had
such interactivity and reinforcing effects.

Map of the Book
Chapter 1 has outlined the phenomenon of peak car use, the rise and rise of rail in
the world's cities, and the increase in urban densities as cities turn back inward to
redevelop rather than going farther and farther out. These patterns appear to suggest the end of automobile dependence. Some patterns that might explain why this
is happening have been suggested, but much more analysis is needed. There are
also many implications for further enabling such a process. Here is how we have
approached these matters in the chapters that follow.

- Chapter 2 provides a more scientific assessment of the end of automobile dependence, based on a comparison of 44 cities that uses the comprehensive and accurate data of the Global Cities Database, which we have been developing, extending, and updating since 1979. This will also enable us to pursue in detail such
  emerging factors as the decoupling of wealth and car use. The chapter will focus
  on cities in more-developed and wealthier parts of the world. It also opens the discussion of what levels of car use can be called an end to automobile dependence.
- Chapter 3 sets out some new data on emerging cities in midrange economies as
  well as in China and India. These cities are also showing signs of reaching the plateau in automobile dependence, as they have reached spatial limits much sooner
  than expected.
- Chapter 4 seeks to understand how the end of automobile dependence is occurring, and what are its roots in economic, political, and cultural systems as
  expressed in terms of a new theory of urban fabrics. This will enable us to discuss
  how the end of automobile dependence can be facilitated and guided toward the
  most productive and sustainable outcomes. The chapter stresses that we have
  three cities within each city, and each needs a different approach in this time
  of transition. It sets out what all automobile-dependent cities should be doing
  to ensure that they can manage this transition and pursue policies enabling the
  old walking city fabrics (and those of new centers seeking to be more walkable),
  rejuvenating transit city fabrics (including new transit city expansions), and promoting the kind of policies that can work in the newer automobile city fabrics.
  Chapter 4 suggests different car-use targets for each type of urban fabric in order
  to accelerate the end of automobile dependence.

- Chapter 5 examines the role of transportation modeling and planning in the creation of automobile dependence and both how this modeling needs to change if it is to better reflect new trends and also how cities can move beyond car-based planning. The chapter suggests that only by considering the nuances of different urban fabrics with different transportation and land-use needs will transportation planning be able to recreate its role in guiding cities into the future.

- Chapter 6 examines some of the chief barriers to enabling cities to manage the transition to reduced automobile dependence. The chapter does so by examining five questions that confront most cities trying to overcome automobile dependence: How important is density compared with transit services in reducing automobile dependence? What are the myths and truths about the impacts of density? Can density be "greened"? What are alternative ways of funding transit? And how fair is it for transit systems not to price congestion?

- Chapter 7 shows how we can accelerate the achievement of a new urban planning paradigm for the twenty-first century, one that no longer assumes automobile dependence, but instead actively designs urban environments that can function reliably and conveniently on alternative modes, with the automobile playing a very much reduced and more manageable role in urban transportation—and a more refined, more civilized role. Citizens, government, and industry all play a part, but work best when they are integrated around this rapidly emerging urban vision.

- Finally, chapter 8 imagines what cities will be like when the end of automobile dependence has been achieved. In particular, this last chapter will analyze what automobile-dependent cities might be like in a future free of carbon emissions, as all cities must reduce carbon emissions by 80 percent by 2050 and 100 percent by 2100. The decoupling of wealth and automobile dependence is critical to understanding the overall decoupling of wealth and fossil fuels. Is it possible to imagine cities with 50 percent less car use as well as renewably based transportation for all our needs? Throughout the twenty-first century, the continuing reduction in oil-based automobile dependence will be essential—and now it can be envisioned.

2

Urban Transportation Patterns and Trends in Global Cities

We have been tracking automobile dependence in metropolitan areas since the late 1970s, beginning with data collection back to 1960. This places us in the unique position to provide a 45-year perspective on the development of automobile dependence, from 1960 to 2005. Chapter 1 provides this historical perspective for 26 cities using a set of more limited data that were consistently available back through all decades from 1960 to 2000. The present chapter focuses on a detailed examination of a much more comprehensive set of data variables for a sample of 44 cities in order to demonstrate clearly what has been happening in land use and transportation over the decade between 1995–96 and 2005–06, when car use peaked in many industrialized nations.

In our 1999 book, *Sustainability and Cities*, we provided an overview of the patterns of automobile dependence in 46 cities worldwide, using data from 1990. Subsequently we conducted a study for the UITP in Brussels entitled the *Millennium Cities Database for Sustainable Transport*, which contained completed data for 84 cities in nearly all regions of the world (Kenworthy & Laube 2001). Since 2007, we have undertaken to update the 1995–96 data to 2005–06 data on a selection of about half these cities covering a core set of variables. Such detailed data collection is extremely time consuming and labor intensive, and the updated data, partially reported in this chapter, have taken some six years to complete.

Cities examined in this chapter are all from wealthy regions and were chosen as our first targets for the update because they generally had better data available than did cities in less-developed regions. Rapidly developing cities in emerging economies, some of which we are working on now, generally need specialized assistance through research students and take longer to update, due to the much greater difficulty in assembling data (see appendix). Nevertheless, chapter 3 does contain some data perspectives on two such cities (Sao Paulo and Taipei), which we have been able to partially address so far.

The cities examined here in this chapter are presented in table 2-1. New Orleans, Portland, and Seattle are not included in the trend analysis for American cities, since data were only collected for the first time for 2005.

Throughout this chapter, tables and figures show some key data for cities in 2005–06, as well as the overall trends for cities in 1995–96 and 2005–06 in the different

Table 2-1. List of global cities examined in this chapter.

USA	Australia	Canada	Europe	Asia
Atlanta	Brisbane	Calgary	Berlin	Hong Kong
Chicago	Melbourne	Montreal	Bern	Singapore
Denver	Perth	Ottawa	Brussels	
Houston	Sydney	Toronto	Copenhagen	
Los Angeles		Vancouver	Düsseldorf	
New Orleans			Frankfurt	
New York			Geneva	
Phoenix			Graz	
Portland			Hamburg	
San Diego			Helsinki	
San Francisco			London	
Seattle			Madrid	
Washington			Manchester	
			Munich	
			Oslo	
			Prague	
			Stockholm	
			Stuttgart	
			Vienna	
			Zurich	

regions.[1] In order to explore these data systematically we have attempted to answer the following key questions:

1. How do cities in the United States, Canada, Australia, Europe, and prosperous parts of Asia compare in critical factors that characterize automobile dependence? Are they diverging, converging, or are they maintaining their differences?
2. Is urban wealth decoupling from automobile dependence?
3. What has been occurring in key factors that underpin automobile dependence, such as densities and centralization of work, transportation infrastructure, and transit service and performance?
4. How have mobility patterns changed in the use of cars, public transit, and non-motorized modes?
5. Have some of the major outcomes of urban passenger transportation systems, such as energy consumption, emissions, and fatalities, been reduced over the study period?
6. Taken collectively, and examining some linkages between these questions, is there any evidence for the end of automobile dependence in these predominantly wealthy cities?

An Overview of the Global Trends in Automobile Dependence

The 45-year data perspective shows that the average percentage increase in car vehicle-kilometers per capita in cities from 1960 to 1970 was 42 percent; from 1970 to 1980, 26 percent; and from 1980 to 1990, 23 percent (Newman & Kenworthy 2011b). This was clearly the great epoch of car-dependence growth in the world's major cities. Since then growth has ebbed. From 1995 to 2005 in the 41 cities we studied for trends, car use per capita increased on average by only 7.2 percent, or less than one-third what was typical in the 1980s, or one-sixth the growth level in the 1960s.

Trends from 1995 to 2005 for the 41 cities in the United States, Canada, Australia, Europe, and Asia are shown by region in table 2-2. Twenty-seven variables were examined, and we found the results below in relation to the trajectory of automobile dependence in these cities. A summary and discussion of the overall trends for all regions is provided in the conclusion to this chapter and summarized there in table 2-3.

Wealth, GDP, and Transportation

It has long been held that wealth is a key driver of urban mobility. As people become wealthier they travel more, especially by automobile. Lave (1992) cast this as an "irresistible force" and asserted that increasing car use is an inevitable and unavoidable outcome of increasing wealth; indeed, he saw the automobile as sitting atop a

Table 2-2. Trends in key automobile-dependence characteristics in major cities of the United

	USA 1995	2005	% Diff.	AUSTRALIA 1996
METROPOLITAN CHARACTERISTICS				
Urban density (people/HA)	14.9	15.4	3.4%	13.3
Activity density (people + jobs/HA)	22.4	23.6	4.9%	18.8
Proportion of jobs in CBD	9.2%	8.2%	-10.8%	13.3%
Metropolitan gross domestic product per capita	$31,386	$44,455	41.6%	$20,226
PRIVATE TRANSPORTATION INFRASTRUCTURE				
Length of freeway per person (M)	0.156	0.156	-0.2%	0.086
Parking spaces per 1,000 CBD jobs	555	487	-12.3%	367
Passenger cars per 1,000 persons	587	640	9.0%	591
TRANSIT INFRASTRUCTURE				
Total length of reserved public transit routes per 1,000 persons	48.7	71.7	47.0%	169.7
Ratio of segregated public transit infrastructure versus expressways	0.41	0.56	36.8%	2.18
TRANSIT SERVICE AND USE				
Total public transit seat kilometers of service per capita	1,566	1,874	19.7%	3,997
Total public transit passenger kilometers per capita	492	571	16.0%	966
Total rail passenger kilometers per capita	274	341	24.5%	638
MODAL SPEEDS				
Overall average speed ofpublic transit (KM/H)	27.3	27.3	-0.2%	32.5
Average speed of rail (metro and suburban rail) (KM/H)	45.1	47.6	5.5%	46.2
Average road network speed (KM/H)	49.3	50.4	2.3%	43.6
Ratio of public transit versus road-traffic speed	0.57	0.55	-4.7%	0.75
Ratio of rail speed to road-traffic speed (metro and suburban rail)[a]	0.96	0.95	-1.0%	1.06
MODAL SPLIT				
% of all daily trips by non-motorized modes	8.1%	9.5%	18.3%	14.9%
% of total motorized passenger kilometers on public transit	2.9%	3.2%	9.2%	7.5%
PRIVATE MOBILITY				
Passenger car passenger kilometers per capita	18,155	18,703	3.0%	12,114
Car kilometers per real 1995 USD of GDP	0.416	0.300	-27.9%	0.384
Total motorized passenger kilometers per real 1995 USD of GDP	0.603	0.441	-26.8%	0.656
TRANSPORTATION ENERGY USE				
Private passenger transportation energy use per capita (MJ)	60,034	53,441	-11.0%	31,044
Public transit energy use per capita (MJ)	811	963	18.6%	876
Total transportation energy use per capita (MJ)	60,845	54,403	-10.6%	31,920
TRANSPORTATION EXTERNALITIES				
Total emissions per capita (Kg)	265	185	-30.0%	199
Total transportation deaths per 100,000 people	12.7	9.5	-25.2%	9.1

Souce: Author's own date.

[a]Note that this ratio is calculated with the road-traffic speeds and rail speeds for the same set of cities.

States, Australia, Canada, Europe, and Asia.

AUSTRALIA	%	CANADA		%	EUROPE		%	ASIA		%
2006	Diff.	1996	2006	Diff.	1995	2005	Diff.	1995	2005	Diff.
14.0	5.7%	26.2	25.8	-1.5%	49.3	47.9	-2.8%	215.4	217.3	0.9%
20.3	7.5%	38.8	39.9	2.8%	77.3	77.5	0.2%	317.7	330.6	4.1%
12.7%	-4.7%	15.7	15.0	-4.2%	22.2	18.3	-17.6%	11.4	9.1	-19.6%
$32,194	59.2%	$20,825	$31,263	50.1%	$34,673	$38,683	11.6%	$23,593	$21,201	-10.1%
0.083	-4.2%	0.122	0.157	28.7%	0.080	0.094	18.0%	0.025	0.026	5.6%
298	-18.9%	390	319	-18.1%	212	248	17.2%	135	121	-10.3%
647	9.4%	530	522	-1.4%	412	463	12.3%	73	78	7.7%
160.0	-5.7%	56.3	66.8	18.7%	231.0	297.8	28.9%	18.3	33.8	84.5%
1.98	-9.4%	0.55	0.56	2.1%	4.17	5.51	32.0%	0.93	1.42	52.4%
4,077	2.0%	2,290	2,368	3.4%	5,245	6,126	16.8%	6,882	7,267	5.6%
1,075	11.3%	917	1,031	12.4%	1,830	2,234	22.1%	3,169	3,786	19.5%
713	11.8%	339	407	20.2%	1,256	1,597	27.1%	1,286	1,704	32.5%
33.0	1.4%	25.1	25.7	2.5%	28.0	29.8	6.4%	24.0	26.3	9.4%
47.5	2.8%	36.7	39.2	6.8%	42.6	44.6	4.7%	38.2	46.5	21.7%
42.8	-1.8%	44.5	45.4	2.0%	34.2	34.3	0.4%	31.8	30.6	-3.8%
0.78	3.2%	0.57	0.57	-0.3%	0.83	0.88	6.3%	0.76	0.86	12.5%
1.11	4.7%	0.85	0.89	4.7%	1.23	1.29	4.9%	1.20	1.52	26.7%
14.2%	-5.0%	10.4%	11.6%	10.7%	31.7%	34.5%	9.1%	25.0%	26.1%	4.7%
8.0%	6.7%	9.9%	11.3%	14.1%	22.3%	24.5%	9.8%	62.0%	62.9%	1.5%
12,447	2.7%	8,645	8,495	-1.7%	6,319	6,817	7.9%	1,978	1,975	-0.1%
0.272	-29.2%	0.309	0.209	-32.4%	0.150	0.135	-10.0%	0.050	0.060	20.0%
0.433	-34.1%	0.465	0.307	-34.1%	0.281	0.252	-10.3%	0.223	0.288	29.2%
35,972	15.9%	32,519	30,804	-5.3%	15,324	15,795	3.1%	6,447	6,076	-5.7%
1,036	18.3%	1,044	1,190	14.1%	1,243	1,532	23.2%	1,905	2,691	41.3%
37,008	15.9%	33,563	31,994	-4.7%	16,567	17,327	4.6%	8,352	8,768	5.0%
144	-27.8%	179	165	-8.0%	82	35	-57.3%	44	34	-23.1%
6.2	-31.4%	6.5	6.3	-4.2%	5.6	3.4	-39.4%	5.3	3.8	-27.7%

In other words, the road-traffic speeds of cities without metro and suburban rail are not used.

hierarchy of transportation modes due to its "irresistibility" in terms of comfort, convenience, speed, social status, and other features. The essence of his argument was that anyone still using anything other than an automobile was only doing so because they could not afford better. This perspective was based mainly on American experience, where public transit systems and good conditions for walking and cycling, had been systematically destroyed in the postwar era; nevertheless, he extended the idea as a general principle the world over.

For most of this century, the United Nations and OECD have been articulating an agenda that there needs to be a decoupling of growth in gross domestic product (GDP) from such growth-related environmental problems as fossil-fuel consumption (OECD 2011; UNEP 2011). In this book we make the strong case, especially in chapters 3 and 8, that there is considerable evidence for wealth decoupling from fossil fuels generally, and that wealth is now decoupling from automobile dependence. Figure 2-1 shows that, in most of our cities over the 10-year period, there has been a measurable reduction in car kilometers per unit of real GDP (local currencies).[2] It shows that 39 out of the 42 cities reduced their car kilometers per GDP by an average of 24 percent (across the entire 42 cities, the decline was 21 percent). These cities have thus been able to grow their economies while experiencing major reductions in the *relative* amount of car driving associated with this wealth creation. Overall, the data suggest that in the overwhelming majority of cases where real per capita GDP has grown, this wealth creation has decoupled from car use.

In table 2-2, we convert GDP to 1995 US dollars so that regions can be compared. It can be seen that in all regions except Asia, the number of car kilometers driven per dollar of GDP has declined from 1995 to 2005, with the European cities showing the least decline on average. Here we also see that in 2005, US cities experienced by far the most car use for every dollar of generated GDP, Australian cities were a little more efficient in this respect, and Canadian cities were clearly lower than both their US and Australian counterparts. European cities needed less than half the car use to generate the same amount of GDP as in US cities. These have been the same basic patterns observed since we began collecting city data from the 1960s (Newman & Kenworthy 1989). The two relatively wealthy Asian cities of Singapore and Hong Kong had about one-fifth of the car use per GDP as the US cities in 2005. Similar patterns are evident in 1995, except that the gap between the Asian cities and the rest of the cities was much greater in 1995 than in 2005 (these Asian cities increased in their car kilometers per dollar of GDP, while all the other regions declined). A similar situation is observable when we compare the Canadian and European cities because of the small relative decline in car kilometers per dollar of GDP experienced in European cities.

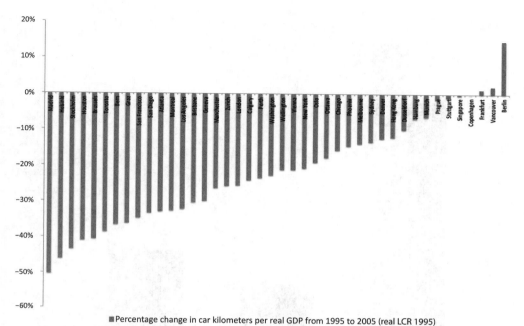

Figure 2-1. Percentage change in car kilometers traveled per unit of real GDP in 42 cities (real local currencies [LCR]). Source: Authors' own data.

In order to see the overall decoupling that has occurred globally, figure 2-2 combines all the cities and shows the growth in GDP per capita compared with the growth in car kilometers per capita (and total motorized mobility, as will be discussed next). The graph clearly demonstrates how the average GDP per capita in all these cities (as measured in 1995 US dollars) has grown significantly, while car kilometers per capita has hardly increased. This decoupling of vehicle-kilometers-traveled (VKT) and GDP has been noted by others, especially in relation to the United States but also in places such as New Zealand (Kooshian & Winkelman 2011; Ecola et al. 2012).

The trends that are contributing to peak car use, including growth of the knowledge/services economy, the urban youth culture and its use of social media, an increasing popularity of urban locations with rising urban densities, and a revival in the use of public transit, can all be contributing to the decoupling of car use from GDP (see chapter 3).

However, 12 of the 42 cities did in fact not only achieve *relative* reductions in the amount of car driving associated with their GDP growth, but also absolute declines in per capita car kilometers of driving (Atlanta, Houston, San Francisco, Los Angeles, Oslo, Toronto, Montreal, Zurich, Stockholm, London, Vienna, Graz). The average decrease in per capita car use for these 12 cities was 6.4 percent.

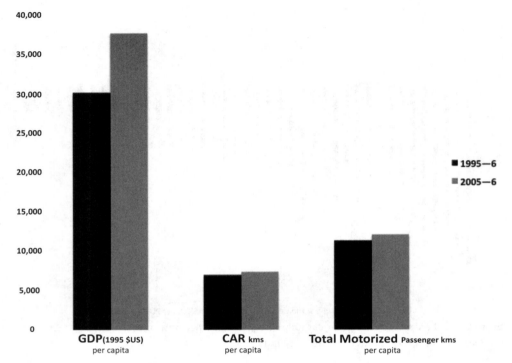

Figure 2-2. Decoupling of GDP per capita and mobility per capita (car mobility per capita and total motorized mobility per capita), averaged for 42 cities between 1995–6 and 2005–6. Source: Authors' own data.

But is car use simply being replaced by other forms of mobility in generating the GDP of an urban region? In case this is so, we combine annual car, motorcycle, and public transit passenger-kilometers and express this per unit of real GDP in the local currency.

Figure 2-3 presents the percentage changes for each city. It demonstrates again that the large majority of cities needed significantly less total personal motorized mobility in 2005 relative to the amount of real GDP they generated, compared to 1995. Only 7 of the 42 cities increased in this factor. Overall, in the 35 cities that reduced in this factor, the average reduction was 26 percent over the 10 years, while across the entire sample, including those cities that increased, the overall reduction in motorized mobility per unit of GDP was 20 percent. The 7 cities to have increased in total motorized mobility per unit of GDP from 1995 to 2005 were Stuttgart, Oslo, Munich, Hong Kong, Frankfurt, Vancouver, and Berlin. In the case of Hong Kong, the mobility increase per capita was all in public transit, with combined car and motorcycle passenger-kilometers per capita actually declining. In the other 6 cities that increased, all the forms of passenger mobility per capita rose. In fact, only 8 of the 42 cities actually declined in per capita total motorized mobility from 1995 to 2005 (Graz, Stockholm, Melbourne, Montreal, Toronto, Atlanta, Houston, and Los Angeles). In summary, in 83 percent of the cities in the analysis, total motorized mobility relative to GDP reduced (i.e., decoupled) between 1995 and 2005.

Figure 2-2 shows that for the entire group of cities, the average total motorized mobility per capita only increased slightly between 1995–96 and 2005–06, while GDP per capita grew significantly. Furthermore, table 2-2 groups the cities into their respective regions and uses real 1995 US dollars for cross-city comparisons. It shows that in 1995, Australian cities had the highest level of overall personal mobility per dollar of GDP. This was followed closely by the US cities, then the Canadian cities with a big drop in this factor, then the European cities with another big drop, and finally the Asian cities, which were lower again but by a lesser margin than the other differences. By 2005, all the groups of cities had reduced their personal mobility requirements relative to GDP, except the Asian cities, which went up. In general, in

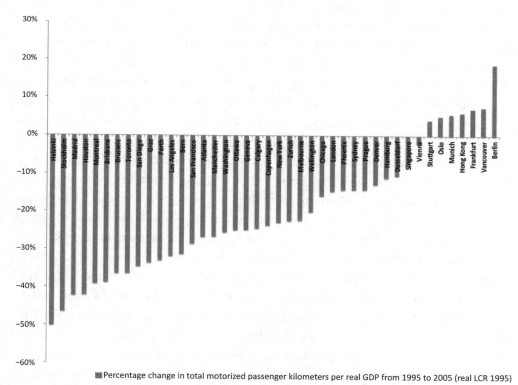

Percentage change in total motorized passenger kilometers per real GDP from 1995 to 2005 (real LCR 1995)

Figure 2-3. Percentage change in total motorized passenger-kilometers-traveled per unit of real GDP in 42 cities (local currencies). Source: Authors' own data.

comparing 1995 and 2005 there seems to be a "flattening" process at work so that the differences in motorized personal mobility levels relative to GDP are becoming a little less pronounced.

In order to understand these results for car use, it is important to look in detail at other data describing each metropolitan area. Table 2-2, presented earlier, shows the key comparative transportation data for 1995 and 2005 by regional groupings of cities. These data are discussed in terms of metropolitan characteristics, private transportation infrastructure, public transportation infrastructure, public transportation service and use, comparative modal speeds, modal splits, private mobility, transportation energy use, and transportation externalities.

Metropolitan Characteristics

Metropolitan characteristics include density (population and jobs), the centralization of jobs, and wealth (as measured by metropolitan GDP per capita, already discussed)—all of which help determine urban form patterns, i.e., the shape of the city and how it is structured to enable it to function.

The importance of urban form in helping to explain patterns of urban transportation, especially automobile dependence and transportation energy use, has been widely discussed (Cervero 1998; Kenworthy & Laube 1999; Newman & Kenworthy 1989, 1999a). As densities rise in cities, per capita car use and transportation energy use decline (Newman & Kenworthy 1989, 1999a). Selectively increasing urban densities, such as in centers linked to quality public transit with good provision for walking and cycling can help to reshape cities for reduced car use and lower transportation energy use by improving the viability of public transit (Thomson 1977; Newman & Kenworthy 2006; McIntosh et al. 2014a). Concentrating jobs can help to counter the low-density, "salt and pepper" dispersal of jobs—which has been shown to lead to radical drops in public transit use, large increases in transportation energy use, and increased car-trip lengths (Cervero & Landis 1992; Baillieu, Knight, & Frank 1991). There is now a reaction to this and a move to focus more jobs and residences in central areas and sub-centers as demand has become more urban and less suburban.[3] Figure 1-14 provided an updated version of our original graph of urban density versus per capita passenger-transportation-energy use, with many more cities globally and a greater range in city type, including less developed cities.

Wealth can also help to shape urban form, but not in any inevitable or single direction. Increasing wealth has been used to buy more urban space—both larger residential lots and bigger houses in distant car-dependent suburbs. This has occurred in particular in the United States and Australia, the large dwellings sometimes derogatorily referred to as "McMansions." There is also a lot of evidence that wealth can be and is used to buy into better locations, which often means higher density, mixed-use environments in inner cities (e.g., Manhattan or downtown San Francisco). Ultimately, how wealth interacts with urban form depends on prevailing cultural priorities and many other factors that determine the attractiveness of different locations and forms of living to different population cohorts at any given time.

Densities

Australian cities remain the lowest-urban-density cities in our sample, followed closely by American cities (table 2-2). Urban density is based on population within an urbanized area. Canadian cities have notably higher urban densities than cities in Australia or the United States. Collectively, American, Canadian, and Australian cities are in the range of about 8 to 25 persons per hectare, or what may be termed low density. European cities remain medium-density (from about 26 persons per hectare up to around 80 persons per hectare), while the Asian high-density cities (generally above 80 persons per hectare up to over 300 per hectare in Hong Kong), represented by Singapore and Hong Kong, lead with an average urban density over five times higher than that of European cities. The change from our earlier work is seen in the increase in density in the auto-oriented cities in the United States and Australia, and the rather slight decline (2.8 percent) in European cities, though the European cities are still over three times denser than American and Australian cities and on average almost twice as dense as Canadian cities.

Table 2-2 shows that "activity density" (population and jobs combined) in all groups of cities shows a stronger positive change than urban density. Percentage increases range from 0.2 percent in the European cities up to 7.5 percent in the Australian cities. While modest, these changes represent a reversal of the growth patterns of these cities since World War II, when densities continuously declined through automobile-based sprawl.

Centralization of Jobs

Job centralization is measured as the proportion of metropolitan jobs located in the central business district (CBD). Most transit systems in the world are still focused on the central city, despite a growth in crosstown or circumferential services in many cities in response to job decentralization. The data show that the absolute number of jobs is still growing in the vast majority of CBDs, although relative to other parts of the city nearly all CBDs in our study show a decline (we don't have the types of jobs, however, and the evidence in several chapters here suggests that knowledge-economy jobs are focussing in CBDs and centers). The data show that in 29 out of 41 cities, the actual number of jobs in the CBD increased from 1995 to 2005 (which of course helps to also increase metropolitan job densities), whereas only 8 of these cities actually increased in the *proportion* of jobs in the CBD. Two cities (Graz and Manchester) remained identical in this proportion. Concentrating jobs that are outside of the central business districts in public-transit-oriented sub-centers is important in creating more polycentric metropolitan areas that are better served by non-auto modes.

Overall, one can say that the central areas of cities are still critical in shaping transportation patterns and that radial transit systems based on rail are increasingly important. But it is also likely that the need for orbital transit connections between other centers is increasing (e.g., the Sheppard Subway line in Toronto, the T1 and T2 light-rail lines in Paris and the London Overground). European cities remain the most centralized in the sample, with over 18 percent of jobs still located in their CBDs. This is over twice the US level of only 8.2 percent, though the Asian cities are not much higher (9.1 percent). In line with their generally less automobile-dependent urban forms, Canadian cities are closer to European levels of job centralization in their CBDs, with an average of 15 percent. Many Canadian cities also have some significant concentrations of jobs in public-transit-oriented sub-centers outside of downtown (e.g., Metrotown on Vancouver's Skytrain and the North York and Scarborough sub-centers on the Toronto subway system). The rail renaissance happening worldwide (Newman, Kenworthy, & Glazebrook 2013) may moderate the decline in job centralization in the CBDs of cities, as well as strengthen the "decentralized concentration" of suburban jobs into TODs. This will be discussed in more detail in chapter 4.

Private Transportation Infrastructure
Three key physical pillars that underpin a city's level of automobile dependence are car ownership, freeway availability, and parking availability in the CBD.

Car Ownership
Car ownership rates (measured in cars per 1,000 persons) show major differences between the city groupings, as shown in figure 2-4. With a rise in car ownership of 12 percent, European cities are creeping closer to Canadian cities as the five Canadian cities on average declined by a little over 1 percent in car ownership. Both Australian and American cities rose in car ownership by 9 percent to 647 and 640 cars per 1,000 persons respectively. Canadian cities now sit at 522 cars per 1,000 persons, well below the Australian and American cities. European cities edged up from 412 to 463 cars per 1,000 persons.

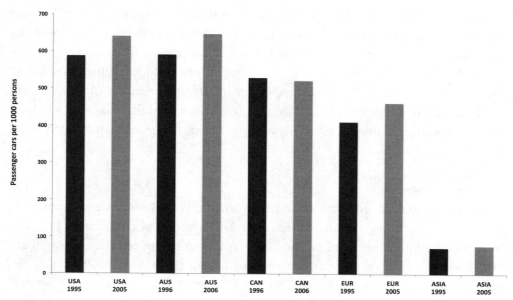

Figure 2-4. Car ownership in global cities, 1995 and 2005. Source: Authors' own data.

Singapore and Hong Kong remain at extremely low levels of car ownership. Singapore tries to keep its car ownership more or less constant, which it did (99 compared to 100 cars per 1,000 persons in 1995 and 2005, respectively), by matching the rate of new car registrations with the attrition rate through the extremely expensive Certificate of Entitlement auctioning system for the *right* to purchase a new car (the car purchase cost is on top of this). Singapore tries to ensure that its road system is not overwhelmed with cars due to constraints on how much road space can be provided and the need to ensure free-flowing conditions for its commercial traffic.

Hong Kong rose from 46 to 57 cars per 1,000 persons, or less than one-tenth of the car ownership in American and Australian cities. This is partly a reflection of the generally high costs imposed on car ownership and use in Hong Kong, which are necessitated by the extraordinarily compact and space-constrained urban form and the physical impossibility of devoting too much space to roads. Hong Kong's urban density is 336 persons per hectare, compared to European cities with an average of 48 persons per hectare, and the automobile-dependent regions averaging only 14–26 persons per hectare.

Hong Kong's low rate of car ownership works hand-in-glove with the astonishing diversity, spatial density, and frequency of its public transit services. Hong Kong's transit options include the ubiquitous red and green public minibus systems, the regular buses, the double-decker trams, the peak tramway (funicular), the light-rail system in the New Territories, the Hong Kong metro system, the impressive KCR East and West longer-distance rail system, and the extensive network of ferry services. Hong Kong is one of the few cities in the world that can boast so many modes of transit.[4] On top of this, despite its sometimes mountainous topography, Hong Kong's dense, mixed-use urban form and pedestrian infrastructure ensure that many trips can be made on foot. Such is Hong Kong's built environment that many trips to local facilities involve predominantly vertical displacement in elevators with a very short walk at ground level.

Freeway Supply

Of critical importance to automobile dependence is the level of freeway provision. Freeways are premium road infrastructure and are symbols of government priorities in transportation infrastructure. The city of Vancouver rejected the freeway plans of the 1960s and never built any. It remains one of the world's most liveable cities, retaining a highly functional, diversified passenger transportation system and increasingly diverse and numerous neighborhoods with low car–dependence such as False Creek (Schiller et al. 2010). It has been understood since the 1970s that urban freeways directly facilitate greater car use and energy use in cities (e.g., Watt and Ayres 1974) through longer travel distances, declining transit systems, and deteriorating conditions for pedestrians and cyclists (Newman & Kenworthy 1984, 1988b, 1999b; Schiller et al. 2010). Now there is an economic priority not to build them.

The evidence gathered on freeway length per person between 1995 and 2005 is mixed (see table 2-2). US cities seem to have stabilized in freeway provision per person, but some continue to build freeways while others do not.[5] US cities such as San Francisco and Portland, Oregon, have removed some sections of freeway in their downtowns and radically improved the quality of the public spaces (the Embarcadero Freeway and the Harbor Freeway, respectively). Freeway provision per person in Australian cities has declined 4 percent on average, and they continue to have little more than half the US level of freeway provision. Canadian cities appear to be providing significant new freeway infrastructure, growing by 29 percent, taking over the lead from the United States. Four out of the five Canadian cities grew in freeway length per capita, with only the Vancouver region declining. European cities have increased by 18 percent in this factor, due to a combination of freeway construction and low population growth. Interestingly, these European cities had 13 percent more per capita freeway provision than Australian cities in 2005. In keeping with their low automobile dependence, Singapore and Hong Kong are the least freeway-oriented cities in the sample, and have only a fraction of the freeway provision per capita of any of the other cities.

Central Business District Parking Supply

Parking provision in the CBD is an important factor in determining the modal split for trips to those space-constrained parts of all cities. The availability of parking, much more than price, determines the attractiveness of car commuting to the central city (Newman & Kenworthy 1988a). High levels of parking will encourage the most energy-consuming trips to work by car, while well-loaded, radial rail systems will use the least energy.

The data in table 2-2 suggest that parking supply in the CBDs of the most auto-oriented cities is generally on the decline—and significantly so. In American cities, parking per 1,000 workers in CBDs declined by 12 percent, Australian cities 19 percent, and Canadian cities 18 percent. Even Singapore and Hong Kong, the least parking-oriented cities in the sample, declined by 10 percent in CBD parking per 1,000 jobs. European cities, on the other hand, rose by 17 percent, but from a very low base level of 212 spaces per 1,000 jobs up to only 248 per 1,000 jobs, or still only about half the rate of the average US city in 2005, with 487 spaces per 1,000 CBD jobs. Even with this increase, parking rates in European CBDs remain lower than those of Canadian and Australian cities. European CBDs generally boast numerous pedestrian-only zones and traffic-calming measures. Despite the CBD parking declines in US cities, they are still much higher than in Canadian and Australian cities (298 and 319 spaces per 1,000 jobs, respectively). It appears that some cities are actually reducing the absolute number of their combined off-street and on-street CBD parking spaces through both new development taking over parking areas and also increased on-street parking restrictions.

Reducing CBD parking has been shown to support public transit use to the CBD, even in the off-peak travel times. But for public transit to compete better, parking in sub-centers will also need to be reduced. There are multiple advantages involved in lowering the parking supply in the CBDs of cities, including the improvement of the public realm for pedestrians and cyclists. Jan Gehl, the famous Danish architect and urban designer, has explained clearly the multiple social, environmental, economic, and livability advantages to cities of systematically reducing parking and pedestrianizing centers in cities. Copenhagen reduced its central area parking by 3 percent per year until it gradually created the world-renowned pedestrian-only zone that is now the centerpiece of the whole city (Gehl 2010, 2011; Gehl & Gemzoe 2004). Paris is now removing 55,000 on-street parking spaces over a 20–year period (Newman et al. 2009) as they seek to make a highly walkable city even more walkable; they recognize that asphalt for cars is not helping urban productivity.

Public Transportation Infrastructure

This section considers the level of premium transit infrastructure in cities in the form of reserved rights-of-way to speed up transit operations (fully separated rail-system alignments, bus lanes, BRT), and in particular how this variable compares to urban freeways, which are premium road infrastructure built primarily to facilitate fast car travel.

Reserved Transit Route per Person

For public transit to be successful, it must be reliable and legible (easily located and with route clarity) and it must compete in speed with road traffic. Therefore, public transit routes need to be free from general traffic, and their stops and alignments must be easily navigated by users and not subject to change. Regular bus systems provide neither, since they suffer from the traffic congestion caused by private automobile use, and their stops and routes can literally change overnight. This factor is measured here as the one-way per capita length of reserved public transit right-of-way (bus lanes / BRT and rail systems operating on separated rights-of-way, including protected on-street routes for trams and LRT).

The data in table 2-2 show that in all groups of cities except those in Australia, per capita length of reserved public transit right-of-way has generally improved significantly, showing an increase between 18 percent and 85 percent. The exception is the Australian cities, which showed a decline in per capita length of reserved public transit right-of-way of 6 percent (due to growth in freeway provision without investment in enough new rail systems and bus lanes), though they are still on average the second-highest group in this factor, behind the European cities. Singapore and Hong Kong have the lowest amount of reserved public transit route per capita, overall, due to their densities reducing required lengths; in fact, there was an 85 percent increase in reserve route per capita in the 10-year period. American cities have now eclipsed the Canadian cities in this factor, though both groups are relatively low, with 72 and 56 meters per 1,000 persons, respectively, compared to 160 in Australia and 298 in Europe.

In the US cities, the increase in reserved route is shared more or less equally between new bus-only lanes and combined new LRT, metro, and suburban rail additions. In the Canadian cities, new bus-only lanes make up the majority of their additions by a small margin. However, in European cities the 29 percent overall increase in reserved route per person is dominated strongly by suburban rail and some new metro, while the reserved route for trams and LRT both experienced some declines due to overall lack of growth in reserved-system length compared to population. Sometimes cities add tram/LRT lines in mixed traffic, not as reserved route. In the Asian cities, new public-transit-reserved routes are totally dominated by LRT, metro, and suburban rail-network additions (13.2 out of the 15.5 meters per 1,000 persons increase).

Ratio of Reserved Public Transportation Infrastructure Versus Freeways

Reserved transit routes are the corollary of freeways because both are premium, higher-speed transportation infrastructure, but they lead to very different results for mobility patterns. The ratio between these critical transportation infrastructures is important, as it is a yardstick for whether private or public transportation is gaining ascendency in cities. American and Canadian cities have the lowest amount of public-transit-reserved route compared to freeway provision (0.56 or about half as much). Australian cities do better, having almost twice as much reserved public transit route length per capita as urban freeway length. European cities, with their well-developed public transit systems, have a ratio of 5.5, while the Asian cities, which are still rapidly developing in this factor, have 1.4. This characteristic is probably the most striking way to see the differences between these groups of global cities.

The trends show that in every group of cities, except those in Australia, there is a significantly growing ratio in favor of reserved public transit route compared to urban freeways. Australian cities overall, though they have slipped 9 percent in this measure, are still on average much higher than the North American cities.

US cities, while growing 37 percent in this factor, still only have a little over 50 percent as much reserved public transit route as freeways. Canadian cities are now identical to US cities, due to very low growth in this factor of 2 percent. European cities grew 32 percent in this ratio and have some five-and-a-half times as much reserved transit route as freeway. Singapore and Hong Kong increased by 53 percent and now have significantly more public-transit-reserved route than freeway, whereas the reverse was true in 1995. These data powerfully show the declining commitment to automobile dependence in the world's cities.

Public Transportation Service and Use

This section examines three factors from table 2-2 that measure the amount of public transit service and usage. Total annual public transit seat-kilometers of service per person is a measure of transit service supply, which takes account of the different sizes of vehicle (e.g., a typical regular bus compared to a rail wagon). Public transit passenger-kilometers measure transit usage and can be also employed for measuring car travel. The other factor examined here is that part of the public transit passenger-kilometers performed by rail systems (annual rail-passenger-kilometers per person).

Total Annual Public Transportation Seat-Kilometers per Person

In all cities, the level of public transit service per capita is going up. US cities remain the lowest, even though they had the biggest percentage increase (20 percent). Canadian cities are the next highest, but they are a good way ahead of US cities. Then we have the Australian cities, European cities, and finally Singapore and Hong Kong, with nearly four times more public transportation seat-kilometers per person than US cities. Generally the growth was relatively low, with Australian and Canadian cities increasing by only to 2–3 percent, while Singapore and Hong Kong rose nearly 6 percent. The European cities increased almost 17 percent in this factor and certainly added the most public transit service per person in real terms (881 seat-kilometers per person compared to the US cities, with 308).

Total Annual Public Transportation Passenger-Kilometers per Person

This measures the per capita annual travel distance in public transit by people in each city. The Asian cities are the clear leaders, with 3,786 public transit passenger-kilometers in 2005 (and 20 percent growth), followed a relatively long way back by

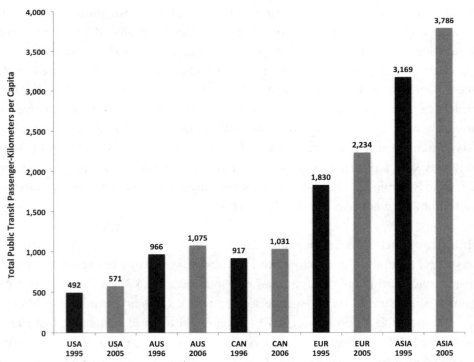

Figure 2-5. Public transit passenger-kilometers per capita in global cities, 1995 and 2005. Source: Authors' own data.

the European cities, with a still healthy 2,234 public transit passenger-kilometers (and 22 percent growth). There is then a rather dramatic falling away in this factor, with Australian and Canadian cities being about equal with 1,075 and 1,031 passenger-kilometers (and 11 percent and 12 percent growth, respectively).

The American cities basically halve these figures again, with only 571 public transit passenger-kilometers, notwithstanding a 16 percent increase. Figure 2-5 summarizes the differences among the groups of cities and how they have changed over the 10 years in this important measure. Figure 2-6 shows the value for each city in the study in 2005 (including Seattle, New Orleans, and Portland, which are not part of the US sample in table 2-2).

Figure 2-6 shows the vast global range in public transit kilometers traveled per person, with the former Eastern-bloc city of Prague having over 5,000 public transit passenger-kilometers per person (14.2 kilometers of public transit travel per day for every man, woman, and child!), while at the other end, Phoenix weighs in with a mere 117 annual public transit passenger-kilometers per person (or 320 meters per person per day!). Indeed, the lowest nine cities are American, followed immediately by an eclectic mixture of "underperforming" public transit and automobile cities, namely Manchester, Perth, Chicago, Geneva, and Ottawa.[6]

At the other end of the spectrum, Hong Kong and Bern have very high public transit passenger-kilometers per capita of between and 4,000 and 5,000 kilometers, but then the values drop away significantly to Vienna, with just over 3,000 kilometers, and Munich and London, with only slightly lower figures.

Total Annual Rail-Passenger-Kilometers per Person

The contribution of rail versus other modes to the overall performance of the transit system is an important topic, given the new "golden age" of rail currently being experienced worldwide (Newman et al. 2013). Table 2-2 shows that the European cities are clearly "rail cities." In 2005, they had 72 percent of all their public transit passenger-kilometers on rail, up from 69 percent in 1995, and their 10-year growth was 27 percent. In actual total rail use per person, the two Asian cities have more travel by rail (1,704 compared to 1,597 passenger-kilometers in Europe), but this constitutes only 45 percent of these two Asian cities' total public transit use. In the Asian cities, buses clearly still play a pivotal role, though the rail component is creeping up (from 41 percent in 1995), and the growth in rail use was the highest of all the groups (33 percent).

In the remaining groups, the American cities grew by 25 percent, and rail in 2005 constituted 60 percent of total public transit travel, up from 56 percent in 1995. Rail was even more important in the Australian cities, constituting 66 percent of total public transit travel in both 1996 and 2006. On the other hand, the Canadian cities, while enjoying a 20 percent growth in rail use, only had 40 percent of their public transit passenger-kilometers by rail, up from 37 percent in 1996.

Modal Speeds

Speed of travel is a key factor in any analysis of transportation choice. In this section, we explore five very important factors in any urban transportation system: the overall average public transit system speed, the average speed of urban rail systems (heavy-rail, metro, and suburban rail systems combined, but excluding the partially on-street rail modes—trams and LRT), the average road-traffic speed, the ratio between public transit and road-traffic speed, and the ratio between average rail speed and road-traffic speed.[7] Average road-traffic speed covers seven days a week, 24 hours per day, not just peak periods.

Ratio of Overall Public Transit Speed to Road-Traffic Speed

Our previous research has shown that it is not the absolute speed of any one mode in a city that necessarily determines its attractiveness, but rather the relative speed between modes. People tend to choose the mode that provides the fastest service, so if cars in a city are operating at 30 kilometers per hour and rail delivers an average speed of 40 kilometers per hour, rail will represent an attractive modal choice. On the other hand, if in another city cars operate at 45 kilometers per hour and the rail system still only works at 40 kilometers per hour, rail will be less attractive (Newman & Kenworthy 1999b; Newman et al. 2013).

The data in table 2-2 show a mixed situation for the ratio between public transit and traffic speeds; in some cities it is improving, suggesting an extra advantage to transit users, while in others it's going down. In Canadian cities the ratio between transit and road-traffic speeds is very slightly down (less than half a percent), and in US cities it is down by 5 percent, whereas in Australian cities it has improved by about 3 percent. In the 20 European cities, the ratio has improved in favor of transit by 6 percent, and in the case of the two Asian cities by 13 percent. Basically, it is the two most rail-oriented groups of cities that display a more promising trajectory in the speed-competitiveness of transit.

The data overall show that in US and Canadian cities, the average speed of public transit is barely above half that of the car, while in Australian cities it is above three-quarters. The average public transit speed in the European and Asian cities is only a little below the road-traffic speed (0.88 and 0.86, respectively,

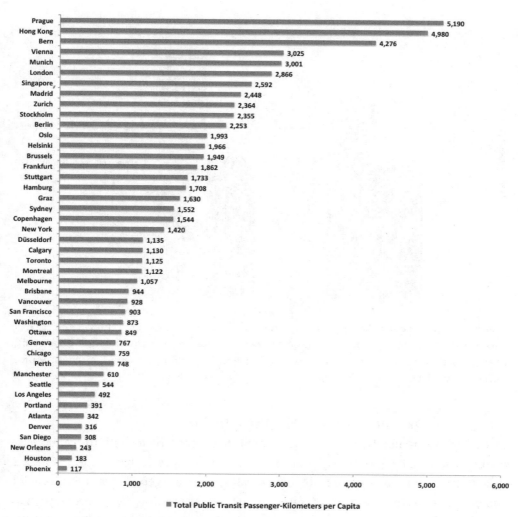

Figure 2-6. Public transit passenger-kilometers per capita in 44 global cities, 2005–6. Source: Authors' own data.

of the average road-traffic speed), and the trend is in a clear positive direction for public transit. Metro and suburban rail generally offer the most competitive speeds. Tram and LRT systems can compete with cars in certain circumstances but tend to have lower speeds because they are generally installed in denser settings with more closely spaced intersections and closer spacing between stops along their routes. Where either trams or LRT operate on reserved rights-of-way and also have pre-emptive green-wave traffic signals (e.g., in Zurich), they can compete much better with the car.

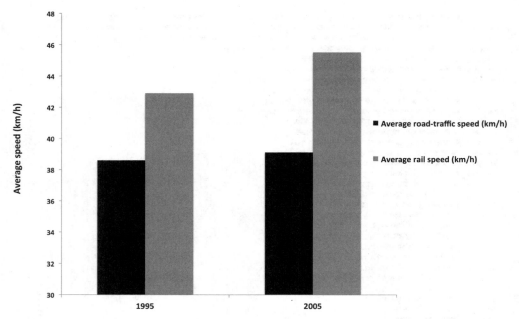

Figure 2-7. Average speed of road traffic and rail (metro and suburban rail) in 35 cities, 1995–6 and 2005–6. N.b. This includes only those cities in the database that have relevant rail systems. Average road-traffic speed and average rail speed reflect the data for the same 35 cities. Source: Authors' own data.

Ratio of Rail-Transit Speed to Road-Traffic Speed

Metro and suburban rail systems are clearly able to compete better with the car because of their protected rights-of-way and higher operating speeds than buses. Table 2-2 shows that even in the United States, where rail systems are generally not so prevalent and developed as in other parts of the world (with the exception of some cities such as New York and San Francisco), still the speed of rail is just a little below that of general road traffic (0.95), and it has remained essentially the same over the decade (showing just a 1 percent decline). The Canadian cities have the slowest rail systems compared to road traffic, with a 0.89 ratio, though this has improved by nearly 5 percent over the decade. In Australian cities, the suburban rail systems have enhanced their speed competitiveness by 5 percent and stand at 1.11 times the road-traffic speed. However, it is not surprising that in European and the Asian cities rail systems compete best with private transportation. Rail systems in European cities are 1.29 times faster than road traffic, which is a 5 percent improvement over 1995. The two Asian cities are even more dramatic, with their rail systems offering speeds that are 1.52 times faster than road traffic, up a remarkable 27 percent from 1.20 since 1995.

Figure 2-7 averages the data for all cities between 1995 and 2005, showing the average road-traffic speed versus the average rail speed and how rail is increasing its speed advantage.

Figure 2-8 shows this ratio for the 35 cities in 2005 where each city had either a metro or a suburban rail system, or both. The graph shows that the average rail system speed in cities varies from a high of over twice as fast as road-traffic speed in Düsseldorf and very high also in Hong Kong, Bern, and Hamburg, each having a ratio of between 1.6 and 1.7. The slowest rail systems compared to road traffic are in Chicago, Toronto, New York, and Washington, with ratio values between 0.69 and 0.85.

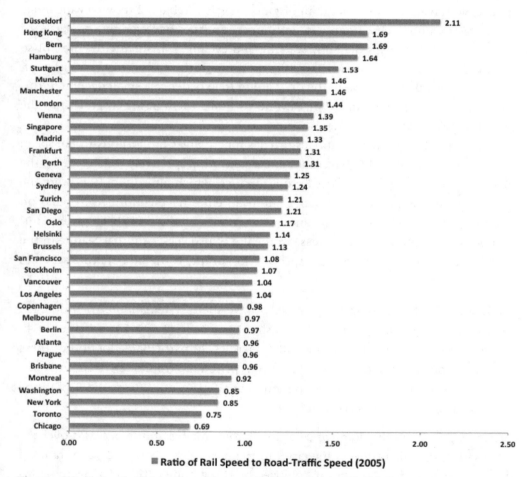

Figure 2-8. Ratio of rail-transit speed to road-traffic speed in 35 global cities, 2005. N.b. Only cities that have either metro or suburban rail systems or both are included here. Source: Authors' own data.

Modal Split

Here we examine two key variables: the percentage of total daily trips by non-motor-ized modes and the percentage of total motorized passenger-kilometers undertaken by public transit. Total motorized passenger-kilometers consist of car, motorcycle, and public transit passenger-kilometers.

Percentage of Total Daily Trips by Non-motorized Modes

In this chapter, both private and public transportation are measured in passenger-kilometers. However, non-motorized modes of transportation (NMM), namely walk-ing and cycling, is generally measured through the number of trips reported in household travel surveys rather than distance traveled. Table 2-2 shows a wide range in this factor among city groupings, with American cities having only an average of 9.5 percent of daily trips made by walking and cycling. Canadian cities are not so far ahead at 11.6 percent. Australian cities do better in this factor, with 14.2 percent. However, Australian cities were the only group to experience a small decline in this factor (from 14.9 percent in 1996). Beyond Australia there has been growth in the modal share of NMM in all cities surveyed.

The use of non-motorized modes reaches much larger proportions in European and Asian cities, with 34.5 percent and 26.1 percent, respectively. Interestingly, the biggest jump in usage was in the European cities, which already in 1995 were the leaders in this sample of cities. Many European cities have continued to build on traditions of walking and cycling, and more recently bike use has been given a fur-ther boost through the rapid increase in the use of pedelecs.[8] Another feature of the worldwide ascendancy of cycling, especially in Europe, is the bike-sharing schemes appearing in cities:

> Between 2008 and 2013 the number of bike-share systems more then doubled from 213 operating in 14 countries using 73,500 bicycles to 535 schemes in 49 countries, with a total fleet of 517,000 bicycles. In particular, adoption of these systems outside of Europe soared over that period, up from one system in Wash-ington, D.C., to around 143, with more than 50 percent of the world fleet in the Asia Pacific region, especially in China.[9]

Figure 2-9 shows the dominance of the European cities in use of NMM over the other cities studied. The top nine cities in the use of NMM are European, ranging from 37.1 percent to 51.9 percent, followed by Hong Kong with 36.0 percent. How-ever, the next 11 cities are also European, meaning that no cities except Hong Kong cut into the European dominance of walking and cycling. The bottom four cities,

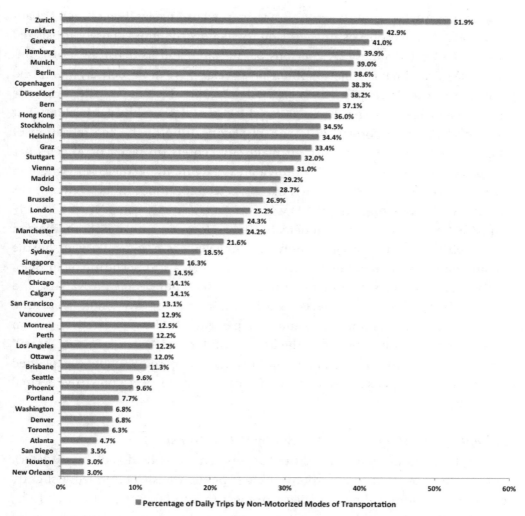

Figure 2-9. Percentage of daily trips by non-motorized modes of transportation in 44 global cities, 2005–6. Source: Authors' own data.

unsurprisingly, are American (New Orleans, Houston, San Diego, Atlanta), none of which have even 5 percent of daily trips by these modes. Toronto is the first non-US city with 6.3 percent NMM, but then the next five cities are also American, with NMM between 6.8 percent and 9.6 percent of daily trips. By far the most NMM-oriented city in the United States is New York, with 21.6 percent of daily trips undertaken by NMM.[10]

Perhaps somewhat surprisingly, Los Angeles is actually the third-highest NMM user in these 13 American cities, with 12.2 percent of trips made by foot and bicycle (Los Angeles County only). However, the Los Angeles–Long Beach Urbanized Area, centered on Los Angeles County, is now the most densely urbanized area in the United States (27.6 persons per hectare), and its density is now similar to key Scandinavian metropolitan areas (e.g., it is more densely urbanized than the Stockholm region (25.7) and Oslo (27.0) and is only a little less dense than Copenhagen's Finger Plan region, which has 29.2 persons per hectare). But Los Angeles's urban form is different, displaying little of the centralization of these three European cities in their main city centers (in fact, Los Angeles has 3.4 percent of its jobs in the downtown area, a figure unparalleled anywhere in the world—even in Phoenix, which has 4.9 percent of it jobs in its "center"). Los Angeles's relatively high use of NMM for an American city can at least be partly explained by the more uniform density factor. However, unlike in Scandinavian cities, which are quite cycle-friendly, Los Angeles has a generally very hostile urban public realm dominated by roads and parking, a strong culture of automobility, and some areas that are often not safe, which put people off walking and cycling (Davis 1990). Copenhagen, Stockholm, and Oslo, with similar densities, have 38.3 percent, 34.5 percent, and 28.7 percent NMM use respectively, or an average that is nearly three times the use of NMM in Los Angeles. This factor will need to grow in any city wishing to improve its urban productivity; as explained in later chapters, walkability is enabling the growth of new knowledge-related urban jobs.

Percentage of Total Motorized Travel by Public Transit
This factor measures public transit use against car use (which is discussed later). The results show that in all groups of cities public transit performed a slightly higher proportion of the motorized passenger task in 2005 than it did in 1995. However, this role is still very small in US cities (3.2 percent). In Australian cities it is 8.0 percent, and in Canadian cities a little better at 11.3 percent. By contrast, public transit systems in European cities account for 25 percent of motorized travel (eight times more than in the United States and over three times more than in Australia), while in Singapore and Hong Kong it is a massive 63 percent. If one included taxi passenger-kilometers in private transportation and took a new percentage, public transit's contribution would be even a little lower in each case, but not significantly so. The importance of this factor will be discussed more in the case studies in chapter 3.

Figure 2-10 shows the results for the entire sample of 44 cities, with Hong Kong leading the world by an extraordinary margin (83.8 percent of all motorized

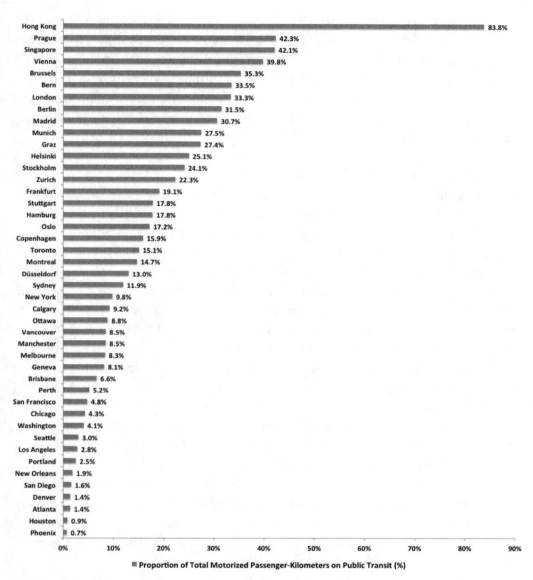

Figure 2-10. Percentage of total motorized travel on public transit in 44 global cities, 2005–6. Source: Authors' own data.

movement is public transit–based!). Prague is a distant second but also very high, with 42.3 percent, and is almost identical to Singapore, with 42.1 percent. The next 16 cities are all European, ranging from 15.9 percent (Copenhagen) to 39.8 percent (Vienna). At the other extreme, Phoenix has a somewhat embarrassing 0.7 percent of motorized travel by public transit, followed by Houston, Atlanta,

Denver, San Diego, New Orleans, Portland, Los Angeles, and Seattle, all with 0.9 percent to 3.0 percent public transit travel. New York, with just under 10 percent of total travel by public transit, is the only American city to even approach its northeastern neighbors in Canada (Montreal, with 14.7 percent, and Toronto, with 15.1 percent). It's interesting to see that climate must play very little part in this range of data, suggesting that urban fabric is much more likely to explain the variations (see chapter 4).

Private Mobility and Peak Car Use

Private mobility is represented in table 2-2 by annual car-passenger-kilometers per person and shows the regional patterns in this variable. The patterns are highly predictable, with American cities clearly the global leader (18,703 km) followed a considerable way back by Australian cities, with 12,447 kilometers. The Canadian cities are the really interesting group, given their North American status, because they have only 8,495 passenger-kilometers per year by car. Canadian cities are 68 percent higher in density than American cities, and this is a key reason for their lower car dependence. The European cities follow here, with only 6,817 kilometers, and then the private mobility figures for the two Asian cities plummet to a mere 1,975 kilometers per person, meaning that American cities are roughly ten times higher in their car mobility than these dense Asian cities.

A key point about these 2005–06 car use data is the fact that the increases since 1995–96 are modest. American and Australian cities each only increased about 3 percent, while Canadian cities declined by 2 percent. The Asian cities basically remained constant, while the European cities were the only ones to register a more significant increase of 8 percent over a 10-year period. These data appear to be in line with the global trend in many developed countries described in chapter 1; total vehicle–kilometers of travel by car in whole nations was slowing in growth up until 1995–96 and then peaked around the 2005 mark (Puentes & Tomer 2009; Millard-Ball & Schipper 2010; Newman & Kenworthy 2011b; Gargett 2012).

Figure 2-11 shows the car use per capita in passenger-kilometers for each of the 44 cities in this analysis in 2005. Atlanta, Denver, Houston, and Washington have over 20,000 car-passenger-kilometers per capita, and indeed the top 11 cities are American, interrupted only by Perth in Western Australia, with 13,652 kilometers per capita. Unsurprisingly, the two lowest-car-use cities are Hong Kong (910 km) and Singapore (3,040 km), followed by a series of European cities (Brussels, Vienna, Berlin, Graz). There is a difference of over 26 times between Atlanta and Hong Kong in car use per capita.

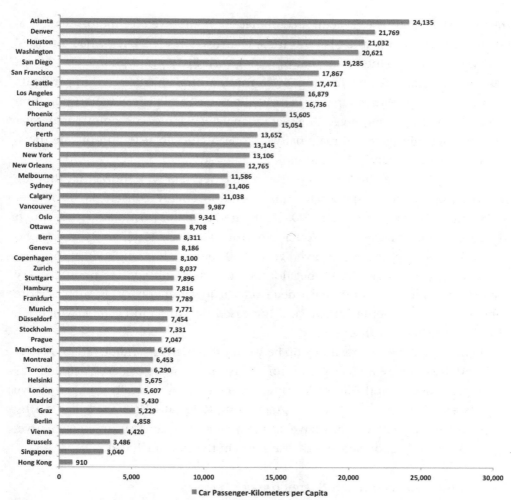

Figure 2-11. Car-passenger-kilometers per capita in 44 global cities, 2005. Source: Authors' own data.

Transportation Energy Use

The issue of oil consumption in urban transportation has always been a primary focus of our research on cities. This section examines the two key variables of per capita consumption of energy in both public and private transportation systems (and the total resulting from this).

Private Passenger Transportation Energy Use per Person

Table 2-2 shows that all groups of cities in this study, except Australian and European cities, have on average reduced their per capita demand for energy in private passenger transportation—US cities by 11 percent, Canadian cities by 5 percent, and the two Asian cities by 6 percent. A combination of improved technologies and stabilizing car use appear to be behind these changes.[11] The US and Canadian cities' vehicle fleets were so inefficient that trimming their fuel consumption over 10 years was achieved mainly by downsizing. By contrast, Australian cities grew in per capita car use by 14 percent (measured by vehicle-kilometers) and per capita transportation energy use by 16 percent, suggesting that urban vehicular fuel-consumption rates per kilometer actually increased marginally. European cities increased in private transportation energy use by only 3 percent.

Even with this decline in energy use in US cities, table 2-2 shows that they are still the highest private-passenger transportation energy consumers, with over 53,000 megajoules per capita in 2005, compared to major Australian cities, which averaged 36,000 megajoules.[12] Canadian cities are even lower at 31,000 megajoules. European cities use on average 15,800 megajoules, while Singapore and Hong Kong use a mere 6,000 megajoules. Such stark differences point to very important lessons that must be learned from the lower-energy cities, such as more compact land use, better transit, and increased walking and cycling, which are discussed throughout this book.

Figure 1-14 shows the relationship between urban density and private-passenger transportation energy use per person for a very large sample of developed and less developed cities around the world using the more geographically comprehensive 1995 data set. The first version of this graph using 1980 data (Newman & Kenworthy 1989) and subsequent versions have all maintained the same strong power curve, regardless of the year of data and the variation in the cities included.

Total Public Transportation Energy Use per Person

Energy use per capita for public transit is for the most part relatively small when compared to use per person for private-passenger transportation. In American cities public transportation energy use per person is less than 2 percent of the private figure, Canadian cities are 4 percent, Australian cities 3 percent, European cities 10 percent, but in Singapore and Hong Kong public transit energy use is 44 percent of the total, due to the much larger comparative role played by public transit in these cities. Due to increases in transit services and more energy-consuming features such as air-conditioning, public transit energy use per person has risen consistently in all cities (14–41 percent increases). Whether this actually raises CO_2 output depends on whether private-transportation energy use declines due to more use of public transit and also on where transit energy-use increases are sourced (many electric transit systems depend on hydro, nuclear, and renewable power sources such as wind (e.g.,

Calgary runs its LRT system on wind power alone). The global trend is toward renewables, as set out in chapter 8.[13]

The important thing is that public transit has huge energy-conserving potential. US cities use 963 megajoules per person to carry 3.2 percent of their total motorized mobility. Singapore and Hong Kong use only 2,691 megajoules per person (or less than three times more energy) for 65.3 percent of their entire motorized mobility (over 20 times the role of public transit in US cities). Given changes to city structure and other factors that favor greater use of existing transit services, public transit has the potential to support a massive amount of any city's mobility needs with comparatively little energy use or greenhouse-gas impact. Public transit systems also use far less energy per passenger-kilometer-traveled (PKT) than cars. US public transit is most energy-consumptive (2.1 MJ/PKT), but cars still consume 38 percent more (2.9 MJ/PKT).

Public transit in American cities is more energy consumptive than elsewhere partly because most of the service (65 percent of public transit vehicle-kilometers of service) is provided by less energy-efficient buses (and to a lesser degree demand-responsive minibuses), and much of this service is run in lower-density suburban areas where passenger loadings are very light, especially in the poorly used demand-responsive services.[14] It is also because American urban buses in 2005 had an average energy consumption of 31.3 megajoules per kilometer. By contrast, buses in Australian cities consumed 21.9 megajoules per kilometer, and those in Canadian cities, 24.9 megajoules per kilometer. It appears that buses in the American cities suffer the same "gas guzzling" affliction that has characterized the American car fleet. Public transit in Singapore and Hong Kong consumes only 0.70 megajoules per passenger-kilometer-traveled compared to cars, at 3.3 megajoules per passenger-kilometer-traveled (nearly five times more). Buses in these two Asian cities consume 23.5 megajoules per kilometer. Despite the fact that buses (and minibuses) in these two cities still provide 76 percent of the public transit service, the regular buses are very highly utilized due to the high-density urban form, and their average energy consumption is only 0.95 megajoules per passenger-kilometer-traveled (though the minibuses are rather more consumptive at 1.96 megajoules per passenger-kilometer-traveled). Rail in the Asian cities is the really energy-efficient mode, consuming 0.24, 0.55, 0.34, and 0.27 megajoules per passenger-kilometer-traveled for trams, LRT, metro, and suburban rail, respectively.

Overall, an increase in public transit energy use can probably be considered beneficial for energy consumption and climate change issues in cities because it reflects greater use of public transit. This is true overall, even in American cities, though it also seems clear that more public transit needs to be provided by the much more energy-efficient rail systems.[15] For US bus systems to be more energy-efficient and contribute

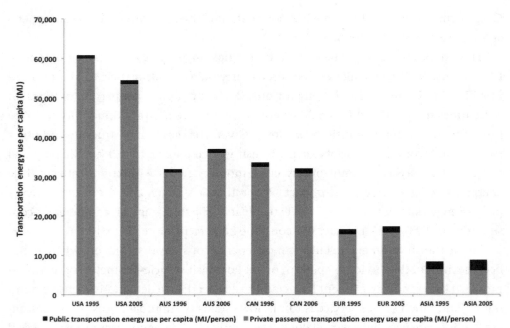

Figure 2-12. Private and public transportation energy use per capita in global cities, 1995 and 2005. Source: Authors' own data.

to climate-change mitigation, they need to be improved technologically, and ideally to run on renewables. At the same time, land-use densities and urban form need to be more supportive. One way of making buses more energy-efficient, aside from techno-logical change, is to radically curb the congestion that plagues American road systems and unfairly penalizes the bus services that use only a fraction of the road space of cars (Bradley & Kenworthy 2012). Another way is to run them more strategically as feeders to more rail stations and urban sub-centers where transit-supportive densities can be found (McIntosh et al. 2013; Newman & Kenworthy 2006).

Figure 2-12 shows the trend in private and public transportation energy use in the city groups in 1995 and 2005, while figure 2-13 shows the 2005 data for the whole group of 44 cities, with the cities sorted from highest to lowest on the basis of their private-transportation energy use. The range is quite simply extraordinary, with Atlanta at 75,000 megajoules and Hong Kong at 4,200 megajoules per person—18 times different. For private-passenger transportation energy use, European cities, without surprise, dominate the bottom half of the graph, while public transportation energy use shows no really clear pattern across all the cities. The exceptional city is Hong Kong, where public transit energy use per capita is 3,686 megajoules per capita, or very close to what is consumed per capita in cars in that city.

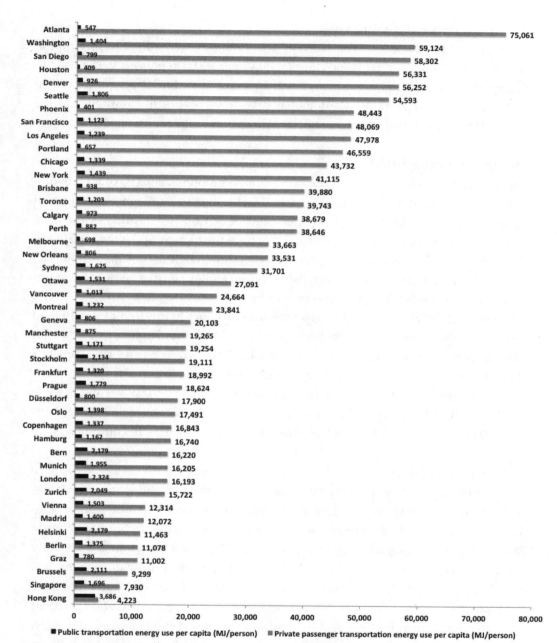

Figure 2-13. Private and public transportation energy use in 44 global cities, 2005. Source: Authors' own data.

Transportation Externalities

The final data in table 2-2 are for two key transportation externalities, transportation emissions per capita and transportation fatalities per 100,000 persons.[16] The need to dramatically reduce GHG in the period to 2050 has been outlined by the IPCC (2013) and is pursued in chapter 8. Many global cities have begun this journey, and the United States has started the process with new carbon limits for cars in 2014.

Transportation Emissions

The data presented here represent the sum of carbon monoxide (CO), volatile hydro-carbons (VHC), oxides of nitrogen (NO_x), and sulfur dioxide (SO_2) emissions from all transportation sources in each city on a per capita basis. Consistent with previous data, table 2-2 shows clearly that the American cities have the highest per capita transporta-tion emissions in the world (185 kg per capita), followed by the Canadian cities (165 kg) and Australian cities (144 kg), with the European and Asian cities being more or less equal and very much lower than everywhere else (35 and 34 kg, respectively).

Trend-wise, all groups of cities show significant declines in this factor from 1995 to 2005 (European cities declined by 57 percent, American cities 30 percent, Australian cities 28 percent, Asian cities 23 percent, and Canadian cities 8 percent). Overall, it appears that regardless of the city, transportation emissions are trending down, which can be explained mostly by better technology, aided by the slowing down and in some cases reversal of the growth in car vehicle-kilometers. In order to reduce these emis-sions 80 percent by 2050, both of these trends will obviously have to continue.

Transportation Fatalities

The data in table 2-2 make it very clear that transportation fatalities are on a signifi-cant downward trend in this sample of wealthier global cities. The American, Austra-lian, European, and Asian cities all recorded similar percentage declines of between 25 and 39 percent (average 31 percent). The Canadian cities, which in 1996 already had comparatively low transportation deaths, declined only a further 4 percent. It is also clear that among these groups of cities, it is those in the United States that have the highest number of fatalities (9.5 per 100,000 persons), Australian and Canadian cities are almost identical (6.2 and 6.3 respectively), while the European and Asian cities are also similar and the lowest in the sample (3.4 and 3.8, respectively). Phoe-nix has the highest fatality rate, with 14.6 per 100,000, while Berlin loses 2.0 persons per 100,000 to transportation causes (Vienna and Stockholm have 2.1). The range in the United States is also quite large, with New York, the most public-transit-oriented US metropolitan area, recording only 6.4 transportation deaths per 100,000 persons.

Conclusions

Some overall conclusions can be drawn regarding the transportation patterns and trends in global cities and how they relate to the end of automobile dependence. To do this we answer the questions we posed at the beginning of the chapter. Table 2-3 contains the overall trend for all cities in the study, from which many of the conclusions below are drawn.

(1) How do cities in the United States, Canada, Australia, Europe, and prosperous parts of Asia compare in critical factors that characterize automobile dependence? Are they diverging, converging, or are they maintaining their differences?

The data show that, in nearly all factors that we use to characterize automobile dependence, the American cities are still the most dependent on the automobile. These cities are followed by the Australian cities, which on many factors, including actual car use, are significantly less than the American cities. Canadian cities on most factors are then a step down again in automobile dependence, including being significantly lower in car use than American and Australian cities. We then find another drop to the European cities in automobile dependence, with most of the factors in these cities being significantly better again than in the Canadian cities (less car use, higher public transit use, better use of non-motorized modes, etc.). Finally, the two Asian cities make again a large drop away from the European cities in having very low dependence on the automobile, due mainly to their very high densities compared to all other cities and a commensurately high level of development of public transit systems and non-motorized modes.

The strong differences between the cities in many of the automobile-dependence factors have been maintained since our 1995 study. However, the litmus test of automobile use, actual car use per capita (car VKT per person), has changed somewhat in the size of the gap between the different cities. Table 2-4 summarizes the differences in car VKT per person that existed between pairs of city groups in 1995 and 2005. It is clear that the difference between US cities and Australian cities has reduced, with the significant growth in Australian car use and only modest growth in US cities. On the other hand, the difference between Australian and Canadian cities in car VKT per person has widened considerably, again because of the rather large growth in Australian urban car VKT and only slight growth in Canadian cities. Going in the other direction, there has been a slight narrowing in the gap between Canadian and European cities. Finally, in the other direction, the difference in car use per capita between European cities and the two Asian cities has widened slightly as European cities have grown in car use, while Singapore and Hong Kong remained almost identical over the decade.

Table 2-3. Overview of trends in automobile dependence in 41 cities, 1995–2005.

Metropolitan Characteristics	Percentage Change 1995–2005
Urban density	–1.0%
Job density	7.4%
Proportion of jobs in CBD	–14.2%
Metropolitan gross domestic product per capita	24.7%
PRIVATE TRANSPORTATION INFRASTRUCTURE	
Length of freeway per person	10.8%
Parking spaces per 1,000 CBD jobs	–4.5%
Passenger cars per 1,000 persons	9.0%
PUBLIC TRANSIT INFRASTRUCTURE	
Total length of reserved public transit routes per 1,000 persons	26.4%
Ratio of segregated public transit infrastructure vs. expressways	28.2%
PUBLIC TRANSIT SERVICE AND USE	
Total public transit seat-kilometers of service per capita	13.7%
Total public transit passenger-kilometers per capita	19.7%
Total rail passenger-kilometers per capita	25.8%
MODAL SPEEDS	
Overall average speed of public transit	4.0%
Average speed of rail (metro and suburban rail)	6.1%
Average road network speed	0.8%
Ratio of public vs. private transportation speeds	3.8%
Ratio of rail speed to road-traffic speed (metro and suburban rail)	4.8%
MODAL SPLIT	
% of all daily trips by non-motorized modes	8.8%
Proportion of total motorized passenger-kilometers on public transit	8.4%
PRIVATE MOBILITY	
Passenger-car passenger-kilometers per capita	4.0%
Car kilometers per real 1995 USD of GDP	-23.4%
Total motorized passenger kilometers per real 1995 USD of GDP	-22.4%
TRANSPORTATION ENERGY USE	
Private-passenger transportation energy use per capita	–3.8%
Public transit energy use per capita	22.5%
Total transportation energy use per capita	–2.9%
TRANSPORTATION EXTERNALITIES	
Total emissions per capita	–33.8%
Total transportation deaths per 100,000 people	–28.8%

Source: Authors' own data.

Table 2-4. Difference in per capita car use between city groups, 1995 and 2005.

Difference between each city group in car VKT per capita	1995	2005
American and Australian cities	5,195 km	4,402 km
Australian and Canadian cities	1,266 km	2,179 km
Canadian and European cities	1,793 km	1,582 km
European and Asian cities	3,388 km	3,604 km

Source: Authors' own data.

Perhaps of greatest significance is that GDP per capita rose by an average of 25 percent in real terms across the cities (when expressed in 1995 US dollars). Increase in wealth is clearly one thing that cities universally aim for, but these data show that it is now a neutral factor in terms of automobile dependence. Perhaps the more recent trends outlined in chapter 1 and elaborated in other chapters, are suggesting that economic advantage favors the end of automobile dependence and that this will be a major factor in determining economic advantage in future years. This decoupling of wealth from automobile dependence is a very important message for the world's cities, as the great challenge of the UN's climate-change goal is to reduce carbon emissions 80 percent by 2050, and it is not feasible to do this unless oil use is decoupled from wealth. Oil use and wealth have been coupled for much of the twentieth century, but now we must hope for a future without oil while we continue to grow in GDP.

The decoupling of wealth and car dependence will be taken up in chapter 3 on emerging cities, in chapter 4, where we can help to explain it in terms of different urban fabrics, and in chapter 6, where we discuss how we can now imagine a long-term future without automobile dependence. What these data show is that wealth can be channeled into ways that diminish automobile dependence and improve overall productivity. These policies include higher-quality and more-extensive public transit systems, better public environments that encourage walking and cycling, and transit-oriented developments (TODs) that provide less auto-dependent lifestyles in better locations. These policies are now being chosen in greater frequency, and their economic impacts are positive.

A case can now be made that wealth generation in cities, which clearly depends on people-intensive jobs and services in the twenty-first-century economy, requires much more spatial efficiencies, especially in central locations where the knowledge economy is locating. Rail, cycling, and walking are very spatially efficient and attract dense economic activity; cars and buses are not spatially efficient and disperse economic activity. Perhaps this mechanism is at the heart of the trends we have been observing in twenty-first-century cities.

(2) What has been happening in key factors that underpin automobile dependence, such as densities and centralization, transportation infrastructure, public transit service and performance, and other factors?

In terms of the key factors that underpin automobile dependence, such as densities, centralization, transportation infrastructure, and public transit service, the results on the whole are positive for the cities here, though some trends seem mixed. Activity densities in cities have generally risen, with job densities growing more than urban density. The most auto-dependent regions (the United States and Australia) and Asian cities have increased in both urban and job densities, while Canadian and European cities have stabilized or declined slightly in urban density. The importance of the central business district (CBD) as a location for jobs has generally declined in relative terms (only 10 cities maintained or increased their share of CBD jobs—Graz, Hong Kong, Vienna, Manchester, Melbourne, Montreal, Berlin, Hamburg, Atlanta, and Phoenix), but the great majority (71 percent) have nevertheless increased in their absolute number of CBD jobs. Research needs to be done on whether genuine public transit–served sub-centers are also attracting intensive urban economy jobs, as do the CBDs.

Infrastructure for private transportation (car ownership, freeways, and CBD parking) presents a mixed picture. Overall, freeway length per capita in the 41 cities has increased. However, the American and Australian cities have remained stable and have reduced a little, respectively. Meanwhile the Canadian cities rose along with the European cities, with the two Asian cities recording the smallest possible rise, from 0.125 to 0.126 meters per person. Overall, it can probably be concluded that in these more developed cities the era of building significant new urban freeways as a solution to transportation problems has probably passed.

Parking supply in the CBDs of cities has reduced even further, with only European cities showing something of an upturn. Data suggests that this global pattern results from a combination of factors:

- the growing importance of urban rail in cities,
- the burgeoning growth in central-city living, sometimes on former commuter parking lots, and
- the continued growth in CBD jobs without commensurate increases in parking supply.

Car ownership, on the other hand, is on the rise everywhere except for the Canadian cities, though the increase in Singapore and Hong Kong is tiny. But in every city these cars are being used less.

Transit infrastructure is essentially growing everywhere. In the global sample, the reserved length of public transit route per person has increased by over 26 percent, and the ratio between reserved public transit route and freeways has increased similarly. Australian cities were the only ones to go against this trend, with a small decrease in this factor due to freeway growth outpacing the development of new reserved-route public transit lines. Backing up this increase in quality public transit infrastructure, there have been strong increases in public transit service. Seat-kilometers per capita have increased by 14 percent across the cities, with all regions showing growth in this factor, mainly due to rail.

Further, the speed performance of public transit has improved across the global sample (a 3.8 percent increase), especially the ratio of public transit speed relative to road-traffic speed (a 4.8 percent increase). Only the American cities declined a fraction in this factor and the Canadian cities remained at the status quo, while the other regions increased. Within this perspective, it is the rail speed relative to road-traffic speed that has improved the most, and the best cities are over 1.5 (Asian) or over 1.3 (European), with American cities not yet breaking the 1.0 barrier. US cities measured 0.96 in 1995 and 0.95 in 2005, and clearly need to improve.

(3) How have mobility patterns changed, such as the use of cars, public transit, and non-motorized modes?

Car use per capita in these cities appears to be stabilizing in its growth, or in some cases is already declining. Twelve out of the 41 cities achieved reductions in the amount of car driving (car VKT per capita). The cities that reduced were Atlanta, Houston, San Francisco, Los Angeles, Oslo, Toronto, Montreal, Zurich, Stockholm, London, Vienna, Graz. The average decrease in per capita car use for these 12 cities was 6.4 percent. In actual car travel (car-passenger-kilometers), the overall growth in car use in these 41 cities has been minimal (4 percent), with the Canadian and the two Asian cities reducing marginally in this factor.

Public transit use is generally a success story in all the cities. Public transit passenger-kilometers per capita increased by 20 percent across all the cities, while the rail-transit component increased 26 percent. In addition, the proportion of total motorized passenger-kilometers by public transit improved across the sample by 8 percent. These changes have occurred across all groups of cities and so they represent very strong, consistent trends toward reduced automobile dependence.

The use of non-motorized modes is also substantial, with an overall increase of 8.8 percent across the cities as a whole. The Australian cities were the only group to register a small decline in this factor, though Australian cities remain higher than US and Canadian cities in walking and biking.

(4) Have some of the major measures of urban passenger transportation systems, such as energy consumption, emissions, and fatalities, improved over the study period?

Private-passenger transportation is the biggest consumer of energy in the transportation sector in cities. Overall this factor has reduced by just less than 4 percent. This has been led by the American cities, with quite a significant drop of 11 percent (though from a globally high starting point). Canadian cities have reduced a little (5 percent), and also the two Asian cities (6 percent). However, European and Australian cities have increased in energy use for private-passenger transportation.

Public transit energy use per capita, which in 2005 represented less than 5 percent of the per capita private figure across all cities (1,360 compared to 28,302 MJ per capita), increased overall by 23 percent (every group of cities increased in transit energy use per capita from 1995–96 to 2005–06). Globally, we are trying to reduce energy use in every sector, but an increase in public transit energy use can be viewed more as a positive trend than a negative. This is because it indicates an increase in public transit service, backed up by significant increases in public transit use and also because public transit energy is at least partially sourced from renewables (especially electric modes) and has the potential for a more rapid change to renewables than the much larger and complex fossil-fuel-dependent private-transportation sector.

Transportation-sector emissions of sulfur dioxide, carbon monoxide, nitrogen oxides, and volatile hydrocarbons have all experienced very large drops from 1995–96 to 2005–06, with an overall average decline for the sample of 34 percent. Every group of cities achieved relatively strong drops, the Canadian cities being the least pronounced. Given that car use, the main source of these emissions, has increased across the whole sample by 5 percent, it can be assumed that the reductions are primarily due to much improved vehicle-propulsion systems and emissions-control technologies.

Another very consistent success factor in this global perspective is the large reductions in transportation deaths, averaging 29 percent overall. All groups of cities reduced significantly in this factor, with the Canadian cities again having the least significant drop (but from an already comparatively low figure in 1995). Again, it would appear that a major source of improvement is in vehicle safety features.

(5) Taken collectively, and examining some linkages between these questions, is there any evidence for the end of automobile dependence in these predominantly wealthy cities?

The data in this chapter, when taken collectively, suggest that automobile dependence is on the wane. This is highlighted most strongly by

1. the number of cities that have actually reduced their car use per capita over the 10-year period examined, which actually had an end point (2005) right at the beginning of the proven peaking and subsequent decline in car use per capita in so many countries (2004–05) as discussed in chapter 1;
2. the increasing speed competitiveness of public transit systems led by growing metro and suburban rail networks;
3. the fairly consistent upturn in the fortunes of public transit and especially urban rail (which seems to be having a new "golden age");
4. the growth in the use of walking and cycling in many cities;
5. the global upturn in the density of cities after years of decline;
6. the continuing strong and mostly increasing importance of central-city areas, despite a relative decline in jobs located there; and
7. finally and perhaps most significantly, the fact that both car use and total motorized mobility appear to have decoupled from GDP growth in nearly all of the cities studied.

What Does This Mean for the End of Automobile Dependence?

The trends indicate that a decline in automobile dependence is setting in. But there are still a huge number of cars on the streets of the world's cities, and in many cases this number is still growing. How far will automobile dependence have to decline before we can say the end has come?

Color plate 1 shows the percentage of total travel for all modes (including walking and cycling) in all the global cities. The data come from each mode expressed as person-kilometers not just trips, hence it includes the distances traveled. This is a very rare set of data, a description of which can be found in Kenworthy (2014).

The overwhelming picture shown by these data is that even in the least automobile-dependent cities there is still a lot of car use as a proportion of total travel. Yet we have seen from the data in this chapter that the actual per capita use of cars (measured in person–kilometers of travel, or PKT) in these cities is much less, with the figure for US cities double that of Australian cities, four times that of European cities and ten times that of Asian cities, on average. Why is this?

To answer this, we must understand that the city's share of person–kilometers of travel (PKT) by different modes is the hardest test we can use to determine whether a city should be considered auto-dependent or not. This is because it is not the percentage of "trips," but the percentage of actual distances traveled. Because walking and biking trips are so short, they do not contribute many person-kilometers, and so it is very hard to have them contributing much to the percentage of total travel, even though they may actually be meeting a lot of important mobility needs in terms of the trips undertaken. Motorized modes (cars, public transit), contribute much more to total travel distances because they service longer trips, which are out of the reach of walking or cycling. So in fact it is very hard in any city to get the proportion of total annual travel by car down to very low levels unless the city really has a very low modal split for cars and the city is so compact that even those car trips are quite short, such as in Singapore and Hong Kong. These are the only cities in our study that have less than 50 percent of total travel by car, and these two cities are about as far away from automobile dependence as one can get among wealthier cities (Tokyo, with its extraordinary rail systems, was similar in 1995).

In color plate 1, there are only six cities where the automobile constitutes less than 60 percent of total annual urban travel requirements (Brussels, Berlin, Prague, Vienna, Singapore, and Hong Kong), and again, only in Singapore and Hong Kong does the automobile represent less than half of all mobility. But do we really need to get as low as 50 percent of all urban travel by car for a whole metropolitan area before we can say that auto dependence has ended? We don't think so. Pinup cities for sustainable transportation, such as Copenhagen or Zurich, still have 72 percent and 67 percent, respectively, of total travel by automobile, despite their reputations for exceptional use of walking, cycling, and public transit. Are these latter two cities "auto-dependent" or not? Clearly not, even though two-thirds to three-quarters of the running around people do is by car. We would never talk about a city like Munich as being "automobile-dependent," yet 65 percent of the actual kilometers people have to travel are still by car. Frankfurt has 72 percent of its total person-kilometers by car. Is it car-dependent? Absolutely not. It is entirely possible to not own a car but to bike, walk, and use public transit to access almost everything. Jeff Kenworthy lives in Frankfurt and lives without a car. As he says, "I do not have a car and I use my bike, my own feet, and transit to access everything I need, and it is easy. A car is a nuisance for most daily needs. . . . You have to park it, negotiate one-way street systems (bikes are allowed in both directions on all streets), and it gets stuck in traffic. I do not find Frankfurt automobile-dependent the way I have found it living in Perth and most American cities."

Ending automobile dependence in US cities could mean that less than 80 percent of annual total travel is undertaken by automobile and still falling. As can be seen in color plate 1, around 80 percent of travel by car is basically where the worst European city (Geneva) sits. We have always used European cities as clear examples of cities that are not auto-dependent. Geneva is not automobile-dependent; it has a different character. Geneva, like all European cities, has a strong mix of modes and choices available for many trips. If one lives in a European city, for the most part one has a choice of how to travel for a majority of daily trips. So we would suggest that a US metropolitan area where auto dependence has ended (but where a huge number of cars are still used) would be one where 75 percent or less of its total annual travel is by car. No US metro area yet approaches this figure, but US cities are trending down-ward. Even the New York tri-state region has still about 88 percent car travel, despite the huge impact of New York City, where the figure is dramatically lower. One could safely say that New York City by itself is not an auto-dependent city.

That might not sound very ambitious, but when one considers that most of the US cities are more than 95 percent auto travel it is in fact a major shift. Getting from a Houston/Atlanta picture to better than a Geneva picture is a big shift, but if you make that shift step-by-step, any city can then claim to have ended their dependence on cars.

Based on all this, we conclude that:

1. The end of automobile dependence is clearly not the end of the car, and future automobile travel needs to become sustainable through renewable fuels and tech-nological efficiency. The automobile needs to do less damage, take up less space, and become simply a useful tool, not something that is absolutely indispensable for every trip (this is expanded in chapter 6).

2. If a metro area such as Houston or Atlanta, where 98 percent of travel is by car, can be shifted to one where only 75 percent is by car, then one can clearly say that auto dependence has ended. The character of the city will have changed forever. The city will have real options for reaching most activities without a car. This is achievable and indeed it is the trend.

3. If we are to be consistent with our terminology (as we have used it in the past in relation to travel patterns in cities) and therefore be clear about what the title of this book really means, auto dependence can then be said to have ended in a city when it has overall about 75 percent or less of total travel by car. This is hardly the end of the car, but it is the end of complete dependence on it. Color plate 1 shows 18 cities where about 75 percent or less of total travel is by car. All are Euro-pean or Asian cities that are clearly not automobile-dependent. The first non-European/Asian cities that come close to this figure are Montreal and Toronto

(around 83–84 percent car travel), Canada's two big public transit metropolises, suggesting that these two cities are well positioned for ending their dependence on the car if the right policies can be followed.

4. In chapter 4 we will outline a better way to understand this through our theory of urban fabrics based on automobile-city, transit-city, and walking-city urban types, which can be found within virtually all cities. We show how the end of automobile dependence is best understood in terms of the management of cars and other options in these three distinctly different parts of the city. Here we shall also see that the above-minimum average target for ending automobile dependence (75 percent car use for a whole metropolitan area), can be quite different for the different types of urban fabric within any city. We suggest in chapter 4 that in public-transit-oriented urban fabric a figure of more like 50 percent or less total travel by car could be achieved, and in walking city fabric 25 percent or less car use should be expected. The more that these types of urban fabric can be encouraged, including selectively changing auto city fabric into transit or walking city fabric, the easier it will be for whole metropolitan areas to end their automobile dependence.

3

Emerging Cities and
Automobile Dependence

We have shown that we are seeing the end of automobile dependence in the developed world as cities decline in car use, even as they grow in wealth. But what is happening in global cities in the developing or emerging economies of the world, such as China, India, Latin America, and Eastern Europe? Authors such as Schafer and Victor (2000), who have been linking mobility and wealth for many years, predict that the emerging nations of the world will increase their motorized mobility more than four times by 2050.

Because data collection in lower-income and often less organized cities is very resource-intensive, frequently requiring specialized, skilled assistance from native-language speakers to build necessary relationships, our data focus has largely been on cities with the resources to gather, analyze, and export the data more easily. However, we need to try to answer the big question posed for this chapter.

To understand how change is happening we are going to use decoupling theory, which helps us to see how cities are facilitating economies to create wealth while reducing automobile dependence. Decoupling is now a major global agenda for enabling sustainable development—increasing livability and reducing poverty, on the one hand, while reducing the use of fossil fuels and other environmental impacts at the same time. Decoupling is well under way in the developed world and the first signs are there in the emerging world as well, so we will summarize these trends to see the big picture, using the emerging cities of mainland China and India. The actual mechanisms for understanding how decoupling works are best gained through case studies. We have chosen three emerging midrange cities: Prague, Sao Paulo, and Taipei.[1] These case studies use less-comprehensive data than those in chapter 2, but they do provide evidence that car use in these rapidly motorizing environments is also hitting a wall, for a variety of reasons. These reasons seem mostly to relate to the dense structure of their cities and the consequent inability to cope with the physical space demands of automobile dependence. They also appear to be showing a decoupling of car use from wealth.

Decoupling Theory

Development economists have been struggling with how to support economic development while lowering consumption. The United Nations Environment Programme's (UNEP) International Resource Panel addresses this theme in the report *Decoupling Natural Resource Use and Environmental Impacts from Economic Growth* (UNEP 2011) and suggests it is entirely possible to decouple wealth from fossil fuels. There are others who suggest that only by extreme reductions in personal lifestyle and reduced economic growth will it be possible to solve our environmental problems (Jackson 2009). The UNEP panel focuses on decoupling: "reducing the amount of resources such as water or fossil fuels to produce economic growth and delinking economic development from environmental deterioration" (p. 4). All agree that decoupling is a necessary process but may not be sufficient for lowering resource consumption as economic opportunities increase.

It has been shown that there is a point where environmental issues begin to be prioritized once basic human needs have been met. The Environmental Kuznets Curve (EKC) is used in order to understand how a range of environmental outcomes deteriorate in the early phases of economic development and then improve as economies grow, producing an inverted U-curve as seen in Figure 3-1 (Grossman & Kruger 1995; Brock & Taylor 2004), particularly as urbanization accompanies this growth. McGranahan et al. (1999) have shown the same thing specifically for cities in what they term the "urban environmental transition": as a city's people become wealthier and more secure, their range of environmental awareness grows from concerns about the immediate indoor household, to concerns about the neighborhood (e.g., pollution due to poor cooking fuels and bad waste disposal), and so on—to the district, the city (e.g., regional air pollution), and ultimately the global environmental level (e.g., climate change).

Even if the concern results in action once cities have become wealthier, the world cannot afford to wait until the emerging economies grow through these economic stages (Sachs 2015). Climate change is now driving the world to cut back 80 percent on fossil fuels by 2050, and this will not be possible through the developed world alone (IPCC 2014). At the same time, many emerging cities have their own issues—such as smog in Chinese cities and the multiple externalities

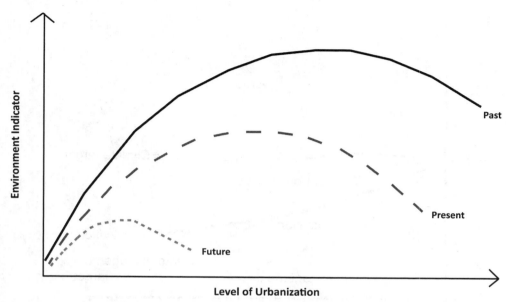

Figure 3-1. Shifting the Environmental Kuznets Curve. Source: Wan and Kahn (2012).

from excessive traffic in all emerging cities—that motivate them to decouple wealth from automobile dependence at a much earlier rate than economists would have predicted.

The Asian Development Bank's 2012 report on Green Urbanization in Asia suggests that Asia may reach the point of improving its environmental outcomes sooner in its economic development trajectory due to the continent's rapid and dense form of urbanization (Wan & Kahn 2012), as outlined in figure 3-1.

Decoupling in the Developed World
The three figures below (figures 3-2, 3-3, and 3-4) show the decoupling of wealth from environmental outcomes in general in the Netherlands, and the decoupling of wealth and fossil fuels in both the UK and Denmark. Similar curves can be shown in all developed countries. The processes by which this is happening are outlined in UN reports and publications from groups such as the World Resources Institute. They involve the kind of technological changes outlined in Hargroves and Smith (2005), Smith et al. (2010), and von Weisacker et al. (2009) and include radical resource productivity, renewable energy, and electric sustainable transportation systems as well as structural changes in cities like those outlined in this book.

The key to understanding how rapidly these changes can set in is to see that once the peak in fossil fuels begins, the decline is exponential and thus can dramatically fall

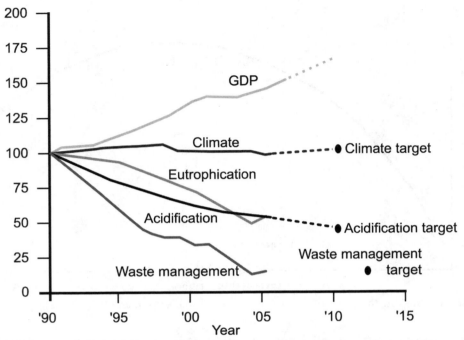

Figure 3-2. Decoupling of GDP and environmental problems in the Netherlands from a 1990 baseline. Source: Compiled from data provided by the Netherlands Environmental Assessment Agency (2007).

away. However, the fear has always been that this decline in coal and oil use (as well as associated structures like automobile dependence) in the developed world will be swept away by the emerging world. Surely the people in the developing world want to be like America and seek wealth through the same kind of fossil-fuel consumption trends? Surely the Chinese and Indians will want cars just like in American cities?

China's Decoupling

In the past decade China has begun a move away from its early phase—"development at all costs"—to a clean-energy pathway. This has been a planned transition to manage excessive problems of urban air pollution and congestion; it has taken a decided focus on reducing the need for so much automobile dependence. It has shown some dramatic changes in recent years that are summarized in the figures below.

A part of this has been the rather dramatic shifts in the central government's original take on the Chinese automobile industry as one of the four pillars of Chinese industrialization. Guo et al. (2014) explain how China's automobile industry can be divided into four clear phases:

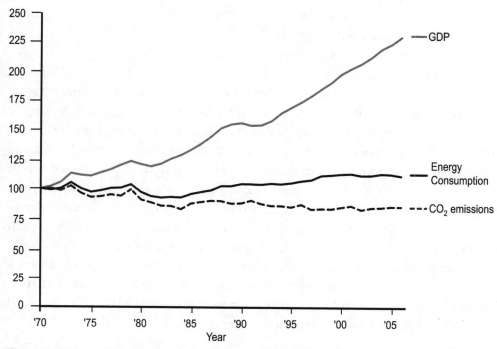

Figure 3-3. Decoupling of GDP and energy / greenhouse emissions in the UK from a 1970 baseline. Source: Compiled from data provided by DETR (2000) and WRI (2009).

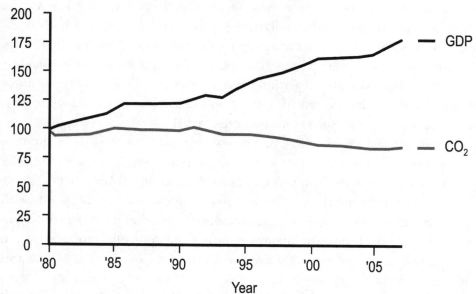

Figure 3-4. Decoupling of GDP and greenhouse emissions in Denmark from a 1980 baseline. Source: Compiled from data provided by the Development Data Group (2008).

Startup Phase (1956–1978)

Growth Phase (1979–2000)

Prosperity Phase (2001–2010)

Stationary Phase (2011–present)

The progression is basically one of initial elation and optimism, similar to the heady post–World War II days in the United States with its love affair with the car and its massive ramping-up of production, to a not-so-gradual realization that the impacts of automobiles—and the land-use patterns and infrastructure that go to support them—are simply unsustainable for China and have to be slowed down or reversed. We see this not only in expanding programs to build metro systems and high-speed rail systems (chapter 1), but also in major efforts now to curb car-ownership growth in large cities. The best-known of these efforts are Shanghai's auction system for the right to purchase a car (introduced in 1994 before large-scale motorization started and hence the most effective of all in China so far), and Beijing's more-recent lottery system to win the same rights to purchase a car, but by chance. These changes are further documented in Zhao et al. (2013, 2014) and Chen and Zhao (2012), and the relative merits of each are discussed.

Car Use

China used the automobile industry to help propel its economic growth. Private-vehicle ownership was only first allowed in 1984, and not until the 1990s, after a period in which automotive manufacturing was oriented to trucks, did it begin to focus on cars. Private-vehicle ownership rose from around 2 million in 1994 to almost 8 million in 2001 and then to 73 million by 2011 (*China Automotive Industry Yearbook* 2012). However, the congestion levels in cities grew very rapidly, as Chinese cities are very dense and do not have the land-use patterns or the transportation infrastructure to cope with such a massive influx of vehicles.

Chinese cities, shaped over millennia by walking and more recently by bicycles, were simply overwhelmed by automobiles being imposed on very tight walking city fabrics (see chapter 4). Air quality deteriorated dramatically (Wan & Kahn 2012), leading to a new set of policies that have been promulgated as part of their twelfth five-year plan (2011–15). These policies introduced Transportation Demand Management (TDM), which directly involves reducing the desirability to access a car, and a large-scale shift toward public transit opportunities. In effect, TDM attempts to curb the demand for private-vehicle travel so that it matches the existing transportation infrastructure, rather than trying to endlessly increase the supply of that infrastructure to meet ever-expanding demand. There is some evidence that a new era of managing growth in car use is emerging. Chinese automobile production has peaked. After the Chinese automobile manufacturing industry became the biggest in the world in 2009 it has begun to plateau in its production, with only 0.8 percent growth in 2011 after decades of double-digit growth.

Really effective and significant TDM is rarely practiced in Western cities, but it is now firmly on the Chinese urban agenda. Car ownership is now being controlled in most major cities through curtailing the quota of new car registrations with a system, originally pioneered by Singapore, by which people must bid at an auction for a "Certificate of Entitlement" that confers the right to purchase a car. Vehicle quotas have been enacted in Shanghai, Beijing, Guangzhou, Guiyang, Hangzhou, and Tianjin. Also, many of the large cities have adopted other means of TDM; Nangjing and Shenzhen, for example, are both using parking restrictions as a way of better managing the car. Many other cities have imposed numbered license-plate restrictions to limit the days people can drive, but drivers are often able to get around such rules wherever they are implemented.

Urban transit is being radically revamped and prioritized. This is being achieved within cities by the building of metros in 39 cities so far, with a total of 86 more either under construction or planned. Also, other cities are building light-rail transit (LRT) or bus rapid transit (BRT). Figure 3-5 shows metro network growth in China.

Two examples of the dramatic changes in urban transportation are the metros in Shanghai and Beijing. Shanghai (Line 1 opened in 1993) and Beijing (Line 1 opened

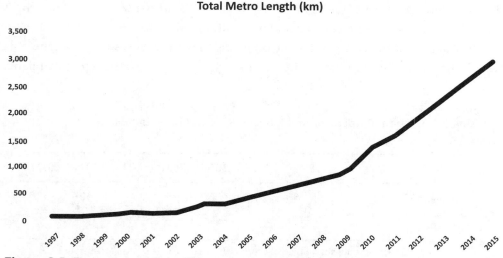

Figure 3-5. Dramatic growth in Chinese metro-system length, 1997–2015. Source: Compiled from data provided by CESG (2014).

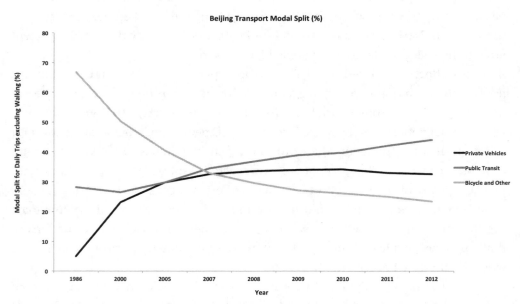

Figure 3-6. Travel modes of Beijing residents' daily trips, by percentage (excluding walking), 1986–2012. Source: Compiled from data based on Beijing Transport Development Annual Report (2013).

in 1969) began the major phase of Chinese metro building in the early 2000s and have demonstrated to the rest of China how successful they can be, now with 8 million passengers a day in Shanghai and 9 million passengers a day in Beijing—the highest metro patronages in the world (Newman & Matan 2013a, 2013b). Shanghai's metro is some 434 kilometers long and was built in a decade.

An example of the changes that are occurring in such cities is shown in figure 3-6, which shows that Beijing's growth in the mode share of car use, after replacing biking,

Table 3-1. Growth of ridership on high-speed rail in China (in millions of passengers per year).

	2007	2008	2009	2010	2011	2012	2013
Ridership of China Railway High-speed (CRH) Services (in millions)	61	128	180	291	440	486	530

Source: Qiao (2013) and english.peopledaily.com.cn/90778/7754100.html (accessed 23 April 2012).

has now in turn been replaced by the growth in mode share of public transit (BT 2013). This is significant and necessary, because the use of bicycles plummeted in Beijing from 63 percent of daily trips in 1986 to just 14 percent in 2012 (see figure 3-6). Importantly, the modal split of private motor-vehicle use (cars and motorcycles) has peaked and is now in decline. Guangzhou has similarly stopped its growth in private-vehicle modal split at just over 40 percent of daily trips as its metro begins to take over (GTD 2012). These private-vehicle modal-split data for both cities also include a large component of electric motor scooters and electric bikes, which are also defined as private motor vehicles and now number more than 250 million across the country.

A further dramatic change has been the growth in high-speed rail between cities: there are now over 8,500 kilometers of high-speed rail track across the country. The trends in patronage are given in table 3-1.

The result of this kind of growth in electric public transportation can now be seen in the decoupling of China's GDP from oil and coal (see figure 3-7).

The switch to more electric transportation, especially mass-transit modes, could ease the congestion problems in Chinese cities, especially if accompanied by more

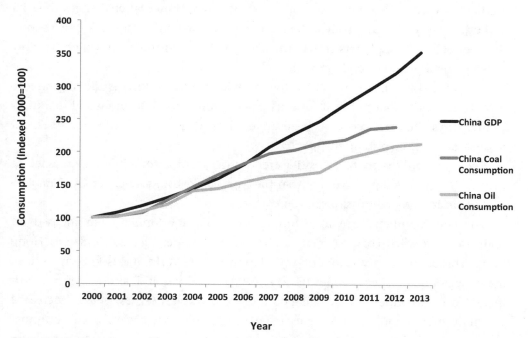

Figure 3-7. Chinese GDP vs. coal and oil consumption, showing decoupling. Source: Compiled from data provided by the Chinese Bureau of Statistics (CBS) Annual Yearbook (2013).

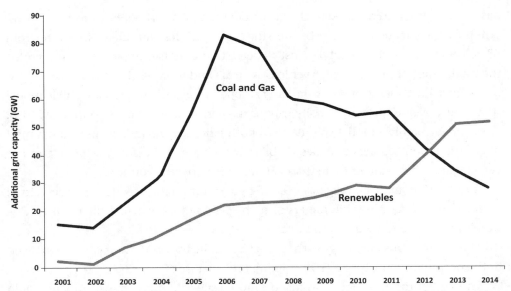

Figure 3-8. The transition from coal to renewable energy sources in Chinese power production. Source: Sheehan (2014).

widespread use of controls over car ownership, as described above. However, if they are based on coal-fired power stations then the environmental challenges of GHG and urban air quality are likely to be unchanged or worsened. Figure 3-7 also shows that China has decoupled its growth of GDP from coal consumption, which has now peaked after a period of rapid growth.

As reported by Sheehan (2014), there is evidence that China is moving rapidly toward the phasing-out of coal from its power production and industrial manufacturing. The switch from coal has been driven mostly by a change to renewables and natural gas, as shown in figure 3-8.

Thus, not only is there a positive trend away from automobile dependence in China, there is also a positive sign that the world's biggest producer of GHG may be peaking in its carbon emissions.

The chosen urban form for Chinese economic development has focused on high-rise towers in redevelopment and new development areas, similar to Hong Kong. This high density is among the highest in the world and is known to have many agglomeration economies (Glaeser 2011). However, it is also associated with increased externalities such as air pollution and congestion, as well as increased greenhouse emissions, and such extreme density has not always been accompanied by commensurate increases in mixed land use and transit-system expansion to encourage more walking, cycling, and public transit use (e.g., there are parts of eastern Shanghai—Pudong—that have extreme density, but also a lot of gated communities based on cars). Thus, there is now a policy focus on how to move away from coal-fired power and oil-based car use in order to improve air quality, reduce congestion, and meet stated goals of reducing carbon intensity. The interventions have been rapid, as with most Chinese economic planning. The first evidence is now appearing that Chinese greenhouse emissions are unlikely to follow the trajectory of the industrialized West and that the Environmental Kuznets Curve shown in figure 3-1 will occur much earlier.

Indian Decoupling

The same patterns of decoupling from oil and coal have been demonstrated in India (see figure 3-9 for coal and oil); even though the consumption growth is still occurring, it looks like it is peaking. As outlined in chapter 1, there are significant commitments now to Indian cities developing electric public transit systems and their popularity is immediately evident: Indian cities are highly congested, so fast rail across the top or underneath the traffic is transformative in its impact.

The data on China and India indicate that decoupling is well underway. The mechanisms in China and India are best understood in terms of their cities, which have rapidly urbanized and are now seeking to manage their environmental issues, including their automobile usage. What is obvious is that their cities are nothing like American and Australian cities and are never going to develop the kind of automobile dependence evident in Atlanta and Houston or even Melbourne and Perth. They will have a few patches of automobile dependence, mostly in developments far from the main centers, but generally they are going to address transportation and land use in much more dense and mass-transit-oriented ways.

Midrange Cities and Decoupling

As the detailed data on Chinese and Indian cities are difficult to obtain, the best way to assess the mechanisms for how cities are decoupling wealth from automobile dependence is by examining some midrange-economy cities where it was also expected that wealth would lead to further car dependence, as Chinese and Indian cities are not as developed as Western industrial economies.

In this chapter, we present data on three midrange cities from Eastern Europe, Latin America, and Asia. Sao Paulo is Brazil's largest metropolitan area (with 19.9 million people), Prague is the capital of the Czech Republic (with 1.2 million people), and Taipei is the capital of Taiwan (with 6.4 million people). The GDP of these cities is in the midrange on a per capita basis.

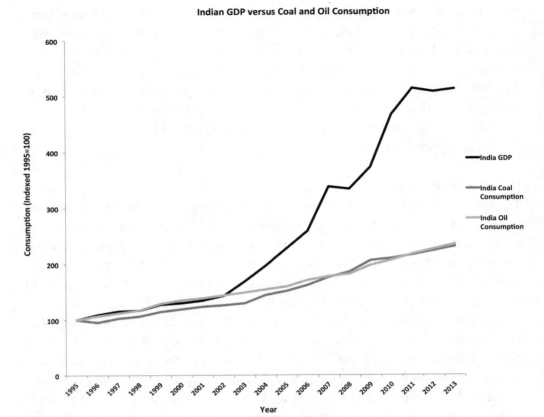

Figure 3-9. Indian GDP vs. oil and coal consumption showing decoupling. Source: Compiled from data provided by the World Bank (2014), Indexmundi data portal (2014), and the US Energy Information Administration (EIA) (2014).

These cities have in recent decades all experienced a dramatic increase in the presence of private motorized traffic. Prague, a medium-density European city with an extensive transit system, has advanced rapidly since the breakup of the Eastern Bloc and subsequent economic liberalization and growth, with a spectacular increase in cars and traffic since the Velvet Revolution of 1989. Taipei is the main urban center of Taiwan, one of the four "Asian Tigers" (the others being Singapore, Hong Kong, and South Korea), which industrialized and grew dramatically from the 1960s through the 1990s, increasing steadily in car and especially motorcycle ownership. Taipei, indeed, can be characterized as a "motorcycle city" (Barter 1999). The Sao Paulo Metropolitan Region (SPMR) embraces 39 municipalities and now, with over 20 million people, is a major economic engine of Brazil. It includes the city of Sao Paulo, which alone is a megacity of over 10 million people. It has a reputation akin to Bangkok for traffic congestion, with an unusually high rate of helicopter use for intra-urban travel (Phillips 2008). A key question of relevance to comparable medium-income urban environments worldwide is whether or not there is also evidence of a decoupling of car (and motorcycle) use from growing GDP per capita.

Sao Paulo

The detailed data on the Sao Paulo Metropolitan Region (SPMR), which we have collected for 1996 and 2011, suggest strongly that Sao Paulo's most obvious transportation problems stem from the cars and motorcycles that have such a large impact on the region's public environments, especially evident in the city's legendary traffic jams. Perhaps surprisingly, these two modes still only make up about 30 percent of the city's daily trips, despite the GDP per capita of the region having risen by 153 percent in real US dollars, and in real local currency by 126 percent, from 1996 to 2009 (US$13,438 in 1995 dollars). The congestion and sheer impact of traffic stems primarily from the physical inability of the present city fabric and infrastructure systems to cope with the aggressive and unrestrained space demands of cars and, to a lesser extent, motorcycles (see figure 3-10). This is because so much of Sao Paulo's very dense, mixed-use urban fabric, which was never built for the automobile (although freeway length per person grew by 111 percent from 1996 to 2011), has no chance of properly handling even its still comparatively modest levels of car and motorcycle ownership (365 and 73 per 1,000 persons in 2011) (see figure 3-11). Cars and motorcycles therefore have a visual and physical impact that is very disproportionate to the magnitude of their actual role within the total passenger-transportation system.

Many of the city's outward appearances and problems would perhaps suggest an urban region that is moving inexorably toward a sprawling and automobile-dependent model of development akin to that of the United States, whereas the overall facts from the data collected for both 1996 and 2011 suggest otherwise. The overall picture can be summarized as follows:

- Sao Paulo is a dense urban region that is actually getting denser (85.5 persons per ha, up 10 percent from 1996).
- It remains highly centralized in terms of jobs (28 percent), and the CBD is serviced by an increasingly extensive rail system (metro and commuter rail).
- The amount of public transit service is very high by global standards and is increasing significantly (vehicle- and seat-kilometers per capita rose by 32 percent and 21 percent, respectively, over 15 years). While buses remain clearly dominant within the transit system (in 2011 they constituted 75 percent of all public transit vehicle

Figure 3-10. Sao Paulo's very high-density urban form makes it ideal for public transit and non-motorized modes but problematic for accommodating cars. Source: Jeff Kenworthy.

–kilometers of service in the region), their growth in numbers is faltering compared with that of rail, and the region is moving toward a much greater role for its metro and suburban rail systems (bus use in terms of passenger-kilometers per capita declined by 4 percent, while metro use rose 45 percent and suburban rail rose 139 percent).

- The relative speed of public transit compared to the car has improved and is comparatively good when compared to typical automobile cities (up 11 percent to 0.79). The metro and suburban rail systems both have average operating speeds that far surpass that of the road system (traffic speed averages 25.4 kilometers per hour, compared to 37.5 and 40.0 kilometers per hour for the rail services).
- Analysis of modal splits and trip making suggests that cars and motorcycles did not increase their share, but have actually experienced a small negative trend from 1997 to 2007 (from 32.0 percent to 29.6 percent), while public transit has increased its share from 32.9 percent to 36.4 percent of daily trips. (The latest Household Travel Survey was conducted in 2007.)

Figure 3-11. Accommodating cars in any high-density urban area mixed with pedestrians, cyclists, and public transit is a major problem, especially in parts of Sao Paulo like those pictured here. Source: Jeff Kenworthy.

- The combined use of public transit and non-motorized modes for daily trips (70 percent) remains very dramatically higher than in any automobile cities. Sao Paulo is even significantly higher than in the more attractive European cities that have traditionally been strongholds of public transit and non-motorized modes.
- The relatively small proportion (30 percent) of daily trips that are undertaken by car and motorcycle in the SPMR are causing most of the damage in terms of congestion, air pollution, traffic noise, and traffic mortality, and are chiefly responsible for the region being increasingly characterized as a traffic disaster.
- Actual car use per capita has increased somewhat in Sao Paulo but not as much, perhaps, as the clogged road system would suggest (car-passenger-kilometers per capita increased 10 percent over 15 years). US cities still have 4.5 times more car use per capita, and the indications are that Sao Paulo will not and cannot even contemplate auto-dependence levels anywhere near those of typical automobile cities, wherever they are located.

- Motorcycle ownership and use are dramatically up (3.4 times higher ownership and 2.7 times more person-kilometers per capita) and are high compared to most other cities, but motorcycles remain small players in the overall mobility system, with both per capita car and public transit use *each* individually exceeding motorcycle mobility by factors greater than 10.
- Public transit boardings and passenger-kilometers per capita show relatively strong growth (27 percent and 14 percent, respectively, over 15 years) and this is especially true of rail (62 percent growth in boardings and 94 percent in passenger-kilometers on the combined metro and commuter rail systems). Though buses are still the mainstay of the public transit system, their percentage share is declining (82 percent of total public transit passenger-kilometers in 1996 and 69 percent in 2011).
- The cost recovery from Sao Paulo's heavily used public transit system is very much higher than in typical automobile dependent cities and almost breaks even (91 percent). (See figure 3-12.)
- Overall transportation emissions per capita (CO, NO_x, SO_2, and volatile hydrocarbons [VHC] from all transportation modes) have declined by 15 percent and are significantly below those in the automobile cities.
- The proportion of Sao Paulo's total motorized transportation task accomplished by public transit is the same in 2011 as it was in 1996, an astonishingly high 46 percent and some 15 times greater than that in the auto-dependent US cities.

At least partly due to the above-mentioned facts about the evolution of Sao Paulo from 1996 to 2011, the region displays a clear decoupling of car use from growth in real local GDP. From 1996 to 2011, the car-kilometers per unit of real GDP (in Brazilian reals—R$) fell by 48 percent (0.466 km to 0.240 km per real R$).[2] Similarly, total motorized travel (cars, motorcycles, and public transit) per unit of real local GDP has also fallen by 50 percent (1.344 to 0.679 passenger-km per real R$).

Despite some trends toward more freeways, a deteriorating ratio between the length of quality reserved public transit route and the length of freeways, and a still very high transportation death rate (14.1 per 100,000 persons, compared to the average for US cities of 9.5), the SPMR is absolutely not displaying any of the key characteristics of any automobile-dependent region. What the analysis does show is that it is clearly an *automobile-saturated* region, where even its medium level of car ownership, compounded by a dramatically rising motorcycle fleet, simply cannot be accommodated in an urban structure not designed around the car and

Figure 3-12. Urban rail is critical to the future of high-density, rapidly motorizing cities, and its use is growing rapidly in Sao Paulo (Luz station on the commuter rail system). Source: Jeff Kenworthy.

one that has no chance of simply building its way out of this congestion with new roads. The fact that 70 percent of daily trips are still dependent on public transit and non-motorized modes shows rather that investment should be primarily directed into these modes, thus consolidating this significant advantage compared to auto-dependent regions.

Furthermore, without some physical, economic, or other restraints on the ownership and use of cars (and motorcycles), there appears to be little chance for Sao Paulo to control the congestion that cripples both cars and buses or to stop the relative decline of bus use, as described in this case study. To ignore the need to control congestion will perpetuate and worsen what is already a morally questionable situation for the millions of people who collectively make over 4.4 billion bus boardings per year and are forced to travel at an average speed under 17 kilometers per hour because of the cars that clog all available road space. This is not much better than the typical average speed for an urban bike trip. Buses annually transport 50 billion passenger-kilometers in the SPMR and yet add a burden of only 1.6 billion vehicle-kilometers to the road system in order to achieve this mobility service for the population. Cars carry 80 billion passenger-kilometers per annum but add a burden of 56.0 billion vehicle-kilometers. Thus, the public bus system that reaches and serves more people than the present rail system and contributes 62 percent as many passenger-kilometers as the car, with only 3 percent as many vehicle-kilometers, drowns in the congestion created by unrestrained use of cars.

The physical realities and constraints of the SPMR mean that automobiles and motorcycles cannot provide people with the mobility they need within their one hour per day travel-time budgets (Marchetti 1994). Buses suffer similar problems. There thus appears to be an adjustment process occurring at an urban system level. This urban system adjustment, perhaps hidden by the more imposing picture of road chaos and the sheer physical impacts of so many vehicles squeezed into a space that cannot contain them, is characterized by

- densification and limits on the spread of the city;
- failure of extra road capacity to solve traffic problems (compounded with the fact that new high-capacity roads destroy too much of the city's physical fabric and are extremely expensive);
- rail becoming a favored mode because of its inherently superior relative speed, made much more striking by the fact that buses cannot compete on the roads in speed terms due to a lack of fair allocation of road space; and
- increasing attraction of rail station precincts as sites for development because of accessibility advantages.

In conclusion, Sao Paulo is not becoming an automobile-dependent city. In fact, both car use and total motorized mobility over the 1996 to 2011 period decoupled significantly from growth in GDP, despite the fact that the city is perceived as a rapidly motorizing environment where major increases in wealth are supposedly driving equivalent increases in car use and mobility in general. On the contrary, Sao Paulo is a large metropolitan region that is maintaining a strong public transit and walking orientation in the face of a physically devastating increase in cars and motorcycles, which alone are simply unable to meet the mobility needs of the region. As a result, Sao Paulo appears to be undergoing a painful process punctuated by traffic mayhem.

The region demonstrates the clear physical limits on how much a dense, rapidly industrializing urban environment can support car and motorcycle use before hitting a wall of mobility limitations, environmental impacts, social inequity, and

severe negative livability outcomes. This collision inevitably forces other adjustments, the beginnings of which we see reflected in the data on Sao Paulo, especially
the decoupling of mobility from real growth in GDP. Sao Paulo has been able to
increase its GDP per capita by 126 percent (real local currency), while its per capita
mobility by cars and motorcycles (passenger-km) has grown only 15 percent over
15 years and public transit mobility by only 14 percent. These adjustments are the
seeds of a more regenerative response by the region involving a limit on, and ultimately a reversal in, the growth of automobile use, and the ascendency of non-auto
modes, while still allowing the region's economy to grow in real terms. At present,
one of the key missing items in this adjustment process, in common with most
other cities in the world, is the direct, region-wide control of congestion (Bradley &
Kenworthy 2012). If the city were able to control congestion through a Singapore
or London process, it would increase GDP per unit of car mobility even more dramatically than it has been doing.

Taipei

Taipei is the capital of Taiwan, or the Republic of China; the island was formerly
known as Formosa. Taiwan is one of the four "Asian Tigers" known for their very
rapid economic growth since the 1960s. The Taipei metropolitan area consists of
Taipei City and Taipei County (now New Taipei City), an area that today consists of
around 7 million people. Taipei has a well-developed public transit system consisting
of a metro, some suburban rail services, and a complex and largely integrated bus
system. It is, however, better known in transportation terms, along with a handful of
such other Asian metropolises as Ho Chi Minh City and, to a lesser extent, Bangkok
and Jakarta, for its extremely high rate of motorcycle ownership.

In fact, Barter (1999) classified Taipei as a "motorcycle city." This was distinct
from other, more-typical classifications of cities, such as walking cities, public
transit cities, and auto cities, typologies conceived mainly on the basis of the
transportation evolution of cities, which today are part of the developed world
(see chapter 4). Likewise, "motorcycle city" is also distinct from more-recent classifications of large global cities (Priester et al. 2013) and German cities (Klinger
et al. 2013) through cluster analysis, the first of which led to six distinct city
types, termed auto, public transit, non-motorized mode, hybrid, paratransit,[3] and
traffic-saturated cities. Taipei in this latter analysis fell into the "traffic-saturated
cities," along with Ho Chi Minh City, Jakarta, Kuala Lumpur, Bangkok, Cairo, and
Tehran.

Taipei is also a very dense Asian urban environment, with a density in 2006 of

170 persons per hectare, which places it firmly in an urban category where walking, cycling, and public transit tend to be very important components of the urban transportation system. It also means that it has a very constrained and compact urban form where space, especially road space, is used very intensively and is at a premium. These physical factors, combined with rapid economic growth and rising consumer expectations surrounding mobility, make Taipei an interesting case study of what may be happening more widely in the Asian region in urban transportation in a period of very rapid motorization.

Taipei is a metropolitan region that has clearly experienced some sweeping changes in its urban transportation system from 1996 to 2006 (the latest year of data we have been able to assemble). On the one hand, motorcycles have increased in number dramatically, while on the other, cars have also increased in number, though more modestly. The key findings are:

- Urban and job density have declined over the decade (–26 percent and –21 percent, respectively), though Taipei retains very high densities by global standards (170 persons/ha and 76 jobs/ha); the decline is probably a boundary issue.[4]
- Centralization of jobs into Taipei's CBD has increased marginally (7 percent), which coincides with the rapid development of the Taipei metro.
- Wealth, expressed in both real US dollars and real New Taiwan (NT) dollars, has grown very significantly over the decade (32 percent and 95 percent, respectively). At $20,502 (US dollars, 1995) in 2006, the city is still well below the overall average for all the cities examined in chapter 2 ($37,700), but it is relatively close to the average for Singapore and Hong Kong ($21,201) after such growth.
- The freeway length per capita in Taipei has increased by over three times, from 0.011 to 0.035 meters per person. Although this is a large increase, the overall 2006 figure is still rather low by global standards, though a little higher than its two neighboring Asian cities, which had 0.026 meters per person in 2005.
- Available parking in the newly defined CBD is a lot higher than in 1996 (a 337 percent increase), but at 119 spaces per 1,000 jobs is still extremely low by comparison to most other cities.
- Transit lines have been rationalized and reduced (a 65 percent decline), though the supply of high-quality reserved route for public transit has increased significantly (117 percent), especially the metro network expansion. This is a process that many developing cities need to make as a way of creating faster and more competitive public transit.
- Car ownership has increased moderately (28 percent), but at 224 cars per 1,000 persons is still relatively modest (all the other cities in this study average 512).

However, on this factor it is very much higher than Singapore–Hong Kong, which average only 78 cars per 1,000 persons.

- Motorcycle ownership has grown dramatically (149 percent) and stood in 2006 at 491 motorcycles per 1,000 persons! The average for all the other cities in the Global Cities Database was 28.
- Road-traffic speed is very slow by global urban standards (17.0 km/h), and it has not changed over the decade.
- Public transit service per person (vehicle-kilometers) has declined overall (–10 percent), but increased in its rail component, while the seat-kilometers of service per person have expanded by about 1 percent, despite a drop in bus service.
- Public transit speed has improved in overall terms (18 percent) due to the rail system and bus rationalization, and the ratio of public transit system speed to general traffic has improved by 16 percent. The metro speed (32.7 km/h) is nearly twice as fast as road traffic, while suburban rail (47.0 km/h) is 2.7 times faster.
- Overall, trip-making rates have increased by 26 percent (3.38 trips per person per day in 2006), and non-motorized and public transit mode shares have grown slightly at the expense of private motorized modes (a 6 percent and 3 percent increase, respectively).
- Car use per person (vehicle-kilometers) has increased over the decade by 16 percent but still stands at only 2,100 kilometers per person, a very low rate compared to that of all the other cities in our sample (7,312 km), but considerably higher than the Singapore–Hong Kong average of 1,333 kilometers.
- On the other hand, car passenger travel (passenger-kilometers per person) has declined by 7 percent, due to a reduction in average occupancy.
- Motorcycle vehicle and passenger kilometers have grown by 73 percent and 48 percent, respectively, and at 2,158 kilometers and 2,438 kilometers per capita are very high compared to other cities (a meager 104 km and 133 km per capita, respectively).
- Public transit boardings and passenger-kilometers per capita have grown to a significant degree (29 percent and 16 percent, respectively). Annual boardings are now a healthy 340 per capita (compared, for example, to the European cities, with 386), and the proportion of the total motorized passenger transportation by public transit has even increased slightly from 25 percent to 26 percent, despite the rise in car and motorcycle use.
- Total passenger transportation energy use per capita has risen 12 percent over the decade, but transportation emissions and transportation deaths per capita have declined dramatically (48 percent and 65 percent, respectively).

Taipei, like Sao Paulo, clearly has a motorization problem in terms of the growth in vehicles, their usage, and all that this implies for the integrity of the public realm and livability of the city. But it is also clear that, as in Sao Paulo, adjustments are taking place that mean that the region is not succumbing to private transportation in its aggregate mobility patterns. On the contrary, many of the trends are very positive.

Finally, if we examine the vehicle-kilometers of travel per unit of real GDP (in NT$) in 1996 and 2006, we find that car kilometers and motorcycle kilometers per unit of real local GDP declined by 41 percent and 11 percent, respectively. When these two pillars of private mobility in Taipei are combined, the overall decline was 29 percent. Considering total motorized mobility by combining the car, motorcycle, and public transit passenger-kilometers per unit of real local GDP, we find that here too there is a decline of 42 percent. It therefore appears that, despite the apparent motorization trend, urban travel in Taipei in every component has decoupled from GDP growth and it is happening at a very advanced rate.

Prague

Prague, the capital of the Czech Republic, is a medium-size European city that today has a population of around 1.3 million and is the largest city in the Czech Republic and the 14th largest in the European Union.[5] Clearly, it is very much smaller than Sao Paulo and Taipei. In the period from 1995 to 2005, Prague's population, in common with that of many "shrinking" European cities, declined from 1,212,655 to 1,181,610, a reduction of 2.6 percent. It occupies a relatively compact administrative area of 485 square kilometers, which, if considered as circular, has a radius of only about 12.5 kilometers. And only about 55 percent of this area (267 km^2) is urbanized, the rest being forest, agriculture, and undeveloped land.

Prague contains a beautiful medieval center, famous worldwide for its historic landmarks and listed by UNESCO as a World Heritage Site. Mobility in this area is strongly oriented to walking and cycling as well as public transit, since it is served by a very extensive tram system and many metro stations. Outside of the historic inner area, much of the post–World War II development consists of Communist-era concrete high-rise buildings set in windswept and bleak open spaces, though frequently linked closely to the city's metro system or connected to metro stations by feeder buses.

From 1948 to 1989, Prague, then the capital of Czechoslovakia, was under Communist rule and lay behind the "Iron Curtain." After the 1989 Velvet Revolution, Prague became part of a parliamentary republic. In 1993, Czechoslovakia split into the Czech Republic and Slovakia. Since 1989, Prague has rapidly motorized and, like most former Eastern Bloc cities, this motorization has put heavy pressure on an urban fabric and transportation infrastructure system designed primarily around non-automobile modes. In 1981, while Prague was still under Communist rule, the number of cars was 284,756 for 1,183,000 people (or 241 per 1,000 people) a not-insignificant car-ownership rate, considering the Communist-based socioeconomic and political situation (Institute of Transportation Engineering of the City of Prague 2006). By comparison, car ownership in Copenhagen in 2005 was still only 333 per 1,000.

By 1990, just after the Velvet Revolution, the number of cars had grown slowly to 336,037 (about 5,700 extra cars each year) for 1,215,000 people, or an ownership rate of 277 per 1,000 people. However, after that the number of cars grew much more rapidly (Institute of Transportation Engineering of the City of Prague 2006). By 2005, Prague had exceeded 500 cars per 1,000 people, a car-ownership rate that surpassed even that of Montreal, Toronto, and Vancouver and was only a little behind the high car ownership of German cities such as Düsseldorf (516) and Stuttgart (531) in 2005.

This rise in car ownership was followed by a steady growth in car use. In the 10 years from 1971 to 1981, daily car vehicle-kilometers of travel grew from 3,543 to 4,338 million, and then nine years later, in 1990, it was 5,848 million. However, in only one decade, from 1990 to 2000, the figure leapt to over 2.5 times higher (15,131 million km) and has grown steadily since (Institute of Transportation Engineering of the City of Prague 2006).

On the other hand, Prague also has a remarkable public transit system. Our data show that in 2005 it had 2,085 kilometers of bus lines, 559 kilometers of tram line, 54 kilometers of metro, and 160 kilometers of suburban rail line, or nearly 3,000 kilometers of transit routes within its relatively compact form, which equals nearly six kilometers of transit route within every square kilometer of its total land area. Perth, a city of similar population size, had less than one kilometer of transit route in every square kilometer. Melbourne is recognized as having one of the most extensive tram systems in the world, but in 2006, Melbourne's trams had a total system length of 341 kilometers (compared with 559 kilometers in Prague), despite having low densities and thus a need for longer transit lines. In 1995, Prague had an astonishing 907 annual public transit boardings per capita, by far the highest in the hundred cities surveyed. Prague massively exceeded even one of the world's great public transit cities, Zurich, which had 505 boardings per capita in 1995, as well as eclipsing the public transit giant Tokyo, with 611 boardings per capita (Kenworthy & Laube 2001).

It is therefore interesting to dissect urban transportation in Prague a little more carefully to see what has been happening in this period of rapid motorization and again to examine the extent of changes in mobility in the city in the face of this apparent onslaught of cars and car use. Is Prague becoming an automobile-dependent city, or are there signs of a more regenerative approach?

Prague is a city of stark contrasts in both the character and aesthetics of its built form. However, both its more typical European-style five-story apartment buildings with shops underneath and its high-rise neighborhoods, all serviced relatively well by public transit, make the basic structure of the city more amenable to walking, cycling, and public transit use than to the automobile or indeed the motorcycle. Its very extensive, expanding, and heavily utilized public transit system also acts as a bulwark against car and motorcycle mobility. From 1995 to 2005, Prague's transit boardings per capita grew by 16 percent to 1,051 per capita annually, or nearly three trips for every man, woman, and child per day. Further, the annual distance traveled by public transit increased from 4,321 to 5,190 transit-passenger-kilometers per capita, or over 14 kilometers per day on public transit for every person.

Nevertheless, it is very clear that motorization has developed at a high rate since the end of Communist rule. It could perhaps be said that cars have been taken up with even more relish than in other European cities, as part of an overall trend toward greater personal freedoms, opportunities, consumerism, and wealth since democratization.

If we consider car use in relation to wealth, we find that from 1995 to 2005 car kilometers per unit of real local GDP reduced by 1.6 percent (0.0128 to 0.0126). A similar though stronger picture emerges when we combine all motorized mobility by car, motorcycle, and public transit. In 1995, there were 0.036 total motorized passenger-kilometers per Czech koruna (CZK), and in 2005 there were 0.031, a reduction of over 14 percent. Put another way, Prague's real wealth grew from CZK243,303 per capita in 1995 to CZK400,523 in 2005, or a 65 percent increase, while the total motorized mobility (car, motorcycle, and transit) used to generate each Czech koruna declined by 14 percent.

If we wish to compare Prague's car use relative to GDP with that of other global cities, we need to use a common currency—in this case, 1995 US dollars. Even though Prague in 2005 had 0.249 car-kilometers per 1995 US dollar, which is atypically high for a European city (an average in this study of 0.134 in 2005), it is still less than the that of the auto cities of the United States and Australia–New Zealand, which average 0.297 and 0.272, respectively.

Nevertheless, it is also clear that there has been a tangible and significant increase in the spatial intensity of car use in Prague and its impact on the physical environment. This is visible, for example, in more traffic, more parked cars, and more impact on the public realm of the city, perhaps giving the impression of a city heading quite strongly toward automobile dependence.

As in the case of Sao Paulo and Taipei, the data point strongly to a city where the visibility and prominence of the car belies the car's actual overall role in urban mobility. The reality is that cars and motorcycles, for all the environmental impact they have in a compact city like Prague, which has not been built for them, account for only 25 percent of the trips undertaken in the city, and that this is actually a reduction relative to 1995 when they accounted for 29 percent. The proportion of total daily trips by public transit has grown significantly, from 46 percent to almost 51 percent, while non-motorized modes account for 24 percent (almost identical to 1995). And with respect to the proportion of total movement by motorized means, Prague's public transit system accounted for over 42 percent of passenger-kilometers-traveled in the city in 2005, compared to auto cities, which rarely achieve more than 10 percent (though Prague did reduce from 49 percent in 1995).

Combined with an already evident decoupling of GDP growth from growth in car use and mobility generally, this suggests that Prague is not succumbing to automobile dependence or becoming an automobile city. Rather, it is maintaining its basic character as a city strongly oriented to public transit and resilient enough to find a way through the very rapid growth in car numbers and car use. Prague is reaching limits, and system adjustments are taking place that are beginning to stifle the role that the car can play in the urban system; the role of public transit is being reasserted.

Prague has some cultural features that have probably helped in this process. Clearly, the city is culturally oriented to public transit, as evidenced by its extraordinary per capita public transit use, and this is at least partly due to its heritage as one of the former Eastern Bloc cities, most of which developed extensive and highly utilized public transit systems with very cheap fares as part of the social and political philosophy of the Communist era, though this built upon a public transit tradition covering most of the period from the 1880s on. Also, Prague is the sixth-most-visited city in Europe, with around 4.1 million foreign tourists annually, many of whom use the public transit system.[6] Any public transit trips by tourists are included in the Prague public transit usage data.[7] The city literally cannot afford to lose the attractiveness of its historic quarters due to excessive impacts from the automobile, nor can it easily accommodate further increases in private motorized mobility. Prague's future lies quite clearly in continuing its decoupling of GDP from car mobility, and it is unlikely to sacrifice its heritage streets, buildings, and public spaces for anything less.

Conclusions

The case studies of cities experiencing rapid motorization rates and apparently capit-
ulating to the automobile, with obvious congestion and a general increase in the
presence and impact of cars (and motorcycles), in fact present a different story when
examined at an urban system level through a wide variety of data. One thing is clear:
none of them are in any way near to or are even capable of progressing close to typical auto-city levels of car dependence. In fact, it would appear that physical limits
are already being reached, making higher levels of private motorized mobility very
problematic if their transportation systems are to remain functional. These limits
already appear to be creating a turnaround in the usage of non-motorized modes
and an upturn in public transit systems, especially urban rail. That these cities have
been able either to hold their own, or even to somewhat increase their share of total
motorized mobility by public transit over a 10–15 year period, is some indication
that these cities are all "hitting the wall" in the motorization path much sooner than
cities in North America and Australia, which grew up with and were designed around
the space needs of cars.

It is also interesting that while many cities in the developed world have shown
a decoupling of car use and total passenger mobility from GDP growth over the
1995–2005 period (see chapter 2 and Kenworthy 2013), the same is proving true
for these much less wealthy cities. It is not hard to see why this may be happening.
All cities, especially emerging cities, are growing into a new global economy where
the numbers of intensive urban economy jobs and services jobs are growing the
most rapidly. These jobs require land uses that are spatially efficient, thus utilizing
dense city centers where rail, bikes, and walking are by far the most efficient means
of transport. Such jobs are even more obviously required in the dense cities of the
twenty-first-century emerging world, and hence it is likely that the need to avoid
automobile dependence will become paramount at a much earlier phase of these cities' economic growth than in the cities of the twentieth century.

It is very important for policy makers in such rapidly developing cities to realize the already evident positive patterns and not to assume that they are fighting a
losing battle with motorization. It gives hope and initiative to the whole transpor-
tation-policy-making environment to realize that automobile dependence, far from
being the "irresistible force" it has always been assumed to be (Lave 1992), is actually
something that can and is being reversed. While public environments and congestion can and possibly will get worse in such cities as more vehicles are squeezed into
confined spaces, it is more likely that motorization is actually losing the battle. It
appears to be simply unfeasible to find an accommodation with the automobile and

motorcycle that allows such dense cities to remain both functional and livable. The theory of urban fabrics outlined in chapter 4 will enable us to understand this better and to see how these dense, congested, and rapidly developing cities can proceed.

Cities in the emerging world are adjusting and reversing aspects of the motorization problem because of spatial physical limits and a growing awareness of the economic benefits in decoupling wealth creation from car mobility. Once this is realized more globally, then urban policy can dramatically assist and accelerate this process in any city. It is possible to see the end of any trend toward automobile dependence in currently motorizing cities, an end that is approaching much faster than perhaps anyone may have thought possible.

So let us conclude by again asking our original question: What is happening in global cities in the developing or emerging economies of the world, such as cities in China, India, Latin America, and Eastern Europe? Are they following an inevitable path towards motorization and automobile dependence as they develop, or are they also decoupling economic growth from automobile dependence?

Our answers:

- Emerging cities are generally growing fast, but are not following the trajectory of automobile dependence as found in US and Australian cities.
- Decoupling economic growth from automobile dependence is now happening not only in the world's developed cities, but in the emerging cities of the world.

A special 2013 issue of the journal *Transport Reviews* was focused on the peak-car-use phenomenon, with data from the world's cities suggesting that a structural change was under way. One article, from David Metz, suggested that even the emerging cities of the world may now be moving toward "peak car" as they are choosing to build major rail infrastructure and are maintaining their dense urban forms (Metz 2013). Our analysis would suggest that this could be expected, and it is a highly significant development for the world's emerging cities.

In the next chapter, we will outline a new theory of urban fabrics that enables us to understand why these trends to reduced automobile dominance and dependence are occurring both in the developed world's cities and also in these newly emerging cities of the developing world.

4

The Theory of Urban Fabrics:

Understanding the End of Automobile Dependence

Cities are shaped by many historical and geographical features, but at any stage in a city's history the patterns of land use can be changed by altering its transportation priorities. An understanding of how cities work, based on walking, transit, and automobile fabrics, will therefore enable a more fundamental understanding of the rise and fall of automobile dependence. In this chapter we show how different urban fabrics have developed from different transport types and how they should be recognized, respected, and regenerated as the basis of town planning. In doing so we will find a way to understand automobile dependence and how it can be shaped into a more sustainable and regenerative approach to cities. In particular, the theory will help us to explain why it appears that walking and transit fabrics are now valued more highly—economically, socially, and environmentally—than automobile fabric, and how to manage each fabric more appropriately.

We show this through using academic research based on urban data collected from cities around the world, some of which has been summarized in chapters 1 and 2, together with the practical work of city planning, in which we have both been involved.

One of our research partners over the years, Leo Kosonen, has been working in a small Finnish town called Kuopio for 20 years using the main ideas in our previous text (Newman & Kenworthy 1999a) and attempting to see how a different approach could be taken toward the all too common tendency toward automobile dependence that is built into so many planning systems around the world. With Kosonen, we have developed a new theory we have called urban fabrics (Newman, Kosonen, & Kenworthy 2015; Kosonen 2007; Rainer et al. 2012). Urban fabrics are the material reality created by certain urban lifestyles and functions; our theory shows how they are shaped primarily by transportation infrastructure.

History of Urban Fabrics

Italian physicist Cesare Marchetti (1994) and Zahavi and Talvitie (1980) were among the first to show that there is a universal travel-time budget of a little over one hour on average per person per day.[1] This "Marchetti's constant" has been found to apply in every city in our Global Cities Database (Kenworthy & Laube 2001), as well as in data on UK cities for 600 years (Standing Advisory Committee on Transport 1994). Further analysis of 2005–06 complete travel data by mode (walking, cycling, public transportation, cars, and motorcycles) on 41 global cities (see color plate 1) using average modal travel speeds, showed that the mean and median travel times per day were 66 and 65 minutes, respectively (see Kenworthy 2014 for the travel data used).

The biological or psychological basis of Marchetti's constant seems to be a need for a more reflective or restorative period between home and work, but if travel time is too long people become very frustrated due to the need to be more occupied rather than "wasting" time between activities. Many functions are carried out while in automobiles as well as while on transit, biking, and walking during travel time that are not considered to be wasted (e.g., conversations with other commuters, phone contact, social networking using mobile devices, or active exercise), but these are less orientated toward the primary functions of work and thus are valued less (Mokhtarian & Chen 2004).

Marchetti's constant therefore helps us to see how cities are shaped (Newman & Kenworthy 1999a, 2006). Cities grow to being about "one-hour wide" based on the speed by which people can move in them. If cities go beyond this they start to become dysfunctional and therefore begin to change infrastructure and land use to adapt again to this fundamental principle (Van Wee et al. 2006).

So far the world has seen three main city types emerge: walking cities, transit cities, and automobile cities, with most cities today having a mixture of all three urban fabrics. The fundamental problem with the past 65 years of town planning has been the belief that there is only one type of city: the automobile city. The rediscovery of the other city types has been a fundamental factor in the reduction of automobile dependence as a paradigm in town planning.

The original typologies are set out in figure 4-1 (Newman & Kenworthy 1999a),

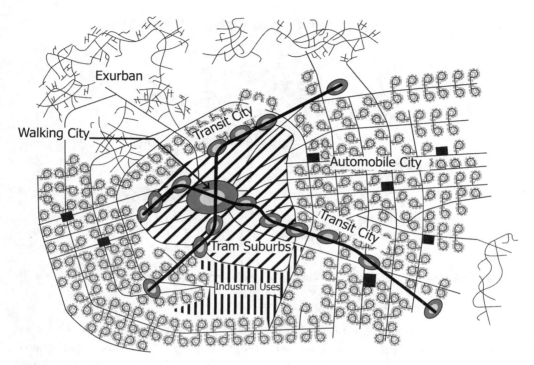

Figure 4-1. The automobile city: a mixture of three city types. Source: Newman & Kenworthy (1999).

and the version used by Kosonen (2007, 2014) is set out in figure 4-2, showing that the three fabrics actually now fully overlap. The significance for policy is sorting out why the walking and transit fabric need to be supported, not just driven over by automobile fabric planning and perceptions.

1. Walking Cities have existed for the majority of human settlement history, since walking, or at best animal-powered transportation, was the only form of transportation available to enable people to get across their cities, with walking speeds of around three to four kilometers per hour. Thus walking cities were dense, mixed-use areas of generally over 100 persons per hectare with narrow streets, and were mostly no more than three to four kilometers across, or roughly two kilometers in radius. The most intensive part was within a one-kilometer radius of some central point such as the main city square or plaza.

Walking cities were the major urban form for 8,000 years, but substantial parts of cities like Barcelona, Ho Chi Minh City, Mumbai, and Hong Kong, for example, retain the character of a walking city, even though today they are of course

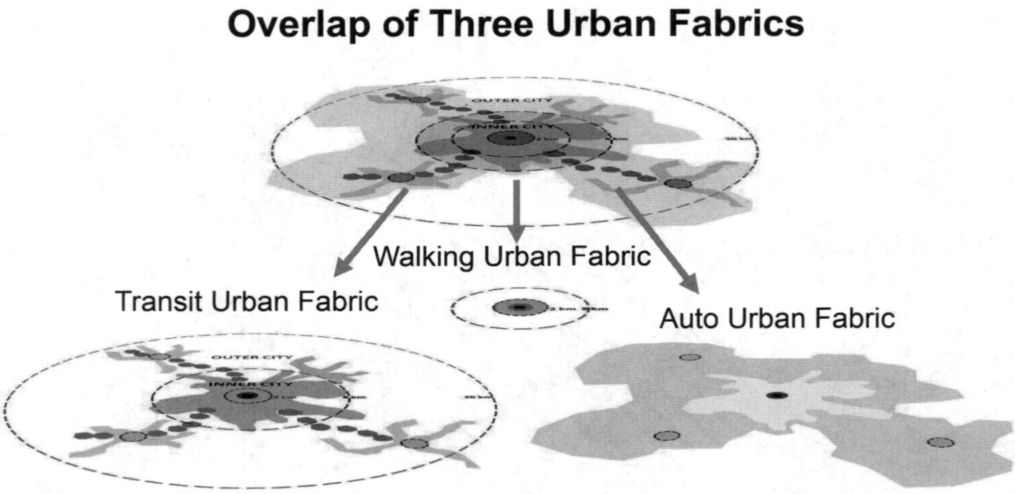

Overlap of Three Urban Fabrics

Figure 4-2. The Automobile City, Transit City and Walking City, based on an original diagram form Newman and Kenworthy (1999).

much larger than four kilometers in diameter. Kraców and Venice are, even today, mostly walking cities. In squatter settlements common to many Latin American, African, and South Asian urban environments, the urban fabric is usually a walking city with narrow, winding, and often unsealed streets suitable only for walking.

In wealthy cities like New York, London, Paris, Vancouver, and Sydney, the central areas are predominantly walking cities in character, though they struggle to retain their walking urban fabric due to the competing transit city and automobile city, which now overlap with it. Many cities worldwide are trying to reclaim the fine-grained street patterns associated with walkability in their city centers, and they find that they cannot do this unless they respect the urban fabric of ancient walking cities (Gehl 2010). Many modern cities are trying to create new urban centers and need to learn from this theory how to make them truly walkable (see color plates 2, 3, and 4).

2. Transit Cities, built from about 1850 to 1950, were first based on trains (after 1850 the steam train began to link cities and then became the basis of train-based suburbs), followed by trams (from the 1890s) that extended the old walking city. Both trains and trams could travel faster than walking—trams at around 10–20 kilometers per hour and trains at around 20–40 kilometers per hour. This meant that cities could now spread out in two ways, with trams forming the inner transit city, 10–20 kilometers across (that is, a 5 to 10 km radius, with an average around 8 km), and with trains forming the outer transit city, 20–40 kilometers across (10 to 20 km radius).

The resulting public-transit-based urban fabric was different depending on whether it was developed around trams or trains. Trams create linear development (trams, being slower and having more closely spaced stops, lead to strips of walking urban fabric).[2] Trains create dense nodal centers along corridors (following faster heavy-rail lines with walking urban fabric around stations, like pearls along a string). Densities could be less (around 50 persons per hectare) as activities and housing could be spread out further, although they could also be significantly denser than 50 persons per hectare. The key character was proximity to this new kind of transportation mode.

Subways in Paris, London, and New York, which started running in the nineteenth century, were essentially designed to extend the walking city like trams did. The early subways, such as in Paris, had many stops a short distance apart and traveled around 15 kilometers per hour, and so they spread the walking city into an inner transit urban fabric extending to a radius of around 8 kilometers, as we see with trams. Later subways were faster and averaged around 30 kilometers per hour, extending this central area even farther out. But as we see in cities like London, a series of centers generally emerged around these lines, similar to the urban fabric generated by trains.

Since 1950 the new areas of the inner transit urban fabric (originally based on trams) have been based mainly on conventional bus lines running from new areas to the center, such as in Kuopio and other small transit cities of Finland. Some new tram-based neighborhoods, such as Vauban in Freiburg, Germany, and Pikku Huopalahti in Helsinki, have been constructed during the last decades with increasing commitment to tram city urban renewal, which is now accelerating in many cities (Newman et al. 2013).

Trains supplemented by buses are the basis of outer transit urban fabric. These can go out much farther than the traditional tram and metro networks. The train/bus fabric is based on corridors of dense sub-centers created by public transit with an average speed of around 40 kilometers per hour. These developments now go out 20 kilometers or more from the city center, depending on the speed of the trains. Busways and BRT are now doing the same without trains in newer areas of many cities wherever they are freed up from traffic.

Most European and wealthy Asian cities retain this transit urban fabric, as do the old inner cores in US, Australian, and Canadian cities. Many developing cities in Asia, Africa, and Latin America have the dense corridor form of a transit city, but they do not always have the public transit systems to support them, so they become automobile saturated or motorcycle saturated. Singapore, Hong Kong, and Tokyo have high densities in centers based on rail mass rapid transit linkages, and this dominates their transportation modal split. Cities such as Shenzhen, Jakarta, and Dhaka have grown extremely quickly with dense, mixed-use transit urban fabric, but the development is based predominantly on buses and paratransit. The resulting congestion shows that their intensity of activity demands mass public transit. Most of these emerging cities are now building the public transit systems that suit their urban form, and in fact Shenzhen opened a metro system in 2004. China and India are building innumerable metro rail systems to support their dense transit urban fabric, as explained in chapter 1.

New fast trains can extend the transit city far beyond the previous maximum distance of about a 20-kilometer radius (see the case study on Perth outlined in chapter 6 and in McIntosh et al. 2013). When fast trains averaging 80 kilometers per hour are built across big cities, then a new kind of transit city fabric emerges around each of the main stations. Cities that are looking to create transit urban fabric (such as New Urbanist concepts) need to see that the public transit systems are not just design traits, but are essential to making such fabric happen and allowing it to function efficiently (see color plates 5, 6, and 7).

3. Automobile Cities, built from the 1950s onward, could spread beyond the 20-kilometer radius to some 80 kilometers in diameter (that is, up to a 40-kilometer radius) in all directions, and at low density, because automobiles can average 50–80 kilometers per hour as long as traffic levels are low. These cities spread out in every direction due to the flexibility of automobile travel, investment in automobile infrastructure, and zoning that separated activities.

Buses were used as a supplementary service to the automobile (and to rail systems, as outlined above) and became subservient to automobiles in the new automobile urban fabric. Automobile cities provided limited public transit—mostly unattractive and infrequent bus services to support their sprawling suburbs—and within a generation such areas became the basis of automobile dependence (Newman & Kenworthy 1989) and automobility (Urry 2004). Many cities that developed since 1950 have used their growth to build automobile-dependent suburbs as their main urban fabric.

Automobile cities that are looking to create public transit options are often without reasonable densities around train stations and are finding that they need to build up the numbers of people and jobs near stations in order to create enough activity to support transportation options without extensive feeder systems and park-and-ride. Therefore they are building transit urban fabric and walking urban fabric to support these modes with walk-on transit users.

Many European and Asian cities are now building some suburbs outside their old transit urban fabric, where access to transit services is feasible but distant and where it requires car, bus, or bike connections (Nilsson et al. 2014). The densities of these suburbs tend to be higher than those in US or Australian suburbs. In Asian cities especially, the use of private automobiles is often supplemented by large numbers of motorcycles that seem to thrive in transit urban fabric where travel distance is usually shorter, parking is easier, and maneuverability through congestion is better. In cities and parts of cities that are built around the automobile, there is a similar need to recognize the urban fabric and respect it for what it contributes to the urban economy. However, there is also a need to see that there are real problems associated with the dominance of such automobile fabric, especially where it extinguishes the best features of walking and transit fabric. This is happening less now that the qualities of walking and transit fabric are being recognized, but the history of town planning did create a modernist one-size-fits-all approach in which the automobile city was the main model (Newman et al. 2015; see color plates 8, 9, 10, and 11).[3]

The Theory of Urban Fabrics: Areas, Elements, Functions, and Qualities

In tables 4-1, 4-2, and 4-3, we set out the basic features of the theory of urban fabrics in terms of areas, elements, functions, and qualities for each urban typology. These tables are based on the daily practical experience of the city of Kuopio, Finland, over the past 20 years as it applied the theory in its planning needs, as well as in our experience working as planning advisors in many cities in Australia, New Zealand, and North America. The tables show:

1. Fabric areas: the spatial dimensions and boundaries outlined above for each urban fabric;
2. Fabric elements: physical components, which are the working buildings and infrastructure that enable each urban fabric to function in its own way;
3. Fabric functions: the habits, ways of life, and business functions of the users and providers in each fabric; and
4. Fabric qualities: the measurable outcomes in terms of urban form, transportation, and economic, social, and environmental qualities in each urban fabric.

Table 4-1. Fabric areas and fabric elements.

	Walking City	Transit City	Automobile City
Fabric Areas	0–2 km	2–8 km	8–20 km
	1–2 km (less intensive)	8–20 km (less intensive)	20–40km (less intensive)
Fabric Elements			
Street widths	Narrow	Wide enough for public transit	Wide enough for cars/trucks
Squares & public spaces	Numerous, due to very little private open space	Less numerous, due to more private open space	Uncommon, due to much greater private open space
Street furniture	High level for pedestrian activity	High level for public-transit activity (bus stops, shelters)	High level for car activity (signs, traffic lights)
Street networks	Permeable for easy access, enabling high level of service for pedestrians	Permeable for pedestrians, networks to reach transit stops & corridors, enabling high levels of public transit service	Permeability less important, enabling high levels of service for cars on freeways, arterials, and local roads
Block scale	Short blocks	Medium blocks	Large blocks
Building typologies	High density: min. 100/ha typical	Medium density: min. 35/ha typical	Low density: <35/ha (usually around <20)
Building setbacks	Zero setbacks	Minimal setbacks for transit noise	Large setbacks for car noise
Building parking	Zero for cars, seats for pedestrians	Minimal for cars, seats for pedestrians and public transit users	Full parking in each functional area, little seating for non-auto users
Level of service for transport mode	Pedestrian services allow large flows of pedestrians (high levels of cycling also provided for)	Public transit services allow large flows of transit users	Car capacity allows large flows of car users

Source: Peter Newman & Leo Kosonen.

Table 4-2. Fabric areas and fabric functions.

	Walking City	Transit City	Automobile City
Fabric Areas	0–2 km	2–8 km	8–20 km
	1–2 km (less intensive)	8–20 km (less intensive)	20–40 km (less intensive)
Fabric Functions			
1. Movement/ accessibility functions	High by walking	Medium by walking	Low by walking
	Medium by public transit	High by public transit	Low by public transit
	Low by car	Medium by car	High by car
2. Consumer services - shopping - personal services	High local—esp. niche services	High in corridors— esp. sub-centers	High everywhere— esp. shopping centers
3. Large-scale consumer services - hypermarkets - warehouse sales - car yards	Low	Medium	High
4. Process Industry functions	Small—more white collar	Medium—more labor-intensive, e.g., hospitals, education	Large—more blue collar
5. Face-to-face functions (knowledge economy/ people-intensive) - financial + admin - creative decision making - knowledge exchange - the arts	High	Medium	Low
6. Car-less functions	High	Medium	Low

Source: Peter Newman & Leo Kosonen.

Table 4-3. Fabric areas and fabric qualities.

	Walking City	Transit City	Automobile City
Fabric Areas	0–2 km	2–8 km	8–20 km
	1–2 km (less intensive)	8–20 km (less intensive)	20–40 km (less intensive)
Fabric Qualities			
1. Urban form qualities			
- Density	High	Medium	Low
- Mix	High	Medium	Low
2. Transport qualities			
- Car ownership	Low	Medium	High
- Level of Service (L.O.S.)	High L.O.S. pedestrian	High L.O.S. public transit	High L.O.S. car
- Transportation activity	High pedestrian activity	High public-transit activity	High automobile activity
3. Economic qualities			
- Development infrastructure costs per capita	Low–Medium	Medium–Low	High
- GRP per capita	High	Medium	Low
- Labor intensity	High	Medium	Low
4. Social qualities			
- Difference between rich & poor	Low	Medium	High
- Ability to help car-less	High	Medium	Low
- Health due to walking	High	Medium	Low
- Social capital	High	Medium	Low
- Personal safety	Variable	Variable	Variable
- Traffic accidents	Low	Low	Medium to high
5. Environmental qualities			
- GHG per capita	Low	Medium	High
- Oil per capita	Low	Medium	High
- Footprint per capita	Low	Medium	High

Source: Peter Newman & Leo Kosonen.

Tables 4-1, 4-2, and 4-3 show that there is a significant set of differences between these three kinds of urban fabrics. This theory of particular urban fabrics being created in a close functional relationship with three different kinds of transportation priorities is at odds with the modernist urban concept that is almost universally applied to cities and which is predominantly an automobile city set of fabric areas and fabric qualities.

As automobile dependence ends, cities moving beyond car-based planning need a more coherent set of planning norms. The new paradigm and theoretical understanding of future cities can be assisted by seeing the value of urban fabric theory in strategic and statutory planning.

Strategic and Statutory Planning Responses to Automobile Dependence: Recognize, Respect, and Rejuvenate Urban Fabrics

How then do we begin to practice town planning based on the theory of urban fabrics? How do planners manage cities in the rapidly changing conditions outlined above and where the twentieth-century modernist certainties about automobile urban fabric are now losing their appeal? We will speak more specifically about how to move beyond car-based planning in chapter 5, using some new transport-planning methodologies. This chapter is more about how town planning methodologies—both strategic and statutory planning—can be used to enable cities to address automobile dependence. The importance of recognizing, respecting, and rejuvenating the three main urban fabrics are therefore now outlined.

1. Recognizing the Urban Fabric

The first step is to ensure that various urban fabrics can be recognized through the use of mapping. A number of reports, books, and journals already do this but sometimes miss the significance of the three fabrics. Even our own data comparisons have not always clearly highlighted them, though the different transportation systems were quite clearly creating different areas. For example, in Newman and Kenworthy (1989) we defined the CBD, which is generally the old walking city; the inner area, based on pre–World War II transit city areas; and finally the remaining parts, the outer areas or automobile-dependent suburbs.

The Finnish Environment Institute (SYKE) has taken the core ideas of the theory of urban fabrics and applied them to an analysis of all Finnish cities (Schulman et al. 2014). They have used transportation data as the basic element to separate areas. Similar maps based on transportation data were the basis of the VAMPIRE (Vulnerability for Mortgage, Petrol, and Inflation Risks and Expenditure) maps developed by Dodson and Sipe (2008), as shown in color plate 12.

A similar distinction between the three areas can be seen in London in color plate 13.

The Spatial Network Analysis for Multimodal Urban Transport Systems (SNAMUTS) model, developed by Curtis and Scheurer (2010), has examined many cities in terms of their transit networks and services (see figure 4-3). These can be used to help recognize walking, transit, and automobile urban fabrics.

2. Respecting the Urban Fabric

If cities are shaped by their transportation systems, then the most important policy and planning direction for each component of the city should be to respect the fundamentals of each fabric. If this is not done, then the imposition of new transportation systems over the urban fabric will render them largely dysfunctional. This can be seen in most city centers with excessive automobile traffic and especially in high-density emerging cities in Asia, Latin America, and elsewhere, where motor vehicles have flooded the old walking and transit urban fabrics in a short space of years and these areas simply cannot cope.

The core idea in respecting the fabric is that the main elements, functions, and qualities need to be reflected in the statutory plans for each of the areas of the city, based on their inherent urban fabrics.

Respecting Walking Urban Fabric

The new economy of cities requires walkable urban centers in order for them to create the intense interactions needed in the knowledge economy. Thus walkable centers must be respected. The best way to achieve this is to respect each element:

- Provide walking infrastructure that can cope with pedestrian flows that are the highest priority of the transportation system in the area;
- Don't widen streets, or insist on setbacks;
- Ensure that walking space is sufficient and that traffic signals are timed with long periods for pedestrian flows;
- Enable laneways to be connected and active;
- Encourage high density and mixed use;
- Keep parking to an absolute minimum;
- Ensure there are cycleways on each street in the walking city area apart from pedestrian streets;
- Provide some controls over the amount of traffic permitted to enter and do not allow fast one-way streets with green waves at traffic lights in pedestrian and cyclist areas.

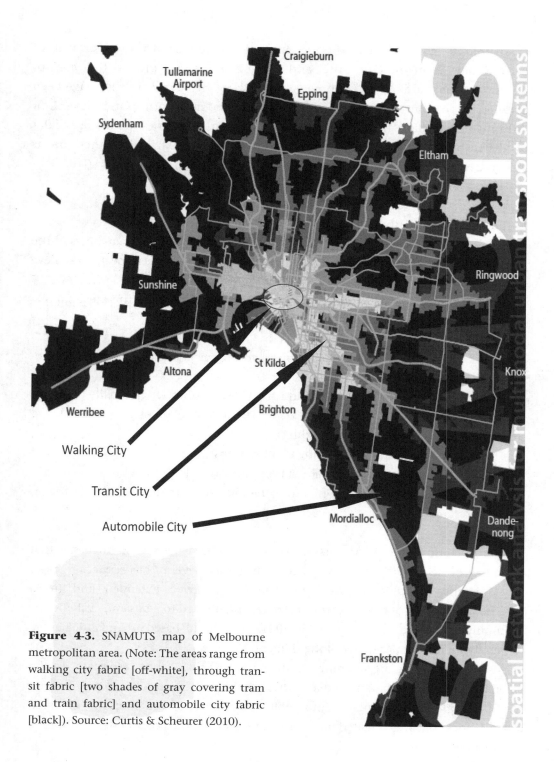

Figure 4-3. SNAMUTS map of Melbourne metropolitan area. (Note: The areas range from walking city fabric [off-white], through transit fabric [two shades of gray covering tram and train fabric] and automobile city fabric [black]). Source: Curtis & Scheurer (2010).

In Kuopio, the 1994 Plan first recognized and respected the importance of urban laneways in the city center and began a restoration process that continues today. There are now 10 kilometers of walking city laneways that have been restored for that purpose. Melbourne, New York, and many other cities have similarly instituted plans that respect their walking urban fabric—with spectacular results in terms of increased pedestrian activity and walking city functions, as well as demand for more walking urban fabric (Gehl et al. 2006; Gehl 2010; Gehl & Gemzoe 2004).

Respecting Transit Urban Fabric

The high spatial efficiency of the transit city enables the economic outcomes of the intensive urban economy as well. Thus transit urban fabric needs respect. To achieve this, plans should:

- Provide public transit as the major transportation system in the area, supplemented strongly by walking and cycling;
- Ensure that corridors are well connected;
- Maintain roads as wide enough for buses and trams but not high-capacity automobile use;
- Optimize all the necessary transit infrastructure to ensure a high quality of service (e.g., passenger information systems, shelters, system maps, etc.);
- Provide minimal setbacks on buildings;
- Provide cycleways on roads leading to all stations;
- Build up the density of centers along train lines and along tram lines;
- Keep parking to a minimum and constrain the amount of car traffic as appropriate.

Transit fabric in Kuopio was first recognized in 1993, when the planners saw that a number of neighborhoods were going to have their level of bus services reduced unless a series of other neighborhoods could be renewed, extended, and linked together in a "string of pearls" corridor. This eventually led to a bus and cycle/pedestrian-only bridge that was completed in 2001; the new bus-based urban fabric has led to rapidly increasing patronage along that corridor.

Many other cities are building up their transit urban fabric, especially in the emerging cities of China and India as they confront the unresolvable problems of trying to cope with too many automobiles, motorcycles, and trucks in cramped urban fabrics that were created and designed for non-motorized modes and transit (Newman et al. 2013).

Respecting Automobile Urban Fabric

The functionality of automobile urban fabric is so embedded into most urban planning systems that it hardly needs to be elucidated, but in order to maintain such fabric the following elements need to be respected in the plans for these areas:

- Separate functions into clear residential, industrial, retail, and other uses, but where it is reasonable, mix the functions that need to be mixed;
- Provide large setbacks on all buildings, but avoid inefficiency where noise conditions make this feasible;
- Don't increase densities and mixed use without underpinning them with good public transit systems;
- Protect existing high-capacity roads where needed, especially for freight, and where possible include space for mass transit and cycleways;
- Provide sufficient automobile parking without the old suburban mall model of acres of asphalt.

Planning regulations for many cities have treated each part of the city as though it is either part of the automobile city urban fabric or soon will be. The challenge for town planning in this time of transition from auto dependence is how best to find combinations of the automobile city with the walking city and the transit city. This is a challenge in terms of developing new greenfield areas and also rejuvenating older urban fabrics, especially in the middle suburbs or "grayfield" areas, and in the so-called older-generation edge cities (Garreau 1991; Newton et al. 2012). There are, however, some automobile urban fabric areas that will need to be respected for what they are: automobile-and-truck-centric urban fabric with little flexibility to be anything else. Not all automobile city areas can become TODs based around new transit lines. The right balance is different for each city.

3. Rejuvenating the Urban Fabric

All cities are constantly remaking themselves and extending one or another of their urban fabrics. The theory of urban fabrics suggests that the functionality of the city depends considerably on whether they are being built to respect their transportation systems and their associated fabric elements.

Rejuvenating Walking Urban Fabric

Traditional walking centers can be rejuvenated by using the elements of a walking city shown above in tables 4-1, 4-2, and 4-3 above. Walking city centers and transit city corridors (with their walking city centers) can also be built into new automobile-dependent areas. In Newman and Kenworthy (2006), the theoretical basis of how viable walking centers are created is set out using the "ped shed" concept, around one kilometer in radius, and the kinds of densities found to be associated with an economically viable center.

A pedestrian catchment area or "ped shed," based on a 10-minute walk, creates an area of approximately 300 hectares for walking speeds of maximum five kilometers per hour. If a walking city center is required, then a density of at least 100 persons per hectare is needed, based on the data collected in the Global Cities Database. This gives an idea of a bare minimum of the kind of activity that a town center would need: approximately 30,000 residents and jobs within this 10-minute walking area of 300 hectares. The range is from around 22,000 to 55,000 people and jobs. This number could provide for a viable town center based on standard servicing levels for a range of activities.

Lower numbers than this means services in a town center are nonviable and it therefore becomes necessary to increase the center's catchment through widespread dependence on driving from much farther afield. This also means that the human design qualities of the center are compromised by the need for excessive amounts of parking and road infrastructure. Of course, many driving trips within a walking "ped shed" still occur, but overall they constitute a very much lower proportion of total trips. However, if sufficient amenities and services are provided, then only short automobile trips are needed, which is still part of making the center less automobile dependent and thus respecting the walking urban fabric.

"Footloose jobs," particularly those related to the global economy, can theoretically go anywhere in a city and there is considerable evidence that such jobs are locating in dense centers of activity due to the need for networking and quick face-to-face meetings between professionals. High-amenity, green, walking-scale environments are better able to attract such jobs because they offer the kind of environmental quality, livability, and diversity that these professionals are seeking. As Florida says: "Economic growth and development, according to several key measures, is higher in metros that are not just dense, but where density is more concentrated. This is true for productivity, measured as economic output per person, as well as both income and wages" (Florida 2012a).

Talent levels are also higher where density is more concentrated. This holds for both the share of college graduates and the share of knowledge, professional, and creative workers. Leinberger (2014) has found that the top six most-walkable cities in America have 38 percent higher GDP than the rest of American cities. Thus, the market for walking urban fabric is likely to continue increasing,[4] and planners will need to change their strategic and statutory guidelines to enable this.

Rejuvenating Transit Urban Fabric

One of the important elements from urban fabric theory is the need to enable density in centers along the transit line. For a transit corridor to work, it needs areas of sufficient density strung along it to enable the transit system to be viable. This density seems to have as its minimum around 35 people and jobs per hectare of urban area, or about 10,000 residents and jobs within this 10-minute walking area (Newman & Kenworthy 2006). Transit corridors need to offer the quickest way for as many residents as possible to get along a corridor, which is probably already congested with cars and buses.

Some transit centers will have a lot more jobs than others, but the important physical-planning guideline is to have a combined minimum activity intensity of residents and jobs necessary for a reasonable local center and a public transit service to support it. Other authors support these kinds of numbers for viable local centers and public transit services as outlined in these urban fabric tables (Pushkarev & Zupan 1977; Ewing & Cervero 2010; Frank & Pivo 1994; Cervero et al. 2004). The number of residents or jobs can be increased to the full 10,000, or any combination of these, as residents and jobs are similar in terms of transportation demand. The more residents and jobs in excess of 10,000 within this one-kilometer or 10-minute walking area, the more effective will be the transit center.

Either way, the number suggests a threshold below which public transit services become noncompetitive without relying primarily on bus and automobile access to extend the catchment area. Bus linkage is an important new transit-corridor urban fabric and this is expanded below, based on experiences with the Perth Southern Railway line. Often planners are under pressure to provide park-and-ride, which can destroy the possibility of building density around public transit stops and can ruin the quality of the public realm, unless it is placed underground. In the automobile city urban fabric, it is hard not to provide park-and-ride facilities for a new transit line. The best combination of transit and auto city fabric will create a highly contested area. Sometimes it will be necessary to get the train line in and then slowly regenerate around train stations as market forces begin to take over and drive a better use of station precincts than just asphalt. Many new automobile-dependent suburbs have densities around 12 persons per hectare or less and hence have only a maximum of about one-third of the population and jobs required for a viable public transit center. When a center is built for such suburbs it tends just to have shops with job densities little higher than the surrounding population densities. Hence the "ped shed" never reaches the kind of intensity that enables a walkable environment or can ensure viable public transit. The public realm of such centers is dominated by roads and parking. Many New Urbanist developments are primarily emphasizing changes to improve the legibility and permeability of street networks, with less attention to the density of activity and its transit infrastructure (Falconer & Newman 2010). As important as such changes are to the physical lay-out of streets, the resulting centers may not be able to attract viable commercial arrangements and have only weak public transit. However, transit centers can be built in stages, with much lower numbers to begin with, provided the goal is to reach a density of at least 35 persons and/or jobs per hectare through enabling infill at higher intensities.

Rejuvenating Automobile Urban Fabric

The analysis so far suggests that recognizing, respecting, and rejuvenating walking and transit urban fabric can occur in ways that significantly reduce the need for auto-mobile use. What then should be done to respect and rejuvenate automobile urban fabric? Just as automobile fabric has been imposed over transit and walking fabric in the past, we would suggest that it is time for a greater mixing of transit and walking fabric into the automobile city.

The automobile-dependent suburb will not easily change its fundamental fabric. Nor will the associated truck-dependent fabric of warehouses, industries, and large-scale shopping/distribution centers that surround most cities. These places will need to be respected for their economic function, as their functions will rarely be able to fit into walking and transit fabric, nor will these areas be suitable for transit and walking fabric. These large-scale, spatially inefficient land uses are naturally part of an automobile- and truck-related fabric. There are, however, large tracts of automobile urban fabric that are showing their age and are ready for a new future with less car dependence. These areas have been part of the consumer economy rather than the knowledge economy, and although both are needed, the big issues of managing a competitive, sustainable global city in the twenty-first century have moved inexorably toward creating more of the walking and transit fabrics that are critical to this creative people-intensive economy.

In order to enable the automobile urban fabric to transition into a more sustainable future, it will need new forms of low-automobile- or no-automobile-based transportation as well as maintaining those parts that are always going to require spatially inefficient land uses. It is possible to imagine combinations of electric vehicles, biofuels, and methane (solar derived) that could enable this transition to occur (see chapter 6). Such suburbs also lend themselves to development along the lines of the permaculture and Transition Town movement, with their goals of local self-sufficiency and local food (elaborated in Newman & Kenworthy 1999a; Newman et al.

2009). Having more space can become an asset for such community-based activities and also for collecting solar energy (Newton & Newman 2013). However, they will still need transportation and hence the role of green cars and fuels will be essential, as they will not be able to keep within travel-time budgets otherwise and oil-based mobility will be phased out.

There is also a clear trend setting in of trying to create more walking and transit urban fabric, and some of this will be part of automobile urban fabric. One of the ways this is happening in the United States is the redevelopment of large, nonviable, car-based shopping malls and airports with their vast parking areas and the concurrent introduction of better public transit services (Calthorpe 2010).

Another potential way forward is suggested by the dramatically successful new Southern Railway in Perth, Western Australia (McIntosh et al. 2013). The railway was built deep into a totally automobile-dependent corridor that is some 75 kilometers long. This choice of corridor was criticized by transportation planners when it was first suggested, as it had none of the kind of dense land use necessary for a viable urban railway system, as outlined above. In other words, it was a railway built into automobile fabric, not transit fabric. But it has worked, with patronage levels of 80,000 people a day—far exceeding the levels predicted and within a fraction of the timeframe predicted to build up use along the line.

This success seems to be due to a system that respects the automobile fabric and yet provides a real public transit option distinctly better than the previous bus system that collected just 14,000 people a day within the corridor. The characteristics of the system are as follows:

- The train is able to out-compete the road traffic by being much faster, with a maximum speed of 130 kilometers per hour and an average speed of 90 kilometers per hour down the middle of a freeway. (The freeway speed limit is 100 kilometers per hour.)
- Stations are set an average of about 7 kilometers apart, not the traditional 1- to 2-kilometer spacing.
- Buses are integrated into the stations along main roads at crossover points over the freeway/railway alignment, thus facilitating very quick and easy transfers to and from the train.
- Integrated ticketing also provides easy transfers.
- Some park-and-ride facilities as well as kiss-and-ride (passenger drop-off) are provided.
- There are new TODs (rather than just park-and-ride fabric) developing at key stations.

The automobile fabric is now beginning to adapt and create a more public-transit-oriented urban fabric around some of the stations, with denser land uses being attracted to the station catchments. In the first five years of operation, the value of land has increased some 42 percent higher in the station catchments than in the suburbs around the rail corridor (McIntosh 2014b). Thus, the first signs of a transit fabric are emerging within the automobile fabric, though the primary fabric of the corridor was built around the automobile.

In his book *Suburban Transformations*, Paul Lukez describes a number of American developments that attempt to do transit-based renewal in automobile city areas including Tysons Corner, Virginia, outside of Washington, DC; the former "edge city," built around automobiles, is being rebuilt around a train line and two tram lines with associated transit fabric (Lukez 2007).

Using the Theory of Urban Fabrics to Explain the End of Car Dependence

The value of the theory of urban fabrics is in its predictive capacity and hence its inherent use in town-planning strategy, as well as in town-planning statutory functions, with its variable approach to regulatory requirements that distinguishes between different areas and their distinctive urban qualities.

It is possible to see two major structural changes in cities that are likely to be part of the global phenomenon of automobile-dependence decline. One is that the structure of cities based on car use began reaching a limit, and the other is that urban culture and economy have also begun to change and no longer favor car-based mobility. This is a major global transition that may have passed unnoticed if it had not been for the dramatic decline in car use that followed it.[5]

1. Urban Structural Limits, Relative Travel Time, and Space Constraints

If cities are structured around their transportation priorities, then it should be possible to explain the end of automobile dependence in terms of the theory of urban fabrics.

All cities have combinations of the three city types, because most retain dense centers that still function as walking cities and many still have rail-based suburbs built around rail stations before cars became dominant. Some, like Stockholm, developed their public-transit-based urban form from the 1950s onward (Cervero 1998). The last 80 years have seen the growth in transportation mostly around the automobile city while the old walking and transit city components have been reasonably static, as the car was a quicker and more convenient option. Many cities destroyed their old walking and transit city fabric.

However, in the past decade it would appear that the automobile city has reached its limits, and a new type of city is emerging with a different structure. This can be seen by examining the trends in average speeds for car use compared to those for rail-based transit. Despite the difference in city types around the world, it seems that the twenty-first century is the period during which the limits on global car-based urban growth are being reached. This will be explained by referring to two groups of cities: the denser cities of Europe, the Middle East, and Asia, and the low-density cities of America and Australia.

The new data from the Global Cities Database shows that traffic speeds have stabilized in the world's cities and that public transit speeds have increased, as outlined in chapter 2. This factor underpins the peaking of car use and the resurgence of rail use in cities, as the relative speed of travel by different modes primarily accounts for the development of different urban fabrics.

Data collected from a significant cross section of cities from 1960 to 2005 demonstrate that the speed of urban rail systems in relation to cars has been increasing, as the latter face growing congestion. Table 4-4 shows data grouped by region (America, Canada, Australia, Europe, and Asia).

Although these data are only current through 2005 and the peaking of per capita car use seems to be centered around 2004 in many places, it can be postulated that the process involved is likely related to a tipping point involving a gradual change in the relative competitiveness of public transit versus cars, which reaches a critical point and then cascades (Gladwell 2000). And of course we are not arguing that this factor is the only one involved in peak car use, so there are cumulative factors involved in reaching such a tipping point. Table 4-4 also highlights another critical factor in the argument put forward in this chapter by showing the ratio of metro/suburban rail speeds (trams and LRT excluded) in each group of cities compared to the average general road-traffic speed for the same cities (i.e., only those cities which have the rail systems).[6]

First of all, it can be seen for the cities analyzed here that while globally the ratio of overall public transit system speed compared to general road traffic has increased from 0.55 to 0.70 between 1960 and 2005, the ratio of rail system speed to general road traffic has gone from rail being slower than cars in 1960 (0.88) to a situation in 2005 where rail was, on average, faster (1.13). And this trend has shown a steady increase.[7]

Within the regions it can also be seen that, even today in American and Canadian cities, public transit overall is barely half as fast as general traffic speed, whereas their rail systems are about 90–95 percent as fast, meaning that in many cases they are

Table 4-4. Ratio of overall average public transit system and rail speed to general road-traffic speed in cities, 1960–2005.

Comparatve Speeds in Global Cities	1960	1970	1980	1990	1995	2005
Ratio of overall public transit system speed to road speed						
American cities	0.46	0.48	0.55	0.50	0.55	0.54
Canadian cities	0.54	0.54	0.52	0.58	0.56	0.55
Australian cities	0.56	0.56	0.63	0.64	0.75	0.75
European cities	0.72	0.70	0.82	0.91	0.81	0.90
Asian cities	—	0.77	0.84	0.79	0.86	0.86
Global average for all cities	0.55	0.58	0.66	0.66	0.71	0.70
Ratio of metro/suburban rail speed to road speed						
American cities	—	0.93	0.99	0.89	0.96	0.95
Canadian cities	—	—	0.73	0.92	0.85	0.89
Australian cities	0.72	0.68	0.89	0.81	1.06	1.08
European cities	1.07	0.80	1.22	1.25	1.15	1.28
Asian cities	—	1.40	1.53	1.60	1.54	1.52
Global average for all cities	0.88	1.05	1.07	1.11	1.12	1.13
	1960	1970	1980	1990	1995	2005
Ratio of overall public transit system speed to road speed	0.55	0.58	0.66	0.66	0.71	0.70
Ratio of metro/suburban rail speed to road speed	0.88	1.05	1.07	1.11	1.12	1.13

Source: Newman, Kenworthy, & Glazebrook (2013).

competitive with the car, especially in dense urban centers where clogged highways are losing out to fast rail systems time and again. Australian cities do a little better, with public transit overall now being only about 25 percent slower than cars, while the rail systems are now on average about 8 percent faster and have generally been improving their competitive position since the 1960s and 1970s. When major corridors into city centers are considered, the rail systems are at a clear advantage.

European cities have mostly always had quite competitive rail systems in terms of speed, but they have hit a high in this 45-year perspective by reaching an average speed 28 percent greater than that of cars. Indeed, their overall public transit systems, as a result of their fast rail, are on average 90 percent as fast as the car. It is interesting to note, however, that their rail relative speed dropped from 1.07 to 0.80 during the 1960s, when these cities opened up to the car and built a lot of roads. Something similar occurred in Australian cities, but after the 1960s rail speeds relative to the car rose quite consistently. In both cases, the new freeways quickly filled with traffic and rail once again quickly asserted its speed-competitiveness.

The limits to car growth are demonstrated in such data and support why we are probably seeing such limits reached in Chinese and Indian cities, as set out in chapter 3.

Asian cities have very fast rail systems compared to their crowded road systems, where in 2005 rail speeds were an extraordinary 52 percent higher. This has fluctuated somewhat over the decades, but rail speeds on average were never less than 40 percent better than cars, even in the 1970s. To the many emerging cities struggling with the car, such data give hope that rail systems can help them to develop a very different kind of overall urban transportation system that is not so overwhelmed by the automobile, and can further enhance the kind of transit urban fabric that they favor. In the emerging cities, traffic speeds were very slow (below 25 km/h) and bus speeds always slower than the average traffic speeds. Bangkok had a traffic speed of 14 kilometers per hour and a bus speed of 9 kilometers per hour in 1990. Thus, as these emerging cities build rail (often above or below the traffic) the data will be reflected in dramatic public transit speed improvements. This is now demonstrable in China and India and is driving their commitment to fast rail systems within and between their cities. The global end to automobile dependence can be seen in these relative speeds of public transit and road traffic.[8]

The remarkable growth in urban rail in China and India suggests that these cities may have hit the physical-constraints wall much sooner than did European cities and certainly far sooner than American cities. Daily experience of the streets in these cities suggests that the old walking and transit city urban fabric is saturated with cars, and from here on the growth will largely plateau. Of course, these cities too are capable of sprawling, and some of the new high-rise cities are little more than "vertical sprawl," but they are always denser than cities in the United States or Australia. It is simply not physically possible to turn a dense Asian city into an American city without demolishing the whole thing and starting again. Sprawling, car-based suburbs of the very low-density kind that are found in Australia and the United States are rare in China and India, where land constraints, including unsustainable destruction of essential food-producing areas and cultural preferences for high-rise, are likely to mean their growth will largely be based on walking and transit forms from here on.

Judging from this analysis, European levels of car ownership and significantly lower levels of car use would be the most that would be expected in China and India, more probably with around half the levels of where car use plateaued in Europe.[9] The data presented in chapter 3 and recent announcements in India have suggested that this is the kind of plateau in car use that they are seeking, as traffic congestion has far exceeded acceptable levels, and new rail systems are planned to enable better access (Jayaram 2012). Thus, it is possible to understand that the Metz hypothesis discussed in chapter 3 (Metz 2013) on the early peaking of car use in emerging cities has a basis in urban fabric theory.

The cities of America and Australia grew mostly in the automobile city era, and as a result they are much lower in density (usually by a factor of 10). Car ownership and car use grew to a much higher level but are now plateauing and declining. They seem to have hit the same wall as the denser cities, but at a much higher level of car ownership and use, and with much more space given over to the car. However, they have reached a limit on the growth of freeways and other urban space for cars (e.g., parking is being restricted heavily in most developed cities, especially in centers, or is even being reclaimed for housing and public space, as in Portland, Oregon), and hence average traffic speeds have plateaued or reduced.

The 19 lower-density cities in Australia (4 cities), the United States (10 cities), and Canada (5 cities) for which we have 1995–96 and 2005–06 average road-traffic-speed data (24 hours / 7 days per week), show an overall average road-traffic speed in 1995 of 46.8 kilometers per hour and 47.4 kilometers per hour in 2005. In terms of the regional averages, Australian cities in 1995 averaged 43.6 kilometers per hour and declined to 42.8 kilometers per hour, the Canadian cities rose slightly from 44.5 kilometers per hour and 45.4 kilometers per hour, respectively, and the US sample was similar (49.3 km/h and 50.4 km/h).[10]

Thus the same mechanism can be understood to have set in over the past decade: the urban structure or fabric of the city has prevented any further growth in car use, congestion has remained totally uncontrolled, and the only way forward has been with alternative transportation, especially urban rail.

The relationship between car use and transit use is exponential, and thus relatively small increases in the use of public transit can lead to significant reductions in car use. This is confirmed in the previously mentioned concept of the "transit leverage effect," which shows that one extra passenger-kilometer by public transit substitutes for multiple car-passenger-kilometers (generally in the range of 3 to 9), mainly through the trip-chaining that transit users employ on their journeys (Neff 1996; Newman & Kenworthy 1999a) in the transit city.

2. Urban Economic and Cultural Change

The biggest change in the economy during the period leading up to and including the period of car-use decline and rail growth has been the digital transformation and the consequent knowledge/service economy. Despite this being global and enabling long-distance communication, it has in fact been a concentrating force in terms of city structure and fabric.

As shown in chapters 1 and 2, new data on global cities reveal a universal increase in density in the past decade or so after over 100 years of decline. The intensive urban economy and digital jobs are focused in city centers, as these are where the creative synergies between people occur (Kane 2010). Old CBDs have been transformed back into functional walking cities and, in those cities that have done this best, have attracted the most capital and young talent to work there (Gehl 2010; Matan & Newman 2012). Other centers along the old transit city rail lines (tram, metro, and suburban rail lines) have also made similar transformations, and the linkages between them have become the basis for the revival of the transit city. Universities, health campuses, and IT-job clusters have created their own people-intensive economy centers for jobs and have attracted housing and transit to link them together.

Other parts of the economy, such as manufacturing, small and large industry, freight transport, and storage, have remained car-based (and truck-based) and are outside this new knowledge, people-intensive economy. They will remain so, but they are also not located where the main growth in jobs or the growth in wealth is occurring. Thus, the automobile city economy and culture has become somewhat distinct from the new regenerated urban economy of knowledge and services and its basis in walking city and transit city locations. Walkability and wealth are now closely linked (Leinberger & Lynch 2014).

If the automobile-based economy had continued to scatter land use and economic function, it would not have been possible for the rise in rail to occur. Rail focuses activity and that is now happening in rapidly accelerating ways. Thus, there is obviously a close link between the urban structural change and the value of time saved by rail outstripping cars in the journey to knowledge-based centers. The three modes of rail, cycling, and walking are all highly spatially efficient in terms of the numbers of people they can bring together into small urban spaces. Figure 4-4 is a series of photos showing how 40 people can fit into urban space using cars, a bus, or bikes. The spatial efficiencies of these three modes are set out with walking and biking as well in table 4-5. The most spatially efficient are trains, which can be a single-carriage light rail at 4.3 people per square meter, or a train with about 10 carriages, so their spatial efficiency is huge.

The intensive modes are all capable of causing major rises in urban land value, as they help create the potential for knowledge-economy interactions. The dispersive modes of cars and buses do not create such job opportunities and hence are not linked to such large increases in land value. The value-capture mechanism associated with the intensive modes will be discussed in chapter 6 as a means of seeking funding for transit and walkability.

As with many economic changes, there is also a cultural dimension to this transformation that might explain the rapidity of the changes observed above, as well as the demographic complexion of the change. Young people (especially those involved in intensive urban economy jobs) are moving to reduce their car use and switch to alternative transportation faster than any other group. Younger, educated people are moving to live in the walking city or transit city, as these locations more readily foster the kind of urban experience and culture to which they aspire (Florida 2010), as well as the people-intensive economy to which they belong. Thus, such people feed the market that enables the rail revival and city center renewal to continue. Hanes (2015) shows how millennials (25- to 34- year-olds with four-year degrees) in the United States are now flocking into depressed cities such as Baltimore, Cleveland, St. Louis, Nashville, New Orleans, and Detroit, where they can find affordable, dense old neighborhoods which they then help to restore. The article states: "Young people want dense, diverse, interesting places that are walkable, bikeable, and transit-served" (p. 30).

A driving force behind this cultural change to a more urban lifestyle is the use of social-media devices (Florida 2010). On transit or when walking (and even to an extent while biking) people are already connected by their smart phones and tablets.[11] Such mobile devices are hardly usable, at least not safely, while driving a car.[12] The Davis, Dutzik, and Baxandall (2012) report shows that the mobile phone is a far more important device than a car for younger people. This is a cultural revolution that contributes to the end of automobile dependence.

Amount of space required to transport the same number of passengers by car, bus, or bicycle.
Event info at www.UrbanAmbassadors.Org/ShootYourCommute - Photos by www.tobinbennett.com   Des Moines, Iowa - August 2010

Figure 4-4. Spatial impacts of cars, buses, and bicycles carrying the same number of people. Rail will be three to five times more spatially efficient than bus (see table 4-5). Source: Urban Ambassadors, Des Moines, Iowa; photos by tobinbennett.com.

Table 4-5. Space requirements of different transport modes for particular operating conditions.

Mode	Capacity Scenario (users/hour/lane[a])	Speed (km/h)	Space demand (m2/user)
Pedestrian	23,500	4.7	0.7
Bike[b]	5,400	12	8.0
Motorcycle[c]	2,400	12	17.5
Car (urban street)	1,050	12	40
Car (expressway)	3,000	40	47
Bus (55 seats)	7,700	10	4.5
Tram (250 seats)	24,000	10	1.5
Metro rail	40,000	25	2.5

Source: GTZ (2004, p. 10).

Notes: These figures are not maximum values or typical speeds for all situations, but rather present the space required under various conditions.
[a]The width of a lane is assumed to be 3.4 meters.
[b]Assuming one user per bike.
[c]Assuming 1.1 users per motorcycle
All public transport modes are assumed to be 80 percent full.

Baby boomers gained freedom and connection with cars; millennials don't even need cars. They like to save time on a fast train but they also like to use the time constructively, communicating with their friends and co-workers through smart-technology devices. They are thus attracted to live/work/play areas such as the walking city or transit city. Culturally, the car is no longer feeding the economy or the cultural needs of this digital generation (now around half of the adult world in most car-dependent cities), which is partly reflected in the decoupling of car use from wealth that was discussed in chapters 2 and 3.

The end of automobile dependence is occurring because the intensive modes of transportation (rail, walking, and cycling) are needed to enable intensive economic functions; and the dispersive modes of transportation (bus and car) are needed to enable the less intensive, dispersed economic functions of the consumer economy. Thus, the combination of rail, walking, and cycling are required in walking and transit city fabric for this creative, global-economy part of the city. And the combination of bus and car are required in the automobile city fabric for the more consumer-based part of the city. As explained above, these cities overlay each other, and the need to balance the modes and the different urban fabrics remains. The trends, however, suggest that the automobile city fabric is now less needed while the walking and transit city fabric is more needed in cities of both the industrialized world as well as in those of the emerging economies.

The peak in car use and the continuing rise of rail into what might even be called a new golden age of rail are both enmeshed in this return to the more urban lifestyle that is now part of American and Australian cities as well as the traditionally denser cities of Europe and the emerging world. Thus, the end of car dependence can be explained by the theory of urban fabrics as a combination of urban structural limits together with urban cultural and economic change that together enable us to see a different kind of urban future emerging. Cities that are responding to the powerful new agenda for building rail systems and regenerating their walking and transit fabric can enable this new, less car-dependent city to emerge. However, if a city does not adequately develop or build the rail infrastructure or allow the regenerative urban redevelopment processes to occur, then it can easily miss out on this important social and economic change. The biggest threat is if car-dependent cities do not recognize that the golden age of the car, and the car-dependent suburb, is over, and that their economic and cultural development will stagnate along with their automobile-dependent urban fabric unless new transit and walking infrastructure and fabric are built into their areas.

Best Practices in Regenerating Urban Fabric

1. Regenerating the Walking Cities of New York and Melbourne

Copenhagen is probably the most famous city to have regenerated its central city fabric as a walking city. This transportation and land-use-planning trajectory, along with that of Melbourne, New York, and many other cities worldwide, has been facilitated by the work of Danish scholar, architect, and urban designer Jan Gehl and his firm Gehl Architects. Gehl is one of the most internationally recognized urban designers and has made substantial contributions in over 40 cities around the world (Matan 2011; Matan & Newman 2012; Gehl 2010). He has demonstrated that with each improvement to the pedestrian environment comes an increase in the level of activity in a city's spaces.

The biggest current example of a city implementing sustainable streets, introducing bike-sharing schemes, and reclaiming public space is New York. To become a sustainable city and to accommodate an additional one million people by 2030, the City of New York and the New York State Department of Transportation (NYDOT), headed by Commissioner Janette Sadik-Khan, hired Gehl Architects in 2007 to survey the pedestrian environment in New York. Unsurprisingly, the survey found that New York has many pedestrians; however, it also found that many of the sidewalks were overcrowded, there were few places to sit, and although New York has many public places, many were difficult to access and exhibited an unwelcoming environment (as measured through numbers of youth and older users). It was determined that people were primarily walking only for transportation purposes—they were on the streets to move quickly from A to B—rather than to spend time in the public realm and enjoy the city.

Following the conclusion of the surveys, the City of New York and NYDOT have been rapidly implementing changes to the public realm and to the walking and cycling environment with the aim of using road capacity more efficiently. The most visible changes include new plazas throughout the city, most notably at Times Square, and the redevelopment of Broadway into a "boulevard" (New York City Department of Transport 2010). In addition, the city and NYDOT have been rapidly building bicycle paths throughout the city (over 200 miles / 322 kilometers between June 2007 and November 2009, with a plan to have an 1,800-mile / 2,896-kilometer bicycle network) and extending sidewalks and other pedestrian infrastructure. Most of the changes have been quick, simple infrastructure adjustments such as repainting road surfaces and redistributing road space through bollards, planting boxes, and folding chairs.

The closing of Broadway to cars at Times Square has been the most visible symbol of the city's "pedestrianization." On May 23, 2009, Broadway was closed to through traffic at Times Square between 47th and 42nd Streets, initially as an experiment. This was made permanent in February 2010. The closure has resulted in a "seven percent improvement in traffic flow" (Gehl Architects 2011, n.p.n.), with northbound taxi trips found to be 17 percent faster after the Broadway shutdown (comparing Fall 2009 to Fall 2008) (City of New York 2011; New York City Department of Transportation 2010). The closure has shown significant economic benefits to the businesses at Times Square, with 71 percent projecting revenue increases after the closure (City of New York 2011).

The changes in New York did not happen smoothly, and they created much controversy. The City and NYDOT persevered, however, and now the results are becoming evident. Throughout the city, pedestrian rates have increased, pedestrian injuries are down in the project areas by 35 percent, and 80 percent fewer pedestrians walk in the roadway in Times Square (City of New York 2011; Taddeo 2010). Between June 2007 and November 2009, cycling to work doubled in New York, with commuter cycling increasing by 35 percent between 2007 and 2008 (New York City Department of Transport 2010).

These changes to the city's multimodal transportation system demonstrate how quickly changes can be made to improve the walkability and public realm in a walking city. The reality is that it is relatively easy to reclaim the walking city from the automobile. The Commissioner explains these changes: "Until a few years ago, our streets looked the same as they did 50 years ago. That's not good business. . . . We're updating our streets to reflect the way people live now. And we're designing a city for people, not a city for vehicles" (Taddeo 2010, n.p.n.).

Interestingly, back in 1961 journalist and urban activist Jane Jacobs, writing from New York, was quite prophetic about what needed to be done in cities such as New York. She asserted:

> Attrition of automobiles operates by making conditions *less* convenient for cars. Attrition as a steady, gradual process (something that does not now exist) would steadily decrease the numbers of persons using private automobiles in a city. . . . Attrition of automobiles by cities is probably the only means by which absolute numbers of vehicles can be cut down. . . . What sort of tactics are suitable to a strategy of attrition of automobiles? . . . Tactics are suitable which give room to other necessary and desired city uses that happen to be in competition with automobile traffic needs. (Jacobs 1961, p. 377)

Fifty years after writing this, the attrition she longed for is finally happening in her favorite city!

The City of Melbourne shows perhaps the most dramatic results of all the Australian cities in illustrating how positive changes to the public realm can result in synergistic increases in walking and improvements to city life, offering "a remarkable case study in an emerging pedestrian city, having shown some dramatic, positive change in its pedestrian character and public sphere in the relatively short span of twenty years" (Beatley & Newman 2009, p. 134). The City of Melbourne deliberately focused on restoring and strengthening the city's traditional grid pattern and redesigning sidewalks and alleyways to create an interesting, walkable urban environment. Two surveys (1993–94 and 2004) have been made by Gehl and the City of Melbourne, measuring and monitoring the changes and enabling a decade of work to be evaluated. The surveys demonstrate that there have been:

- An increase in the number of people walking in the city center. On weekdays in the evening this number has increased by 98 percent (from 45,868 in 1993 to 90,690 in 2004), and in daytime by 39 percent (from 190,772 in 1993 to 265,428 in 2004);
- An increase in public space by 71 percent via creation of new squares, promenades, and parks (from 42,260 m² in 1994 to 72,200 m², plus Birrarung Marr Park's 69,200 m² in 2004) and an increase in the number of people spending time in these urban spaces;
- More places to sit and pause, with an increase in the number of cafés and restaurants (from 95 in 1994 to 356 in 2004), a threefold increase in café seats (from 1,940 in 1993 to 5,380 in 2004), and an integrated street-furniture collection;
- In 1992, there were 738 dwellings in the Melbourne CBD. By 2002, this had already grown to 9,895 (Gehl et al. 2004), with rapid increases every year since then, leading to a resident population of around 30,000 by 2014, with 6,000 apartments being built in 2013 and 2014;[13] and
- Improved economic activity in the city's streets, including the revitalization of a network of lanes and arcades (Gehl et al. 2004).

Melbourne and New York illustrate the regeneration of the walking city. Around the world there are many other examples of this growing cultural and economic shift toward creating walkable urban cores and redistributing city space from automobiles to people, reinvigorating the walking city, and at the same time reducing the ecological footprint of cities.[14]

2. Regenerating Transit City Fabric through Regional Transit and TOD Planning in Perth

The majority of public-transit-oriented development planning is based around constructing isolated demonstrations of the efficacy, viability, and market attractiveness of TODs (Arrington & Cervero 2008). What's needed is a strategic plan that sets out extensions to the public transit system and foresees how transit city fabric can be built around it to encompass the whole city, including its dispersed automobile city fabric.

A plan for Perth has been assembled that demonstrates just how effective such a regional approach to transit and TODs can be (Hendrigan & Newman 2012). Figure 4-5, below, presents the results of a detailed analysis that builds up only transit city fabric over the next 30 years of urban development in the largely automobile city fabric of Perth.

First, a range of heavy-rail, light-rail, and BRT systems would be built into the urban fabric using realistic and practical options over the next few decades. The urban development would then be focused around each of the rail-station precincts—both along the new transit lines and the old lines.

Designs were created that examined all the best sites in the urban rail-station system, with no higher densities than 5- to 8-story buildings. The results showed that the next 30 years of urban development (residential and commercial) in one of the OECD's fastest growing cities could be accommodated in the regional TOD structure (see figure 4-5).

If Perth were to do this, it would move decisively toward accomplishing the 75 percent overall automobile use (in person-kilometers), a maximum of 50 percent automobile use in its transit fabric, and a maximum of 25 percent in its walking fabric; these are believed to create the character of a city that has ended its automobile dependence (see chapter 2 and the conclusions to this chapter).

The economics of the Regional Transit and TOD Plan for Perth were also assessed, showing substantial savings. The plan would:

- Double and then triple the public transit patronage;
- Reduce the sprawl—potentially to zero;
- Save AUD$3.9 billion in residential infrastructure costs;
- Save 1.14 billion metric tons of greenhouse gases per year (50 percent less per household);
- Save $2.6 billion in transportation costs for new residents over 50 years;
- Reduce health costs and improve worker productivity by AUD$403 million per year (a 6 percent increase in worker productivity was estimated).

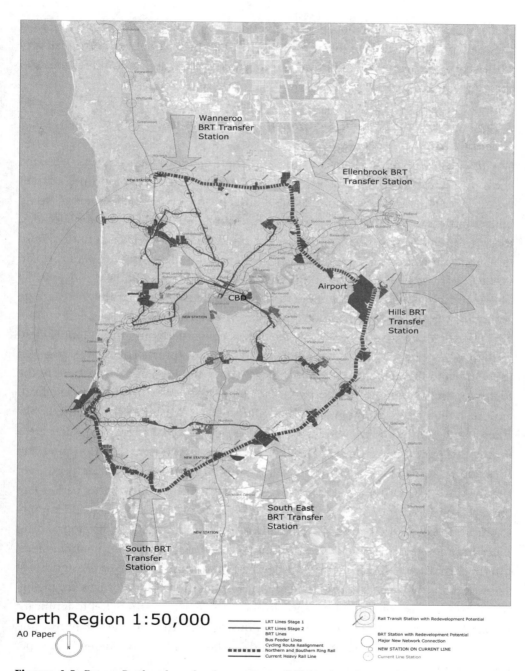

Figure 4-5. Future Perth urban development possibilities, based on public transit and TOD. Source: Hendrigan & Newman (2012).

Reducing automobile dependence will improve any urban economy, so a regional approach will improve it most, as this will bring a network of transit city fabric required to enable widespread improvement in transportation, lifestyle, and economic choices.

3. Regenerating Automobile-Dependent Middle Suburbs: Greening the Grayfields

Not all areas in all cities will be able to have a new rail line and a TOD, as suggested above for Perth. Many suburbs in cities will remain far from the rail lines of their transit city era. Is it possible to imagine a different future for such suburbs? Newly built suburbs on the urban fringe will be impossible to redevelop for many decades; these greenfield suburbs will need to have some imaginative transportation solutions that can reduce their automobile dependence, but in reality such planning can do little of structural value. Solutions could likely focus on voluntary and possibly informal relationships between residents and businesses of such far-flung areas (e.g., community-based car-sharing and van-pooling arrangements).

However, there are other areas between these new suburbs and the old transit and walking cities where it is possible to imagine a different future. These areas are often called the middle suburbs, or the "grayfields." These middle suburbs were built in the highly optimistic and economically vibrant post–World War II period in American and Australian cities, and they were built almost solely with the car in mind. Public transit and non-motorized modes were not a serious consideration in such areas during this period. This time was also known as the "grand transportation plan" era based on the Chicago- and Detroit-area transportation studies. A high proportion of the freeways that currently exist in cities were constructed during this period (see chapter 5 and Kenworthy 2012). These areas extend out from around 10–30 kilometers from the central city and are generally quite low in density. Redevelopment in most automobile-dependent cities in recent decades has focused on the inner areas, often referred to as "brownfields" as they had (and some still do have) significant areas of redundant industrial land ready for regeneration. Much of this redevelopment, however, is now complete, and although there will continue to be significant demand and focus on the redevelopment of brownfields, there are new opportunities opening up in the middle suburbs—grayfields—where land is also inherently cheaper due to its location.

The grayfield suburbs are nevertheless often well located in terms of distance from the city but they lack good public transit, as they were not considered to ever need it. As these suburbs have aged, they have often lost services. There are often many small houses on large lots, which are generally valued simply for their land area. They are thus ready for redevelopment.

In many cities where there is a fear of increasing density, these grayfield suburbs are redeveloped with simple infill of one to three small houses on the 1,000- or so square-meter lots. This kind of redevelopment is very suboptimal. It often removes the large trees from a neighborhood and does nothing for the improvement of local infrastructure and services. It is often aggressively opposed by resident groups, who fear a loss of land value and amenity. There is no ability to provide underground power, water-sensitive design, and new public spaces, or even to improve local services in nearby shopping areas. There is little chance of providing much variety in the form of the housing, for example, for aged persons or students. Most of all, it continues to provide little option for reducing car dependence.

The alternative is what we have called "greening the grayfields" (Newton et al. 2012). It requires that a whole precinct or neighborhood become involved in the redevelopment process. A city-planning exercise will require intervention that re-plans the 20–100 houses in an area. Some heritage houses can be retained, but the whole area will have much greater potential to enable the kind of denser land development that provides many of the new green opportunities, which are outlined in chapter 6. By assessing designs at various densities, it is feasible to make opportunities that can create much better housing and urban areas for everyone in the area, as well as provide many more houses, thus also helping to keep prices down. If reasonable densities can be achieved, the case for new public transit or transit upgrading is greatly improved, along with some small shops or a café.

Only a few examples of grayfields that have been greened are available. The iconic redevelopments of Vauban in Freiburg or BedZED in London (Newman et al. 2009; Rauland & Newman 2015) are indeed in middle suburbs, though the majority of grayfields are not redeveloped into such systematic and creative new communities. The next phase of redevelopment will need to be much more creative if automobile dependence is to be overcome in this next urban challenge.

Conclusions

Every city is made up of three types of urban fabric: walking city, transit city, and automobile city. They need to be recognized, respected, and regenerated. Regenerating urban fabric in the three areas of any city will require creativity by town planners, who will need different manuals for built-form typologies (elements, functions, qualities) that fit the different urban fabrics.

The value of the urban fabrics theory can be demonstrated in town-planning regulation that respects the different urban fabrics, and also in strategic planning that can enable different urban fabrics to be rejuvenated for twenty-first-century values and outcomes. The next chapter will look at how transport-planning tools can be crafted to respect and regenerate different urban fabrics, not just automobile fabric.

So what does it mean to "end automobile dependence" in the three urban fabrics? Each of the urban fabrics has a different fundamental physical form that can enable different travel distances and different combinations of modes. The reduction in car use and the rise of sustainable modes will thus be different in each urban fabric.

From the discussion in chapter 2 we concluded that strongly automobile-dependent cities would need to work toward an overall metropolitan average of around 75 percent car-passenger-kilometers rather than the 95 percent of total travel that car usage tends toward today. This is what we suggest should be the goal for automobile fabric, which needs to decline in car use and begin to move toward a much greater proportion of other modes.

For the transit city areas, there will already be a much higher use of other modes and shorter distances for all modes. The goal of around 50 percent or less car use in the transit city is likely to be more realistic than suggesting that this area should remain similar to the automobile-dependent suburbs at 75 percent.

For the walking city centers, there is little room for cars. We therefore suggest that these high-walkability areas should aim for levels around 25 percent or less in total car use. The Hong Kong metro area's current share of car and motorcycle travel is about 15 percent, so it is not unrealistic to suggest that 25 percent car use is possible in less dramatically dense walking-scale neighborhoods.

Any city can look carefully at its different urban fabrics and then begin to set out how its elements, functions, and qualities can be better expressed in these distinct urban fabrics. Transportation infrastructure and appropriate urban design elements should then be built to enable reaching the goals of no more than 25 percent automobile use in the walking city fabric, no more than 50 percent automobile use in the transit city fabric, and no more than 75 percent automobile use in the automobile city fabric. With this in place, any city will find a different urban quality will emerge, and it will not be automobile-dependent.

5

Transportation Planning:

Hindrance or Help?

Transportation planning methods and practices have helped the automobile-dependent city to evolve. They have been based on what has been derogatorily termed a "predict and provide" computer-modeling approach, which treats traffic analogously to a liquid, something that retains its original volume regardless of the container into which it is placed—in this case, the capacity of the road infrastructure that accommodates it. This chapter will show how traffic is more like a gas that can be either compressed or allowed to expand, depending on the capacity provided for it. Historically, technical and computer-model-based approaches to transportation have fallen far short in providing the policy direction and vision required in developing well-functioning transportation systems in cities. As the age of the automobile diminishes, a more human-focused, holistic approach is needed. The global knowledge economy is focused in cities, and the jobs that now increasingly underpin urban economies are not dependent on the further extension of the automobile city fabric that traffic models are so adept at providing. These new jobs, as well as the many other benefits from reduced automobile dependence, will require the protection and extension of walking city and transit city fabric. This means an entirely new focus for the transportation planning profession and how computer models are used for future urban and transportation planning.

Since World War II, transportation planning has for the most part treated the automobile and the urban fabric it creates and supports as being the primary concern in all cities. Keeping car traffic moving smoothly, regardless of the urban fabrics through which the traffic pours, has had devastating effects on the walking and transit fabrics outlined in chapter 4.

In many cases, these traditional modeling shortcomings endure until today. For example, the recent UK pronouncements about the expectation of significant new traffic growth over the coming decades,[1] the Aberdeen Western Peripheral Route,[2] and the Lancaster Northern Bypass, to name just a few current issues in the United Kingdom alone, have all the hallmarks of this now widely discredited predict-and-provide approach. In Australia and America the same predictions about traffic growth continue to be used in justifying new roads, despite peak-car trends, and those predictions never consider how there could be different approaches in different parts of the city, as explained by the urban fabrics theory in chapter 4.

Unfortunately, the emerging nations have tended to uncritically import these post–World War II traffic-modeling approaches. Partly as a consequence of the conceptual framing of transport problems inherent in these models, focusing almost entirely on the impossible dream of congestion removal, many are building freeways at an alarming rate (e.g., India and China began this trend but many other emerging countries are trying to solve their congestion in this way). Assistance from the World Bank (WB) has been central to this approach, as the WB has uncritically accepted these modeling techniques and big-road policy solutions.

Evaluations of major infrastructure projects by Nicolaisen and Driscoll (2014) have shown constant errors between what was predicted and what was delivered in the way of usage patterns; in Australia, similar research questions the value of the modeling and the assessments done on freeway projects (Odgers & Low 2012).

Counter to this rather negative story, there is now clear evidence that other approaches are possible and can yield very different results for cities (Goodwin 1997). Instead of treating traffic as a liquid—or a fixed given—there is now extensive evidence that traffic behaves more like a gas, expanding to fill the space available and compressing to cope with reduced road capacity.[3] This simple conceptual model can change the approach to congestion management from the traffic-as-liquid idea that has been so dominant for most of the twentieth century.

This chapter outlines the origins and provides a brief history of transportation planning, in particular the computer-based models that have been extensively used to predict and plan cities' future transportation infrastructure. It shows how the processes have had little regard to the diverse nature of the urban fabrics making up every city, as described in chapter 4, but have largely assumed that the automobile and its road and parking needs are appropriate and can be applied freely nearly anywhere. The chapter explains how these processes have helped facilitate automobile dependence and how they now must be changed to reinforce and accelerate an end to that dependence.

Perhaps the most important and influential of the technical procedures in transport planning is the land-use transport-modeling process, which emerged in the mid-1950s as a distinct area of study.

Self-Fulfilling Prophecies

Building large road systems changes the nature of the city, making it more automobile-dependent. In general, modeling has assumed that land use is "handed down" by land-use planners and that transport planners are merely shaping the appropriate transport system to meet the needs of the land-use forecast. This is not the case. One of the major reasons why freeways around the world have failed to cope with demand is that transport infrastructure has a profound feedback effect on land use, encouraging and promoting new development wherever the best facilities are provided (or are planned). Most of the major US cities, such as Chicago, New York, and Detroit, which built extensive freeway systems as proposed by their grand transportation studies (see the next section in this chapter), found that the freeways spread land use and generated more and more traffic until, very soon after their completion, the freeways were already badly congested. Sometimes this even occurred at opening, because urban sprawl had intensified to such an extent during the planning and construction phase that the road facilities were already out of date. Many studies now refer to these issues under the rubric of "induced demand" (Goodwin 1997; Zeibots 2007; Siegel 2007), and the USEPA now requires that environmental assessments of the transport-emissions impacts of new highways and freeways formally take into account that more vehicle–miles of travel (VMT) are generated by these projects than the traffic models typically predict (Newman & Kenworthy 1999a).

Once cities are locked into a primarily road-based system, a momentum develops that is very hard to stop. The typical response to the failure of freeways to cope with traffic congestion is to suggest that still more roads are urgently needed. The new roads are then justified again on technical grounds in terms of time, fuel, and other perceived savings to the community from eliminating the congestion. This sets in motion a vicious circle or self-fulfilling prophecy of congestion, road building, sprawl, more congestion, and more road building.[4]

This pattern is not only favorable to the vested interests of the road lobby and some land developers, but it also builds large and powerful government road agencies whose bureaucrats see their future as contingent upon being able to justify large sums of money for road building. This commitment often translates into direct political activity in which policy makers and politicians are influenced by narrow or biased technical advice. In this way, road authorities can become de facto planning agencies, directly shaping automobile fabric and land use in a city and having a large vested interest in road-based solutions to transport problems.

A Short History of Road Planning

The watershed for land-use transport modeling was the publication in 1954 of Mitchell and Rapkin's *Urban Traffic: A Function of Land Use*, which first drew attention to the fact that traffic is dictated by land-use decisions (Brown et al. 1972).

The immediate postwar period, as we discuss in greater detail below, was a time of huge economic optimism and growth, when the car was seen as the future of urban transport. The conceptual breakthrough provided by Mitchell and Rapkin, accompanied by the rapid evolution of computing power, led to a meteor shower of multi-million-dollar transport studies in North America, Australia, Europe, and elsewhere. The purpose of these studies was to plan for anticipated growth in population, jobs, and traffic flows as far ahead as 20–30 years such that there would continually be an equilibrium between the supply of transport facilities and demand for travel as it arises from land use.

The concept of the "grand transportation study" was embraced with enormous enthusiasm: virtually every developed city at some point between about 1955 and 1975 undertook at least one major transportation study. In the United States since 1962, urban areas over 50,000 people have been required to do land-use transport studies on a regular basis to qualify for federal road funds. These studies were widely acknowledged as being unashamedly highway-oriented (Brown et al. 1972). Governments vigorously promoted them, partly because they were a high-profile vote-winning exercise that appeared to be tackling transport issues, and partly because of the political influence of the road lobby and a handful of international transport consulting firms with close links inside transport bureaucracies the world over, who very quickly adopted, and to some extent monopolized, the then-esoteric technical modeling procedures. There was a huge amount of money to be made from "grand transportation plans" during the 1950s through to the 1970s, and transport consulting firms were only too eager to adapt their technical expertise to fit the political and community expectations of the time.

The first major transportation plans to appear were the Detroit and Chicago Area Transportation Studies (1955–56 and 1959–62, respectively; see Weiner 1999), which were very much along the lines described above. These two studies pioneered the technical procedures we know today as the land-use

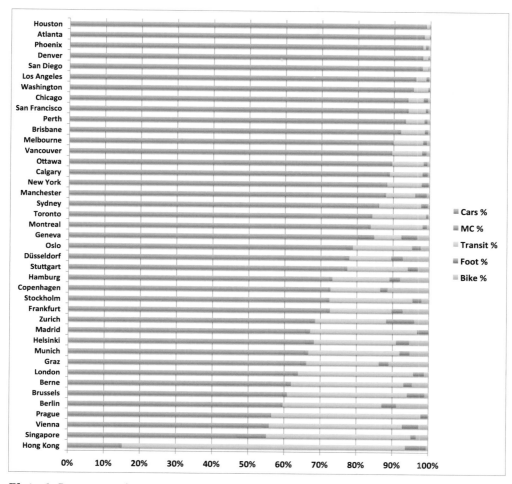

Plate 1. Percentage of travel by all modes in global cities based on person-kilometers for each mode, 2005. Source: Kenworthy (2014).

Plate 2. The old walking city of Weinheim in Germany. Source: Jeff Kenworthy.

Plate 3. Barcelona's walking city fabric (La Rambla). Source: Jeff Kenworthy.

Plate 4. Vancouver has been rapidly extending its walking city fabric through many dense new pedestrian and transit-based developments throughout the region (New Westminster near Sky-train station). Source: Jeff Kenworthy.

Plate 5. Paris has a classic dense transit city urban fabric served by its Metro and suburban rail lines. Source: Jeff Kenworthy.

Plate 6. Melbourne retained its trams and has some very attractive transit city fabric. Source: Peter Newman.

Plate 7. Portland has been building new transit city fabric through extension of its MAX light-rail and streetcar system, pictured here in the Pearl District redevelopment with high-density, mixed-use development. Source: Jeff Kenworthy.

Plate 8. Low-density automobile city fabric, which spreads and destroys surrounding bushland and food-growing areas (Perth, Western Australia). Source: Jeff Kenworthy.

Plate 9. Dubai has shaped itself significantly around the automobile but is now installing metro and LRT lines in association with dense urban development (note the metro line cutting across the freeway junction on an elevated viaduct). Source: Jeff Kenworthy.

Plate 10. One of Dubai's impressive Metro stations. The Metro and new LRT lines are beginning to shape a more transit-oriented future for the region. Source: Jeff Kenworthy.

Plate 11. Automobile city fabric in Perth, Western Australia, is being transformed by building new urban rail systems in the center medians of freeways. Source: Christine Finlay.

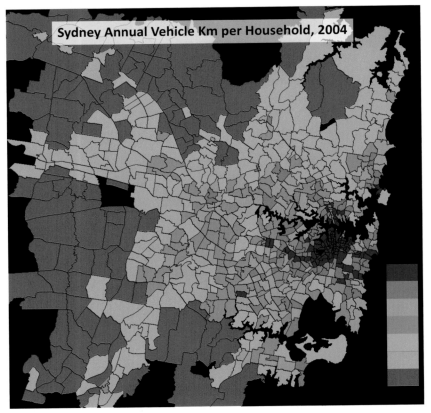

Sydney Annual Vehicle Km per Household, 2004

2.3 – 7.6
7.6 – 10.1
10.1 – 12.6
12.6 – 15.0
15.0 – 18.4
18.4 – 24.5
24.5 – 39.0

Plate 12. VAMPIRE map of Sydney showing the various urban fabrics with their different vulnerabilities to fuel-price-related mortgage stress. (Note: Blue areas basically indicate walking urban fabrics, green areas more transit-oriented urban fabric, and the red/orange areas mainly automobile city fabric.) Source: Dodson & Sipe (2006).

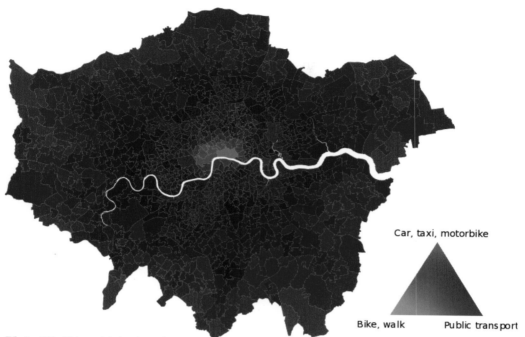

Car, taxi, motorbike

Bike, walk   Public transport

Plate 13. Urban fabrics based on transport modes, London. Source: Compiled from UK census data (2011).

Plate 14. Singapore office tower illustrating the green floor space ratio by using a green wall. Source: Peter Newman.

Plate 15. Singapore's KTP Hospital with community garden on its roof. Source: Peter Newman.

Plate 16. KTP Hospital in Singapore, first health campus to demonstrate the de-stressing value of biophilic design. Source: Peter Newman.

transport-modeling process (Black 1981). These technical procedures have been refined and tuned over the years but have evolved into what is generally referred to as the "conventional" land-use transportation planning study (or the standard approach to conducting a major transportation study). In fact, it has been said that there is "a generalised international urban transportation planning process"—UTP (Ben Bouanah & Stein 1978).

This process can be characterised by the following major tasks (see Black 1981):

1. Formation of goals and objectives;
2. Inventories of the present situation (mainly Household Travel Surveys, or HTS, to determine a population's trip-making frequency, purposes, modes, and other characteristics), which are then used in four key mathematical steps to determine essential data: trip generation, trip distribution, modal split, and traffic assignment (hence the other commonly used term: Four-Step Gravity Models);
3. Forecasting of new land-use plans and their resulting traffic, modeled on the baseline set of data developed under the previous step;
4. Analysis of alternative transport networks to cope with predicted travel; and
5. Evaluation of various alternatives according to costs, benefits, impacts, and practicality, followed by recommendations.

So what is wrong with this approach?

The Science Unmasked

Part of the prevailing philosophy during this period was that transport planning was largely seen as a value-free, objective science that was carried out by equally objective traffic experts, mostly males. Traffic was viewed as an independent and unavoidable—indeed immutable—physical phenomenon, and there were few questions raised about the validity or even the desirability of attempting to cater for all projected growth. Technical manuals and standards for road design to cope with growing traffic were developed apace, and the work of transport planning was left mostly in the hands of single-discipline technical analysts.

The fact was, however, that these highly technical and expensive studies were neither scientific nor value-free, but were strongly influenced by their social setting. The 1950s and early 1960s were a very optimistic, certain, and prosperous period, characterized by economic growth and consumption-oriented lifestyles. Car ownership was booming, and the political expectation, at least in the United States and Australia and for a time in Europe, was that the automobile would be the future of urban transport. Planning was based on a standard of one or two cars per family. Priority was therefore given to automobiles and road construction, and the pillars of transport planning became mobility and speed. Accessibility largely took a backseat to mobility, meaning in simple terms that a 200-meter walk at 5 kilometers per hour to a corner shop for a liter of milk became a 5-kilometer drive at 50 kilometers per hour to a "big box" shopping center. The approach was to "construct away" any problems caused by cars, especially the traffic queues and increasing number of traffic accidents and deaths, through better road systems (Gunnarsson & Leleur 1989).

Thus right from the outset, land-use transport studies tended to be strongly associated with planning for roads and cars rather than a balance of transport modes, and most of the US and Australian land-use transport studies pioneered the building of elaborate highway and freeway systems (Brown et al. 1972).

However, these are by no means value-free, objective technical procedures, and there are numerous ways that they can be biased to facilitate certain outcomes. The transportation studies of this early era pioneered large-scale road and highway planning because the technical procedures were oriented to the car and the social and political expectations of the 1950s and 1960s, were based around burgeoning car ownership and sprawl (as will be discussed below). In the process, public transit—especially rail—was glossed over and effectively eliminated from consideration in many cities (e.g., Denver, Detroit, Phoenix, Houston, and most other US cities). Stopher and Meyburg (1975) show this clearly when they discuss how public transit was dealt with technically in the modal-split stage of the US studies: "The earlier in the process that transit trips could be estimated and removed from further consideration, the more efficient would be the resulting highway travel forecasting procedure." The analysis would then proceed, with most forecasting based on private-transport growth and the associated land-use patterns. Once such low-density land use is in place, public transit is more often than not based on an inefficient and infrequent bus service (often merely demand-responsive buses in very low-density areas), walking is reduced to taking the dog around the block, and bikes are hardly used at all, even by children. Car usage proliferates and a massive increase in road funding is then needed to provide the highway capacity for the "grand plan" needs and to keep the system from collapsing altogether.

The modeling process does not address walking and bicycling in any meaningful way, due to the fact that the models are set up with a set of origin-destination zones (O-D zones) and are designed to measure trips from one zone to another. Shorter intra-zonal trips, which are possible by foot and bicycle, are hardly dealt with, but are placed in a kind of "throw-away" category called "centroid connectors" and not modeled effectively. In addition, the smaller-scale effects of local density increases or mixed land use within an O-D zone are not brought out in the model results. The density of population and jobs within each zone is an average and therefore considered to be uniformly distributed. The distribution of that density within a zone is therefore not modeled properly or reflected in policy conclusions (e.g., high-density, mixed-use TODs around rail stations, which can greatly alter overall travel patterns).

The shortcomings of these traditional four-step models are dealt with in a comprehensive way by Atkins (1986) through a detailed review of over 50 critical studies. Atkins shows clearly how in every respect, at least up until that time, there were major deficiencies and flaws in conventional transport-modeling studies. These problems cover the models' performance and accuracy, their structural deficiencies or specification errors, and a mismatch between the capabilities of the models and the purposes for which they are used. Most important, this last aspect shows how they are not good predictive tools and are of little use in examining genuine policy options designed to affect change in cities. The specification errors are inherent in the data-collection process; the development of the zones and networks; the trip-generation predictions; the trip-distribution, modal-split, and traffic-assignment stages; calibration and validation; and finally in forecasting ability.

Such problems can still be found today in terms of the way problems are framed and solutions are presented. This is because most models are still premised more on a supply-side approach of greater road infrastructure to solve circulation problems and other perceived transport inadequacies in cities, rather than on an approach which, for example, asks: "How do we change the existing dependence on cars by providing more sustainable and cost-effective alternatives?" One of the papers reviewed by Atkins sums up the experience with traditional transport modeling in this rather damning way: "It might be said (with due apologies) of computer-based transportation modeling that 'never before in the history of human conflict has more money been spent by more people with less to show for it'" (Drake 1973, p. 1).

Most of the reaction to the traditional transport-modeling process has come from continental European cities that found that their historic urban fabrics, based around walking and transit (spatially the major part of most European cities), did not fit the models. The solution to the problems continental European cities were facing did not come out of relying on the guidance of technical transport-planning methodologies. Rather, it came out of a political process involving a sense of vision that had to be fought for as hard as anywhere in the world, and it had to go largely against the mechanistically determined view of the future as prescribed by conventional transport planning. Monheim (1988) relates, for example, the difficulties faced by those wishing to close off streets in the center of Nürnberg to create a pedestrian network. The transport planners claimed that it could not be done because of the volumes of traffic using the streets. However, it was done and their worst fears did not materialize, because between 71 and 80 percent of the traffic simply dissolved in each of the four stages as pedestrianization progressed between 1972 and 1988—Museumbrucke and Fleischbrucke in 1972–73, Karolinenstrasse and Kaiserstrasse in 1972–73, Bankgasse and Alderstrasse in 1982, and Rathausplatz in 1988.[5] Nürnberg now has one of the world's most beautiful central cities and an underground railway to service it. Munich did the same thing in the 1970s and has an equally impressive pedestrian zone (see figure 5-1).

This process, followed by many European centers, of deciding between a mechanistically determined future for their cities and one that involved a strong degree of self-determination is neatly summarized by Herman Daly. In referring to the self-fulfilling nature of many energy-consumption predictions, he also effectively sums up the basic choices involved in setting a city's transport agenda:

> We can make a collective social decision regarding energy use and attempt to plan or shape the future under the guidance of moral will; or we can treat it as a problem in predicting other peoples' aggregate behaviour and seek to outguess a mechanistically determined future. As the art of foretelling the future has shifted from the prophet to the statistician, the visionary, goal-oriented element and the accompanying moral exhortation have atrophied, while the analytical, number crunching has hypertrophied. (Daly 1978, p. 232)

Evidence of the battle fought in Europe between these two different approaches to transport planning is partly seen in comments by the mayor of Munich, who said in 1975 that "With every million we spend on roads we will be closer to murdering our city," and the mayor of Vienna, who asserted that "unlimited individual mobility . . . is an illusion. . . . The future belongs to the means of public transportation [and this will be] a driving force of city renewal" (Gratz 1981).

The Failure of Model-Based Transport Planning

In the broad sweep of cities around the world, conventional transport-planning practices and wisdom cannot claim to have left behind a proud legacy. Nowhere is this more evident than in the traffic chaos characteristic of many US cities, such as Atlanta, Houston, and Los Angeles. A similar situation is evident in Australia, though it hasn't reached the proportions found in the United States. After decades of

Figure 5-1. Part of Munich's extensive pedestrian zone. Source: Jeff Kenworthy.

following the advice of practitioners using land-use transport models as one of their basic *modus operandi*, cities have been left with few apparent solutions to their traffic problems, and in many cases few options other than to endure the traffic chaos on the roads or provide token gestures such as high-occupancy-vehicle (HOV) lanes. The traffic problem, which escalated in the United States in the 1980s, was seen partly in the era's proliferation of books and articles about congestion, with titles like *Metropolitan Congestion: Towards a Tolerable Accommodation* (Larson 1988), *Resolving Gridlock in Southern California* (Poole 1988), and *"Managing" Suburban Traffic Congestion: A Strategy for Suburban Mobility* (Orski 1987). (Other articles and books on the subject published during this period include, for example, Cervero 1986, Pratsch 1986, Cervero 1984, and Gleick 1988.)

The overwhelming impression is of cities that can only hope to throw palliatives at a problem that has much deeper causes, though they rarely recognized the pivotal role being played by transport planners. Frequently suggested policies such as extended or early work hours, carpools and vanpools, computerized traffic lights, or discounts on transit are hardly going to alleviate or significantly arrest the problem. The only solution was to civilize the car through technology, not to end its dominance in planning. Technological wizardry was also sought through the Intelligent Highway System launched in the United States in 1995, representing a conglomeration of traditional highway lobby interests and the IT industry to create a system that would essentially micromanage traffic flows on the road system during peak hours in order to provide a better relationship between supply and demand.[6] This program involves research into what causes congestion on a micro-level so that drivers can relate to the street system in a totally interactive way, being told which routes to take in order to avoid snarls, when to enter freeways from ramps to ensure a reasonable flow of traffic, and at what speeds to travel to maximize traffic flow (Gleick 1988). One of the key ideas is that somehow, if congestion is understood in a more detailed way, roads and people can be manipulated through electronic surveillance to keep traffic flowing. It is also sometimes suggested that California, for example, should double-deck all its freeways, but perhaps as "tollways," to encourage those who can afford it to pay the appropriate economic price for the privilege of moving around the freeway system at peak hour (Gleick 1988; Poole 1988).

The disturbing part about all these approaches is that they are seeking to treat only the symptoms of an ailing transport system, albeit in ever more technically sophisticated ways. This overlooks the root causes of the problems, which lie largely in inefficient land-use patterns and in transport policies that prioritize road-capacity increases over serious transport-demand management (TDM), including proper road pricing (Whitelegg 2011) and provision of higher-quality public transport, cycling, and walking infrastructure. The process of developing these technological solutions can create an unrealistic expectation that technology alone will solve the problems of the automobile-dependent city.

A small digression into the issue of new technologies and fuels for propulsion systems demonstrates this point further. Many still believe that alternative fuels and new types of cars will be the panacea to the problem of oil vulnerability which will see the world's supply of conventional petroleum become increasingly problematic and expensive (see chapter 8). To realize how persistent such thinking can be, one only has to consider the current hype over electro-mobility in Europe, which seems intent on replacing one kilometer of petrol/diesel driving with one kilometer of electrically powered driving, as though there are not already very good social, economic, and environmental reasons for fundamentally reducing car use (Kenworthy 2011a).

Obviously, technological innovation is a crucial element in progress and problem solving and will always be sought, but there is a constant need to weigh such innovation against other issues and to incorporate a more holistic vision of a future society. In the case of transport energy, the reality is that large-scale fuel production from biomass, coal, and oil shale has overwhelming economic and environmental as well as climatic and human adaptation problems, which makes widespread use of these alternative fossil fuels for transport very unlikely.[7] New automobiles such as electric cars, although dramatically improved technologically from years ago and increasingly seen in cities today, are still years away from widespread market penetration, due mainly to the intense capital-investment requirements in changing an entire automobile industry, as well as fuel production, the distribution system, and the technical support network, over to electricity. The frenzied search for alternative fuels in the 1970s and early 1980s after the first two oil crises, in 1973 and 1979, and the ongoing manifestation of this technological "silver bullet" approach in electro-mobility today, all serve to delay the search for deeper transport and planning solutions that will produce a better overall quality of life in cities.

Transport planning as a whole seems slow to respond to the new imperatives in cities and the failures of the past. There is a tendency to hang onto entrenched beliefs even after they have been shown to be false. For example, roads are still justified partly on the basis of simple cost-benefit analyses involving savings in fuel, time, and sometimes emissions, time being the key item, which usually constitutes 70–80 percent of all monetized economic benefits. This occurs notwithstanding the widely documented Marchetti's constant of a 65- to 70-minute overall travel-time budget in cities through the millennia, regardless of the dominant transport mode, and studies showing that time savings due to speed increases in fact do not occur, but are rather just used to travel farther (Marchetti 1994; Newman & Kenworthy 2006).

It is very clear that from an urban systems perspective the analyses are wrong and that fuel, time, and emissions are really costs of new urban road projects in cities, particularly in those already highly dependent on cars (Newman & Kenworthy 1984, 1988b; Newman, Kenworthy, & Lyons 1989). The fact that major new roads are sometimes still touted as solutions to congestion seems to suggest something of an inability to learn from past events. Almost 50 years of experience has demonstrated the futility of building more-extensive road systems to relieve congestion, and the environmental and quality-of-life implications for cities sticking with that approach are dramatic and widespread.

And yet the "roading" approach still persists. Bremen, a city in northern Germany renowned for its progress in car sharing and non-motorized mode use, still struggles with the issue of a major bypass (Whitelegg 2012a, 2012b), as does Aberdeen in Scotland with its extremely expensive Aberdeen Western Peripheral Route. Lancaster's Northern Bypass, which cost £130 million for 4.5 kilometers (£29 million per kilometer), is another recent example of excursions into this less-than-fruitful, indeed destructive approach to transport strategy. Recent UK government pronouncements also herald a continuation of a "predict and provide" approach, with a staggering estimate of between 34 and 55 percent more vehicle–miles of travel in England between 2010 and 2035 and rejection of the "peak car use" hypothesis.[8]

As if all of the foregoing evidence were not sufficient to show the inability of freeways to provide real solutions to traffic problems, there is now evidence showing that pulling freeways down has increased quality of life in those areas where it has occurred and has not resulted in traffic problems. Bringing together various sources, there are innumerable historical and more recent examples of "trip-degeneration," as it was termed by the late John Roberts (TEST 1992). By 1998, there were already at least 60 documented cases worldwide where roads were closed or traffic capacity was reduced and 20–60 percent of traffic disappeared. It was not rerouted as would occur if traffic were like a liquid, but it simply contracted as would be expected if traffic were like a gas. Examples abound:

- In London the Tower Bridge was closed in 1994 due to structural problems; after three years traffic was still not back to original levels.
- Part of London's ring road, the Ring of Steel, was closed in 1993; traffic fell by 40 percent.
- London's Hammersmith Bridge (30,000 vehicles per day) was closed to all traffic except buses and cyclists due to structural problems. A survey of commuters that was conducted a few days before closure and with the same people afterward showed that 21 percent no longer drove to work. They switched to public transit, walking, and cycling, and congestion in surrounding areas did not markedly increase.
- In New York City in 1973, one section of the West Side Highway collapsed and most of the route was closed. A 1976 study of the remaining portion, based on traffic counts three years prior to closure and two years after, showed that 53 percent of trips disappeared, and of those trips 93 percent did not reappear elsewhere.
- In 1989, an earthquake destroyed the Embarcadero Freeway in San Francisco and it was not rebuilt; the predicted chaos never materialized. The whole waterfront area of San Francisco was revitalized, even though today there is still traffic along a surface road.

- In 1996, the upper deck of San Francisco's Central Freeway was torn down due to instability following earthquake damage; traffic chaos did not materialize.
- In 1992 in Melbourne, the Swanston Street Transit Mall was created when a street carrying 30,000 vehicles per day was closed to regular traffic. During the lead-up period, traffic chaos in surrounding streets was vehemently projected; after the closure there was no chaos. Some increase in volume was found on surrounding streets, but it was well within the capacity of the streets to handle this increase.[9]
- In Portland, Oregon, the Harbor Drive Freeway along the Willamette River waterfront was closed in 1974 and then removed, and a linear park was created (Tom McCall Waterfront Park). Traffic chaos did not materialize, but the whole downtown was revitalized with LRT, people, places, and markets, and sound urban design for pedestrians and transit users (see figures 5-2 and 5-3).
- In Seoul, South Korea, the Cheonggye elevated expressway, 6 kilometers in length running through central Seoul, was torn down between 2003 and 2005, along with Cheonggye Road beneath it, which together carried 168,000 vehicles per day; no traffic chaos ensued. In fact, the traffic engineer interviewed in the documentary film made about the project reveals that the overall average traffic speed in the city of Seoul actually rose by 1.2 kilometers per hour, contrary to the normal expectation of gridlock. This project has led to a general "road diet" approach in Seoul, emphasizing new bus lanes, improved subway operations, and more walkable environments. The city is being greened (Schiller et al. 2010).[10]
- There is now an ongoing movement to remove freeways.[11]

These projects add to the almost 50 years of successful pedestrianization schemes in European cities such as Munich, Copenhagen, Köln, Nürnberg, and so on, which have also showed that significant amounts of traffic do not reappear following road closures but instead the cities become more livable and sustainable.

Transportation Decision Making and BCRs

Apart from the four-step transportation planning model, the other major transportation planning tool is cost-benefit analysis, which produces the benefit-cost ratio, or BCR. BCRs have been a significant part of transportation decision making and a BCR of at least 1.5 is generally required for a project to be considered economically acceptable. BCRs are dominated by travel-time savings supplemented by cost savings due to reduced accidents and vehicle emissions.

Figure 5-2. River Place Development in Portland along the Willamette River near to where the Harbor Drive Freeway was torn down. Source: Jeff Kenworthy.

Edmund Bacon, the famous American urban planner and architect from Philadelphia and outspoken critic of automobile-based planning, provides a useful comment on the consequences of overzealous application of BCRs in the formulation of urban transport policies:

> The sad thing is how often the planners in the United States seize mindlessly upon the latest fashionable planning gimmick. The cost-benefit ratio was one of the first of these, a "scientific" method for determining where a highway should be placed by adding up the costs of alternative highway routes and comparing these with a quantification of the value in dollars of the time saved by the highway user. This was adopted universally as the only right way to do things until its continued use imposed such outrageous consequences that it dawned on someone that saving the highway users a few seconds of time would be less socially and economically desirable than destroying irreplaceable landscapes, historical sections of cities, coherent neighbourhoods, or networks of human relationships. Underlying it all was the failure to realize that the development of policy through

Figure 5-3. Pioneer Courthouse Square in downtown Portland, site of a former car park. Source: Jeff Kenworthy.

the manipulation of numbers is always bound to be wrong because numbers by definition leave out the unquantifiable variables: human passions, beloved traditions, human will, and it is these which are really important. While cost-benefit analysis and its many successors have been discredited, basic understanding of the destructive effects of relying primarily on numbers in the formation of public policy still has not penetrated the consciousness of the planning profession in the United States, and that profession is gradually committing suicide in consequence, persisting in the delusion that it is a science—which it never was and never can be. (Bacon 1988, p. 2)

Despite Bacon's assertion nearly 30 years ago, the practice of transportation decision making did not change a lot. Much of this decision making still lacks a broader strategic framework, and until this is in place, meaningful economic analyses remain elusive. However, this is now changing and the tools to improve BCRs have begun to appear. Since the Eddington Report in the United Kingdom in 2006 on how transportation impacts on the economy, BCRs can now include what are called wider economic benefits (WEBs). There has been a renewed interest in how transportation BCRs can reflect the wider economic impacts of infrastructure on cities. WEBs are calculated from the "agglomeration economies" that are associated with synergies between jobs due to close co-location. These are the benefits derived from face-to-face contact, information exchange, and networking only available to industries working close to each other. They are the closest that urban economists have come to measuring the benefits of density in cities (Trubka 2012).

When the UK government was planning the biggest piece of infrastructure in modern Europe, the Cross Rail project in London, they were only able to find a BCR of just under 1.5. As it was in the middle of the GFC-related downturn there was a lot of scepticism about whether such a project was a good idea. However, when they brought in WEBs to the BCR, the value rose to more than 3. The train was obviously going to add dramatically to the economy of London by promoting the knowledge-economy-intensive job generation related to the intensive mode of travel into and across central London. The project went ahead.

The other decision-making tool to go along with BCRs is an assessment tool called avoidable costs. This assesses the economic costs and benefits of redevelopment associated with a new project, especially a rail project that can enable redevelopment to occur, and compares it to business-as-usual greenfields urban sprawl. Trubka et al. (2008) have done detailed calculations on avoidable costs in Australian cities, and these results are set out in chapter 6. Most decisions on transportation do not yet include avoidable costs or wider economic benefits, but if they did they would invariably find that rail projects were more economically beneficial than road projects.[12]

A third factor that is rarely considered in technical economic assessments of infrastructure is the importance of land-value capture—how transport, especially rail, causes land values to increase and hence can be used to help finance the infrastructure. This approach will be outlined further in chapter 6. If value-capture potential is included, then the spatially efficient modes of rail, bike, and walk are likely to be the ones that can lead mostly to intensive urban economy jobs; if bus and car modes are seen as the preferred modes, then a spatially inefficient consumption economy is likely to be the main result.

Technical Failures

Even when judged on the basis of whether the technical procedures are producing accurate predictions of, for example, future traffic flows, relationships between public and private transport and how all modes economically interact with land uses, the overwhelming weight of evidence has been on the negative side if it is primarily focused on automobiles (Atkins 1986; Southworth 1995; Schiller 2010). It is one thing for a transportation land-use model to accurately reproduce the present situation. It is quite another for it to reflect accurately what may happen in the future under a complex array of urban pressures and forces, or what the result might be where a city is given a glimpse of a future quite different to what exists today. There is a danger that the modeling process is so shaped by existing patterns that it is unable to respond correctly or creatively to significantly different circumstances (e.g., markedly higher localized TOD densities), or to meaningfully incorporate significant factors outside its usual outlook (complex climate change, social changes, or qualitative changes in the city environment that demand new approaches). Conventional transport modeling is simply too geared to extrapolating and magnifying existing patterns to be of significant use in guiding cities toward an alternative future. The future being demanded today in all cities is for a low-carbon, regenerative approach to the urban environment, which at the same time delivers a high quality of life.

Perhaps the most powerful factor that now undermines the traditional four-step transport and land-use planning model is the decoupling of wealth from car ownership and car use (see chapters 2 and 3). A critical input to the model takes income and computes both car ownership and use based on a series of assumptions that may have been valid in early-1960s American urban development. However, it is most certainly not valid today, as explained elsewhere in this book. It is very evident that people, especially younger people in the developed world, are choosing more-urban locations and sustainable transportation options that are obviously not predicted by the model. They are not buying cars the way they were predicted to and they are not using them in anything like the same way as earlier generations did. Some are not even bothering to get a driver's license. These models must now be put aside or adapted to enable them to include other choices like these.

In particular, the techniques of transport planning are not well suited to predicting human responses to qualitative changes in the character of a city or the way people may respond to a new transport option. Transport planning is a victim of the modernist idea that complex systems can be reduced to simple relationships. The models may suggest little if any response to these complex issues, and yet the changes may be quite rapid and marked. For example, a city may make a major effort to humanize its central city through urban design improvements, city art and festive marketplaces, pedestrianization schemes, and other traffic-limitation strategies. At the same time it may decide to install or upgrade rail services, with the result that people may discover new ways of experiencing their city. This can begin to set new relationships between transport and land use, including reductions in parking, greater demand for central and inner-city housing, joint development of high-density, mixed-use TOD complexes around stations, better pedestrian and bicycle links and facilities, and still more public transit. Travel behavior and housing options can change quite rapidly under these circumstances, in ways that transport modeling does not anticipate or incorporate well. Yet transport modeling could not anticipate or incorporate such outcomes into its simple car-based assumptions. A conventional transport-planning study could not recommend that such changes be made to a city, and hence they are usually achieved through political approaches and market responses that override the modelers.

Technical models do need to be improved, but they must always answer questions set by a strategic approach to what a city sees as its key needs. What is most needed is a clear vision or goal that can enable all modes of transport to be optimized within a desired land-use plan. Without this, transport planning will have an increasingly deadened sense of purpose within the profession and an inability to provide policy makers with sound guidance. Decision makers, who must cope with an increasingly complex set of demands related to local, regional, national, and global sustainability needs, provision of more-diverse housing options, social and community needs, and depressed financial situations, often find many of the prescriptions from traditional transport analyses blinkered and unworkable.

In summary, the technical world of transport planning finds it difficult to get beyond a view that the city's future can be predicted and provided for by mathematical equations based on often-debatable transport economic and behavioral theories biased to automobile-dependent outcomes. Relative transport costs, resource-efficiency measures, narrow cost-benefit analyses, and other abstractions from the world of transport modeling are not in themselves adequate to the task of guiding decision making and fulfilling diverse community expectations about the future of a city and its quality of life. Without a wider social and environmental as well as broader economic context, transport planning often loses sight of other important forces and is always at risk of working in a vacuum, producing answers that are of little or no use to politicians, the community and business leaders, or the long-term sustainability and liveability of cities.

Planning with Vision

It is very rare to find a transport-planning treatise that makes a clear statement about the broader intent of the work, a statement that sets a clear human context or vision and gives the mathematical and modeling work substance, direction, and meaning. *Transport and Reurbanisation* (Klaassen et al. 1981), historically, was one of the first works to break this mold. While clearly translating its transport prescriptions for cities into mathematical modeling terms, transport was strongly directed toward encouraging a process of "reurbanisation," which the authors saw as crucial to the total life and meaning of the city. Their work sets a human context for their transport-planning expertise. They describe "reurbanisation," their ultimate goal, in the following way:

> The process thus set going is one of once more turning degenerated urban patches into city quarters with living cores, fulfilling a real economic, social, and cultural function, a process of reurbanisation. Its ultimate fascinating objective is the revival of the old core cities, fascinating to many individuals who have learnt in hard practice that living near to nature means mowing the lawn every week, driving downtown in long queues every morning, and driving out of town in long queues in the evening; that a suburban home means buying a second car for their wives so that they may flee the periphery, etc. The more people realise all this, the less they will want to leave the inner city if they are still there, and the stronger will become the desire to live just there, leading a modern life in an old town full of atmosphere. (p. 36)

With the benefit of hindsight, re-urbanization is in fact what many cities have been embracing since that time. In the case of Australian cities, this started as "urban consolidation"; the US cities have their "smart growth" programs; and countless European cities have been and still are regenerating former industrial and port areas into vibrant new post-industrial communities (e.g., Hafen City in Hamburg, Rotterdam, Malmo, and Frankfurt).

It would still appear today that if transport planning is to provide any clear policy guidance to decision makers confronted with how to respond to car dependence and congestion, the planners' approach must incorporate some more-radical visions of compact land-use patterns, both in new developing areas and through selective infill and redevelopment in older areas. The way technical transport studies are conceived, as well as the policies and prescriptions that result from them, can then be geared towards achieving those visions. Even if some of the solutions seem unachievable within prevailing social, economic, and political realities, the fact that an attempt has been made to provide an alternative vision is a step forward, which creates momentum. In particular, it can begin to give substance to the idea that a better balance between cars and other modes is possible. Once started, this momentum can gradually filter its way through communities, bureaucracies, and the political arena and finally result in concrete change—as has been the case, for example, in Portland, Oregon, and Perth, Western Australia.

Circumstances also change, which makes what is achievable a constantly changing thing. For example, in Perth 27 years ago it would not have been conceivable that the city would now have electrified three existing rail lines, constructed a 33-kilometer line to the north and a 70-kilometer line to the south, and be actively pursuing the development of a LRT system and further heavy-rail extensions and new lines. Nor would it have been thinkable that all these changes would also be allied to efforts at rail stations to provide a focus for land-use development. These changes did not come out of traditional transportation-planning analyses, but there is a chance that they could have, given the right issues, contexts, and goals to shape the transportation-planning process.

At the same time a parallel process occurred in central Perth, where a dull and unsafe city center was transformed through a series of interventions led by the Danish urban designer Jan Gehl (Gehl 2009, 2010). All of Gehl's suggested interventions came from walkability data collected in Perth streets and compared to other cities; none of these policies and strategies could have come from the traditional transport model.

To a great extent all the strategic approaches just mentioned have taken place in Portland, Oregon, over the last 25–30 years, at least in the central and inner-city areas, as described in the section below. Other cities, too, have shown surprisingly rapid land-use adaptation and success with their new rail systems. For example, Washington, DC, and in particular some Canadian cities such as Vancouver have numerous examples of integration between new rail systems and high-density, mixed-use development (Newman & Kenworthy 1999a; Schiller et al. 2010). Los Angeles's rail development was linked in its planning phases to proposed major new commercial and mixed-use developments (Keefer 1985), and this has occurred both around its new Metro stations on the Red and Purple lines (e.g., at Wilshire and Vermont, and at Hollywood and Vine) and around the light-rail system (e.g., at Del Mar station on the Gold line). But Portland remains a stand-out example, because it was the first in the United States to break the transport modelers' hold on city planning.[13]

The Portland, Oregon, Experience

Portland's long fight to get away from the early technical transport studies and their overwhelming road orientation is summarized by Edner and Arrington (1985) in the following way: "Initial political stirrings for a transit option were substantially unsupported by comprehensive technical studies. The thrust was to wean Portland away from a highway-based system and buy time to develop a balanced alternative using transit and limited highway improvements" (p. 14).

This involved doing some new technical studies with an emphasis on public transit, but this time under the auspices of Oregon's governor, who was convinced that change was needed:

> The key question facing the Governor's Task Force (GTF) was whether transit was a viable alternative to freeway investment. Sixty-eight system configurations for the region were ultimately evaluated. These configurations were identified as alternatives to PVMATS (Portland-Vancouver Metropolitan Area Transportation Study) and its highway emphasis. That study, initiated in 1959 but not formally adopted until 1971, assumed that transit ridership and operation would stabilize and, at worst, continue a trend of decline into the future. (p. 14)

Like nearly every "grand plan" from the 1950s, Portland's transportation study was roads-oriented and virtually assumed the demise of public transit. However, the GTF's report provided the first technical justification for public transit, based on a range of factors including positive environmental effects; but more importantly, according to Edner and Arrington:

> It set the stage for developing the technical and political decision-making capability for regional transit planning. The GTF report was a crucial element in the decision to withdraw the Mount Hood Freeway. . . . This technical justification initiated a linked technical/political decision-making process. . . . Freeways were de-emphasized to the benefit of transit and a CBD focus. (p. 15)

They summarize the decision to build a rail line instead of a freeway as "a major shift in the functional and philosophic role of transit in the region . . . [which] ruptured the political fabric of transportation decision making, realigning the roles and responsibilities of many political and technical actors" (p. 2). In Portland, transportation planning was really forced through a political process, especially one involving the community, to take on new directions. There was little evidence that the transportation profession was about to provide the initiatives itself.

It is interesting that in Portland the process of planning and building the Metropolitan Area Express light-rail system, or MAX, met with a lot of cynicism, particularly in the press. A competition was run to find the best name for the system. "A Streetcar Named Expire" finally won. However, MAX is now a big success, both as a transport system and as a focal point for new development. Howard (1988) reported, shortly after the opening of the first line in 1986, that benefit-assessment districts established in the downtown area to return to the community some of the private-land-value increases of the system "have proven very successful, partly because the system is so appealing to the public that the development community is jumping on the bandwagon to expand the scope of that program" (p. 172). Having made the big break and built a railway instead of a freeway, Portland found the next steps to be easier. The only arguments in Portland about MAX became which community should get the next extension (see figure 5-4).

Making Transport Planning a Better Tool in Reshaping the Auto-City

There is nothing inherent in the actual techniques of the land-use transport-modeling process or the other technical procedures of transport planning that will *inevitably* produce road-biased results. It is more the way decisions are made about how to use the techniques. Historically, road planners have dominated this exercise. If a genuine attempt is made to consider alternatives to urban sprawl and more freeways, and if this attempt is accompanied by a community-engagement process such as Perth's *Dialogue with the City* (see Schiller et al. 2010), it is possible to give new direction to the transport-planning process. It is also possible to build in more-sophisticated

Figure 5-4. Portland's Saturday/Sunday market, a revitalized area based on light rail, where a major freeway would have been constructed. Source: Jeff Kenworthy.

feedback mechanisms where transport and land use are dealt with in an iterative manner, one progressively affecting the other. This would in all likelihood be an improvement over existing practices, though the results of such models are still subject to considerable debate and inconsistency and are by no means guaranteed to come up with prescriptions that will assist cities in transitioning to lower car dependence (Webster, Bly, & Paulley 1988).

Ultimately, it comes back to the first stage of the process: the formation of goals and objectives. In the past, and unfortunately still today in many places, land-use transport modeling has chased something of a fairy-tale world where transport demand and supply are meant to be kept in equilibrium by planning road systems to cope with projected traffic volumes—a sort of "transport utopia." The pressing requirement was, and often still is, to try to keep ahead of congestion. Interestingly, even after decades of experience in US and UK cities of building freeways while congestion relief remained an elusive goal, large new roads are still called for today and justified for their supposed ability to relieve congestion. Fundamentally, in too many places a genuine alternative, such as minimizing unnecessary private motorized travel, has not really been embraced. Too often, walking and bicycling are not considered in any serious way, while public transit is often still seen as an addendum to the main game of catering for private mobility. In many cases there is very little meaningful variation in the different scenarios provided by transport studies—just minor variations on a fundamentally road-oriented theme.

A change to more comprehensive planning requires better specification of the goals and objectives of transport studies and more emphasis on public transit in the models. Since the 1980s, there has been a rapid growth in new light-rail systems throughout the United States and Canada (commencing in Edmonton in 1978 and then Calgary and San Diego in 1981). These new systems have been introduced largely as broader community or politically led initiatives in response to a dire need for mobility alternatives, rather than as technical decisions from conventional transport analyses. This political- and community-driven response reflects widespread disenchantment with automobile dependence and the problems it creates, such as: congestion; local, regional, and global environmental impacts; and social and economic inequity in transport. Rather than promoting greater freedom, unbridled personal mobility derived from mass prosperity and automobile use have created high levels of individual frustration when a car is the only alternative for most trips (Eno Foundation 1988).

Urban and transport planners everywhere can assert their role in the development of cities through new goals and objectives for transport–land-use modeling based around balancing the roles of various modes of transport, minimizing total motorized travel in the urban system, and reducing the costs of urban land-development through reducing urban sprawl—in short, creating more-sustainable and indeed regenerative cities. There is no compulsory reason why transport planning should favor roads and suburban sprawl to the exclusion of other modes and more-compact patterns of development. As stated in the last major Australian urban "grand plan," the Sydney Area Transportation Study (SATS 1974), with regard to land-use transport modeling:

> Some of the inputs into the models are based on assumptions of a political nature or those containing value judgements. . . . Transportation models cannot directly give answers to policy questions, nor can they derive transportation system alternatives. Final decisions cannot be reduced to a set of mathematical equations. (p. II-1)

Conclusion

The urban fabrics theory described in chapter 4 has major implications for the way that transportation planning is practiced. Up until now, the models employed in conventional transportation planning have been relatively blunt instruments, applied with no regard to the different kinds of urban fabrics that exist in cities and the need to respect them. The models have really been used in a modernist one-size-fits-all approach, where large roads have been seen as a solution everywhere. They have been punched through old walking and transit fabrics, destroying their human amenity and walkability and undermining or destroying the transit city parts of metropolitan areas.

Cities should no longer apply these models at such an aggregate and simplistic level across cities, intended to achieve results that most frequently optimize infrastructure for the automobile. It is possible to envisage a future where the useful transportation modeling and planning tools that have been developed and refined over decades can now be applied more selectively, with very different guiding objectives in mind in different parts of cities, as opposed to just facilitating free-flowing automobile traffic.

These models have the capacity to be run with different aims in mind, in much the same way that Portland opened up its traffic model to produce a series of public-transit-based future scenarios for the region, instead of more highways. Given that the models divide cities up into a series of origin-destination zones, with a great deal of underlying base data describing each zone, transportation planning can be practiced at a more fine-grained level, where walking, cycling, and transit are analyzed and prioritized rather than the car. This will mean paying a lot more attention to the importance of short intra-zonal trips, which often rely on foot or bike. It may be that these zones do have to be redefined and perhaps made even smaller in order to pick up the fine details of walkability in the walking and transit city fabrics. There are important nuances and differences in the less automobile-dependent qualities of different parts of the city that need to be enhanced or extended, as shown by Gehl (2010) and other pedestrian-oriented urban designers.

Under this kind of future scenario, the key to making transportation planning a better contributor to policy development does not lie in giving what amounts to open-ended briefs, such as asking computer-modeling studies to predict traffic 20 years into the future or how many new roads are going to be necessary to cope with it. History shows that under this kind of direction it is almost assured that within the logic of the models' own analysis, enough traffic will be foreseen to justify any number of new roads and just about anywhere, regardless of the inherent characteristics of the urban fabric. This is how the grand transportation studies of the 1950s, '60s, and '70s universally recommended elaborate freeway networks and presided over a massive decline in public transit. It is how they aided and abetted the destruction of so much walking and transit city fabric and helped to extend the automobile city over vast areas.

Even asking traffic models to assess whether traffic projections alone justify the construction today of a particular road tends to take the decision out of context with other important values, visions, and directions in the city, which are often in direct opposition to the idea of building more road capacity (e.g., the aforementioned conflict in Bremen between building a new ring road and all its sustainable public transit achievements to date). The internal workings of traffic models tend to generate self-fulfilling prophecies of traffic and future road needs without consideration of the broader implications or the special qualities of walking and transit fabrics that now need to be respected, revitalized, and extended for many reasons, especially in support of the move worldwide toward intensive urban economy jobs that thrive in these urban fabrics but not in auto-based urban fabrics.

The traditional transport model is a "hammer" approach, which treats every problem like a nail; to use it is an invitation to perpetuate or strengthen dependence on the car and a sure way of generating a sense of powerlessness within public planning about influencing the future land-use and transportation directions and possibilities of any city. Yet cities everywhere are taking back the initiative, which can reclaim a more people-oriented city. Gehl (2010) outlines hundreds of cities now making this transition away from traditional traffic planning, at least in their city centers.

The next phase of mainstreaming this approach is to adapt the transport-planning tools so that they can make a contribution to much less auto-oriented planning. Making transportation planning and models work to find better solutions to extend walking and transit city qualities, and to ameliorate wherever possible the automobile city fabric of the last decades, holds great potential to revitalize the transportation profession. Again, this is especially so when one considers that the economy of so many cities is increasingly reliant on spatially efficient intensive urban economy jobs that require more spatially efficient transportation modes. In effect, the transportation-planning profession needs to reinvent itself from one that emerged in the twentieth century, with the car as the basis of all its traffic models and economic analyses, to one that is today based much more on facilitating walking, cycling, and public transit.

To shepherd this process, there needs to be a strong vision of ending automobile dependence in the city and then guidance from transportation modeling about how to achieve that. Questions about the need for new roads should not be put in terms of "Is the new road justified on traffic grounds?" Typically, traffic models are very likely to conclude that it is. Rather, we should be asking questions such as:

- Will the new road help to end automobile dependence and protect and revitalize the walking and transit city fabrics, and will building it contribute to or detract from this?
- What are the alternative options for a city in assessing a road proposal, and how do these alternatives relate to a range of other objectives associated with respecting the different urban fabrics of the city? These objectives might include, for example, environmental protection, urban regeneration, reduced resource and fossil-fuel consumption, livability of neighborhoods, accessibility and mobility for all groups in the community, transportation safety, and healthy outcomes.

Collectively we need to be able to say what we would like the city to look like in 20 years' time. That means making decisions about whether we want walking, public transit, or automobile priorities in different parts of the city. Specifically, this means asking quite different questions of the transportation planning process than have been asked in the past, questions such as:

- What sort of improvements in the urban environment do we want?
- What qualities and diversity do we want in urban lifestyles? Consider, for example, qualities like communal spaces where once only through-streets existed, mixed land uses as opposed to rigid zoning, more variety in dwelling styles and density, and greater sociability versus increased privatism.

- What do we want the central city and sub-centers to look like?
- Do we want strong centers, and what should the balance be in modes of access to and within these centers and how does this work out in terms of road widths, setbacks, and parking requirements?
- What kind of overall population and job densities should the city aim for to minimize car dependence, and where should higher densities be concentrated?
- What goals can be set in terms of reducing car dependence? For example, such goals might include parking levels in the CBD and other centers, future modal splits for various types of trips, goals for walking and cycling, and targets for reducing overall per capita car use, in line with the 25 percent / 50 percent / 75 percent of total travel by car in different urban fabrics of the city, as mentioned in previous chapters.
- What goals can be set for extending or introducing new rail systems to help reduce car dependence?

Working within this type of visionary framework and with close regard to the different urban fabrics of the city, transportation planning can make a more constructive contribution to urban policy and practice. The new transportation model, incorporating more sophisticated BCRs and other improved economic evaluation tools as described in this chapter, also needs to have sections for each part of a city's urban fabric, with different assumptions and expected outcomes for each section. The model needs to optimize levels of service for walking and cycling in walking city fabrics, optimize levels of public transit service for transit city fabrics, and optimize automobile levels of service in the automobile city fabrics but only if other transit fabric extensions cannot be achieved. If such changes are not made, the profession will not be able to respond to the nature of the global knowledge-based economy and its need for walking and public-transit-based urban fabrics. Cities are already competing on the basis of their walkability and transit options. The last thing that is needed is another round of self-fulfilling prophecies of increased road and traffic from computer models telling communities across the city that they must accommodate more traffic. In simple terms, "predict and provide," one-size-fits-all planning, which treats traffic as a kind of immutable liquid that will simply flow over everything if not catered for, needs to be replaced with a "debate and decide" approach that treats traffic as an expandable or compressible gas in the intensive areas of a city (walking and transit fabrics) and that allows cities to shape a regenerative future for themselves based on a decline in automobile dependence across the whole city.

6

Overcoming Barriers to the End of Automobile Dependence

Although the end of automobile dependence is well underway, the trends toward urban living, human-focused planning, and investment in transit, biking, and pedestrian infrastructure will need to continue for several decades in order to deliver the quality of urban fabric we need. Any significant change involving technology, culture, legal systems, governance, business models . . . will require time to settle into becoming a substantial social transformation (Diamond 2009; Beilharz & Hogan 2006; Geels 2011). One important result of the turn in fortunes is that planners in government, community, and industry have begun to see a very different future emerging. Instead of serving business as usual, the approaches to urban land development and transportation policy have shifted. Market leaders, progressive governments, and strong communities can now sense that by implementing policies that reduce automobile dependence they will be on the right side of history. This chapter outlines these major directions forward and shows how they can be built on to enable the end of automobile dependence.

The two broad areas of policy that need to be addressed in order to continue on the path to ending automobile dependence are re-urbanization and reorienting transportation priorities—just as we first set out in 1989—though now they are so totally interlinked it is difficult to separate them. However, the two most significant sets of issues still surround *doing density well* and *doing transit well* and especially how they can be done together. Thus, the issues that need to be addressed in order to fully implement policies to end automobile dependence are set out in a series of questions related to density and transit. The answers to these questions will help cities proceed in their dismantling of the structures, perceptions, and thinking that prevents the end of automobile dependence.

1. Is increasing density enough to end automobile dependence?[1]
2. What are the myths and truths about density increases?
3. Can alternative funding for transit be used to integrate solutions to reduce automobile dependence?
4. How fair is it to public transit not to price traffic congestion?

1. Is Increasing Density Enough to End Automobile Dependence?

Density, in residential and job land use, is about the number of people wanting to be in the same place. It's not hard to see that the more people who want to be in the same place, the more that a mass transit system will be needed, so it's also not surprising that there will be a relationship between density and transportation. Our work over several decades has been about finding thresholds that can help in making the relationships between density and transportation transparent (Kenworthy et al. 1999; Newman & Kenworthy 1989, 1999a, 2006). The famous graph of density versus gasoline consumption per capita (figure 1-14) has led some people to believe that we are suggesting that only density will fix automobile dependence. So the question is often asked: "Is density enough? Can't you just fix the poor use of public transit by improving services?"

Making mass transit functional depends on many factors (Vuchic 2005). At its most fundamental level, mass transit not only depends on density to support it but also on the frequency of its services. Even the densest places will not have much public transit patronage if frequent service is not provided.[2] Some transport academics have been making these service-level relationships much clearer and more transparent (Bruun 2007; Mees 2000, 2009a, 2009b). Some, like Mees, have suggested that service levels alone can overcome automobile dependence; he has described "the density delusion" as being the biggest barrier to improving public transit. Mees believes that focusing too much on achieving the appropriate density distracts planners from the need for better coordination, management, and organization across agencies and organizations working on transportation. He does not find density to be a convincing explanation for the differences in public transit performance in global cities. We argue on the contrary that population density is a multiplier for any public transit services that are provided. In particular, public transit use can be multiplied many times by population density increases, as has been shown over and over in the TOD literature (e.g., Cervero & Ewing 2010). Casting increased density as being delusional does create doubt in the mind of policy makers, however, and this doubt becomes a barrier to the end of automobile dependence.[3] It therefore needs to be addressed in order to support and strengthen the trend away from automobile dependence. This is not to mention the fact that higher-density development can be highly liveable (see the next section on the "Myths and Truths of Density"). Much of our own research and publishing over many years has tried to allay such fears and doubts by showing the amenity and convenience potential of well-executed compact, mixed-use development within sound urban-design principles for the public realm (e.g., Kenworthy 1991; Newman & Kenworthy 1991). Cities like Vancouver are now showcasing the political appeal of "density done right."[4]

The value of providing better transit services without waiting for density increases is incontrovertible. The data set out in chapter 1 on the rise of rail show how this has happened in many low-density cities as well as the more traditional transit cities with their greater densities. Perth's electric rail system, which has been developed in different stages beginning in 1988, shows the capacity of rail modes to provide superior faster services to which people will flock even from low-density areas, provided the stations are fed properly with access modes. Use of Perth's rail system has exploded from 7 million passengers a year in 1992 to nearly 80 million in 2014. But the value in increasing services while also increasing density is far more powerful. The more people who have access to public transit service, the better the chances are of these people using the service. There is a scale and density factor that operates to enhance and multiply whatever operational advantage can be provided through better services and such things as integrated ticketing.

Public transit usage differences between cities are less strongly correlated with density than is car use. Our own analyses show this in the wealthy cities with an r-squared of 0.58 between public transit boardings and urban density, and 0.82 with car use and urban density.[5] This is a big difference, and it is even greater with non-motorized modes (NMM) (an r-squared of only 0.47 with density). There are lots of qualitative urban-design, topographical, infrastructure, mixed land-use, and other kinds of factors that determine non-motorized mode use, but one will not find very high NMM use in any low-density environments zoned for single use, whichever way you look at it. Use of NMMs is limited strongly by trip distances, and the lower the density and the more single-use an area is, the longer the trip lengths and the less viable it becomes to walk or ride a bike.

The level of public transit service, of course, does not depend on density alone. Some cities have poorly serviced or simply poor public transit infrastructure and so will not have the same level of service of a city of similar density with much better or even exceptional infrastructure and service. Zurich and Bern are good examples of cities that have much higher public transit usage than higher-density cities of similar size.

This is because they introduce "quality factors," as follows:

- They provide very high levels of public transit service, much of it on rail;
- Their services are very well-timed, reliable, and integrated;
- The vehicles are generally very comfortable, clean, and well maintained;
- All the buses and trams operate with green waves (public transit vehicles trigger a green light ahead of cars, thus giving them a speed advantage and allowing them to reach key stations at the same time to enable people to change vehicles easily) and there is also a preponderance of reserved routes with a good speed advantage over cars;
- The ticketing system encourages committed users with annual passes; and
- The passenger information is high quality and the waiting environments are generally pleasant.

These added-quality factors that the Swiss are so good at, on top of the density advantage in their cities, are so pronounced compared to many other European cities of similar density, that Zurich and Bern "outperform" their density and become outliers on the graph.

Increasing population density is not easy in many cities, as we discuss in the next issue. In the eastern suburbs of Melbourne, density appears to have become a barrier to good public policy, and this influences Mees in his analysis. However, this is no excuse for dismissing the value of density. Melbourne's density has actually gone up faster than that of any other Australian city. Furthermore, most cities in the world today are diverse enough to warrant and sustain many different housing and urban-environment preferences—and these are not all anti-density. Many, in fact, are pro-density based on living in a more lively, convenient, and interesting community with attractive, hospitable public spaces, short distances that can be traveled easily by bike or on foot, and more diverse and frequent public transit services.

The relationship between urban density and car use per person for just the fourteen Australian and US cities in this more recent database shows that there is a negative relationship (r-squared of 0.22) between density and car use. When the full set of higher-income cities available in our Global Cities Database are represented, instead of the fourteen used by Mees in the critique about the US and Australian results, the explanatory power of urban density on car use increased from 22 to 53 percent (Newman & Kenworthy 2012).[6] The result for the larger sample of 58 cities shows that 84 percent of the variance in car use across a global sample is explained by urban density.

It is acceptable, naturally, to explore relationships within different regional samples. However, selective data can be very misleading. The relationship between higher density and increased public transit use is not shown only between city comparisons but also within cities. The power of the relationship between public transit use and density is shown even more dramatically within the cities that we have examined, as explained below and in Newman & Kenworthy (2006).

Los Angeles has a reputation as a mega-sprawling, low-density region, but Los Angeles County is now the major part of the densest urbanized area in the United States. It has an urban density approaching that of the Copenhagen and Stockholm metropolitan areas and yet it has very mediocre overall public transit use per capita, a fraction of that for the two European cities. This is due, at least in part though not exclusively, to relatively poor public transit service infrastructure and service provision, with only a comparatively small but growing (and so far very successful) rail system. Los Angeles has a legacy of decades of neglect of public transit options in favor of automobiles, and it is not possible to rectify this in just a few years. Other factors accounting for its overall low use of public transit include the generous provision for automobiles symbolized by the extensive freeways around which the dominant automobile system is built. But it is also true that as the Los Angeles rail system and new higher-speed bus services are expanded, Los Angeles public transit use continues to grow well in excess of population growth and it recorded the highest per capita public transit use growth between 1995 and 2005 of the 10 major US cities in our global cities update (Kenworthy 2011b). Density at the same time is increasing. Again, both density and transit service levels are important in determining a city's use of public transit.

The extent of the density correlation will be affected by other factors such as the level of services and other behavior factors, as pointed out by Ker (2011). The Swiss cities are good cases where public transit outperforms their density levels due to exceptional service provision. However, in no city have we found that density did not play an important role in determining public transit patronage. In Melbourne and Sydney, detailed regression analysis of their transportation greenhouse-gas emissions by local government area showed that density explained 56 percent and 71 percent of the variance, and transit access/services explained 61 percent and 58 percent of the variance; in other words, both were significant and interrelated (Newman 2006b). In chapter 1, we found density and transit services together explained most of the variance in VKT per capita across 40 years of Global Cities Data.

Density is not a delusion; it is a real factor in shaping the overall orientation and performance of the transportation system in every city we have studied. If we could find even one city that did not show some kind of positive relationship between density and transportation, then we would begin to wonder about the significance of density. But we do not.

In response to the question of whether increased density alone is enough, we say that public transit improvements are also needed—but the two go together, they are totally intertwined. The polycentric city of the future will need carefully planned and implemented centers with real density increases. These will be linked together across the city by high levels of public transit service, thus providing the framework for the low-density suburbs to have the necessary transit base for their future viability and resilience. These are key ways of introducing walking and transit city fabric into automobile city fabric and making the latter more sustainable without wholesale change. Density and transit services together form an indivisible partnership in the effort to alter urban fabrics and aid in the end of automobile dependence.

2. What Are the Myths and Truths about Density Increases?

Increasing density is a contentious issue in most cities, but we must take on the issue if we are to continue to enable the end of automobile dependence. There is obviously a case for designers to make density more attractive and for planners to make the amenity better around denser housing and high-rise offices. However, there are many times when the designer and planner never get a chance to show their skills, as any density increases are challenged politically.

This section provides an overview of the density issue and summarizes the myths and truths about density. We hope that the sustainability credentials of density can be better understood by showing the broad perspective. As suggested in the section above, density is a multiplier of benefits from public transit. This section will show, from many perspectives, that it is a sustainability multiplier.

The relationship is very strong between increased urban density and lower consumption of transportation fuel per person in the world's cities, as presented above and in earlier chapters. This alone would suggest there is a good case for density being seen as a sustainability multiplier: for each step in increasing density there would appear to be a large reduction in consumption of transportation fuel.

The most important set of cities in terms of a need for density increases are the highly automobile-dependent cities of North America, Australia, Canada, and New Zealand. However, there are moves to lower the density in all cities in Europe, Asia, and Latin America as part of the need to accommodate different lifestyles. The reactions to density myths and truths are therefore of relevance to all cities; however, our focus here is on low-density cities, with a particular focus on our home town of Perth (perhaps the most automobile-dependent large city in Australia) in order to illustrate how our findings can be applied to similarly sprawling cities.

Ten Density Myths

Myth 1: High-Density Housing Is Bad for Your Health and Creates Social Problems

Most people in the world live in high-density housing, though, as shown previously, there are huge variations in density. There is no correlation between these levels of density and ill health, though increasingly there is a lot of evidence that walkable environments are much healthier—and walkability needs density (Giles-Corti, Ryan, & Foster 2012). Health levels relate mostly to income (Eckersley et al. 2005; Marmot & Wilkinson 2006; Newman & Kenworthy 2006). Poverty is the biggest cause of ill health. Hong Kong has over 300 people per hectare—nearly 30 times Perth's density—but has high life expectancy and low infant mortality, just like Perth. If industrial pollution is high then building densely within the air shed will increase respiratory problems, but this can be more effectively addressed directly within the industries, and letting cities sprawl in order to reduce exposure to pollutants just increases the pollution due to cars.

There is little evidence that social problems such as crime are increased in high-density areas. Crime is also mostly related to poverty (Fischer 1976; Kelly 2000; Knox 1982). In America, the higher the density the lower the crime rate, though this is most likely because low-density cities are poorer (Newman & Kenworthy 1989). There is a lot of evidence that low-density urban areas have higher crime rates due to fewer "eyes on the street"; further, they have greater rates of obesity illnesses (now more prevalent than those caused by smoking) and greater rates of depression, both due to lower walkability (Frumkin et al. 2004; Haigh 2006; Newman & Matan 2012b).

This idea of high density causing health and social problems has likely been carried over from the time of tenement houses and overcrowded slums. We believe there are two primary origins of this myth:

1. Biologists once suggested that it was unnatural to live in high density, and they conducted tests with rats and monkeys in overcrowded conditions that showed how their social organization collapsed (Lorenz 1966; Morris 1968). None of this

research seems to have been repeatable (i.e., it was poorly done and others can't see the same effects). And when such studies are made of human conditions, no evidence of density *causing* health and social problems can be found (Baldassare 1979; Wilson 1976).[7]

2. Since the Industrial Revolution there has been a long-held view that disease was spread through the air (via "miasma"), and thus the early town planners in Britain sought to reduce densities to provide a "wholesome supply of good air" (Jefferson 1909; King 1978). Disease was afterward discovered to be caused mostly by waterborne germs, but the myth continued. In the 1960s, poor people in the United Kingdom, Australia, and America were put into high-rise public housing; the result was health problems and crime, with high-rise being blamed. Now, though, crime and health problems are higher in low-density poor suburbs, especially those with higher levels of public housing, but we don't tend to blame the low housing density—nor should we. The source of the problem in both cases is linked much more to the social situation of having large concentrations of people clustered together with similar problems, for example, high unemployment, poor education levels, and social breakdown in one form or another. This is why in most cities today, for example, public housing is no longer concentrated in a few areas but is distributed throughout the city in smaller collections.

After studying all the evidence on density and social impacts, Freedman (1975) concluded that "crowding is not generally negative and it does intensify human reactions to other people." More recent work by Florida (2005) and Glaeser (2011) supports this hypothesis. Higher density can produce negative effects if we don't design it well to encourage good human interaction, but it can also make for beautiful and human cities that stimulate interaction.

There are cases where the dark side of human interaction has been enabled by higher density, perhaps through concentrating people with social problems in poor public housing. But at the same time, the most creative cities with intense human community are usually the densest places. Manhattan has both Harlem and Greenwich Village, London has both Brixton and Chelsea, Sydney has both Redfern and Paddington. Indeed, in these cases the regeneration of Harlem, Brixton, and Redfern has happened rapidly in recent years, transforming them into highly desirable, trendy locations, especially for creative people. Most planners and housing providers now stress the need for mixed housing, mixed incomes, and mixed cultures as well as good urban design in shared spaces that facilitate face-to-face interactions (Bay 2011; Landry 2008). There is also substantial evidence that having good governance and good management systems in high-rise housing can avoid social problems and create many opportunities for the growth of community (Conway & Adams 1977; Gehl 2010).

Myth 2: High-Density Housing Will Lower Land Values and Create Slums

There is little evidence of land values collapsing when higher-density housing goes into an area. In most cities, land values are related to amenity—access to recreation sites, the ocean, good schools, services such as health, employment opportunities, and proximity to rail lines (Newman et al. 2014). As people move to areas with more amenities, the pressure to subdivide goes up. If zoning for higher density is increased, then land values increase (McDonald & McMillen, 2007). Density is also most often associated with highly accessible central and inner areas where land values are elevated.

Thus, even in America where densities tend to be lower, the highest-density areas, such as Manhattan, inner San Francisco, or Washington, DC, generally have the highest land values. If anything, there is a problem with density causing land values to go up so much that they cause poorer people to be displaced as rents become too high (Sassen 1994). This gentrification is why a proportion of affordable housing is on the agenda for most planners dealing with the density issue (e.g., through density bonuses for upscale housing to cross-subsidize more-affordable dwellings).

More high-density affordable housing in well-located areas is an important priority for automobile-dependent cities. If present trends continue, the auto-dependent city will be highly divided into "eco-enclaves surrounded by Mad Max suburbs" (Newman et al. 2009).

Most low-density cities are known for particular cultural activities, but due to the distances involved in bringing people together, this is often much less intensive (as suggested by Henderson 1977). Thus writers such as Jacobs (1961) have documented the more intense life of dense cities. Landry (2008) and Florida (2012b) have similarly examined the need for cities to come back in and increase their density if they are to create more cultural diversity and creativity. Creativity is now the basis of many new business opportunities in cities (Storper & Scott 2009).

Myth 3: Nobody Likes High-Density Housing

There are many cultures amenable to dense, high-rise housing, notably in Asia, Europe, and Latin America. There is a long tradition of living in close proximity for security and ease of access between friends and family (Newman & Hogan 1981).

English traditional culture favors the village and rural spaciousness (in literature this is called "pastoralism"), especially after the Industrial Revolution with its dense slum housing. In Australia, Canada, and the United Kingdom, many migrants were escaping the poverty of public housing (the "council flats" syndrome) and came seeking a suburban life. There has, however, always been a more urban tradition in cities, such as London and Manchester, with their amenity and attractions (Williams 1985) and in the United States, as noted by writers, such as Mumford (1938), Jacobs (1961), and Gratz (1989), who gloried in their urban environments. As outlined in chapter 4, millennials in North America are now seeking out and helping to revitalize the dense, walkable, transit-oriented neighborhoods of America's forgotten cities such as St. Louis and Baltimore.

Housing markets in Australia, and more dramatically in Perth in recent years, have increased in the proportion of households that favor location over housing type; that is, they choose high density because of its access to amenity (Government of Western Australia 2013; Kelly et al. 2013). Location has always meant a lot in cities.

Many people will want to remain in a low-density neighborhood but they appreciate the benefits that higher-density centers nearby can bring to their area, including better transit, shops, childcare, and even aged-housing options. As dense centers are built the attitudes toward them start to soften, especially where the urban public realm is of a high quality, as it is in Vancouver, where higher-density housing areas set in walkable, green environments have proliferated over recent decades, especially family-oriented apartments (Punter 2003).

Myth 4: The High-Density Problem Is Caused by Population Increases, and This Should Be Stopped or People Should Be Put in Country Towns

Population movements between cities are mostly part of the global economy, and only few countries, such as North Korea, are trying to opt out of that. Stopping participation in the global economy means that cities go into immediate economic decline. Some cities such as Detroit in the United States and Liverpool in the United Kingdom did not adapt to the changing global economy and so went into decline (Newman 1986). Few communities or politicians are going to accept economic decline as their policy for the future.

Perth, for example, is a boom town and its population growth is mostly caused by immigration from overseas. Australia has always been a migrant country, and the growth of the economy is linked to this flow of people from across the world as they follow the new jobs. Mostly, people who come to Australia have specific skills or business investments. Refugees are a small proportion of the migrants and are protected by international legal obligations. If the economy crashed, then the "population problem" would be solved: people would transfer to somewhere else to find a peaceful place with opportunities. Any city that tries to damage its economy in order to stop population growth is unlikely to get very far before it becomes politically impossible to continue, due to the damage done to the rest of the population. It is not likely to be used as an immigration-control device. No city has found a mechanism for preventing migration. Even the Soviets could not control the growth of Moscow, though they had set a notional limit on its future size. Hence, cities will mostly continue to work to attract more people and to use the growth opportunities created by the influx.

Some nations have migrant schemes that require new arrivals to first live in country towns. Some newcomers stay (e.g., the Western Australian country town of Katanning has a multicultural mix of workers), but most move to cities such as Perth where the economic, educational, and health-care opportunities are greater. Country towns in Australia and North America are mostly in decline, and few policies have worked to reverse this decline (Newman 2005b). Government incentives in terms of country-town housing, grants, and the like have never changed the overall growth of major cities.

Population growth is not a bad thing if its growth imperative is used to generate more-sustainable cities (Newman 2011). It is difficult to reshape a city that is stagnant. Every city needs to see its growth plan as an opportunity to create a better city—one that has a reduced footprint and greater liveability. If low-density sprawl characterizes the development, though, it will simply be a wasted opportunity; growth now needs to be directed into ending automobile dependence.

Myth 5: High-Density Housing Removes Trees, Places for Children to Play, and Opportunities to Grow Food and Collect Rainwater

New cities built as car cities after World War II had large allotments. Australian suburb allotment size of a quarter acre (1,012 m²) was a substantial area, designed to accommodate a septic tank's overflow and to have a rainwater tank, a vegetable garden, some trees, a clothesline for drying clothes, perhaps a chicken enclosure, and plenty of grass for children to play on—and of course a large garage for several cars. This lifestyle was heavily subsidized for returning servicemen in the postwar years (as it was in the United States), and it continues to be subsidized as it provides for the unique "Australian lifestyle"—or indeed the unique "American lifestyle" (Gleeson 2006). These are the car-dependent suburbs of today.

Like all New World cities, Australian and American cities now have sewerage systems and good water supplies, and the size of the houses has slowly grown such that they are now four times bigger than houses in the 1960s, while the block size has been reduced to around the 400-square-meter mark. Still the campaign rhetoric of save-our-suburbs groups calls for maintaining the low-density suburb as though suburbs have remained unchanged since the 1950s and have a moral right to remain as they were in the popular imagination (Troy 2004; Gleeson 2006; Newman 2005a; Recsei 2005).

Every decade of housing reaches a point where redevelopment is necessary. The model that seems most acceptable to low-density-dominated local planning systems in the United States and Australia is to allow backyard infill with several small units (Newton et al. 2012). In this way all the trees, grass, and vegetable patches are replaced with brick houses, asphalt, and brick pavers. Apparently, this can be acceptable because it is not high-rise. However, it adds very little to an area because there are no infrastructure changes or service improvements, nor many improvements to the urban public realm to offset density increases. In particular, such development does not lead to increased greening of a suburb, as all the trees are often removed in the process.

Higher density that actually greens the urban environment is possible and is much more likely to be supported by our communities. Tim Beatley has taken the idea of "biophilia,"[8] or the innate need for humans to interact with nature, and applied the idea to cities (Wilson 1984; Beatley 2010). The biophilic city brings landscaping into and onto buildings, walls, roads, and concrete water courses in order to bring nature into every element of the built environment (Kellert et al. 2011; Beatley 2010). The benefits are considered to include the cooling of the city (especially as the urban heat-island effect grows faster with climate change), reduced storm-water surges as rain is slowed down in the same way it is in a forest, reduced energy needs in buildings due to the mantle of insulation from plant life, improved biodiversity, and improved health. Health improvements are of particular interest to many people who see density as antithetical to health. High-rise development enables better infrastructure and services, and it incorporates space for trees, play areas, intensive landscaping (such as biophilic green walls and roofs), and even intensive food gardens with water collection and recycling (Newman 2012; Newman & Matan 2012a).

Perhaps an element missing from the biophilic urbanism story is that it will help with the end of automobile dependence, as public-transit-based density will provide the first and best places to demonstrate the new technologies of green roofs and green walls. This is especially true since a big source of opposition to higher density is that it creates a "concrete jungle" and that it simply increases local traffic, whereas if high-density development is transit- and walking-oriented, it leads to decreased use of cars and, with good design, can have plenty of green, soft surfaces.

The need for a radically new approach to bringing nature into cities has never been more obvious than in the endless modernist, cookie-cutter high-rise towers of the emerging megalopolises of the world, especially in Asia, which are usually surrounded by little more than grass and concrete and where biodiversity loss continues apace (UNEP 2011). Singapore has bucked the Asian cookie-cutter high-rise tower syndrome through its visionary planning over many years, particularly its recent commitment to biophilic urbanism. It now appears to be a leader in this new approach to city building (see color plates 14, 15, and 16).[9] Singapore demonstrates that high-rise creates new options for greening that low-density suburbs cannot. Green roofs and green walls need verticality, as in a forest, and suburbs are more like steppe or a grassland in their overall environmental form. As Singapore becomes a city in a forest through its landscaping on buildings as well as between them, it is possible to see a new kind of high-rise greening emerge.

All these examples of biophilic urbanism demonstrate that the critical density increases needed in cities through TOD (and discussed especially in chapter 4) will be made considerably easier through this innovation. Thus what appear to be "only" urban greening exercises, carried out through urban design of the public realm and different approaches to the architecture of buildings, really do have a much deeper and important role in ending automobile dependence. They help to create a built form that is fundamentally less needful of car use and which provides a revival of walking and transit city fabric.

If planners and architects are unable to green their cities even as others are succeeding in doing so, there will be negative consequences and growing pressure for lower-density housing with its own private green space. Perhaps biophilic urbanism is a way to facilitate green and attractive cities that are also far more efficient in resources. Removing any stigma of density, rightly or wrongly conceived, would be a significant planning contribution that can help in ending automobile dependence.

Myth 6: High-Density Housing Consumes More Energy and Produces More Greenhouse-Gas Emissions

Some arguments against high-rise housing suggest that these building types are dangerous to the future of the planet, as they consume more energy and produce more greenhouse gases than single, detached, low-density housing (Low et al. 2005; Troy et al. 2003; Newton & Tucker. 2011). This is not true according to both first principles of architectural design and ongoing scientific evaluations.

The argument hinges on high-rise housing having large energy-consuming areas such as public lift spaces, public parking, and public common areas for spas and swimming pools. The data that are used to support this invariably include buildings with high-energy-consumption areas (mostly very wealthy) compared to the whole low-density housing stock, which mostly do not have such facilities as spas and swimming pools (Myors, O'Leary, & Helstrom 2005). This is wrong scientifically (Beattie & Newman 2011; Perkins et al. 2009).

The history of architecture shows that one of the key reasons for compact houses was to share walls in order to conserve energy for heating and cooling (Anderson et al. 1996; Wilson & Boehland 2005). Thus, most evidence comparing high- and low-density housing (using similar wealth levels) shows that high density actually consumes *less* energy, as heating and cooling are the biggest factors (Breheny 1992; Thormark 2002).

The need for green building as part of a low-carbon/high-performance building industry is constantly being demonstrated (Friedman 2014; Fraker 2013). Green housing types should be built at every density and height. However, the biggest difference in energy consumption between housing types is in their associated transportation energy needs. Here the main factor is location, and in most car-dependent cities, as in Australia, this is easily measured by how far the housing is from the CBD (Trubka 2010a). Denser central/inner-city housing requires between 4 and 10 times less transportation energy than does housing in low-density outer/fringe suburbs (Kenworthy et al. 1999; Trubka 2010a, 2010b, 2010c), as explained by the theory of urban fabrics in chapter 4.

High-density housing is most amenable to areas closer in, and hence most high-density housing is generally not only lower in its building energy consumption, it is much lower in its transportation energy consumption. As fuel and electricity prices rise, this energy factor will continue to be a major reason why high-rise housing will be needed in increasing amounts, especially if well located (Curtis et al. 2009; Rodriguez 2013). Many Canadian cities, such as Toronto and Vancouver, also have significant high-density (high-rise) housing in their suburbs, mostly around rail stations. These TODs have both lower building-energy and lower transportation-energy costs for the people who live there.

Myth 7: High-Density Housing Is Not Necessary for Environmental Sustainability, as Renewable Energy and Electric Vehicles Will Mean That We Can Drive as Much as We Like

This is a new argument by those who concede that high density can indeed save energy, but perhaps, they say, high density will not be needed anyway, as renewables and electric vehicles will mean that we can have fossil-fuel-free cities and low density. Indeed, the renewables/EV combination (which is essential) has become a rationale for sprawl.[10]

Even with renewables and electric vehicles, our cities are still car-dependent, with rapidly growing suburbs consuming prodigious amounts of land for houses, roads, and car parks. By 2050, when the world needs to have lowered fossil-fuel consumption by 80 percent, there will still be huge areas of American and Australian cities, indeed areas around most cities, with low-density, car-dependent suburbs. To become independent from fossil fuels, these areas will need to have totally converted to renewable sources of power and electric vehicles, as will be discussed in chapter 7.

Moving to renewably powered vehicles will not address the problem of traffic and its associated social, environmental, and economic problems, especially given the new urban economics requiring intensive land use served by intensive modes. Roads in automobile-dependent cities are already full. It makes no sense to imagine traffic increases based on electric vehicles if they carry on destroying the walking city and transit city fabrics, just as petrol and diesel vehicles have done. Reduced car use will happen if high-density, well-located housing redevelopment is provided around rail stations and inner/middle suburban areas with good access (Newman et al. 2009). The problem is urban space: accommodating cars in cities surrenders public and private space to automobiles through roads and parking (in automobile-dependent areas, each car needs between five and eight parking spaces in various locations around the city, as well as the extra road space discussed earlier). The need today is to reverse this situation, not to increase it.

Future cities will need renewables, electric vehicles, and public-transit-oriented high-density housing in all its forms—as fast as possible (Newman 2013).

Myth 8: High-Density Housing Development Is Destroying the Heritage Buildings of Our Suburbs

In every era of urban development there are buildings we want to keep because they are beautiful and full of history, and with sensitive restoration they can be given a new life. Most cities conserve their heritage as part of their redevelopment. However, most urban redevelopment is in newly created spaces reclaimed from redundant industry or warehouse sites. Considerable opportunities exist for adding new houses into underutilized urban space, including conversion of selected heritage industrial and warehouse structures to residential and mixed uses (e.g., in Hafen City, Hamburg, there is now an extensive precinct consisting of heritage warehouses converted to apartments).

The most creative cities can undertake restoration and redevelopment that enables a city's economic and social life to grow (Baycan et al. 2012; Florida 2005). In the decades since our first book on car dependence was published in 1989, virtually every inner-city area we studied has begun to revitalize and regenerate. Perth's inner areas are mostly good examples of redevelopment. The city of Fremantle has almost doubled its housing stock while restoring its heritage as a nineteenth-century port town.

The biggest issue facing American and Australian cities is the lack of creative higher-density opportunities being enabled beyond brownfield sites (Newton et al. 2012). There are many more opportunities for redevelopment in inner and middle suburbs, but most housing redevelopment is either simple, dysfunctional low-density infill of backyards or very wealthy high-rise. It is possible for car-based cities to hold on to their quality heritage but add considerably more affordable high-rise housing in inner and middle suburbs (Newton et al. 2012). Heritage housing restoration and high-density redevelopment are not incompatible—they are both needed. The prevention of redevelopment in the name of heritage or historic preservation can indeed drive away any development, and hence all the benefits of new green buildings with their new technology and materials is lost.[11] Of course, many buildings should be preserved for the future but there will be many needing to be replaced. Well-designed density with strong green credentials will be the heritage of the future.

Myth 9: High-Density Housing Redevelopment Is Not Helping to Create Sustainable Cities, as It Is Wasting the Materials and Embedded Energy in Suburban Housing

When a suburban house nears the end of its life the question becomes: Should it be redeveloped as part of high-rise housing or restored as a low-density historic house? The argument sometimes presented to stop the high-rise option is that the planet will benefit from not wasting the materials and embedded energy in an existing house (Low et al. 2005; Troy et al. 2003). The mantra has become "the greenest building is the one that has already been built." Thus density should be stopped, as it's better to keep the buildings we already have.

The answer in terms of green outcomes is that any building's materials can be recycled and can thus save most of its embedded energy. There are many ways of reusing building materials. Even a timber-and-asbestos house can be redeveloped; one such building was recycled as a prefab home after the asbestos was removed.[12]

New high-rise housing can use materials with much lower embedded energy and low-carbon/low-cost wall and roof materials, especially if constructed by off-site manufacturing (OSM) and simply joined together on-site. An assessment in Perth of the reductions in embedded energy, basic raw materials, and waste saved shows the huge potential for reductions in basic raw materials with redevelopment back into the inner area using new technologies such as OSM, compared to business-as-usual (BAU) urban development on the fringe: 15 metric tons per person for redevelopment using OSM, compared to 288 metric tons per person for BAU on the fringe (Gardner & Newman 2013).

There is an emerging new model for how the environmental footprint of cities (that is, the impact of their resource use) can be dramatically reduced, which we have called the Urban Sustainability Model (Newman 2011; Rauland & Newman 2015). It consists of new urban infrastructure, new urban form, and new urban management and is based around neighborhoods or precincts. The kind of infrastructure required will enable significant reductions in fossil fuels, water, other materials, and waste (thus reducing the footprint) while enabling cost-effective urban areas that are better places to live. The technologies to achieve this are set out in Rauland and Newman (2011).

The kind of approaches that will produce these outcomes can now be modeled in the design process by using such sophisticated models as CCapCity, produced by Kinesis, building on work done by Landcom in New South Wales (Beattie & Newman 2011). In a study of the Cockburn Coast for LandCorp in Perth we used the model to determine the greatest footprint reductions for the least cost. The green features provided (including renewables, water recycling, green building) are all easily available and would cost just $5,600 extra per dwelling compared to a standard house. The rapid growth and deployment of these technologies in the future will continue to reduce this already very low cost as well as the payback period.

The need to adopt the new urban infrastructure of decentralized energy, water, and waste systems is rapidly becoming mainstream policy (Bunning et al. 2013; Rauland & Newman 2015). The massive gains in decarbonizing a city in a short period of time are appealing to urban policy makers across the globe.

However, such green precincts only work when sufficient density is available, and in the case above it required medium- to high-density buildings to make sufficient quantity for the infrastructure to work. Normal low-density suburbs would not work with such infrastructure. Different management will always be required, as local governance of the infrastructure is needed; this was recognized 40 years ago (Freedman 1975).

High-density housing is a major part of the planetary resource solution, not part of the problem.

Myth 10: High-Density Housing Is Not Good for the Economy

It is true that much of the housing market in automobile-dependent cities has become oriented to the low-density, single-family house (Brueckner 2000; Ewing 1994). However, the new high-density housing market is rapidly growing and many firms are adapting to these new opportunities (Government of Western Australia 2013; Rowley & Phibbs 2012).

In terms of the costs of high-density redevelopment versus low-density urban-fringe development, high density looks much more promising:

1. Urban-fringe housing is generally subsidized by governments. In Australia this is around $100,000 per dwelling (Dowling & Lucas 2009; Trubka et al. 2010a). Similar data are found in American cities (Burchell et al. 2002; Chatman & Noland 2014). In Perth this means $45.4 billion in the next 30 years unless redevelopment occurs on appropriate sites in inner and middle suburbs (Hendrigan & Newman 2012).

2. Urban-fringe housing costs the economy hugely in extra transportation costs due to the extra car travel. In Australian cities each dwelling built on the fringe involves an additional $250,000 in travel cost over the lifetime of the house. In the next 30 years this will cost Perth $133.6 billion just in time lost to travel. Denser cities have 4–8 percent of their GDP spent on passenger transportation (operating and investment costs for all passenger transportation modes); low-density cities have 12–15 percent (Kenworthy et al. 1999).

3. Walkable high-density areas have improved health due to greater walkability, and improved productivity outcomes due to greater attentiveness and fewer days lost. The health-care cost reductions of a less sedentary population can be significant (Trubka et al. 2010c).

4. Much more of the revenue from residents of high-density areas is spent locally on personal services such as restaurants, childcare, and entertainment, rather than on cars and housing with do-it-yourself tools and materials, which invariably draws money out of the local economy.

Trubka et al. (2010a, 2010b, 2010c) outline the economic benefits of redevelopment at higher densities over urban-fringe development in Perth, expected over the next 30 years of anticipated development. They suggest the total benefits would come to around $212.9 billion in savings. The same kind of data can be found on all of the car-dependent, low-density cities we studied, as shown in chapter 4.[13]

Glaeser (2002, 2009) has made studies of the most uncompetitive cities in terms of housing prices and concluded that the largest factor is the lack of high-density zonings that can enable cities to have affordable housing, allow residents to benefit from transportation savings, and allow the city to benefit by lowering investment in new infrastructures. Added to this are the economic benefits from the intensive urban economy that require dense centers to enable the synergies and project innovations to happen. Density makes economic sense for any city.

4. Can Alternative Transit Funding Be Used to Integrate Solutions to Reduce Automobile Dependence?

As automobile dependence is in decline and cities everywhere are building public transit to a record extent, attention inevitably turns to the need for public transit funding. It is becoming increasingly out of the reach of governments alone to fund the construction of major new transit systems simply through their own consolidated revenues or market borrowings. This lack of funding for non-automobile modes of transportation is therefore a major potential barrier in reducing automobile dependence.

Table 6-1 lists a range of alternative funding mechanisms that have been used for public transit delivery and provides examples.[14]

Alternative funding for transit has received a boost in recent years when agencies realized that rail projects have a big factor in their favor: they increase the value of land around stations, thus enabling various land-value-capture mechanisms. The same has not been found with road projects and only rarely for bus projects, as they have much less ability to draw pedestrian-based urban activity to be located near their primary focus points (McIntosh et al. 2014). However, walkability improvements do improve land values and have been used as a basis for funding, though usually in much smaller projects than urban rail (USEPA 2013).

The mechanisms and basis for alternative funding for any major rail project are inherently complex and involve an understanding of the way the real estate market works and the different types of taxation systems and other financial mechanisms enshrined in planning legislation. This section therefore provides some detail on these important matters in order to show how to help remove this financial barrier to the end of automobile dependence.

Land and property value increases surrounding transit infrastructure have been well documented (Cervero 1977, 2004; Cervero & Duncan 2002; Scheurer et al. 1999; Debrezion et al. 2007; Kilpatrick et al. 2007; Duncan 2010; McIntosh et al. 2013). Many cities have used active value-capture mechanisms that simply direct these land-value increases back into the project; for example, Copenhagen built its Metro by handing over a corridor of former defense land as the basis for funding a private/public partnership (PPP), and many Asian cities, such as Hong Kong and Tokyo, use

Table 6-1. Review of alternative public transit funding options.

	Value-Capture Mechanisms
Government Property (Passive)	Sale of surplus property / development rights / air rights
	Sale of naming rights to stations
Government Property (Active)	Direct development of government property
	Joint development
	Returns on government parking
	Government property leasing
	Advertising revenue
Non-Government (Passive)	Tax increment financing & additional taxes hypothecated to public transit
	State transfer duty / Sales taxes
	State land / Property tax
	Local government rates / Taxes
Non-Government (Active)	Benefit area levies (or Special Assessment Districts) through state or local government infrastructure cost recovery
	Differential rates, Specified area rates, Service charges
	Region-wide transport levy
	Existing infrastructure tax hypothecation
	Developer contributions
	Parking levies / Bonds
	Localized parking levies
	Increased cash in lieu
	Metropolitan wide parking levy
	Density bonuses

Source: McIntosh et al. (2014).

Examples and Project location	Agency	Notes
Hong Kong, China (Metro)	MTRC	Used when governments hold their property and receive a benefit when property values increase as improved public transit accessibility is monetized
Washington, DC, USA (Metro)	WMATA	
Sydney, Australia (Heavy Rail)	RailCorp	
New York, USA	MTA	
Philadelphia, USA	SEPTA	
Hong Kong, China (Metro)	MTRC	Mechanisms to capture increases in land values and economic prosperity that positively impact the value of state and local government property and land from public transit
Tokyo, Japan (Metro)	Tokyo Metro	
Hong Kong, China (Metro)	MTRC	
London, UK (Metro)	Crossrail Stations—Canary Wharf & Heathrow Airport	
Portland, Oregon, USA (Streetcar/LRT)	Portland Streetcar Inc.	
Philadelphia, USA	SEPTA	
International implementation		
Atlanta, USA (Heavy Rail)	MARTA	Primarily focused on increases in existing ad valorem taxes that result from increases in property and land value
Dallas, USA (LRT)	DART	
Dallas, USA (LRT)	DART	
Portland, Oregon, USA (Streetcar/LRT)	Portland Streetcar Inc.	
Portland, Oregon, USA (Streetcar/LRT)	Portland Streetcar Inc.	
London, UK (Metro)	Crossrail Business Rate Supplement	Mechanisms to capture all or part of the increases in property and land values and economic prosperity that benefit non-government land and business owners
Seattle, USA (Streetcar/LRT)	Seattle Streetcar Inc.	
Portland, Oregon, USA (Streetcar/LRT)	Portland Streetcar Inc.	
Atlanta, USA (Heavy Rail)	MARTA	
Dallas, USA (LRT)	DART	
Portland, Oregon, USA (Streetcar/LRT)	Portland Streetcar Inc.	
Gold Coast Australia (LRT)	Gold Links	
London, UK (Metro)	Crossrail Community Infrastructure Levy	
Portland, Oregon, USA (Streetcar/LRT)	Portland Streetcar Inc.	
International implementation		
Portland, Oregon, USA (Streetcar/LRT)	Portland Streetcar Inc.	
San Francisco, USA	SFMTA	
New York, USA (metro)	NYC Department of Planning	
Curitiba, Brazil	Rede Integrada de Transporte	

government land around stations to build commercial properties that bring in over 20 percent of their revenue. Passive value-capture is where, through the normal taxation system, private beneficiaries around stations help to contribute some of their windfall gains when a rail line is built. In this way, if sufficient ongoing funding can be raised, then it is possible to bring private capital into helping to build the rail line.

Cities analyze and capture the passive financial benefits created in land and property markets by the use of Tax Increment Financing (TIF). The principle of Tax Increment Financing involves forecasting the net tax-revenue impacts of future land-value increases that are induced from value-improving infrastructure projects and directing this into the financing of a project. TIF has been used extensively in the United States for over 50 years (Sullivan et al. 2002; USEPA 2013; Zhao & Larson 2011). TIF has generally been used to fund urban renewal projects but has in recent years been applied to rail projects.

TIF is considered a "self-financing" way to pay for economic-development projects in US cities where redevelopment projects are financed through induced increases to local government taxes, predominantly through local sales-tax revenues generated by new development. Government officials do not have to impose a new tax but they simply set aside a fund that hypothecates the expected revenue, and thus they can finance the infrastructure through this fund. If the infrastructure is not built, then the revenues will not flow and the fund is not possible. It is like a windfall tax that is generated above what would normally be expected in tax revenues—as long as the rail infrastructure is built.

The first TIF law created in the United States was in California in 1952 and has since spread to all 50 states with TIF spurring the redevelopment of blighted areas. Now the use of TIF schemes to generate project finances has expanded into other areas across the United States.

Some examples of using dedicated land and property taxes for investment in public transit projects in the United States include:

1. Chicago, Illinois—the Randolph/Washington station, the Dearborn subway, and various transit projects within central Chicago's Loop. The City of Chicago allocated $42.4 million in TIF revenue to the Randolph/Washington station (USEPA 2013).
2. Atlanta, Georgia—Atlanta Belt Line, a comprehensive redevelopment and mobility project that will build a network of public parks, multi-use trails, and public transit, including a 22-mile rail line that will serve 45 neighborhoods and connect to the existing MARTA rail service. The project will cost an estimated $2.8 billion, with the Atlanta Belt Line Tax Assessment District generating approximately $1.7 billion of the total project cost over 25 years (Atlanta Belt Line 2014).

3. San Francisco, California—redevelopment of the Transbay Transit Center, a multimodal transportation hub that includes a 1,000-foot-tall office tower, a 5.4-acre rooftop park, and 2,600 new homes. Funding for the $4.2 billion project will come from a variety of sources, including $1.4 billion in TIF funds, of which $171 million will be used to repay a federal loan used for the Transit Center construction (USGAO 2010).

Beyond the United States there has been much less use of TIF for public transit. The UK government amended the Local Government Finance Act (1992) in 2010 to allow for TIF in Scotland, and now any proposal for a TIF project must demonstrate to the Scottish government that the enabling infrastructure will unlock regeneration, facilitate sustainable economic growth, and generate additional public-sector revenues (not just revenue that would have been collected anyway). The Manchester City Deal included the "Earn Back Model," which is a residential-dwelling-based TIF expected to earn £1.20 billion over a 30-year period, and to repay or fund the financing for the investment framework in order to undertake the investment in transportation and other economic infrastructure (Greater Manchester Combined Authority 2012).

The benefits of TIF implementation in the United States include the following (Johnson et al. 2002; Sullivan et al. 2002):

- TIF can provide financing for projects that otherwise would not be fiscally feasible;
- The city loses no tax revenue but gains a valuable infrastructure asset;
- Property owners in a redevelopment zone pay their full share of property taxes, and property owners outside the zone are not required to bear more than a normal tax burden;
- If TIF bonds are used, they are not generally included in a city's general debt obligations, thus enabling private/public partnerships;
- Urban redevelopment is financed from the increases in tax revenues that it generates, not by subsidy from other areas of the city;
- Once TIF bonds are retired, the city and all other affected taxing units regain the advantage of the full tax base and increased tax revenues;
- If the TIF is funded through a bond issue, projects must be well planned and economically feasible in order to attract bond investors, thus TIF guarantees quality projects; and
- Voter approval of other taxing units is not required; a city council may act unilaterally.

The benefits of a TIF framework are not just that a piece of quality transit infrastructure is built, but also that an integrated delivery of denser urban redevelopment around stations is made into a strongly enhanced urban development process. TIF revenues will be higher if densities are zoned at higher levels in the catchment area of the rail project. Such delivery of TODs is rarely achieved, despite most car-dependent cities having the concept embedded, but latent, in their plans (Woodcock et al. 2011).

Proposed Framework for Transit Financing in Car-Dependent Cities

TIF financing will work in any city that has a commitment to rail and is prepared to set up a framework to enable it to happen. We have oriented the framework to apply in particular to automobile-dependent cities based on our experience working on the concept in Perth and other Australian cities based on the work of James McIntosh.[15] Thus, it has a particular focus on implementation in car-dependent cities in order to maximize both city-shaping benefits and potential TIF revenues to defray project costs. The proposed steps to achieve an integrated transit- and land-development funding/financing assessment framework are as follows:

- **Step 1.** Assess the relevant land and property taxing legislation and policies, and define the zone for a Tax Increment District (TID). This is similar to the techniques outlined in chapter 4 on recognizing transit fabric, though in a car-dependent city this may go deep into automobile city fabric. The definition of the area works much better if the expected beneficiary area can be based on experience in other corridors where public transit already exists.

- **Step 2.** Analyze the willingness to pay for public transit accessibility and transit-oriented development (TOD). This depends on collecting data on the value of land over a period of time where it can be assessed in relation to other public transit impacts. A hedonic model for Perth was developed that allowed land-value increases to be discovered due to other factors such as nearness to the ocean, good schools, and other amenities as well as access to rail stations. In the Perth analysis, the heritage rail system (nineteenth-century lines) appeared to raise residential land values by 18 percent and commercial land values by over 60 percent; on the new Southern Line that went deep into automobile-dependent suburbs, the value of residential land within a 400-meter catchment area increased 42 percent over a five-year period following announcement of funding for the line (McIntosh et al. 2014).

- **Step 3.** Conduct TID financial analysis to forecast revenue generation and viability. A model can be generated based on these land-value increases applied to the catchment area established in Step 1 that is based on expected tax-revenue increases. In the Perth analysis, depending on the zoning allowed, the Southern Rail line could have funded between 60 and 80 percent of the actual building capital (McIntosh et al. 2014).

- **Step 4.** Propose a project-specific TIF implementation strategy. In Perth we proposed a Transit Fund be established that could take the TIF and other revenues from grants and from active value capture associated with direct land-development opportunities. It was also suggested that consortiums could be asked to bid to build, own, and operate the system in a private/public partnership based on the Transit Fund and the best-quality outcomes from bids in terms of the route and the financial requirements.

Such an approach can enable a city to build the public transit and the transit city fabric at the same time, thus enabling the transition away from an automobile-dependent city. TIF is a system breaker—if cities want change.

4 5. How Fair Is It to Public Transit Not to Price Congestion?

In order to enable a true end to automobile dependence the role of public transit is critical. We have suggested that, with the market swinging toward public transit, the value of land will inevitably rise in cities that provide public transit as a reasonable option. This will give public transit an edge in the competitive world of transportation funding. But what else is needed to make public transit work? In order to compete, buses and light rail in particular (also pedestrians and cyclists) will need to find a way through the congestion created by cars. How can public transit do this when that congestion is not even priced? Congestion pricing is politically difficult—but is that fair?

Congestion exists in just about every city in the world, from Atlanta to Ho Chi Minh City. Atlanta is the lowest-density city in our global cities database (6 persons per hectare in 1995). In modern times it grew up with the car and was built around the car; it provided massive freeway systems and spread its traffic load out over a vast urban and semi-urban territory as it sprawled outward. It suffers chronic congestion. Ho Chi Minh City sits at the opposite end of the spectrum in every respect—except for its congestion. It was the densest city in our database in 1995 (356 persons per hectare, or 60 times denser than Atlanta) and had no freeways at all. It suffers chronic congestion from a chaotic mixture of cars, motorcycles, and trucks, as well as non-motorized and lightly motorized modes. Every city one can name in the world will to one degree or another suffer from traffic congestion, even if they have developed comprehensive and speed-competitive public transit systems such as those in

Munich or London. For all the success of the Southern Rail Line in Perth discussed above, the freeway along which the line travels is still clogged in the peak period, with little sign of improvement.

This suggests that whatever road capacity a city provides, whatever type of city one is dealing with (whether totally car-dependent, more transit-reliant, more oriented to walking and cycling, or a dynamic mixture of all these modes), and whatever high-quality transportation alternatives are provided, roads still get congested. We deal with the reasons for this below. Conceptually, however, it appears that the best way to tackle congestion involves a two-pronged approach: improvements to automobile alternatives and disincentives to the use of cars. This is similar to the way that density and transit improvements need to complement each other.

There are two ways to manage any piece of infrastructure. The first method is to saturate demand with supply, which is why properly managed landline telephone systems always work. It is also why, in normal circumstances, one can always get water when one turns on a tap and also why one can always use the toilet and not have the system overflow. Demand, in these types of infrastructure systems, never exceeds supply due to there being too much "traffic" for the level of infrastructure provided (or so it is to be hoped!). It is also why the Internet continues to function, notwithstanding the occasional messages about not being able to access a particular website due to "extremely high traffic levels." Sometimes, even in the best of infrastructure systems, demand simply does exceed supply.

But no other system of infrastructure approaches the level of problems associated with traffic congestion. With road traffic, in fact, demand exceeds supply every day. For significant parts of the day in the morning and evening along many major roads, and especially on so-called freeways, there is insufficient supply of road space to manage the level of demand. This leads us to the second and only other way to manage an infrastructure system: demand must in some way be tailored or managed so that it does not exceed supply.

This is where transportation planning in most cities has failed. For decades, especially since the Second World War, one of the main enterprises of transportation planning has been the attempt to overwhelm demand for private motorized mobility with a sufficient supply of road space, in essence, planning and constructing new roads ahead of predicted demand. This approach, as outlined in chapter 5, was supposed to create and maintain a kind of transportation Utopia in which travel demand and the supply of movement space would always be in equilibrium and traffic would essentially move as though we are permanently living at three o'clock in the morning (Kenworthy 2012). This enterprise failed, of course, simply because it is never physically possible to build enough road space to keep pace with travel demand without effectively destroying the city—not in Bangkok, not in Phoenix, not in Montreal, not in Munich. Los Angeles tried it, as did Houston, Atlanta, and just about every other US metropolitan area, but none of them eliminated congestion, many aggravated it, and most tore the hearts out of their walking and public-transit-based fabrics trying to do so (Klein & Olson 1996).[16] Vancouver did not because it decided not to build freeways, and this may be one reason why it also appears to be the first city in the world to opt for metropolitan-area-wide road pricing (Coyne 2014).

So with road-based transportation we are left with the only other way to manage the infrastructure: reducing demand. There are education and behavior-change programs that have been shown to work, such as Perth's TravelSmart (Ashton-Graham & Newman 2013; IPCC 2014). These are programs that encourage people to see why they would be better off getting out of their cars and showing them how best to do it. Changes of 8–15 percent have been achieved.

This kind of behavior change is best achieved as part of further structural change that enables better options to be provided at the same time as disincentivizing the use of cars, especially their use at the wrong time in the wrong place. We have to somehow better control the travel demand so that accessibility is still provided but the mobility approximates the capacity of the road infrastructure to provide for traffic's normal and efficient movement without the daily foul-ups common to cities today. Has this been achieved anywhere? The answer to this question is yes, but only in the case of Singapore, a city-state that has, starting in 1972, kept the real cost of purchasing and driving a car so high that its car ownership is still around 100 cars per 1,000 people and has been for many years, while cities that have a fraction of Singapore's wealth have sailed past it in car ownership (Kenworthy & Laube 2001; Kenworthy 2014).

Singapore is also an excellent example of how such congestion controls can work synergistically with prioritizing public transit and building high-density communities around rail stations on the transit network. So on the one hand, the private car is being controlled or limited, and on the other hand, the alternatives are already being rapidly deployed in a way that adds to the convenience, quality of life, and sustainability of the city. Plans are now being made to see if the entire private-vehicle fleet could be replaced by driverless cars that take up half the space, as they are used twice as much when being shared. However, the loss of private-car ownership entirely is unlikely to work, even in Singapore.

The Dutch have adopted an interesting alternative approach of paying people not to use particular freeways in the peak period through their Spitsvrij, or "Peak Free" project.[17] In order to delay investment in a costly freeway-capacity expansion project, people who use the freeway in the peak are offered a €130 per month deposit in their bank account in advance. Their cars are equipped with monitoring devices and if they use the freeway, contrary to the agreement, a fixed amount of money will be deducted from this €130, so that the participants are obviously motivated to retain the reward. The project has been extremely cost-effective and has performed well in reducing congestion in the peak. It has also delayed investment of €1.5 billion by two years for upgrading the freeway (the question of not ever doing the upgrade, given the success of the program, is strangely not discussed at all, however).

This is a modest success story in four small Dutch cities. In most other global cities, the fact that urban management generally has failed to provide one of the city's major infrastructure systems with a sound way of maintaining a high level of service each and every day is curious at best, especially when such a high standard *is* applied to every other infrastructure system in the city upon which residents rely and it is done as diligently as is humanly possible. It does imply that there is somehow an unacknowledged or unspoken assumption that it is really normal and acceptable to have chronic congestion, while at the same time the rhetoric is quite to the contrary, that we must do something about it.

It is of course possible to do something about chronic congestion and in fact to eliminate it, but it takes a strong degree of political determination to do so. Of course, political action first requires some political consensus or alternatively a crusading politician, such as Ken Livingstone, the mayor of London who pioneered the city's successful central-area congestion charge. The lack of such political will or courage seems to be a stumbling block in most countries regarding the most commonly touted form of congestion control, road pricing. If this were not the case, the world's cities should theoretically be replete with road-pricing schemes. However, comprehensive road-pricing schemes generally seem to be about as politically popular as a cold shower in winter and as slow to be adopted as molasses in the same season. Instead, isolated (though still useful) efforts are introduced, born out of less common political circumstances, which are mainly about charging for entry into constrained areas such as CBDs in peak periods (e.g., Milan, Stockholm, and Oslo) are introduced. Broader road-pricing systems as a means of congestion charging have been known about and talked about for decades but are rarely practiced.[18] A pertinent question is why? To answer this it is useful to examine some underlying assumptions that exist in societal attitudes to congestion.

For decades, capitalism has railed against the inefficiencies and indeed the inferiority of socialism as an economic system for the production and distribution of goods and services. Ironically, however, our appetite for capitalism has been lost in the way we manage our urban road systems. The current approach is much more akin, in key respects, to socialism. Under socialism, the "cure" for a lack of supply of consumer goods in the former Eastern Bloc countries, was simply to queue up. This is what the entire world does twice a day, every day, sitting in stalled traffic. We queue up because there has been no logical market created for road space by which to balance supply and demand.

Road pricing attempts to remedy this situation by creating a market for road space. The theory goes that we should ask people to pay a price for their use of road space. The problem that seems to occur when this economic logic is applied to urban roads is that it implies someone has taken away the road space that is already actually ours and which we have been using mostly free of charge since roads were created (with the exception of toll roads). Someone is now asking us to pay a fee for the "stolen goods." If we already own our own home we are not going to appreciate someone insisting that we now have to pay rent on it. So there is naturally a political reluctance to go down a path that can be likened to such a scenario.

In order to keep traffic flowing anywhere, it may well be more logical and productive to treat the road system as a "commons" that must be regulated for efficient operation and the common good. This could mean instituting a system of random fines for operating vehicles in conditions that are deemed to be unacceptably congested and a system of rewards for bus users in the form of reduced fares for their decision to use a mode that takes a fraction of its fair share of available road space (Bradley & Kenworthy 2012). The same logic can be extended to trams and light rail, which also get caught up in congestion and are therefore unable to compete in speed terms with cars if they are not on their own dedicated right-of-way.

People don't like getting fined for parking their cars illegally. Nor does anyone like getting a speeding ticket for socially unacceptable behavior in uncongested conditions. Nevertheless, everyone accepts such fines, as they should, because they have done something considered by government to be unfair in the broader societal sense. People pay such fines and there is no political fallout. Why? Because as human beings living in cities we accept that constraints on certain behaviors are entirely necessary, even if we don't like it. It is the law. The same basic principle can be suggested for using our cars in congested conditions.

Conversely, if one argues that there is no need to regulate people's use of urban road systems where demand exceeds supply in order to achieve better traffic flow conditions and to improve the operation of mixed-traffic public transit modes, then one could also argue that there is no need to have clearway parking restrictions in the peak period, for which one receives a relatively large fine if one is thoughtless enough to park there and obstruct traffic. One could argue that there is a case for just removing those restrictions. In principle, there appears to be little difference between regulating the traffic system by imposing a fine for parking on roads that stop the free flow of traffic in peak hours, on the one hand, and, on the other, imposing other regulatory disincentives on excessive car use in peak times. Such use also obstructs the free flow of all traffic by cars taking up much more than their fair share of road space and it greatly disadvantages buses, trams, and light-rail modes, which are using far less than their fair share of road space relative to the large number of people they carry.

Bradley and Kenworthy (2012) provide detailed quantitative modeling to demonstrate the fair share of road space for cars and buses and the principles on which fines could be developed for car drivers in peak periods, as well as discounted fares for bus users on the same basis. This would ensure that those who take an unfair share of road space would be penalized and those that take less than their fair share would be rewarded. Similar analyses could be developed for trams and light rail. They call this approach "congestion offsets," borrowing from the carbon offsets concept, which sees a carbon penalty in one area or sector offset against gains in another. In the present case, it is suggested that congestion can be dealt with in a similar conceptual framework of "penalty versus credit."

It should be pointed out that reserved rights-of-way for surface rail modes (trams and LRT) are far more common than dedicated bus lanes (Kenworthy & Laube 2001), so buses as the universally present transportation mode in all cities have most to gain from this approach. All cities need well-functioning middle-capacity modes of transportation. Cars represent low-capacity modes and rail systems represent high-capacity systems, with buses representing the only middle-capacity mode in cities, which are severely and unfairly disadvantaged by congestion.

With twenty-first-century digital systems, a congestion-management system could be introduced without all the inconvenience of the old tollbooth systems. Singapore's system operates entirely by a card displayed in the windshield of the car. The system seamlessly extracts money from bank accounts whenever the tag line is crossed and varies with the time of day and levels of congestion.

In many urban transit systems the ticketing has been replaced with a smart card that enables convenient boarding, and fares can vary with the time of riding as well as the distance. Perhaps what is needed for a twenty-first-century congestion-management system is to have a requirement for the same card in your car as you use for public transit or biking. Whenever you cross a tag line in a car, money is removed from your account; whenever you cross in a train, a bus, or a bike, money is put back in. This would also have the effect of making individual transportation choices much more transparent and accountable in a cost sense. People can make informed choices and become more responsible in those choices. The resulting funds raised could be used for managing the system and building sustainable-transport infrastructure. Our data suggest that such a system would make a lot of money, but those doing the right thing could make money from their transport choices. When 50 percent less car use is reached, the system can stop!

The result of this almost universal congestion situation is that people in cars, buses, trams, and light rail (if these three transit modes are not provided with dedicated rights-of-way) all suffer chronic delays together, but the cause of these delays is that cars take a very high and, one could easily argue from the numbers, unfair share of the available road space relative to the volume of people they move compared to the public transit modes. Bradley and Kenworthy (2012) quantify these matters through detailed modeling, but they also raise a more fundamental moral and ethical issue that is closely linked to the practical problem. A norm in most societies, one that underpins concepts of social equity and social justice, the very pillars of sustainability, is that everyone should have equals rights to everything—to the amenities of the city, its infrastructure systems, and so on. The unfinished business of the global civil rights movements is undergirded by this core principle (Roy 2014).

In the absence of widespread acceptance of road pricing as a system of congestion management (unlike what may be about to happen in Vancouver now),[19] the question for cities of whether bus, tram, or light-rail passengers will be given decent travel options in the absence of reserved-rights-of-way will not ultimately be answered by building bigger or smarter road systems, or even better public transit systems, as badly as they are needed. Perhaps with the new culture of urbanism and the peak car-use phenomenon, there will be political momentum to create a more rational approach. We don't put up with congestion in our water sewerage or telecommunication systems, so why should we accept it with cars?

Conclusions

This chapter has demonstrated that five major barriers to the end of automobile dependence can be overcome:

1. There is no point in fighting over transit services versus population density in urban planning in order to reduce automobile dependence, as both are clearly needed.

2. Density increases can be addressed through rational debate and community

engagement.

3. Density can be used to help green a city.

4. A much larger funding source (land-value capture) is available to help build public transit in car-dependent cities than has been considered in the past.

5. Congestion can and should be controlled, especially in walking city and transit city fabric. Such control can be used to help provide more-sustainable transport options, and it can be done in ways that overcome the political problems of road pricing.

Perhaps a new dawn of market-based rail and density packages will emerge across the world that can help finally end automobile dependence. Perhaps cities can find some politically and socially viable way to deal with the congestion problem. Perhaps automobile-dependent suburbs will embrace redevelopment in ways that enable density to be valued and embraced. Together, such changes will enable the end of automobile dependence to become a fully accepted part of urban culture.

7

The End of Automobile Dependence:

A Troubling Prognosis?

This book has presented a case that automobile dependence is ending. It rose, it peaked, and it is now in decline. This represents the fall of one of the most transformative urban planning paradigms the world has ever seen, certainly of the twentieth century. It suggests that this is happening because of a combination of limits due to space and time as well as resources like oil, but most importantly because of economic and cultural change that is favoring more-intensive modes of transportation (rail, cycling, and walking) that thrive, along with the rapidly growing people-intensive economy, in areas with more intensive land use. In other words, these cultural and economic changes are happening in walking and transit city fabrics, but not in automobile city fabrics.

Cities have been reshaped around the car, with major shifts in every conceivable aspect of city life as residents became more and more dependent on private motorized mobility. The non-motorized modes that had provided mobility in cities for about 8,000 years became more and more marginalized along with the public transit systems that had shaped cities for a hundred years before the car's dominance. Even in today's pinup cities for alternative-mobility paradigms, such as Copenhagen with its emphasis on bikes or Zurich with its world-class transit system, the great majority of person-kilometers-traveled are now by car (see color plate 1).

The reality is that cars are not the naturally dominant mode for cities in the same way that they are for many regional and rural areas—but they are important. They have become dominant, as we have argued in chapters 4 and 5, by out-competing other modes of transportation, destroying the walking and transit fabric of cities and spreading their own auto city fabric across vast swathes of hitherto undeveloped land. In fact, though, the car and car-dependent suburbs do not have any kind of natural superiority; the car has effectively enabled certain economic functions and has now reached its limits. The other modes are fighting back. Cities need a new balance.

To suggest that automobile dependence is ending is a big call, but one for which we believe we have mustered considerable systematic evidence and one where we can now see a better future emerging (see chapter 8). But to be clear, this is not to suggest that the automobile itself is fading out. Clearly it is not. However, we are entering a new era in which the technology of the automobile is likely to be transformed into a less environmentally damaging mode of transportation, certainly from an energy, air pollution, and noise pollution perspective, and even a road safety and convenience perspective if driverless cars become commonplace (see chapter 8). But they are never going to lose their urban space consumption, with some 20 times the space requirement of a rail line, and hence all the issues that this leaves unsolved: massive land consumption from urban sprawl, much of it productive food-producing land; despoiling of urban public environments; huge private-transportation infrastructure requirements; eternal congestion; and so on.

So we have argued that our utter dependence on the car will continue to decrease and the world's cities will move toward a situation in which there is far more balance between transportation modes; to put it as we did earlier in the book, a place like Atlanta, where automobile dependence is now virtually 100 percent, could be able to move toward mobility patterns more like those of a city like Geneva (one of the more modest European cities in terms of its dependence on walking, cycling, and transit), which is wholly different in character from Atlanta. In such a city, most people would no longer be automobile-dependent, even with lots of cars still around (possibly electric driverless cars).

If Atlanta could reduce its automobile dependence from almost 100 percent of total person–kilometers of travel down to around 70–75 percent, this would be transformative in every way; it would be as transformative as the changes that have led the city into its present auto-dependent state. It would mean that in terms of daily trips, around 55 percent could be achieved on foot, bike, or public transit, instead of today's figure of around 13 percent. Such changes would mean that the total distances that people have to travel would be radically reduced (walking and cycling trips, which are short, would replace many long car trips, for example), even though 70 percent or so of the total remaining movement may still be by automobile. And of this radically reduced amount of driving (indeed, reduced total travel distances within the city), virtually all of it by 2100 would be in cars powered with renewable energy. This is the end of automobile dependence but not the automobile, which will remain one of the most significant inventions of all time. What has not been wise or beneficial is how we as human societies in many twentieth-century cities have shaped every aspect of our urban existence around it so that it has become a master and not a servant.

A photographic exhibition in London in 2014 called Carscape demonstrated the transition from the automobile being a luxury item, present only in small numbers in the late nineteenth century and early twentieth century, to becoming the main factor shaping the United Kingdom's urban and rural landscapes throughout the twentieth century.[1] We are suggesting that, by the end of this century, we too will be looking back on a critical 100-year period of change that has been at least as radical for its impact on the way we live in cities as anything the automobile ever achieved in its heyday. The signs of this beginning, as outlined in this book, are well and truly observable and we believe they will continue.

Of course, we are aware that such statements can appear glib, notwithstanding the evidence we have brought to bear on the subject. Indeed they can be perceived as very troubling to many people for very many diverse reasons. We examine a few of these troubling matters below.

1. Economic trouble. There are those who would be concerned, and not without reason, that a major bulwark of national economies, indeed the global economy, has been taken away if automobile dependence were to end. And this would not be just the car itself, the money made from its manufacture and sales, but also the oil that fuels it, because it is already clear that this industry is in a decline phase. What will happen to employment, to all the jobs that cascade through city and national economies that are dependent on the manufacture, sale, maintenance, and repair of automobiles, as well as all the automobile-infrastructure construction projects?

2. Automobile enthusiasts' trouble. Those who simply love their cars will also be troubled. This is also not without reason, since for anyone living in an utterly auto-dependent environment, one might as well just chop off their legs if they were to say they should or could do with less car use. Human behavior and even the human psyche have been altered by the car, and it is not necessarily an easy transition for the many who know no other lifestyle and have not even had any travel experience to understand that whole cities can exist in a highly livable, convenient, and attractive way without excessive car dependence.

What do we say to such people? What does one say to people who hate public transit because they see it is as dirty, crowded, uncomfortable, and slow, a big imposition on their personal freedom and comfort? What does one say to someone who has never ridden a bike in a city and who sees it as a threat to their lifestyle, or someone who may find walking a difficult or an unpleasant experience for any number of reasons?

3. **Sustainable-transport burnout trouble.** Then there are those who see the problems of the automobile and who may have worked tirelessly for decades without a lot of success to try to forge positive change in their own cities, to make them less automobile-dependent. These are the people (students, NGO representatives, freeway fighters, transit and bicycle advocates, and so on) who for decades have sat through our presentations on reducing automobile dependence and for whom the burning question is not "should we do the things we have talked about," but how? They say, "We don't see any progress in our city although we have tried for years," or "It's all very well to show examples of other cities that are changing, but we can't break through here." What is the formula for success? How can we make people sit up and take notice and prepare for or facilitate a future that is not dependent on the car?

These are all troubling questions, and to many readers what we are suggesting in this book may indeed present a troubling urban landscape of the future. In this chapter we therefore attempt to step back a little from our own arguments and stand in the shoes of some of the people described above. We hope we can provide some perspectives on the issues.

1. The Automobile and National and Global Economies

At each point in industrial history, different waves of innovation have shaped our cities. In figure 7-1, the waves of innovation as set out by Hargroves and Smith (2005) can be seen to rise and then fall, with a major economic downturn punctuating each of the industrial phases. Our interest has been in how transportation and associated fuels change the nature of cities and hence facilitate these economic eras (Newman & Kenworthy 1999a). It can help us to see how the history of cities and the future of cities can be explained and also to indicate the emergence of the next era of oil-free cities where automobile dependence has disappeared.

Early industrial innovation began in the old walking cities that were linked by water transportation and began using water power to make industrial products. The limits to this began to be obvious in terms of space and materials; thus, the next phase of innovation that arose from the global economic downturn of the 1840s saw the arrival of the steam engine and railway. Cities began to spread out along rail tracks and to build much bigger production based on steam power and steel. Then in the 1890s the incredible stress of living on top of steam boilers and breathing their coal-based air pollution collapsed into a global depression from which came the amazing innovation of electricity. This enabled electric trams and electric trains to spread the city along corridors and the production systems to be separate from their power source—as well as the delights of lighting a city. These demands increased coal-fired power needs enormously and with growing consequences. By the 1930s, these cities were reaching their limits and a new era was created around the automobile, cheap oil, and highways that enabled cities to spread in every direction and much farther out. Cities were released from their need to be in close proximity to fixed tracks. Now these automobile cities are reaching their limits, just as previous cities reached theirs. These cities can no longer afford the costs of their urban sprawl and the associated vulnerability of living off the oil that needs to be imported from highly unstable regions or highly dangerous environments; at the same time, the creative new people-intensive economy in cities requires a more intensive transportation and land-use system that can only be provided in walking and transit city fabrics. New kinds of cities are needed.

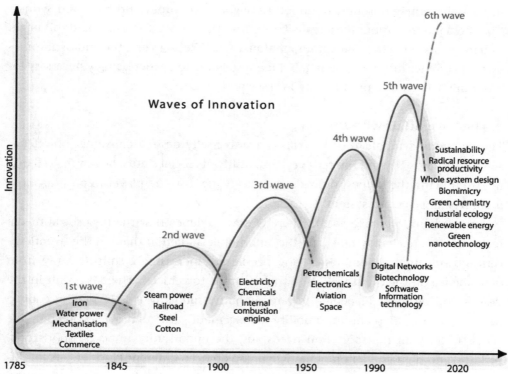

Figure 7-1. The rise and fall of the waves of innovation leading to the Sixth Wave, the green economy. Source: Hargroves & Smith (2005, p. 17), adapted from Schumpeter (1939).

At each stage of innovation cities were mostly able to adapt to the new economic innovations, and while some were left with stranded assets from the previous era, most people could find a better future for their firms and families. But can it now happen around the green economy with reduced automobile dependence? The answer we have presented in this book is that economic change can proceed and indeed is now proceeding with the end of automobile dependence. We have demonstrated that GDP is decoupling from automobile dependence. The new economic competitiveness is already being embraced by those cities that can best demonstrate this decoupling. In figure 7-2, we show the decoupling of GDP from car use in Portland, Oregon, and Washington, DC, two US cities that have done most to build quality rail options along with dense urban centers where walking and transit are the priority.

It is possible to imagine these economic trends setting in to the extent that many cities are left with stranded assets based on the old paradigm of automobile dependence: suburbs that have no alternative to the car becoming less and less valued, toll roads and bridges that cannot pay their way, parking structures that cannot get enough patrons, and quite soon oil-based cars. Some evidence of this has emerged in Australia, where toll-funded tunnels have gone bankrupt in Brisbane and Sydney. Coal-fired power stations are already becoming stranded coal assets. Could this begin to happen soon to stranded automobile/oil assets?[2] Recognizing the end of automobile dependence may be troubling, but it is also going to be increasingly necessary for economic vitality and productivity in the world's cities.

2. The Love Affair with the Car

The changing symbolism of the car as a universally desired consumer object has significance way beyond the car's practical utility. Its social status, however, is changing from being the highest desired object to being just one player in an integrated mobility-management system.

In this book, we have shown there is now evidence that the new social media technologies are already replacing the automobile addiction that fed the twentieth-century industrial economies. Young people are increasingly shifting away from dependence on the car as well as in their attitude to vehicles. There is a shift in the desires and outlooks of people toward mobility; suddenly it is becoming cool to be the holder of a "premium mobility-management card" that gives you complete access to all your transportation needs and the opportunity to access sports cars, pickups, and high-end automobiles when you do need different kinds of cars for different purposes—or no car at all when what you need is simply a quick and healthy journey to work or shopping.

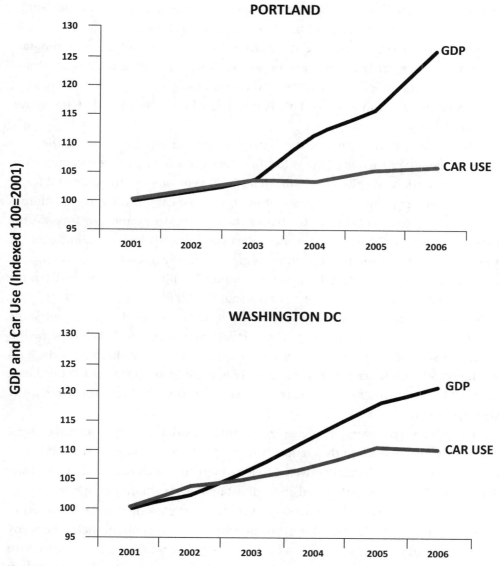

Figure 7-2. Decoupling GDP and car use in Portland, Oregon, and Washington, DC. Source: Kooshian & Winkelman (2011).

Behavior-change projects to facilitate the move away from cars have been shown to help accelerate this process, as many people don't know how to take the first step to end their automobile addiction but are keen to learn (Ashton, Graham, & Newman 2013; Fudge et al. 2013). TravelSmart is one such community-based program to help householders reduce their car use. It has reduced the kilometers–traveled by vehicle by around 12–14 percent in communities across the world—a result that seems to last for at least five years after the program ends. Where public transit is poor and destinations are more spread out, the program may only reduce car use 8 percent or so, but where public transit is good and destinations more concentrated, this reduction in car use can rise to 15 percent (Ashton Graham & John 2006). This is not a revolution, but it has many synergistic positive outcomes.

When people start to change their lifestyles and can see the benefits, they not only persuade their friends of the value, but they also become advocates of sustainable transportation and climate-change policies in general. Governments find it easier to manage the politics of transformation to reduced car use when the communities they are serving have begun to change themselves. An example of this was the development of Perth's rail system. Perth has been progressively rebuilding its rail system since the decision to reopen the Fremantle railway line—first electrifying the old diesel system in the late 1980s, then extending 29 kilometers to the north in the early 1990s and finally 70 kilometers to the south in 2006 (see figure 1-12).

In parallel with the building of the rail line to the south, Perth had some 200,000 households participating in the TravelSmart program. This has helped in the conversion of people from car use to the train, as the Southern Suburbs Railway increased public transit patronage by 59 percent in areas without TravelSmart but by 83 percent in areas where TravelSmart was deployed (Ashton Graham & Newman 2013).

The TravelSmart program recognizes a fundamental principle about cultural change: it works best when the change is supported by a community, when it is part of the development of social networks that support such a change in lifestyle. TravelSmart develops this social capital around sustainable transportation modes. It does this through relationships established with TravelSmart personnel and with others in the local community who are taking the same first steps to get out of their cars. Many people involved in the transition away from car dependence stress the importance of being able to associate with others making the same transition. Today the numbers of people making the journey away from an addiction to car use are outnumbering those who stay, especially in the younger age groups. This is a social movement for the auto-addicted.

A similar transition can be seen in the dramatic revival of many old walking cities in recent years. These central business districts were being killed by monofunctional land-use policies that focused only on commercial and retail activity in the city center and frequently did too much to encourage cars and parking. In recent years these cities have discovered that by making old walking cities attractive for people to come and enjoy the space, to walk around and have fun in the city, not just conduct business, then they can be transformed into places for investment as well as public life. Jan Gehl's analysis is based on how to replace car-oriented space with walking- and bicycle-oriented space, as well as space for people to sit and enjoy the city. The results of this work are easily seen, as the character of a city center can be changed in 15–20 years. Perth is one of these city centers that was once called "dullsville" but in a decade has completely changed character as a place for people (Gehl et al. 2009). There are still many automobiles in central Perth, but the city is no longer automobile-dependent and it's a far better place because of it.

3. The Alternative-Transportation Innovators

Cities everywhere, to greater or lesser degrees, are seeking to change their urban transportation systems and mobility patterns to make them more functional and to bring them into line with sustainability objectives such as resilience to oil vulnerability and adaptation to climate change. At the same time, cities are also striving to make their public environments more livable and attractive by reducing the adverse impacts of motor vehicle traffic, and increasingly the political agenda of many car-dependent cities is to fight for their city to decouple its economic growth from automobile dependence. Many people are working on these matters, but often the key question, as suggested above is, "How do we make it happen?"

The theory of change invariably involves three factors being integrated:

- Industry (which creates markets for new products and services that can bring change very quickly but are generally not based on long-term trends)
- Government (which creates infrastructure and regulation, generally with an eye to medium-term electoral cycles rather than to the long term)
- Civil society (which creates values and visions for the long term)

When these three factors are integrated they are unstoppable, and invariably the magic of sustainable change can be seen when they work together (e.g., Newman 2006c).

But what about cities struggling to end the burden of automobile dependence? Some more specific advice is needed.

What makes some cities more successful at introducing the changes needed to meet these mobility objectives? Why do some cities introduce mobility innovations and move more rapidly than others away from automobile dependence? We have argued in this book that cities are naturally entering a new phase in their automobile dependence. There are many physical, social, economic, and cultural reasons for these changes that are not necessarily driven by any perfectly aimed policies or city strategies. Politicians are simply responding to their electorates, who are demanding a different future. Sometimes these changes are occurring as background processes driven by physical planning-based limits, global markets, technologies, and cultural change expressed as political pressure.

On the other hand there are cities that are real leaders in change, such as the C40 cities that are leading the world in demonstrating commitments to reduce their carbon footprints well beyond those contemplated on a national level. The key question then becomes: How do we respond to these potential changes and what can be done to accelerate and promote them if they are leading the urban system into a more sustainable, indeed regenerative state?

Such a question naturally encompasses a very large range in the types of innovations needed to support and facilitate change away from automobile dependence. Mobility innovations are not just about new technologies or technical systems, though many places focus on technological innovation, attempting to introduce better motor vehicles and energy sources or better traffic- and mobility-management systems through the use of evermore sophisticated IT systems. Many cities are introducing new transit technologies that attempt to provide their residents with high-quality and competitive services, in particular Bus Rapid Transit (BRT), metro systems, and light-rail transit systems (LRT).

Others attempt to control the automobile through a variety of physical, economic, and legislative changes that make the use of private cars less attractive, while at the same time attempting to make other modes more attractive and competitive.

Then there is another group that focuses on urban systems and urban planning. They try to better integrate new urban development in more compact, mixed land-use projects within about 800 meters of stations in order to make walking, cycling, and public transit preferable alternatives to the car, at the same time as providing high-quality lifestyle options in a walkable public realm. Often rail station environments will be the locations for new bike-sharing or car-sharing systems (see figure 7-3). The urban systems approach includes new green technologies in infrastructure as well (Bunning et al. 2013).

All these changes have been described in this book and can have synergistic effects on how far a city can progress toward a more innovative mobility system, one that can change the course of its overall development through technology, economic/social regulation, and urban systems, or in sectoral terms through industry, government, and civil society.

Figure 7-3. A Montreal bike-sharing facility outside a Metro station. Source: Jeff Kenworthy.

This section commences with an overview of our experience with some common factors in innovation in urban mobility worldwide and the specific areas of innovation that seem to be important. We then describe each of these areas and examine additional specific factors that may influence the different types of innovation.

Regardless of the type of innovation involved to change the nature of mobility in cities, there are at least some factors that appear to occur regularly when one tries to understand how innovation occurs. These include:

1. Legacy politicians (e.g., mayors wanting to make changes);
2. Innovative and proactive bureaucrats in specific fields who are change-driven rather than happy with the status quo;
3. Effective civil society groups campaigning for alternative mobility solutions;
4. A consistent message over a long period from thought leaders in universities, the community, or in government about the direction of change needed in a city, and delivered consistently over a long period;
5. An active and well-funded research community;
6. Demonstration projects that start a cascade process of change.

Additional specific factors can be discussed under each area of innovation. The areas to be briefly discussed here with some examples are:

1. Innovation in land-use development in order to reduce dependence on cars;
2. Innovation in alternative transportation systems;
3. Innovation in limiting the dominance of the automobile;
4. Innovation in transportation and mobility-management systems and transportation-related technologies.

Innovation in Land-Use Development in Order to Reduce Dependence on Cars

Traffic arises out of land use; it can be either substantial traffic due to very car-dependent land use (low density and heavily zoned with long travel distances) or much reduced traffic due to more compact, mixed land use that is focused on public transit systems, as described by our theory of urban fabrics. Innumerable cities worldwide are attempting to ensure that new urban development has less "in-built" car dependence from the beginning. What seems to help innovation in this area?

In our experience, changes in land use toward patterns that lead mobility toward less dependence on cars are greatly influenced by *how proactive bureaucrats are within the planning agencies*. An example from Perth in Western Australia is the Livable Neighbourhoods Design Code. Prior to the 1980s and the employment of one highly innovative and change-oriented senior planner in the planning department, all Perth seemed able to do was to roll out low-density, heavily zoned suburbs with curvilinear roads and culs-de-sac that were utterly dependent on the car. The new employee, a graduate in sustainable urban design, started a process whereby planning approval to develop new suburbs would be based on a whole new set of assumptions, such as design for walkability rather than the convenience of the car, grid-based road systems rather than road hierarchies, less generous road widths, more integration with public transit, and so on. This was assisted through outside academic support of the new approach being fostered and a number of innovative planning firms that embraced the new approach. After many years of internal discussion with the department, interactions with the private sector, and consulting with local communities, Perth developed a different statutory basis upon which to determine the design of new communities, one that demanded less orientation to cars. Subdivisions of land will now not be approved unless they conform to these new guidelines. Regional transit and TODs are not covered by such guidelines (Falconer et al. 2010) but are a critical next stage in lessening auto dependence in Perth suburbia.

Other cities, such as Vancouver, British Columbia, and Portland, Oregon, developed unique master plans for their urban regions. These were based on limiting sprawl, preserving green space and agricultural land, and concentrating as much new development as possible around rail stations (see figure 7-4). Part of this innovation was based on:

1. Banning park-and-ride around railway stations in Vancouver and adjacent municipalities, and instead using the land for large-scale compact, mixed-use development;

2. Close collaboration or actual "joint development" between government and the private sector in order to capture at least part of the cost of the new rail system from the private developers who benefit so much from the rail system through rezonings and increased land prices;

3. Intense consultation with local communities, often years ahead of actual change, to secure a consensus for the higher-density development;

4. Very active, well-organized community groups pushing for greener forms of development that are less car-dependent.

Figure 7-4. Public transit–oriented development around the New Westminster train station in the Vancouver region. Source: Jeff Kenworthy.

In all forms of innovation, but especially in alternative land use and living arrangements where peoples' perceptions and emotions are involved, it is very important to provide groundbreaking examples—demonstration projects. Without such projects, whereby people can actually experience the change, it is often difficult to move forward. In Perth, the first TOD around a railway station in Subiaco, an inner suburb, was completed to a high degree of livability, functionality, and beauty under the aegis of a state government Redevelopment Authority that coordinated everything from land assembly, densities, and walkability to the landscape design of streets, the choice of street trees, and a demonstration "sustainable house." This project was a critical breakthrough in helping to change peoples' perception of what higher-density, compact land use can look like and the kind of quality that can be built in.

Innovation in Alternative Transportation Systems

Many cities are consciously endeavoring to provide systems of transportation that are less dependent on the car and better able to confront a future where the assumptions of cheap and abundant oil and unlimited capacities of the biosphere to absorb damage, such as excessive CO_2 output, no longer apply. How do some cities manage to break into a different paradigm of transportation infrastructure provision when others may struggle?

Whether cities can expect to make a dent in the dominance of the automobile will depend on how successful they are at building new public transit systems, especially rail systems, instead of just increasing road capacity, which has been the norm for decades. There are numerous examples worldwide now of cities that are building or have built new metros, LRT systems, and suburban rail systems, many of them mentioned in this book.

The main push for these new systems often comes from one or two sources or perhaps a combination of both. The mayors of many cities have played a major role in the development of new public transit systems, from Mayor Enrique Peñalosa and the Transmileneo BRT system in Bogotá, Colombia, the early U-Bahn and S-Bahn systems in German cities such as Munich (which was also accompanied by mayoral support for pedestrianization of the city center), to people such as Mayor Jaime Lerner in Curitiba, Brazil, who along with many like-minded colleagues developed a unique metro-like interconnected urban bus system with a spine of BRT lines. They reoriented the development of the whole central area along these major spines, changing the CBD from a high-density nodal form to a high-density linear form. It should be added that Curitiba has had consistent leadership over a long period of time about the mobility and planning direction needed in the city. This has survived changes in mayors and the general politics of the city.

In Perth, visionary state-level politicians, determined to leave a positive legacy for the city, pioneered a major expansion of the urban rail system in the 1990s and 2000s, and before that in the 1980s, the electrification of the three existing suburban rail lines. Of great help in this process was the fact that Perth has also had a consistent and clear message delivered through universities via the media and through academic publications over a 35-year period about the need for Perth to reduce its car dependence and develop both alternative transportation and urban development patterns. The synergistic effect of this relationship between legacy politicians and sustained professional academic support has been a powerful combination when sustained over decades, with every election bringing a new public transit issue to the agenda based on academic studies and popular communication through the media.

In Portland, Oregon, a combination of visionary state-level politicians, an extremely well organized and professional civil society network, and innovative bureaucrats ensured that Portland had opened its first LRT line by 1986, 13 years after starting the process. After opening the first line, this building process cascaded into various extensions and expansions of the system, along with a radical redevelopment of the entire central city to a walkable, green, and attractive place. The results are obvious to see in the GDP versus car use decoupling shown in figure 7.2. Part of this process was the tearing down of an elevated freeway along the riverfront in the city and its replacement with a linear parkland. An initial motivation for these early changes, which started at the level of the Oregon governor's office in the 1970s, was the Arab Oil Embargo of 1973. These visionary politicians, supported by academics, groups such as 1000 Friends of Oregon, and key figures in the Portland transit agency, Tri-Met, realized that Portland needed more electric-based mobility to lessen its vulnerability to the shortcomings of an oil-based transit system.

Again, the first LRT line constructed in Portland was a critical landmark event. Before that and during construction, there was tremendous opposition and cynicism expressed toward the new LRT line, especially in the local newspaper. After the opening of the line and the way it interacted with and supported the new life of the downtown area, this opposition largely disappeared. It was the *demonstration project* needed to kick-start a larger enterprise of more widespread change.

Seoul, South Korea, achieved a remarkable transformation of its central area with the tearing down of a 5.8-kilometer, six-lane freeway (Cheonggyecheon) and the digging up of the surface road underneath to reveal a river that had been buried since the 1960s. The city now has a highly utilized and beautiful green river boulevard instead of a giant freeway (see figures 7-5, 7-6, and 7-7). The urban heat island in summer has dropped 3° C, and traffic speeds in central Seoul *increased* slightly after the freeway was removed, even though the roads that were removed had carried some 120,000 vehicles per day. The idea for this project and the technical modeling and backup came through academic input, and there was considerable NGO support, but the project was mainly achieved as part of the successful mayoral election campaign for Lee Myung-bak, who presided over the freeway's demolition and the reconstruction of the corridor into a green, watery oasis. He was elected as mayor of Seoul largely on the back of this stunning landmark project, and eventually he was elected president of Korea.

Likewise, the current revolution taking place in New York City toward bike sharing, traffic-calmed streets, and the humanizing of the public realm of the city has been driven mainly by the independent and innovation-minded Janette Sadik-Khan,

Figure 7-5. The river restoration in Seoul is a site for community festivities. Source: Jeff Kenworthy.

Figure 7-6. The tearing down of the Cheonggyecheon Expressway has allowed Seoul to develop a green heart. Source: Jeff Kenworthy.

Figure 7-7. The new people-oriented corridor in Seoul that has replaced the freeway is a place for contemplation. Source: Jeff Kenworthy.

commissioner of the New York City Department of Transportation, with expert assistance from Gehl Architects, a host of NGOs providing the third-party endorsements, and the political support of Mayor Michael Bloomberg.

On a broader scale, as explained earlier in this book, China is currently building metro systems in their cities at a stunning rate. In this case the central government, after being highly pro-automobile, with development of the auto industry being one of its four pillars of industrialization (see chapter 3), is now realizing that Chinese cities simply cannot cope with unfettered motorization. There is a realization in particular that China's productive food-growing areas are being buried under sprawling car-based development at a rate that undermines the country's ability to feed itself. The forces that led to such changes in thinking are less transparent, but it is clear that expert advice from Chinese academies was part of the change, as were the many protests about air quality from citizens and even some deliberative processes (Zhou 2012; Unger et al. 2014).[3] Thus, the 2011–15 five-year plan was brought forward by planners who saw that a different approach was needed and began to move away from automobile-oriented planning. As a result, funds are flowing on a large scale into urban transit and especially rail projects on an unprecedented scale, and more and more cities are introducing car-ownership restrictions through monthly lotteries or auctions for the right to even purchase a car (similar to Singapore's Certificate of Entitlement system, which attempts to limit new car registrations to the same number that are removed each month and to keep car ownership at about 100 cars per 1,000 people).

Communities around the world are seeking to make their areas more people-friendly, and this usually means an emphasis on sustainable transport modes. Delivering this is usually much harder than creating policy. Pune, India, has tested an innovative deliberative-democracy technique enabling local people to seek win-win solutions that use urban renewal best-practice principles and design (Newman & Matan 2013). This process enables the incorporation of the feedback and values of the community into evolving plans created by a multidisciplinary team of technical experts. This was an iterative process whereby a preferred plan was co-created by participants to determine a preferred urban design plan for the precinct of Dattawadi in Pune. The Pune workshops involved participation from local community members and representatives; to facilitate this, the workshops were held in the local language, with translation into Hindi and English. They looked at how to design their local streets to be more "people-focused"; the process was able to produce an immediate preferred option, and by the end of the day local politicians were able to announce that it would be funded. A similar process in Bangalore was used to help with the funding of a suburban rail system using value-capture and deliberative processes (Newman & Matan 2013).

There are countless further examples that one can point to in which innovation in alternative-transportation systems, often against the dominant paradigm, have been led by politicians at different levels, civil society groups, and academics, as well as, sometimes, by innovative and often somewhat charismatic bureaucrats; the case studies will often show that all three were needed in combination.

Likewise, one can also point to cities where innovation in alternative transportation has been for many years quite unspectacular (e.g., Auckland in New Zealand and Seattle, Washington, to name just two). One can generally trace such lack of progress to bureaucratic ineptitude and indecision, painful lack of leadership, and inconsistent and contradictory policies operating at different levels (e.g., professing that improvements are needed to public transit while prioritizing motorways in capital expenditure). Moreover, such cities are often characterized by insufficient civil society and academic pressure for change by decision makers and politicians in order to maintain accountability and progress. Both cities are now making some progress, with new rail systems and TODs finally being built decades after they were first promised.

Innovation in Limiting the Dominance of the Automobile

As we have explained in chapter 6, cities ideally need to do more than just provide positive alternatives to the car for changing mobility patterns; cities also need to manage travel demand and to control congestion. Here innovation also appears to come mostly through political leadership and civil society, as well as within bureaucracies.

There are two basic approaches to limiting how many cars are purchased and how much they are used—physical means and economic means. *Physical means* for reducing automobile dependence include:

(a) **Traffic-calming and pedestrianization schemes.** These are generally the result of local action and combinations of political willingness/vision, bureaucratic acceptance, and implementation, but they are usually driven by civil society action to create more local sustainable and livable environments.

(b) **Tearing down of existing high-capacity road infrastructure and limitations on new construction.** There are now many cases around the world in which major sections of freeway have been removed from the city in critical locations in order to facilitate change in the nature of the city and its mobility patterns. Again, this innovation stems mostly from the above-mentioned factors of political leadership, bureaucratic support, and civil society. It is also frequently

supported and facilitated by professionals from within the academic community in the form of direct advice to decision makers or direct community action
through the media to publicize the need for change and to give substance to the
lobbying of NGO groups.

European cities remain the best examples of traffic calming and pedestrianization,
with cities such as Frankfurt replete with reduced-traffic lanes in order to make way
for transit-reserved rights-of-way, cycle lanes, and wider footpaths throughout the
city (see figures 7-8, 7-9, and 7-10). Freeway removal is now becoming a worldwide
phenomenon, with the best-known and best-publicized examples of successful high-
capacity-road removal being Seoul (Cheonggyecheon Expressway), Portland (Harbor Drive Freeway), Milwaukee (Park East Freeway), New York (West Side Highway),
Toronto (Gardiner Expressway), New York State (Robert Moses Parkway, which cut off
pedestrians from the Niagara Falls), Paris (Pompidou Expressway), and San Francisco

Figure 7-8. Frankfurt traffic calming along Leipzigerstrasse in the inner city. Source: Jeff
Kenworthy.

Figure 7-9. The traffic-calming and pedestrian-oriented characteristics of European cities has allowed a strong commitment to bikes (as seen here in Amsterdam). Source: Jeff Kenworthy.

Figure 7-10. Traffic calming in European cities and many other cities around the world increasingly involves light-rail systems (Karlsruhe, Germany). Source: Jeff Kenworthy.

(Embarcadero and Central Freeways). All of these involved political courage and deter-mination, community support, creative bureaucracies, and external support from thought leaders in academia and other areas of civil society. They were unthinkable in most cities even 20 years ago—and none of them has elicited even the slightest regrets.

Economic means to reduce automobile dependence include:

(a) Congestion charging/road pricing measures;

(b) Schemes to limit car ownership (and thereby use);

(c) Parking charges; and

(d) Carbon-pricing initiatives.

One of the better-known examples of congestion charging came through a left-leaning one-time mayor of London, Ken Livingstone, who introduced a charge for vehicles entering central London—a project that has helped the bankers and financial sector in central London more than most other government projects. Another well-known example is Singapore with its Area Licensing Scheme (ALS) dating back to the early 1970s, which, like in London today, charged motorists a fee for bringing their cars into central Singapore. Later, the city introduced the Certificate of Entitlement, which means that people wishing to purchase a car have to bid for the right (amount-ing to tens of thousands of extra dollars beyond the purchase price of the car itself). The heritage of the Singapore system dates back to the 30-year, mostly autocratic rule of Lee Kuan Yew. The Cambridge-educated lawyer and prime minister of Singapore not only saw the need to limit cars in the small island-nation (which does not manufacture cars), but also the need to build a first-class public transit system based on rail and not on buses—against the will of the World Bank. Singapore said no to the World Bank's demand for a bus-only system and instead funded its own metro system, heeding strong advice from consultants not so enamored by the Bank's American-dominated anti-rail stance at that time (a position that largely endures today). The stations on the metro system were then used as the focal points around which to construct most of the government-provided housing over the next decades.

Chinese cities such as Shanghai, Beijing, and others have since introduced Singa-pore-style traffic-limitation schemes, with Shanghai opting directly for the Singapore system, while Beijing chose a monthly lottery system instead. Other cities such as Stockholm (Stockholm congestion tax) and Milan (Area C) have central-city conges-tion charges to limit the entry of cars into this part of their cities.

Globally, however, as explained in chapter 6, there are few cities that have had the political courage to introduce such congestion-charging schemes, even in their central areas, or indeed to put in place more general road-pricing schemes that charge motorists for the right to use particular roads at particular times of the day. The notable exceptions are cities that have introduced at least some tollways (e.g., some US cities, Kuala Lumpur, Bangkok, and Shanghai), but these are not very significant in the overall transportation system. There are many cases where road pricing/congestion charging has been put on the table as a policy and even been implemented as a trial scheme (e.g., in Hong Kong), only to be later defeated by negative public opinion and timid politicians.

Carbon pricing is a way of introducing fuel savings into the developing global market for carbon credits (IPCC 2014). As with all the economic instruments, the delivery of carbon pricing will be difficult, but the politics of climate change and oil vulnerability is likely to maintain a consistent and growing pressure on politicians (see next chapter). Michael Sivak has developed very clear data that show the United States rapidly decoupling GDP from both vehicle–miles of travel (VMT) and fuel consumption, so carbon pricing will only assist with this transition.[4]

The next 20 years will see increasing pressure to deliver real reductions in car use, and all the economic techniques for achieving this, especially pricing carbon, are likely to become commonplace—at least they will be on the tables of all politicians and public servants. Now that there is substantial evidence showing the multiple benefits of limiting automobile dependence, it may be that more robust political leadership will emerge to deliver these economic instruments.

Innovation in Transportation and Mobility-Management Systems and Technologies

Many cities are involved with the introduction of new technologies to better manage urban mobility and traffic. Such technologies include:
- Traffic-management systems to keep traffic flowing better;
- Digital control systems replacing train signaling;
- Transit cards and informations systems for planning daily travel;
- Better parking-management systems (e.g., real-time capacity-advisory systems);
- New automotive technologies such as electric vehicles and their required charging infrastructure;
- Autonomous cars (self-driving);
- Car-on-demand schemes such as BMW's Drive Now system and Daimler-Benz's Car-2-Go, which enable people to get quick access to a car without owning one;
- Bike-sharing schemes, including Copenhagen's new public system, which includes a built-in tablet computer on each bike for better navigation and information access to link users with other modes.

Unlike the factors examined so far, for urban innovations in mobility, new technologies, and technical systems, a number of other innovation catalysts are often involved:

1. Strong private-sector research and innovation;
2. Strong public-sector research through universities and well-funded institutes and think tanks;
3. Direct public-sector investment support for new technologies;
4. Bold venture capitalists prepared to invest in new ideas;
5. Well-organized lobbying at high levels of government by commercial interests selling their ideas;
6. Ability of the private sector to read the public mood and public opinion about what motivates people and what people are concerned about, and then use that to develop and sell new ideas;
7. Changing community attitudes; and
8. Technically and politically competent bureaucrats.

The integration of digital information systems into transportation systems is clearly an area of great innovation that promises reductions in automobile dependence. There is now something of a trend toward Multimodal Mobility Management (MMM) or Integrated Mobility Management (IMM), which could see traditional car firms become providers of total mobility packages, with customers buying paid subscriptions to gain access to transport. Such offers would typically see a complete integration of private cars, car sharing, car-on-demand (both electric and normal cars), taxis, car hire, public transit systems, bikes, pedelecs, bike sharing, walking, or other means of mobility as the case may be (see chapter 8).

Success in these kinds of innovations will require much of car makers' ability to deliver technological innovations in hardware and software, through market research, internal change within companies, astute reading of political winds, negotiation skills with stakeholders they would not normally deal with and with those who may normally view a car maker as "the competition" or "a threat" (e.g., traditional public transit operators or umbrella organizations such as Verkehrsverbünden in Germany are often reluctant to deal with car manufacturers, or are even themselves seeking to become the "go to" multimodal mobility provider).

The United States, with its aggressive venture capitalism and well-funded public and private research institutes and think tanks, as well as foundations that fund innovative research, plus a history of powerful lobbying groups (e.g., the highway and automobile lobbies, which have had a profound influence on Washington policy making in transportation for nearly 100 years), is often on the leading edge of many new technologies and their implementation. The Google Autonomous Car, which could potentially reduce the number of traffic accidents and loss of life, is a relatively recent example of the powerful innovation synergies that develop quickly in the United States. Schoettle and Sivak (2015) have suggested that autonomous vehicles could reduce car ownership by 43 percent in the United States without even considering the potential to influence the overall need for a car once shared-travel options become commonplace. Already five US states have changed their traffic regulations to allow experimental autonomous cars into the regular traffic stream. Google is aggressively lobbying for this to be expanded.

Summary of Urban Mobility Change Factors

In providing this perspective on what stimulates or brings about successful innovation in urban mobility, the following factors seem to be highly relevant, though their importance varies according to the nature and type of mobility innovation:

1. Legacy politicians (e.g., mayors wanting to make changes);
2. Innovative and proactive bureaucrats in specific fields who are change-driven rather than happy with the status quo;
3. Effective civil society groups campaigning for alternative mobility solutions;
4. A consistent message over a long period from thought leaders in universities, in the community, or in government about the direction of change needed in a city, and delivered over a long period;
5. Genuine community consultation;
6. An active and well-funded research community committed to public involvement in their city's planning decisions;
7. Demonstration projects;
8. Direct public-sector investment support for the infrastructure to support new technologies (e.g., electric vehicles, MMM digital systems);
9. Bold venture capitalists prepared to invest in new ideas;
10. Well-organized lobbying at high levels of government by commercial interests selling their innovations for overcoming automobile dependence;
11. The ability of the private sector to read the public mood and public opinion about what motivates people and what people are concerned about, and then use that to develop and sell new ideas;
12. Changing community attitudes through a well-informed media and education system; and
13. Technically and politically competent professionals who can see beyond election cycles.

Finally, one can say that the unifying factor in all these matters is demonstration projects (item 7 above). As Jane Jacobs has outlined, cities generate wealth by copying innovations from other cities and improving them (Jacobs 1970, 1985). The next wave of wealth-generating innovation has begun, and we have spent a lot of time documenting the best examples for other cities to copy (Newman & Kenworthy 1999a; Newman & Jennings 2008; Beatley & Newman 2009; Newman et al., 2008; Newman & Matan 2012a). The future will continue to include innovative demonstrations of ways to reduce automobile dependence. In every field of mobility, more innovative demonstration projects are needed in order to create a cascading effect for more widespread and constructive change. As soon as demonstrations appear, the reticence to change begins to evaporate.

This book has highlighted the fact that enough of the change factors have been in place over the past 30–40 years of challenging automobile dependence to enable us to see its decline setting in. The end of automobile dependence will require such factors to be continually refreshed and reinvigorated.

Conclusions

Change is always painful and troubling. We have outlined some potential approaches for easing the pain of change, especially by learning how some cities have been facing the future and innovating in order to reduce automobile dependence. One final suggestion is to set up some Key Performance Indicators (KPI) for each city as it approaches the kind of necessary goals set out in this book. The KPI in land use and in transport planning for ending automobile dependence are:

1. *All, or most, urban land development is in redevelopment.*
2. *The percentage of any urban transport budget spent on sustainable transport by type of urban fabric should be at least Walking City 75 percent, Transit City 50 percent, and Automobile City 25 percent, based on goals to end automobile dependence for each area.*

These KPI should become the agenda for all the change agents in the city—academics, NGOs, and government officials. Together they should map out the different fabrics and outline the various sustainable transport projects within them; innovative business can show how to link urban fabric redevelopment to innovative infrastructure and financing; and politicians can lead the delivery of such projects. There is enough evidence of change to keep us hopeful.

8

Conclusion:

Life after Automobile Dependence

The need to imagine a better future is a defining element of all good public policy. The trends to end automobile dependence are being caused by a range of factors detailed in this book. The interventions suggested are largely social and economic, with a major role to be played by physical planning in addressing them. Looming over this decline in automobile dependence is the need to respond to the major global issue of climate change. This issue is continuing to grow in importance and will affect global and local politics with increasing impact on transportation and urban policy (IPCC 2014). The upshot of achieving a low-carbon city is that this is also a way of achieving a more productive city, a healthier city, a more resilient city, and a more community-oriented city. Increasingly people are seeing that low-carbon houses are high-performance houses,[1] and low-carbon commercial buildings are high-performance buildings that must be built if businesses are to compete in the market. Thus, achieving a low-carbon city is to achieve a *high-performance city*, and so the goals around achieving a low-carbon future will help frame this chapter. In this closing piece we will now look at how we can begin to see a world of cities that no longer use fossil fuels and also at the very important role that ending automobile dependence must play.

The global goals being set by governments, businesses, and NGOs are for green-house gases to be reduced 80 percent by 2050 and by 100 percent in 2100 (IPCC 2014). Considerable progress toward this goal was made on November 12, 2014, when China and the United States, the world's two largest emitters of greenhouse gases, agreed to substantially decouple their economic growth from greenhouse gases. Mostly this has been targeted at the peaking and declining use of coal, but the peaking and declining use of oil is also now on the agenda. California's SB32 legislation in 2015 sets the goal of achieving 80 percent less greenhouse-gas emissions by 2050 and cutting oil use in half by 2030 (Baker 2015).[2] How can this be done?

1. Toward Zero Oil

A zero-oil future has not been defined, and yet it is an imperative in terms of the low-carbon, high-performance cities of the future. It is also necessary, as conventional low-cost oil peaked in 2006, and unconventional oil (tar sands, fracking-derived oil, or deepwater oil such as featured in the Gulf of Mexico "great spill") is expensive. Fracking certainly helped the United States to diminish its oil imports, but now that supply is threatened by price volatility, as outlined below.

The sudden drop in oil price in 2014–15 from over $100 a barrel to around $40 appears to have resulted from a contest for market share, as it has stopped many high-cost oil projects and favored the big low-cost oil producers. The Bank of Canada (2015) suggests:

> Based on recent estimates of production costs, roughly one-third of current production could be uneconomical if prices stay around US$60, notably high-cost production in the United States, Canada, Brazil, and Mexico. More than two-thirds of the expected increase in the world oil supply would similarly be uneconomical. A decline in private and public investment in high-cost projects could significantly reduce future growth in the oil supply, and the members of the Organization of the Petroleum Exporting Countries (OPEC) would have limited spare capacity to replace a significant decrease in the non-OPEC supply. (p. 4)

At the same time as oil supply has been tightening over the last two decades, resulting in dramatic price volatility, there has been a reduction in demand for oil. It is not hard to see why volatility would start to affect demand. Cities, regions, and nations, even households and small businesses, cannot plan and build for the future with such wild fluctuations in oil price (Bank of Canada 2015). They are therefore opting to begin phasing out the use of oil; this can be seen in the response to oil prices when peak-car was first noticed, as suggested in chapter 1. But as we have shown, this is only possible to do because better options are emerging that not only save oil but revive our cities and create new economic opportunities. Due to the processes discussed in this book, demand for oil is dropping with the end of automobile dependence and its multiple benefits; allied with this has been a rapidly increasing vehicle fuel efficiency, with growing shifts to alternative fuels. Goldman Sachs has reviewed the oil price and considers that around 70 percent of the drop in oil price in 2014–15 was caused by increased supply and 30 percent by demand decreases.[3] As this continues, cities will be looking to see how they can more rapidly phase out oil. Reflecting the uncertainty of oil's price volatility, California's senate president, Kevin de Leon, said in relation to their SB32 legislation that "The fact is, an economy based on fossil fuels is an economy built on shifting sands" (Baker 2015, p. 67).

Overarching such considerations about oil's reliability is the growing certainty that it is no longer suitable for the future anyway. Climate-change politics is increasingly looking at oil and how it must be phased out well before any phasing out due to oil supply. In January 2015, the scientific journal *Nature* published research by University College London (McGlade & Eakins 2015) that finds global fossil fuel reserves are approximately three times higher than the amount that can be safely burned by 2050 to keep global warming from exceeding 2° C. Thus, according to their analysis, a third of the remaining oil needs to remain unburnt along with half of the gas and 80 percent of the coal.

Perhaps the scramble for oil market share happened because of the announcement by China and United States that they were taking the climate agenda seriously. In a Deutsche Bank report, Bansal and Kirk (2015) say there will be peak carbon before there will be peak oil. They conclude:

> If the world takes its climate change commitments seriously, then the dynamics of oil will be altered beyond recognition. Oil will become constrained by the level of demand allowed under CO_2 emission limits and this will have implications for the behaviour of countries, companies and consumers alike. (p. 25)

Eventually, as happened with whale oil, the price of petroleum will become irrelevant: there will be no further demand for it as cities and regions adapt to the combination of regulatory-control-based demand reductions and inherent demand reductions due to the end of automobile dependence. As cities continue to decarbonize, they will leave a series of stranded assets such as coal-fired power stations that are no longer needed. Oil-based assets are also going to be left behind and will include highly oil-dependent suburbs and freeways as well as oil-based vehicles. Thus, it is now imperative to begin the shift to removing fossil fuels, including oil, from future urban systems and this process must accelerate if we are to achieve global goals and create more productive, livable cities.

So what kind of future can we imagine? Is it possible to see a rapidly emerging global urban system that is renewably powered? What role will ending automobile dependence play in this transition?

The trends outlined in this book have all highlighted the dramatic decoupling of wealth from oil and car dependence. However, the flow-through of investment into non-fossil-fuel-based power and mobility is not very obvious and seems very slow (IPCC 2014). The more hopeful approach expressed in this book and used as the basis for this epilogue, on the other hand, is based on an understanding of figure 8-1. In the period where GDP and power/mobility were firmly coupled, there was little help from market forces in achieving green-economy outcomes; only demonstration projects of how the market could work were possible (e.g., Vauban in Germany). However, once the decoupling starts it rapidly grows and reaches a critical point where market forces begin to favor the green economy. From here on, exponential decline in the use of fossil fuels is likely and a new world of renewably powered cities can begin to emerge. A different and much more hopeful future can then be envisaged as the structural forces for change all line up.

The future is likely to see a combination of urban system change as well as new technologies. Our book has attempted to show how the structural change involving the decoupling of wealth from automobile dependence is involving both technology and urban fabric changes. We have shown that urban fabric limits for car use are likely to be around 75 percent of total mobility for car-based city fabric, 50 percent for transit city fabric, and 25 percent for walking city fabric. However, it is necessary to show how an overall city limit of around 50 percent car use should also be the goal, along with the remaining 50 percent becoming zero-carbon. Germany has committed to such a target in its Low-Carbon Roadmap and Helsinki is now planning on reducing car ownership to zero.[4]

It is thus necessary to see how urban design and transportation systems can adapt to achieve this non-oil-based future by achieving 50 percent less car use and 50 percent green cars (with zero carbon) for the other half. The challenges of living in a post-petroleum world are likely to increase the need for automobile dependence to continue its decline and indeed come to a very clear end, though the challenges of achieving greater livability at the same time will remain.

The following future technologies and urban systems are emerging and can be imagined as an expanded part of life after oil-based automobile dependence:

1. **Modal Sharing.** Smart-city transportation options using a Multimodal Mobility Management system can enable us to use a "card and not a car" for many of our transportation needs and can be available across all urban fabrics.

2. **Electric Public Transit.** Electric public transit can provide the backbone of all major corridors and link all major centers. This applies within cities and between them. Electric public transit can reduce car use to 50 percent or less in the Transit City corridors.

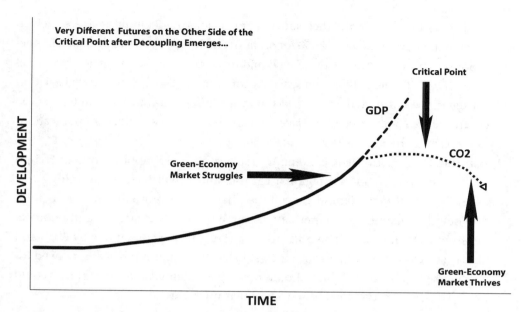

Figure 8-1. The decoupling of wealth from fossil fuels and the critical point of transition to market forces working, with the green economy unleashing exponential decline in fossil fuels. Source: Conceptual model developed by Peter Newman.

3. **Centers.** Urban development can be focused into a regional system of TODs and can ensure that cycling and walking are designed into all urban spaces within such centers and from the immediate surroundings leading into the centers, up to about a 3- to 5-kilometer radius. These walking city areas would have no more than 25 percent car use—and probably a lot less.

4. **Education.** These three changes can be facilitated by linked infrastructure/land-development partnerships and household/business-education programs and behavior-change programs.

5. **Electric Vehicles.** The remaining 50 percent of urban car use (mostly in automobile-city areas where car use is reduced to 75 percent levels) is likely to be plug-in electric vehicles renewably powered through PVs and batteries in homes and smart grids, enabling a city to become 100 percent renewable in its power system (CENEX 2008).

These five policies can replace the vast majority of gasoline use. For diesel, which is the backbone of the freight and commercial system, there are other imperatives. Addressing this will require the following applications of biofuel and natural gas:

6. **Biofuel.** Biofuel is regionally available now at cost-effective prices and is replacing

some diesel use in cities and their surrounding regions. Agricultural areas are likely to develop their own biofuel by 2050 for on-farm and local use, replacing diesel. Biofuel is not suitable for use as a large-scale liquid fuel, but it can be the major local rural fuel by 2050. Biofuel's premium use will be for aviation, though commercial aviation is likely to be greatly reduced, especially in medium-haul routes where high-speed electric rail can be an effective replacement and high-quality digital communications can replace many routine face-to-face meetings.

7. **Natural Gas.** Natural gas can simply replace all diesel applications in freight as well as some urban and regional car use, and it will have a continuing role as an industrial fuel. Natural gas will be phased out eventually by the creation of renewably manufactured methane through biomass gasification and photocatalysis of CO_2 and water. This will enable all freight to be diesel-free by 2050 and all natural gas to be 100 percent renewable by 2100. It also replaces any need for the hydrogen economy, which should now be abandoned as a concept that could never work due to the need to replace all gas infrastructure.

These latter concepts of how oil can be phased out are developed further in Newman (2013) and will not be elaborated here; rather, we'll concentrate on the issues involving automobile dependence in cities.

The above-listed strategies can enable 100 percent oil-free cities and regions by 2050 and 100 percent renewably fueled cities by 2100, with a significantly reduced need for the automobile as well as a more livable set of urban opportunities with continuing rises in wealth—decoupled from the use of automobiles. These five strategies will be expanded below, to show how cities with 50 percent less car use can be imagined and realized, as well as enabling zero oil to become a reality.

2. Smart-City Transportation Options

The digital information systems now available to cities have the potential to either transform our cities away from automobile dependence or to simply prop up the declining years of this dependence. The latter is likely if the only thing we do with smart information systems is to enable more free-flowing freeways through Managed Motorways where sensors only allow traffic to enter a major road when it is free-flowing. The new Google car, which is also managed by sensors and GPS to obviate the need for a driver, is also only likely to add a few more automobiles to heavily congested streets, though its use in a car-share schemes would effectively reduce the number of cars required, as long as the people involved did not also have cars. Approaches that are only simple additions to automobile dependence are not in the long term going to help. They are reductionist in their basic approach; they do not represent structural changes. They can be useful additions but should not be undertaken if they are anything other than highly cost-effective, as judged by rigorous benefit-cost ratios of the kind that are applied, for example, to new rail systems.

The most important use of digital information systems in the cities of the future will be Multimodal Mobility Management (MMM) systems that are operated by using a card that accesses all the digital information needed for twenty-first-century mobility and also acts as a unified means of charging for all transport services, or receiving credits for sustainable mobility behavior, as outlined in chapter 6.

A Card Not a Car

Among the many reasons for people to use an automobile is the need to cover the "first mile" or the "last mile" linking them to public transit. It's simply easier to get into a car rather than walking a long way to a train or waiting for a bus that links to the train or another bus. The next system to revolutionize transportation choices will join together a range of modes into a single easily managed integrated transportation system. This will be needed most in the old automobile-city suburbs where simple connections by walking to a tram or train or even a decent bus service are very often unavailable.

The system would work like this: a provider (probably a private system like a utility in the energy sector, or a traditional car manufacturer looking to diversify its business model, or even a major regional public transit operator) would sign a customer up for a MMM card. This card will enable a person to book a bike share, a car share, a taxi, or a small bus that can link them directly to a high-quality public transit system. Helsinki has announced a few trial schemes to examine how well this can work, and they believe it is possible to remove all car ownership eventually and just own a card that accesses all the modes through sharing schemes.[5] In the Netherlands, the public transport operator has created an option in any ticket purchase of ordering a bike share from a station. This came about because too many bikes were being brought to stations, so instead of bike congestion at stations a seamless integration of public transport and public bikes has been developed.

Booking of train and bike together in the Netherlands occurs using a mobile phone. Such a service could be extended so that a range of modes could be booked to help with any journey. All the information would be available on the customer's mobile phone or tablet, with a GPS-based map showing all the necessary up-to-the-minute information. The connections at either end of the transit trip will thus be fully planned and linked. There could conceivably be competing systems for this service, each one offering something unique that distinguishes it from its competitors (e.g., a provider might offer a mobility guarantee for a particular critical trip, such as to an airport, upon payment of a small insurance premium).

The basis of the system in terms of reduced automobile dependence is in the increased viability of the main transit link through extending its catchment beyond the walking catchment to a much bigger area. A well-planned transit system can indeed enable all the major present automobile-dependent suburbs to be served by this MMM card, offering a range of linkages to a fast train. This will replace the park-and-ride systems that blight station precincts and usually do little for overall public transit use as they cannot work at both ends of a train trip. With car sharing there is a factor of 8–10 private cars replaced for each car-sharing card deployed, as most cars are not used for the majority of the day. Bremen in Germany, which was one of the first cities to pioneer car sharing, has replaced about 1,000 cars in the period when car-sharing vehicles numbered 80–100.[6]

The rapid rise of bike sharing also shows it can work in city centers and inner suburbs, but its extension into car-based suburbs will require a much more intensive information system like that provided by an MMM card. This is due mainly to the bike-hostile environments in which bike sharing would need to operate (low-density, no mixed land use, few dedicated bike lanes, and long distances).

The MMM card can have other advantages, such as frequent-traveler points, access to discount stores, and other inducements to get rid of one's car and join the MMM system. And of course, one of its key advantages, as suggested in chapter 6, is that it can become a unified system for the charging of transport services and the rewarding of sustainable mobility behavior. This provides a highly transparent way for the users of different transport modes to realize the full costs (and benefits or rewards) of their day-to-day transport decisions (including the cost implications of using their cars during peak periods), which in turn enables them to make better decisions about what mode to choose for any particular trip.

It is possible to imagine that a high proportion of automobile-based trips could be replaced by MMM trips by 2050, especially in walking city and transit city areas where so many other options are available. However, for many people the MMM card could work in an automobile city area as well.

3. How Much Can Rail Transit Achieve?

Many transport commentators cannot imagine how rail systems can transform cities. They just see trips that are highly car-dependent and cannot see how fixed rail systems are likely to be able to replace them. But in our view this means that they do not understand how different modes create different urban fabrics and how together they create wholly different transportation outcomes that can transform entire corridors.

How much, then, is it possible to change our cities? Is it possible to imagine an exponential decline in car use in our cities that could lead to 50 percent or less of total passenger-kilometers driven in cars? The key mechanism, as argued in chapter 6, is a quantitative leap in the quality of public transit integrated with buses, bikes, and cars accompanied by an associated change in land-use patterns emphasizing higher densities (and more mixed land uses).

The most important thing about this relationship is that, as the use of public transit increases linearly, the car passenger-kilometers decrease exponentially (see figure 1-13 for relationship between car passenger-kilometers and public transit passenger-kilometers). This is due to the Transit Leverage Effect, a phenomenon highlighted earlier whereby one passenger-kilometer of public transit use replaces many more passenger-kilometers in a car due to direct travel (especially in trains), trip chaining (doing various other things like shopping or service visits associated with a commute trip), giving up one car in a household (a common circumstance that reduces many solo trips), and eventually changes in where people live as they prefer to live or work nearer public transit (Newman & Kenworthy 1999a). This is the change to a different urban fabric propelled by the investment in public transit over car-based infrastructure.

It is feasible that any city could set a target of increases in public transit passenger-kilometers per capita in order to achieve certain target reductions in car use as part of their commitment to reaching the global goal of an 80 percent reduction in greenhouse-gas emissions by 2050.

The biggest challenge in an age of radical resource-efficiency requirements will be finding a way to build fast rail systems back into scattered car-dependent suburban areas. The speed of the transit system is key, and in Perth the new Southern Rail line has a maximum speed of 130 kilometers per hour (80 mph) and an average speed of 90 kilometers per hour (55 mph)—at least 30 percent faster than traffic. The freeway speed limit is in fact 100 kilometers per hour, and like all freeways its average speed is less than 10 kilometers per hour at peak time, with around 40–50 kilometers per hour outside peaks. The result is dramatic increases in public transit patronage, far beyond the expectations of planners who see such suburbs as too low in density to warrant a rail system. The Southern Rail line opened in December 2007 and is now carrying 80,000 people per day, whereas the bus-only system before it carried just 14,000. There is little else that can compete with this kind of option for creating a future in the car-dependent suburbs of many cities.

Fast electric rail services are not cheap. However, they cost about the same per kilometer as most freeways, and the world as a whole (even poor countries, but especially the United States and Australia) has been able to find massive funding sources for building freeways in the past 60 years. In the transition period funding will require some creativity, as the systems for funding rail are not as straightforward. Some funds can almost certainly be found by changing transportation investment priorities from road to public transit funding. Chapter 6 has shown how it is possible to provide private-sector funding for urban rail through land-value uplift processes and legislation.

Public transit funding will therefore naturally also need cities to find innovative partnerships, as described in chapter 6. This will involve financing public transit through the use of taxes or direct payments from land development, as in Copenhagen's new Metro system, or through a congestion tax, as in London. Funding of public transit in congested cities can occur, as it has in Hong Kong and Tokyo, where the intensive requirements around stations means that the public transit can be funded almost entirely from land redevelopment. In poorer cities, the use of development funds for mass transit can increasingly be justified through the transformation of their urban economy (Cervero 2008) and can be financed through the use of land-value capture, now being promoted by the World Bank (Suzuki et al 2015).

4. Reducing Travel Miles through Planning

There are many ways that technology can help to reduce the need to travel. Transportation to meet people by long-distance trips or even short-distance trips within cities may be considerably reduced once the use of broadband-based tele-presence begins to make high-quality imaging feasible on a large scale. There will always be a need to meet face-to-face for creative meetings in cities, but for many routine meetings the role of computer-based approaches will take off rapidly. Cities that are attractive places to meet (walkable, safe, and lively) will thrive even more in these conditions, while suburban areas with little more than scattered houses will find their economies being undermined. The knowledge- and service-based economy is thriving in quality walking city fabric.

As explained in detail earlier in the book, the need to increase densities in car-dependent cities has been recognized for many decades, but recent "peak car" data suggest that densities are increasing as younger people and empty-nesters come back into urban areas (Newman & Kenworthy 1999a, 2011b); the data for this are presented in chapters 1 and 2. The turning back in of cities reverses the declines in density that have characterized the growth phase of automobile cities over the past 60 years. Table 1-3 contains data on a sample of cities in Australia, the United States, Canada, and Europe, showing urban densities from 1960 to 2005 that clearly demonstrate this turning point in the more highly automobile-dependent cities. In the small sample of European cities, densities are still declining due to reductions in population ("shrinkage"), but the data clearly show the rate of decline in urban density slowing down and almost stabilizing as re-urbanization also occurs.

As densities increase, car use will decline exponentially—as shown previously. If a city begins to slowly increase its density then the impact can be more extensive on car use than expected. Density is a multiplier on the use of public transit and walking/cycling, and it reduces the length of travel as well. Increases in density can result in greater mixing of land uses to meet peoples' needs nearby. This is seen, for example, in the return of small supermarkets to the central business districts of cities as residential populations increase and demand local shopping opportunities within an easy walk. Overall, this reversal of urban sprawl will further reduce car use.

The need to develop city centers is now shifting to the need to develop sub-centers across the whole car-dependent metropolitan area in order to help get people out of cars. This process, as explained in chapter 6, aims to create a regional system of TODs. This will ultimately lead to the polycentric city or "decentralized concentration," which consists of a series of sub-centers or small cities in the suburbs all linked by quality public transit, but each providing the local facilities of an urban center, whether on a neighborhood or a regional scale. The public transit lines connecting centers are likely to be both radial and circumferential, obviating the need to come into the center and then out again to make a cross-city trip and increasing the viability of a center by siting an intersection of rail lines there.

The facilitation of TODs has been recognized by all Australian cities and most American cities in their metropolitan strategies (Curtis et al. 2009). The major need for TODs is not in the inner areas, as these have many TODs from previous eras of public transit building (both linear and nodal), but in the newer outlying suburbs. There are real equity issues here, as the poor increasingly are trapped on the fringe, with high transportation expenditures. A 2008 study by the Center for Transit-Oriented Development shows that people in TODs drive 50 percent less than those in conventional suburbs (CTODRA 2004). In both Australia and the United States, homes that are located in TODs are holding their value the best or appreciated the fastest under the pressure of rising fuel prices. They weathered the GFC well, while many of the most car-dependent locations declined through negative equity or collapsed outright as people simply walked away from their "toxic loans" or negative equity traps. The report suggested that TODs would appreciate fastest in up markets and hold value better in down markets. This is the rationale for how TODs can be built as public/private partnerships (PPPs) in rail projects (Dawson 2008; McIntosh et al. 2011).

Thus, regionally connected TODs are an essential strategy for hastening the end of automobile dependence, especially when they incorporate affordable housing. The economics of this approach has been assessed by the Center for Transit-Oriented Development and Reconnecting America, another NGO. In a detailed survey across several states, these organizations assessed that the market for people wanting to live within a half a mile of a TOD (800 meters) was 14.6 million households. This is more than double the number that currently live in TODs. The market is based on the fact that those living in TODs now (which were found to be smaller households, but the same age and the same income on average as those not in a TOD) save some 20 percent of their household income by not having to own so many cars: those in TODs owned 0.9 cars per household compared to 1.6 outside. On average, this frees up $4,000–$5,000 per year. In Australia, a similar calculation showed this would add an extra $750,000 in superannuation (pension funds) over a working lifetime. Most important, this extra income is spent locally on urban services, which means that the TOD approach is also a local economic-development mechanism (CTODRA 2004; Dittmar & Ohland 2008).

TODs must also be PODs—that is, pedestrian-oriented development—or they will lose their key quality as a car-free environment to which businesses and households are attracted and they will fail to provide the much-needed extensions of the walking city fabric into automobile city fabric, as described in chapter 4. Urban designers need to ensure that public space is vibrant, safe, and inviting. Jan Gehl–inspired transformations of central areas, such as those found in Copenhagen, New York, London, and Melbourne, are showing the principles of how to improve TOD spaces so that they are more walkable, economically viable, socially attractive, and environmentally significant (Gehl 1987, 2010; Gehl & Gemzøe 2000). Gehl's work in Melbourne and Perth has been evaluated after a decade of implementation and, in both cases, indicates substantial increases in walkability and the numbers of pedestrians who use the city center for their work, shopping, education, and especially their recreation (Gehl et al. 2009; Gehl et al. 2004). In a post-oil world, developers who claim credibility from scattered urban developments due to their green buildings and renewable infrastructure are likely to find that they simply have a stranded asset unless it has a quality public transit system and a pedestrian-friendly center. All developments will need to extend and enhance walking and transit city fabrics and start to reform automobile city fabric.

At the same time, TODs that have been well designed as PODs will also need to be GODs—green-oriented developments. TODs will need to ensure that they have full solar orientation, are renewably powered with smart grids, have water-sensitive design, use recycled and low-impact materials, and use innovations like modular construction and biophilic urbanism (see Bunning et al. 2013; see also chapter 6).

Examples of TOD-POD-GODs are appearing in many places (see examples in

Newman et al. 2009; Newman & Matan 2012a). An early good example is the redevelopment of Kogarah Town Square in Sydney's inner city, built upon a large city-owned car park adjacent to the main suburban train station that was surrounded by a collection of poorly performing businesses. The site is now a thriving mixed-use development consisting of 194 residences, 50,000 square feet of office and retail space, and 35,000 square feet of community space, including a public library and town square. The buildings are oriented for maximum use of the sun, with solar shelves on each window (enabling shade in summer and deeper penetration of light into each room), photovoltaic (PV) collectors on the roofs, all rainwater collected in an underground tank to be reused in toilet flushing and irrigation of the gardens, and recycled and low-impact materials used in construction; moreover, all residents, workers, and visitors to the site have a short walk to the train station (hence reduced-parking requirements that enable better and more productive use of the site). Compared to a conventional development, the Kogarah Town Square saves 42 percent of the water and 385 tons of GHG per year—and this does not include transportation-oil savings that are hard to estimate but are likely to be even more substantial (City of Kogarah 2009).

Another TOD-POD-GOD is appearing at Cockburn Central in Perth, a completely new center designed around a station on the new Southern Rail. The Department of Housing has created a model housing development called Stella, which was built with modular construction in just 11 days and, compared to normal construction, has been shown to reduce carbon use by 30 percent, waste by 50 percent, construction costs by 12 percent, and aggregate costs by 35 percent due to time savings. Residents can thus expect to save not only on purchase costs and utility costs but also transport costs, as it's next to the station. Such innovations are increasingly popular and can be expected to increase as pressures to reduce carbon globally impinge on land-development decisions (Rauland & Newman 2015).

While the demand for TODs is growing, creating TODs can still present significant challenges, given the complexity of financing TODs and the number of private and public actors involved. TODs are in great demand, which often results in housing priced out of the range of middle- and lower-income households. Thus, along with the other green requirements for TODs there needs to be a requirement of a certain proportion of affordable housing. In Perth, it has been suggested that the 20 or so TODs be subject to new TOD zoning requirements for minimal amounts of parking, maximized density and mix, the inclusion of green innovations, and a minimum of 15 percent affordable housing, to be purchased by social housing providers. This is the kind of transit city fabric, as outlined in chapter 4, that can be extended into all automobile city fabric along each corridor.

5. Renewably Powered Electric Vehicles

Even if a car-use reduction of 50 percent is achieved, as suggested above, by a rather herculean effort, we still have to reduce the oil and carbon in the other 50 percent of vehicles being used mostly in automobile city urban areas. The question should therefore be asked: what is the next best transportation technology for motor vehicles that can fundamentally move us away from fossil fuels? The growing consensus seems to be plug-in electric vehicles (PEV) powered by renewable energy. Plug-in electric vehicles are now viable alternatives due to the new batteries such as lithium-ion as well as hybrid engines for extra flexibility. Many innovative electric motoring devices, such as fold-up cars, air wheels, Yikes, and other devices that can enable personal motorization in the intensive spatially confined areas of our cities, are likely to grow in popularity (Riley 2004). China's 250 million electric bikes and scooters that appeared in less than a decade indicate how quickly electric transportation can happen. Hybrid PEVs are likely in the transition period as electric recharging infrastructure builds up.

For clean, green cities, plug-in electric vehicles not only reduce oil vulnerability, but they are becoming a critical component in how renewable energy will become an important part of a city's electricity grid. The PEVs can serve a storage function for renewables through vehicle-to-grid (V2G) linkages within a smart grid. Thus, electric vehicles are becoming an essential part of how a city can become oil-free (Went et al. 2008).

Electric vehicles will need to be renewably powered; otherwise, if it is coal-based power, the switch to oil-free fuel will be worse environmentally. However, coal-fired power stations are in rapid decline. They are now only a small part of the global power industry's financial investment, which, according to Bloomberg New Energy Finance, peaked in its fossil-fuel investment in 2006, and since then renewables have become the major beneficiary, with more than two-thirds of investment in power (Newman & Wills 2012). Figure 8-2 shows these remarkable changes in the growth of investment in renewables compared to investment in fossil fuels for power.

Coal-fired power stations have now been banned by the United States, the European Union, the World Bank, and even the United Kingdom, where they were invented; more significantly, they are being closed down in the polluted parts of China and so coal has peaked and fallen in the largest greenhouse-gas-emitting nation.[7] The biggest growth in power production is in renewables, with PV solar cells replacing wind as they have become dramatically cheaper. PV is becoming a major distributed energy source; for example, in Perth, 17 percent of homes now have PVs, and together they represent 540 megawatts of power, thus creating a substantial though distributed power station (Mercer 2015). Most of these are in the

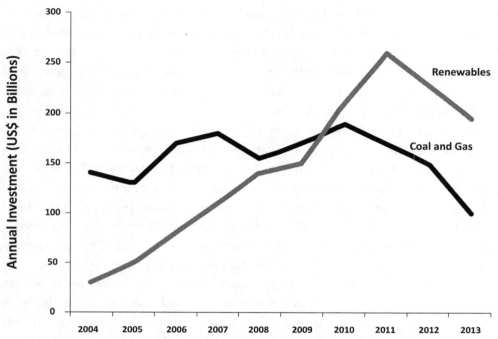

Figure 8-2. Global investment in fossil fuels and renewables for new electric-power generation. Source: Compiled from data provided by Bloomberg New Energy Finance.

car-dependent outer suburbs where homes have larger roofs and where car use is largest, thus suggesting they can readily make the transition to PV-based PEVs (Newton & Newman 2013). Helping this is the rapid growth in home-based battery storage, which is following the trajectory of PV costs. These enable homes to use solar energy at night as well as during the day and will ensure that coal-fired power stations can be phased out everywhere. Demonstration urban developments in which PVs and batteries are integrated into a dense urban fabric that is walkable and transit oriented are already showing that regenerative, carbon-free precincts are possible (Bunning et al. 2013; Newman & Rauland 2015).

To regenerate the present suburbs of most cities will require using whatever urban fabric is there, including the often-dominant automobile city fabric. For these areas electric vehicles will be essential. When electric vehicles are plugged in to be recharged they can be a part of the peak power provision, as they also provide storage in their batteries for the house—not just for the car. Peak power is the expensive part of an electricity system, and suddenly renewables with local storage are offering the best and most reliable option to feed back into the house and even into the surrounding neighborhood through a shared local power system. Hence the clean, green, oil-free city of the future is likely to have a significant integration between renewables and electric vehicles through a smart grid. Thus, electric buses, electric bikes/scooters/golf carts/gophers, and electric cars have an important role in the future oil-free city—both in helping to make its buildings renewably powered and in removing the need for oil in transportation (Simpson 2009a, 2009b), not to mention reducing GHG, local air pollution, and noise emissions.

Electric rail can also be powered from the sun, either through the grid powering the overhead wires, or in the form of new battery-based light rail (without overhead catenaries) that could be built in the middle of highways into new suburbs. The first example of this technology is now running in Bordeaux, and the next generation light-rail public transit is likely to be battery-based with electric power through high-powered contactless charging at stations. These will work better if the stations are green developments with renewable power built into their fabric and available for quick recharging services to trains and to PEVs that can also help in local power storage.

Signs that this transition to electric transportation is underway are appearing in demonstration projects such as those in Boulder, Colorado, in Austin, Texas, in Google's 1.6-megawatt solar campus in California (with 100 PEVs), and in the Honda Zero Carbon Home in Davis, California.

What sort of immediate impact could there be from the implementation of innovative ideas such as these? According to one study, the integration of hybrid EV cars with the electric power grid could reduce gasoline consumption by 85 billion gallons per year in the United States. That's equal to:

- a 27 percent reduction in total US greenhouse-gas emissions;
- a 52 percent reduction in oil imports; and
- $270 billion not spent on gasoline (Kitner-Meyer et al. 2007).

Al Gore has called the smart-grid/renewables/EV transition the "moonshot" of our age, as it has the potential to enable a switch to 100 percent renewables in a decade (Gore 2008).

Looking Forward

There are few guidelines to the future of our cities and regions that enable us to imagine the far future. However, if we do not go through this process of imagination we can get submerged under an avalanche of despair, as people can foresee only disaster once the days of climate change begin to hit more obviously and the days of fossil fuels are finally accepted as over. It is also very good economics to be better prepared for a low-carbon future by creating a high-performance city.

The alternatives all require substantial commitment to change in both how we live and the technologies we use in our cities and regions. The time to begin making needed changes is now, as they will take decades to get in place. But at least by imagining some of the changes suggested above, it is possible to see how we can get started on the track to cities without automobile dependence and its associated fossil-fuel dependence.

The first signs of change toward these emerging technologies and urban systems can now be seen: the dramatic growth in electric transit; the rapid move toward electric vehicles and smart grids, with a 40 percent annual growth in the global use of renewables; the large growth in the use of pedelecs and e-bikes in many places; the emerging use of natural gas and biofuels; new technologies such as Skype and tele-presence; and the emergence of revitalized dense urbanism in a polycentric city framework. Their application into large-scale urban demonstrations is now under way in places such as Kronsberg and Vauban in Germany, Masdar in the United Arab Emirates, the low-carbon cities of China, West Village at the University of California–Davis, and the dramatic example of Singapore, which is not just managing automobile dependence but also, as shown in chapter 6, is demonstrating the greening of density (see color plates 14–16).

The potential for creating cities free of automobile dependence enables us to create oil-free cities that are strongly economically competitive and highly liveable. The technologies and practices outlined above suggest that we can be oil-free by 2050 and renewably based oil-free by 2100. We first need to imagine the changes that are available now in transportation, urban design, and city planning, and then begin the process of change through large-scale demonstrations. As explained in chapter 4, this will depend radically on how much we can protect remaining walking and transit city fabrics and how well we can extend these fabrics into the more extensive automobile city fabrics and thus assist in ending automobile dependence. We remain hopeful that the automobile-dependent city can be replaced with a city that is oil-free, based on options that are viable and attractive. This vision will depend on a substantial reduction in automobile dependence continuing well into the future.

We shouldn't be surprised by the historic agreement on November 12, 2014, between China and the United States—the world's two largest greenhouse-gas emitters—to significantly reduce their carbon emissions. The fundamentals of their decoupling of carbon emissions from GDP have been set in place for the past five to ten years. These include:

- the peaking or plateauing of coal and oil demand;
- the transitioning through the use of natural gas; and
- the rapid growth in renewable sources of electrical power generation.

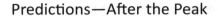

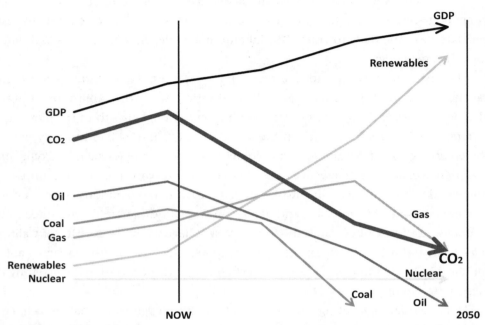

Figure 8-3. The rise and fall of fossil fuels. Source: Concept model developed by Ray Wills and Peter Newman.

Underneath these are the deeper structural changes to decoupling, including:
- radical efficiency gains in all forms of energy use due to smart digital systems and other new technology, as well as new materials in buildings and industry; and
- major reductions in automobile dependence in cities.

These changes will continue. As shown in Figure 8-3, the trend to reduce carbon by 80 percent looks manageable when you simply keep going on the paths that we are beginning to see, as detailed in this book. The opportunities to create a better future for cities in particular, will drive all these trends. Critical to this will be policies that continue to encourage cities to require less automobile use, as well as to require those cars remaining to be renewably powered electric vehicles.

The end of automobile dependence is an important part of the end of fossil-fuel economies.[8] The importance of gathering these trends together and seeing how they can multiply into a global trend is that they can give us hope for our future—as a planet and especially in our cities.

Appendix

Methodology of Data Collection

The data presented in this table (and in chapter 2) come from Kenworthy and Laube (1999) for the 1960 to 1990 data and two other main sources. The Millennium Cities Database for Sustainable Transport (Kenworthy & Laube 2001) was a major international project funded by the UITP (International Association of Public Transport) in Brussels. The project collected a very large set of data for 1995 on 100 cities worldwide over the period 1998–2001. These data were defined carefully in a series of methodological worksheets, which were distributed to people with whom we had contact, to ensure that everyone involved used stable and consistent definitions of all data items. All data provided to us were also reality-checked for accuracy before acceptance into this database. This checking was based on over 20 years' prior experience on the likely magnitudes and ranges for different variables in different kinds of cities. Anything suspicious was double-checked with sources, and often new or corrected data were provided.

The second source of data is the current and ongoing update of the original study using identical definitions of all the variables. The updated data in this chapter are for 2005–06. Work has also been done to update these data to the early 2010s, but it takes many years to collect and establish the database scientifically. Updates would of course be feasible in a more timely manner on fewer cities and with fewer indicators. However, the strength of the global cities data presented in this appendix is in the number of factors that have been considered. This allows greater insight into the many changes that are occurring in cities and enables a more detailed understanding of the changes.

The number of data items collected has been reduced for reasons of resources and time. Also, through experience we have found that this core set of data tells a major part of the story in each city. These updated data have not been systematically published before. The method of collection for both years was first of all a thorough interrogation of all Internet sources for the data. We only collect "primary" data items from

Global Cities Database on 26 cities showing 1960 to 2000 trends in city form, transport

City	1960			1970		
	City Population	Urban Density	% Total Jobs in CBD	City Population	Urban Density	% Total Jobs in CBD
Houston	1,430,394	10.2	10%	1,999,316	12.0	11%
Washington, DC	1,808,423	20.5	27%	2,481,489	19.4	20%
Denver	803,624	18.6	14%	1,047,311	13.8	13%
San Francisco	2,430,663	16.5	20%	2,987,850	16.9	17%
Los Angeles	6,488,791	22.3	7%	8,351,266	25	5%
Phoenix	552,043	8.6	11%	863,357	8.6	8%
Chicago	5,959,213	24	13%	6,714,578	20.3	13%
Perth	475,398	15.6	40%	703,199	12.2	31%
Brisbane	621,550	21	26%	867,784	11.3	—
New York	16,834,500	22.5	30%	18,731,600	22.6	27%
Calgary	249,641	27	41%	403,320	25	30%
Melbourne	1,984,815	20.3	19%	2,503,450	18.1	17%
Sydney	2,289,747	21.3	20%	2,807,828	19.2	17%
Vancouver	827,335	24.9	—	1,082,185	21.6	22%
Ottawa	—	—	—	633,443	34.9	27%
Frankfurt	670,048	87.2	24%	669,751	74.6	21%
Copenhagen	1,607,526	40.1	26%	1,752,631	33.4	19%
Montreal	2,109,509	57.6	—	2,743,208	39	26%
Toronto	1,620,861	36.8	18%	2,089,729	41.4	15%
Zurich	697,434	60	17%	791,761	58.3	15%
Hamburg	1,832,346	68.3	20%	1,793,782	57.5	21%
Stockholm	808,294	65.5	35%	740,486	59.3	28%
Munich	1,046,000	56.6	29%	1,311,798	68.2	26%
London	7,992,400	65.4	32%	7,452,300	61.6	31%
Vienna	1,627,566	91.4	17%	1,614,841	85.4	16%
Brussels	1,022,795	100.3	—	1,075,136	91.1	—

Source: Peter Newman and Jeff Kenworthy.

and infrastructure.

1980			1990			2000		
City Population	Urban Density	% Total Jobs in CBD	City Population	Urban Density	% Total Jobs in CBD	City Population	Urban Density	% Total Jobs in CBD
2,905,353	8.9	12%	3,462,529	9.5	7%	4,385,643	9.2	6%
2,763,105	13.2	17%	3,363,031	13.7	14%	4,006,346	13.5	12%
1,352,070	11.9	12%	1,517,977	12.8	11%	2,120,510	14.9	8%
3,190,690	15.5	17%	3,629,516	16	15%	3,954,824	20.2	13%
9,479,436	24.4	5%	11,402,946	23.9	5%	9,418,370	25.9	4%
1,409,279	8.5	4%	2,006,239	10.5	4%	3,058,459	10.6	4%
6,779,799	17.5	12%	6,792,087	16.6	10%	7,870,265	16.8	9%
898,918	10.8	24%	1,142,646	10.6	21%	1,381,510	11.1	18%
1,028,527	10.2	14%	1,333,773	9.8	11%	1,654,342	9.7	12%
17,925,200	19.8	23%	18,409,019	19.2	22%	19,904,078	18.6	19%
592,743	21.2	24%	710,677	20.8	21%	877,626	20.7	22%
2,722,817	16.4	15%	3,022,910	14.9	11%	3,440,574	14.7	10%
3,204,696	17.6	13%	3,539,035	16.8	12%	4,011,645	19.2	13%
1,268,197	18.4	18%	1,602,502	20.8	13%	2,007,634	23.4	12%
735,854	31.7	26%	907,919	31.3	24%	1,051,609	31.1	20%
631,287	54.0	18%	634,357	46.6	20%	652,412	46.8	19%
1,739,860	30.4	16%	1,711,254	28.6	13%	1,783,349	28.9	13%
2,835,759	33.9	23%	3,119,570	33.8	20%	3,355,825	28.7	17%
2,137,395	39.6	13%	2,275,771	41.5	14%	5,092,398	26.2	6%
780,502	53.7	14%	787,740	47.1	11%	808,907	43.6	11%
1,645,095	41.7	20%	1,652,363	39.8	16%	1,725,764	38.2	17%
647,214	51.3	28%	674,452	53.1	22%	1,807,851	27.4	13%
1,298,941	56.9	24%	1,277,576	53.6	25%	1,306,258	55.3	33%
6,713,200	56.3	30%	6,679,699	42.3	31%	7,259,550	58.8	31%
1,531,346	72.1	15%	1,539,948	68.3	13%	1,622,017	70.3	12%
1,008,715	82.3	25%	964,285	74.9	24%	977,436	74.3	23%

	Car VKT / Capita	PT Service km / Capita (% rail)	PT Passenger-km / capita	Car VKT / Capita	PT Service km / Capita (% rail)	PT Passenger-km / Capita	Car VKT / Capita
Houston	6,829	20.6 (0%)	234.2	8,257	12.6 (0%)	139.4	9,918
Washington	—	32.7 (12%)	570.2	5,671	26.7 (1%)	300.9	7,939
Denver	5,888	15.6 (0%)	245.3	6,933	9.1 (0%)	92.7	8,693
San Francisco	5,656	33.7 (13%)	596.7	7,999	31.1 (10%)	532	9,362
Los Angeles	7,382	19.4 (0%)	244.3	7,850	16.1 (0%)	159.7	9,003
Phoenix	7,188	9.6 (0%)	101.7	8,864	5 (0%)	35.9	9,761
Chicago	4,091	52.1 (39%)	1,015.3	5,769	44.8 (42%)	855.5	7,566
Perth	3,287	67.1 (17%)	907.8	5,224	57.2 (12%)	732.0	6,250
Brisbane	2,608	77.9 (65%)	1,352.3	3,788	57.2 (35%)	953.1	5,861
New York	4,066	60.9 (54%)	1,842.3	4,864	66 (63%)	1,395.3	5,907
Calgary	2,842	30 (0%)	242.4	3,445	30.8 (0%)	319.7	6,069
Melbourne	2,963	75.3 (72%)	1,739.0	4,228	57.3 (66%)	1,221.7	5,582
Sydney	3,757	104.7 (61%)	2,158.0	5,436	70.5 (47%)	1,860.0	6,442
Vancouver	—	36.6 (0%)	—	—	25.1 (0%)	—	6,756
Ottawa	3,503	31.7 (0%)	426.9	—	23.8 (0%)	336.1	5,776
Frankfurt	2,000	—	—	3,500	—	—	4,256
Copenhagen	1,263	72.3 (76%)	1,547.7	3,069	86.1 (60%)	1,381.4	3,462
Montreal	—	—	—	—	—	—	3,267
Toronto	—	48.2 (60%)	1,335.7	—	57.9 (48%)	1,369.5	4,238
Zurich	—	102.7 (88%)	1,944.9	—	92.9 (87%)	1,560.3	4,318
Hamburg	1,560	60.1 (74%)	1,958.7	3,477	74.4 (67%)	1,692.5	4,409
Stockholm	1,804	87.5 (51%)	739.7	3,525	93 (49%)	1,294.5	4,867
Munich	1,516	—	—	2,678	52.1 (60%)	806.2	3,272
London	1,341	121.4 (58%)	2,229.2	1,855	114.8 (63%)	1,995.2	2,529
Vienna	—	71.7 (93%)	1,704.5	—	62.6 (86%)	1,645.2	2,664
Brussels	1,793	64.1 (84%)	1,787.7	2,918	46.9 (61%)	1,462.8	3,891

Note: (%) signifies the percentage of rail-based transit (heavy rail and LRT/trams) operating in the city as part of the total public transit service.

PT Service km / Capita (% rail)	PT Passen-ger-km / Capita	Car VKT / Capita	PT Service km / Capita (% rail)	PT Passen-ger-km / Capita	Car VKT/ Capita	PT Service km / Capita (% rail)	PT Passen-ger-km / Capita
9.1 (0%)	128.3	13,016	16.7 (0%)	215	15,807	19.3 (2%)	183.5
39.9 (25%)	616.1	11,182	37.3 (43%)	773.8	13,050	49.1 (45%)	827
24.9 (0%)	217.6	10,011	21.2 (0%)	198.6	12,820	30.9 (5%)	260.4
50.2 (26%)	925.8	11,933	49.3 (42%)	899.3	12,463	53.3 (47%)	856.2
26.8 (0%)	383.6	11,587	19.8 (0%)	351.6	12,265	29.7 (8%)	408.9
7.2 (0%)	66.0	11,608	9.9 (0%)	123.7	11,542	15 (0%)	108.4
41.6 (44%)	971.1	9525	41.5 (47%)	805.3	10,395	41.9 (46%)	723.4
52.6 (10%)	591.5	7,203	47 (10%)	544.4	8,916	42.3 (27%)	694.9
48.3 (45%)	744.7	6,467	55.1 (49%)	899.8	8,572	63.1 (51%)	831.9
58.1 (58%)	1,285.3	8,317	62.8 (63%)	1,334.3	8,458	62.7 (63%)	1,343
46 (4%)	875.4	7,913	49.7 (18%)	774.6	8,299	49.1 (19%)	1,027.6
52.5 (66%)	778.5	6,436	49.9 (57%)	843.8	7,962	50.7 (58%)	1,025.4
76.9 (57%)	1,510	7,051	94 (58%)	1,769	7,249	76.5 (59%)	1,530.5
45.7 (0%)	839.1	8,361	50.3 (24%)	871.3	6,858	50.2 (30%)	847.7
65.3 (0%)	825.5	5,883	55.9 (0%)	849.5	6,470	45 (1%)	850.4
47 (69%)	1,483.5	5,893	47.9 (68%)	1,148.9	5,618	84.8 (69%)	1,514.7
109.5 (54%)	1,658	4,558	121.3 (56%)	1,606.8	5,402	115 (60%)	1,623.8
63.4 (36%)	888	4,746	60.2 (34%)	951.7	5,380	52.9 (38%)	1,057.5
80.6 (48%)	1,975.7	5,019	98.4 (44%)	2,172.8	5,256	52.9 (37%)	1,087.7
102.3 (84%)	1,821	5,197	148.1 (79%)	2,459.4	5,245	139.7 (75%)	2,433.2
71.7 (58%)	1,501.6	5,061	71 (62%)	1,374.8	5,187	83.9 (63%)	1,577.1
118.8 (51%)	2,124.1	4,638	133.2 (50%)	2,351.3	4,946	122.5 (58%)	2,335.8
65.2 (76%)	1,746	4,202	91.4 (80%)	2,462.5	4,830	99.8 (72%)	2,811.4
119.8 (65%)	1,716.9	3,892	138.4 (68%)	2,405.1	4,088	174.3 (69%)	2,456.8
69 (79%)	1,828.2	3,964	72.6 (72%)	2,430.3	3,909	100.8 (76%)	2,333.6
53 (50%)	1,400.3	4,864	62.7 (48%)	1,427.5	2,648	92.8 (54%)	1,780.9

City	1960			1970		
	Parking Spaces / 1,000 CBD Workers	Cars / 1,000 People	Road Length / Capita	Parking Spaces / 1,000 CBD Workers	Cars / 1,000 People	Road Length / Capita
Houston	497.2	388.1	—	363.1	647.9	11.7
Washington	217.9	289.8	—	295	400.9	5.1
Denver	595.2	479.1	8.8	578.3	522.7	11
San Francisco	135.1	407.4	4.7	154.5	487.9	4.7
Los Angeles	372.8	459.1	4.9	534.8	521.2	4.8
Phoenix	619.2	367.8	15.4	836.3	499.1	12.7
Chicago	83	307.7	4.8	96.3	391	5
Perth	238.8	561.1	14.1	527.1	356.9	13.7
Brisbane	162.2	192.3	7.8	227.6	294.3	7.5
New York	—	270.6	4.3	348.2	—	4.1
Calgary	577.2	323.6	2.8	565.3	409.7	3.8
Melbourne	155.6	224	8.1	295.3	192.1	6.8
Sydney	—	268.1	4.7	86.6	366.4	5.1
Vancouver	—	285.3	7	341	401.7	6
Ottawa	—	279.8	—	—	369.7	—
Frankfurt	110.4	133.3	1.3	189.2	280	1.5
Copenhagen	150.7	88.5	2.8	198.5	199.5	3.4
Montreal	—	192.5	—	—	248.9	—
Toronto	191.8	297.8	1.7	198.2	358.2	2.3
Zurich	—	126	—	112.8	253.9	—
Hamburg	123.7	95.7	1.8	139.1	241.4	2
Stockholm	99.7	143.2	1.5	130.4	274.7	1.8
Munich	—	130.9	1.5	—	261.8	1.5
London	—	156.3	1.5	126.5	222.8	1.7
Vienna	—	93.6	1.2	—	213.9	1.6
Brussels	—	157.3	1.4	—	262.3	1.4

1980			1990			2000		
Parking Spaces / 1,000 CBD Workers	Cars / 1,000 People	Road Length / Capita	Parking Spaces / 1,000 CBD Workers	Cars / 1,000 People	Road Length / Capita	Parking Spaces / 1,000 CBD Workers	Cars / 1,000 People	Road Length / Capita
369.9	602.6	10.6	612.3	607.7	11.7	721	714.1	9.1
257.1	561.4	5.1	252.9	620.1	5.2	281	606.8	5.1
497.6	666.2	9.4	605.6	752.6	7.6	542	693.8	8.7
145.2	543.4	4.9	136.6	603.5	4.6	182	629	4.5
523.6	541.5	4.5	520.4	543.6	3.8	674	563.4	3.6
1,033	498.9	10.4	905.6	643.9	9.6	1,106	533.5	8.1
91.1	445	5	128.2	547.1	5.2	119	603.1	4.9
562.3	474.9	13.3	631.1	522.9	10.7	566	683.8	8.7
268.4	458.1	6.9	321.7	463	8.2	255	635.7	8.3
69.1	411.9	4.7	59.9	483.5	4.6	64	444.8	4.8
425.2	563.5	5	522	630.3	4.9	433	667.6	4.6
270.4	445.8	7.9	337.3	518.3	7.7	308	621.2	8.4
156	489.3	6.2	222.2	530	6.2	201	534.6	6.9
342	453.9	6	443	564.5	5	417	513	4.9
—	473.9	8.4	230.3	510.2	7.1	340	536.7	8.3
241.8	386.9	2	246.3	477.6	2	264	481.7	2
212.3	246.4	4.3	223.2	283	4.6	208	304.4	3.9
313.3	326.5	—	346.8	420.2	4.5	377	437.5	4.5
197.6	462.5	2.7	175.8	606	2.6	206	474.7	4.4
140.3	374.6	3.7	136.7	444.2	4	140	488.7	4.7
148.9	344.4	2.2	177.3	410.2	2.6	176	451.4	2.5
153.3	346.5	2.3	193.2	408.9	2.2	162	424.9	4.8
248.7	359.9	1.7	266.2	468.2	1.8	275	500.2	1.8
120.7	284.1	1.9	—	347.6	2	90	351.3	2
189.5	311.2	1.7	186.5	363.2	1.8	200	384	1.7
185.5	357	1.6	314.1	428.2	2.1	394	468.7	1.9

which to calculate our standardized variables. For example, we do not collect "density figures." Instead, we gather the relevant population or jobs data and then obtain a land-use inventory by which to calculate the urbanized land area of the city and then the density. Likewise, we do not collect other peoples' estimates of, for example, public transit use in cities (boardings per capita), because experience has shown that such figures often fail to reflect the entire transit system, for example, or they are not correctly matched in a geographical sense to the defined metropolitan region. Rather, we go to the original sources, which are the public transit operators, or in the case of the United States, to the National Transit Development Program, where consistent and detailed data on public transit systems in all American cities are carefully compiled.

Once published Internet sources are exhausted, we find the correct institutions, mostly government agencies, that can provide the remaining data, and then we try to locate the relevant people who can answer our questions. For the most part, such requests are honored. Sometimes, however, it is not possible to get cooperation, or the correspondents are unable to release data, or they simply say that they do not have it. In such cases we first of all seek other contacts, because we've learned that even people in the same agency do not necessarily know what information their colleagues hold in other sections. Often the data come to light in this way. In other cases, we are sometimes able to directly measure the data ourselves and this is often quicker than waiting for replies, though it is labor intensive. For example, urbanized land area can effectively be measured from Google Earth in concert with a GIS tool for calculating the area of the resulting shape files. We have checked this method against some cities where urbanized land area is already known from other sources, and the correlation is good. Also, the length of urban freeways can be measured from Google Earth. Where a public transit operator cannot or will not provide us with, for example, their annual vehicle-kilometers of service (relatively rare), it is possible to calculate this from known transit-line lengths and timetables; the same is true with public transit speed, if average commercial operating speed data are not available freely from an operator. Such methods are extremely time-consuming, and it depends on the particular data item whether it can even be measured or not. Many items simply cannot be independently measured or calculated in indirect ways by using other data (e.g., CBD off-street parking spaces).

Overall, these various methods of careful data collection yield the best set of urban data possible in any city. The downside is that the research takes many years to complete and requires enormous patience and resilience. We set out to collect 2005–06 data in 2007, and the data reported here was only finalized in its entirety in 2013; then it still had to be put together into useable forms. So although the data here are already several years old, it would not be possible to finish assembling, for example, a 2015 set of data before 2018 at the earliest; to then analyze and publish it would take another one to two years. Therefore, any set of global cities data will tend to be at least a minimum of five years behind its year of publication unless the significant resources and personnel required to gather it faster can be obtained, perhaps through funding by some major global organizations.

Geographic Area Definitions Used in the Global Cities Database

For the most part, the "cities" in this appendix refer to metropolitan regions, and below is a list of the metropolitan area and CBD definitions used to specify the data in this study.

Metropolitan Area Definitions
US Cities

Atlanta: State of Georgia—Counties of Cherokee, Clayton, Cobb, DeKalb, Douglas, Fayette, Fulton, Gwinnett, Henry, Rockdale

Chicago: State of Illinois—Counties of Cook, DuPage, Kane, Lake, McHenry, Will

Denver: State of Colorado—Counties of Adams, Arapahoe, Boulder, Denver, Jefferson

Houston: State of Texas—Counties of Brazoria, Fort Bend, Harris, Liberty, Montgomery, Waller

Los Angeles: State of California—Los Angeles County

New Orleans: State of Louisiana—Parishes of Jefferson and Orleans

New York: State of Connecticut—Counties of Fairfield and New Haven plus Towns of Bethlehem, Thomaston, Watertown, Woodburg, Bridgewater, New Milford; State of New Jersey—Counties of Bergen, Essex, Hudson, Middlesex, Monmouth, Morris, Ocean, Passaic, Somerset, Sussex, Union; State of New York—Counties of Bronx, Dutchess, Kings, Nassau, New York, Orange, Putnam, Queens, Richmond, Rockland, Suffolk, Westchester

Phoenix: State of Arizona—Maricopa County

Portland: State of Oregon—Counties of Clackamas, Multnomah, Washington; State of Washington—Clark County

San Diego: State of California—San Diego County

San Francisco: State of California—Counties of Alameda, Contra Costa, Marin, San Francisco, San Mateo

Seattle: State of Washington—Counties of King, Snohomish, Pierce

Washington: Washington, District of Columbia; State of Maryland—Counties of Montgomery, Prince Georges; State of Virginia—Counties of Arlington, Fairfax, Loudoun, Prince William; State of Virginia—Independent Cities of Alexandria, Fairfax, Falls Church, Manassas, Manassas Park

Canadian Cities
Calgary: Province of Alberta—City of Calgary

Montreal: Province of Quebec—Grande Region de Montreal selon le Plan des Transports

Ottawa: National Capital Region—Regional Municipality of Ottawa-Carleton, Municipalité régionale de comté Collines-de-l'Outaouais, Communauté Urbaine de l'Outaouais

Toronto: Province of Ontario—Greater Toronto Area, comprising Metropolitan Toronto (City of Toronto), Peel, Durham, Halton, York (2000), Metro Toronto 1960-90

Vancouver: Province of British Columbia—Greater Vancouver Regional District (Metro Vancouver)

Australian Cities
Brisbane: State of Queensland—Brisbane Statistical Division

Melbourne: State of Victoria—Melbourne Statistical Division

Perth: State of Western Australia—Perth Statistical Division

Sydney: State of New South Wales—Sydney Statistical Division

European Cities
Berlin: Land Berlin

Bern (1995): Region Bern, including: Allmendingen, Baeriswil, Belp, Bern, Bolligen, Bremgarten, Diemerswil, Ittigen, Jegenstorf, Kehrsatz, Kirchlindach, Koeniz, Mattstetten, Meikirch, Moosseedorf, Muenchenbuchsee, Muri, Ostermundigen, Stettlen, Urtenen, Vechigen, Wohl; Bern (2005): Raumplanungsregion Bern (VRB)

Brussels: Region de Bruxelles-Capitale

Copenhagen: Hovedstadsregionen, including Kobenhavn Kommune, Frederiksberg Kommune, Kobenhavn Amt, Frederiksberg Amt, Roskilde Amt

Düsseldorf: Landeshauptstadt Düsseldorf

Frankfurt: Stadt Frankfurt am Main

Geneva: République et canton de Genève

Graz: ATS

Hamburg: Freie und Hansestadt Hamburg

Helsinki: Yhteistyovaltuuskunta (YTV) including Helsinki, Espoo, Vantaa, Kauniainen

London: Greater London

Madrid: Comunidad de Madrid

Manchester: Greater Manchester

Munich: Landeshauptstadt München

Oslo: Oslo and Akershus

Prague: Město Praha

Stockholm: Stockholms Län

Stuttgart: Landeshauptstadt Stuttgart

Vienna: Stadt Wien

Zurich: Planungsregionen Zürich, Zimmerberg, Pfannenstil, Glattal, Furttal, Limmattal, Knonauer Amt

Asian Cities

Hong Kong: The Territory of Hong Kong, now the Hong Kong Special Administrative Region

Singapore: Republic of Singapore

Central Business District (CBD) Definitions
US Cities

Atlanta: Downtown Area, bound by Northside Drive, Memorial Drive, Piedmont Avenue, and North Avenue, incorporating Census Tracts (CT) 19–21, 27, and 35

Chicago: The Loop, bounded by Chicago River to the north and west, Lake Michigan to the east, and Roosevelt Road to the south

Denver: Regional Statistical Area 412

Houston: Area inside the Interstate 610 Loop

Los Angeles: Census Tracts—2071 south of Sunset Boulevard, 2073–79

New Orleans: Central Business District area plus Warehouse District area bounded by Ponchartrain Expressway, Canal Street, Interstate 10, and Mississippi River

New York: Manhattan south of 60th Street (called "The Hub" in official documents in the early 1980s)

Phoenix: Census Tracts 1130, 1131, 1141

Portland: Metro 405 Loop

San Diego: Center City

San Francisco: Census Tracts 114, 115, 117, 118, 121–125, 176, 178

Seattle: Elliot Bay to the west, Denny Way to the north, Interstate 5 to east, Royal Brougham Way to the south

Washington: Ring 0

Canadian Cities

Calgary: Community Districts—Chinatown, Downtown East, Downtown West, Eau Claire

Montreal: Arrondissement Ville-Marie

Ottawa: Ottawa Central Area plus Hull CBD

Toronto: Minor Planning District 1e

Vancouver: Downtown neighborhood

Australian Cities

Brisbane: Census Collectors' Districts 3191902–3191904, 3192601–3192603

Melbourne: Inner Statistical Local Area

Perth: Census Zones 101, 130–134

Sydney: Census Collectors' Districts 101–104, 106–107, 109–114, 117, 205, 2003, 2005, 2008, and 2010

European Cities

Berlin (1995): Parkraumbewirtschaftungszonen Stadtmitte and Westliche Innenstadt; Berlin (2005): Bezirk Mitte

Bern: Stadtteil I Innere Stadt

Brussels: Zones 1, 6, 7, 8, 21, and 45

Copenhagen (1995): Statistikdistrikt A Indre By, C Voldskvarternerne; København (2005): Indre By (others are all amalgamated into Indre By)

Düsseldorf: Stadtteile Altstadt, Karlstadt, Stadtmitte, Pempelfort, Friedrichstadt, and Unterbilk

Frankfurt: Ortsteile Altstadt, Bahnhofsviertel, Innenstadt

Geneva: Secteurs Statistiques de Cité-Centre et St-Gervais–Chantepoulet

Graz: 1. Bezirk: Innere Stadt

Hamburg: Stadtteile (Ortsteile) Hamburg-Altstadt (101–103), Neustadt (104–107)

Helsinki: The Helsinki Peninsula, including Vironniemi, Ullanlinna, Kampinmalmi

London: Central Activities Zone (CAZ)

Madrid: Almendra Central, comprising Distritos 1–7 of Madrid Municipio

Manchester: Inner Ring Road area

Munich: Stadtbezirke 1, 2, 3

Oslo: Oslo CBD

Prague: Praha 1

Stockholm: Församlingen—Adolf Fredrik, Gustav Vasa, Hedvig Eleonora, and Kungsholm, plus Redovisningosområdet Jakob and Klara

Stuttgart: Bezirk Mitte

Vienna: 1. Bezirk

Zurich: Kreis 1 Altstadt

Asian Cities

Hong Kong: Comprehensive Transport Study Zones 7–11

Singapore: Planning Areas of Downtown Core, Orchard, Singapore River, Museum, Rochor, Outram, River Valley, Newton

Notes

Chapter 1 Notes

1. The choice of cities for the analysis dates back to the original study by Newman and Kenworthy (1989b) that selected a set of the major cities in each region covering a range of population sizes. The data for this research from the time periods 1960, 1970, 1980, and 1990 were sourced from Kenworthy et al. (1999), while taking the mean values for some cities between 1995 (Kenworthy & Laube 2001) and 2005 (Kenworthy 2011b) as well as recent updates of the database. This has created a set of observations for the year 2000 in order to ensure standardized time periods (10 years) for the econometric analysis. As a general rule, though, the data are patchier for the 1960 and 1970 periods. For this reason our data set, which focuses on cities with the most data over the longest period, uses only 26 cities out of the 46 cities in the longitudinal Global Cities database set. In this sense the data alone in the table in the Appendix represent an original contribution to the field of urban research and a rich resource for others.

2. Increases in passenger-car traffic per capita have major and well-documented environmental, social, and economic impacts on urban function, form, and liveability (Boarnet & Sarmiento 1998; Coevering & Schwanen 2006; Giuliano & Dargay 2006), and this has global significance (IPCC 2013). Reducing car dependence requires an understanding of its causes.

3. At least part of this trend was caused by congestion pricing, which began in 2007; however, the decline has continued even as the pricing has stabilized. See: Phillip Pank, "Welcome to the age of the bike: Cyclists 'must be first' as car use passes its peak" (London) *Times*, 6 Nov 2012.

4. See: *Emerging Trends in Real Estate 2014*, Canada Edition (Online), Urban Land Institute, 2014, pwc.com/en_CA/ca/real-estate/publications/pwc-emerging-trends-in-real-estate-2014-en.pdf (Accessed 28 Feb 2015).

5. See: Emily McWilliams, "Toronto skyline's 'absolute transformation' captured by two photos taken 13 years apart," *National Post* (Online), 17 Jan 2015, news.nationalpost.com/2015/01/17/toronto-skylines-absolute-transformation-captured-by-two-photos-taken-13-years-apart/ (Accessed 28 Feb 2015).

6. See: thefifthestate.com.au/business/trends/cars-are-so-yesterday-young-and-rich-leave-guzzlers-behind/33691 (Accessed 18 Nov 2014).

7. Author Newman: In four years on the Board of Infrastructure Australia, I did not find that the costs of urban rail, per kilometer, were any greater than the costs of building urban freeways; however, rail projects were always better if they were assessed in terms of passenger-kilometers and wider economic benefits (including agglomeration economies). No opportunities to use value capture were taken during this period, but, as set out in chapter 6, this will soon change because the evidence of substantial cost savings are now available.

8. Note that this table underrepresents the number of "modern trams." Switzerland has at least five cities with this mode of rail transit.

9. See: abu-dhabi-metro.com/tag/uae-rail-system (Accessed 21 Dec 2012).

10. See: urbanmobilitychina.com/tag/metro/ (Accessed 6 Oct 2014).

11. Demand-responsive buses are work- or community-related bus services that are not part of regularly scheduled public transit systems. People are generally required to request/book a pickup at a particular time and place, and then the operator works out an optimal route to pick up everyone requiring the service.

12. See: dirt.asla.org/2014/03/10/u-s-public-transportation-use-hits-peak-not-seen-since-the-1950s/ (Accessed 23 Apr 2014).

13. There are alternative views on such trends; see: planetizen.com/node/67997 (Accessed 2 Mar 2015).

14. See: smh.com.au/nsw/dulwich-hill-tram-extension-proving-too-popular-20140402-35y81.html (Accessed 23 Apr 2014).

15. Some studies show that a more complex relationship exists due to the overwhelming desire for better accessibility and an end to urban sprawl, but most prefer houses with gardens, rather than apartments (though a smaller proportion than before); see: switchboard.nrdc.org/blogs/kbenfield/new_realtors_community_prefere.html (Accessed 7 Feb 2015).

Chapter 2 Notes

1. A detailed explanation of the importance and great relevance of the 1995–96 and 2005–06 data comparisons is provided in the appendix.

2. The main aim here was not to compare the relative amount of car driving per unit of real GDP between cities, but how the amount of driving per unit of GDP has changed over the 10-year period between 1995 and 2005 in each city. This can be expressed as a percentage. In examining the decoupling of wealth and car use in individual cities, we have therefore used real local currencies, not US dollars. Our aim is to investigate the possible extent to which growth in mobility and especially car mobility may have decoupled from growth in wealth or GDP per capita. It is thus very important to ensure that both the mobility variables and the wealth data for these cities are kept within the same domain and are not affected by divergent external factors that can come into play in converting to a common currency. Conversion to a common currency can sometimes misrepresent the actual effects of real changes in wealth in local currencies due to specific factors that affect the exchange rate between currencies, which may not be factors in how real changes in local wealth are affecting mobility patterns. For example, the Hong Kong dollar has had a history of changes in its inherent international value

against other currencies, which have been in turn linked to changes in, for example, Hong Kong's relationship to the UK. The Hong Kong dollar was pegged to the US dollar in 1983 (yearbook.gov.hk/1998/ewww/app/app17/index.htm, accessed 21 Sep 2013). Local currencies were converted to real 1995 values using the World Economic Outlook GDP Deflator found at: econstats.com/weo/V005.htm for the country in which each city is located. What affects the value of the US dollar on the international money markets may not be affecting, for example, the value of the euro in the same way. Table 2.2 however, which compares GDP per capita between cities converts all GDPs to 1995 US dollars (a common currency is necessary here).

3. See: *Emerging Trends in Real Estate 2014*, Canada Edition (Online), Urban Land Institute, 2014, pwc.com/en_CA/ca/real-estate/publications/pwc-emerging-trends-in-real-estate-2014-en.pdf (Accessed 28 Feb 2015).

4. Compiling the data on Hong Kong's transit system took over two years and required the collection of each transit data item 18 times before a total could be determined: seven different bus operators, two minibus systems, two tramways, one LRT system, one metro system, two suburban rail operations, and three ferry operators.

5. Freeways are roads with no intersections, no traffic lights, and no direct private-property access. The data measure centerline lengths, not lane kilometers.

6. It needs to be said that there are two important and slightly confounding factors that determine the level of passenger-kilometers by public transit: the actual level of public transit trip making, which naturally pushes the figure up, and the compactness (density) and size of the city, with denser, smaller cities having reduced passenger-kilometers due to shorter trip lengths. Large, lower-density cities can reach higher levels of passenger-kilometers even with modest numbers of transit trips because the distances that must be traveled are greater. Nevertheless, the biggest factor seems to be the actual transit trip rate, since the very dense Asian cities, four-and-a-half times denser than European cities, far exceed the level of passenger travel by public transit in the European cities (70 percent more), despite being so dense and having short trip lengths.

7. The speeds of transit systems used here are weighted by the passenger-hours for each part of the system. The overall public transit system speed is weighted by the passenger-hours for each mode, and within a mode—if there is more than one operator or system—the overall average speed for that mode is weighted by the passenger-hours of each component (e.g., the suburban rail speed for a city with several suburban rail operators is weighted by the passenger-hours-traveled within each operator's services). It should also be noted that all speeds are curb-to-curb speeds.

8. See: bike-eu.com/Sales-Trends/Market-Report/2012/10/Japan-2011-Pedelec-Sales-on-the-Rise-1082814W/ (Accessed 24 Sep 2013). Note that a pedelec is not an e-bike per se, although it is often referred to as such. A pedelec has an electric motor and a battery, but to gain power assistance one must pedal. The bike cannot be driven under electric power alone, independent of pedaling.

9. See: cities-today.com/2014/04/bike-share-schemes-price-healthier-city/ (Accessed 6 Oct 2014).

10. All the New York data in this chapter reflect not just New York City (NYC) but the broader tri-state region with some 20 million people, though the NMM figure is heavily influenced by the patterns in NYC.

11. Michael Sivak's Transportation Research Institute monitors these factors; see: UMTRI, "Sustainable Worldwide Transportation" (Online, last updated 13 Nov 2014), University of Michigan Transport Research Institute, umich.edu/~umtriswt (Accessed 28 Feb 15).

12. One megajoule is equal to 0.0076 US gallons of gasoline; or 1 gallon of gasoline equals 132 megajoules.

13. See: TED Talks presentation by Peter Newman, "Sustainability: Are We Winning?" (Online), 27 Jan 2015, youtube.com/watch?v=6RFiyM89rbk (Accessed 28 Feb 2015).

14. American urban buses averaged 2.97 MJ/PKT and the minibuses used for transit averaged a massive 7.68 MJ/PKT, or over two and a half times higher than cars in 2005!

15. Trams, LRT, metro, and suburban rail in US cities consumed 1.02, 0.64, 0.69, and 1.29 MJ/PKT, respectively, in 2005.

16. Transportation emissions are collected from emissions inventories conducted for cities. The US Environmental Protection Agency (USEPA), for example, has a rolling program of emissions inventories, and many other cities around the world have been conducting them over recent times, due especially to the need for monitoring greenhouse-gas (GHG) emissions. Figures on transportation fatalities are obtained from World Health Organization (WHO) International Classification of Diseases (ICD 10) databases under codes V01 to V99 (2005 data). In 1995, the codes were ICD 9 codes E810 to E825. We do not use police records, which almost always undercount transportation deaths as they do not record deaths in hospital that occur 30 days after an accident.

Chapter 3 Notes

1. Midrange economies are usually defined as the "Asian Tigers," the main Latin American economies, and Eastern Europe, which lie between the Western developed economies of the OECD and the developing-world economies.

2. This measure of decline is also a minimum because the real GDP that has been used is for 2009 (the latest available), while the car use is for 2011; both figures favor an unrealistically high car-travel level per R$ of GDP. The same applies to the total motorized travel per R$ of GDP.

3. Paratransit is demand-responsive transit that does not operate on fixed routes or schedules, such as the jeepneys of Manila, many of the minibus systems in African cities, and the shared taxis or *dolmuş* in Turkey.

4. The decline may be partly due to changes in boundaries that now incorporate more low-density surrounding urban areas in the overall city area.

5. See: czso.cz/csu/2013edicniplan.nsf/engp/101011-13 (Accessed 25 May 2013).

6. Ibid.

7. Even if every visitor to the city took 10 boardings on the public transit system, this would amount to 41 million transit trips. The total number of transit boardings in Prague in 2005 was 1,242 million, so under this assumption tourist traffic would amount to 3.3 percent of usage.

Chapter 4 Notes

1. The actual figure is closer to 1.1 hours per day.

2. Trams were initially horse-drawn; then some systems operated on steam, either with small steam locomotives or with a steam engine at the end of the line pulling the tram along by cables. All tram systems ended up being powered by electricity, as did most of the train systems, apart from those that continued to operate on diesel power.

3. The Athens conference of CIAM in the 1930s, led by Le Corbusier, produced the concept of the Functional City, with land use (for living, working, and recreation) separated from transport as a different function. This set the scene for postwar automobile-based planning, with suburbs placed where only automobiles and secondary buses could service them.

4. See: *Emerging Trends in Real Estate 2014*, Canada Edition (Online), Urban Land Institute, 2014, pwc.com/en_CA/ca/real-estate/publications/pwc-emerging-trends -in-real-estate-2014-en.pdf (Accessed 28 Feb 2015); see also: Emily McWilliams, "Toronto skyline's 'absolute transformation' captured by two photos taken 13 years apart," *National Post* (Online), 17 Jan 2015, news.nationalpost.com/2015/01/17/ toronto-skylines-absolute-transformation-captured-by-two-photos-taken-13-years -apart/ (Accessed 28 Feb 2015).

5. It would also have gone unnoticed were it not for the kind of comprehensive longitudinal urban data sets collected by us over the last 35 years and highlighted in chapter 2.

6. It should be noted that both car and transit speeds are based upon curb-to-curb or "in-vehicle" travel times, not door-to-door travel times. In this sense the relative speed between public transit and cars may be overstated for some trips and understated for others. Higher urban density can do much to shorten access distances and the time required before a transit vehicle can be boarded. In addition, waiting times can be very much reduced where public transit frequencies are very high, such as in Japanese subway systems where peak-period headways can be as short as 90 seconds, or even in, for example, the Skytrain in Vancouver, where peak frequencies along significant sections are two to four minutes. Likewise, cars are not without access times, depending on the nature of the origin and destination of the trip and where parking is to be found. As a rule, public transit is most competitive in speed for trips to centers or major events, which act as temporary centers. In these situations, parking is generally most limited and therefore is least convenient for car users, due to cost and also the walking distance from a car park to a final destination.

7. Note that the data in table 4.4 represent the same city pairs within each year group. From 1960 to 2005 the amount of data increased considerably, so there is a general increase across the table in the number of cities involved in each year.

8. The data also highlight the fact that it is bus systems (as well as tram and LRT systems that are not operating on dedicated rights-of-way) that are dragging down the speed performance of public transit. However, it must also be recognized that buses operate in nearly all cities under intolerable congestion levels that are permitted to continue by not controlling congestion through economic and physical means. It is not the case that buses cannot compete with cars in speed terms in all circumstances, but they will continue to struggle while congestion remains unchecked (Bradley & Kenworthy 2012).

9. Car ownership in Europe has continued to grow until recently, although much more slowly than in the past, and is now showing signs of a plateau in some countries as the streets have filled and other options have to be pursued, as explained in this book. Car ownership is actually declining in some places; for example, five major Canadian cities declined in average levels of car ownership between 1996 and 2006. In addition to the options discussed later, car ownership is also being increasingly affected by car sharing, especially in European cities (e.g., Bremen). Car companies such as Daimler Benz and BMW have also established their own "car-on-demand" systems in some cities (Car2Go and Drive Now, respectively).

10. In terms of parking, between 1995 and 2005 parking supply per 1,000 CBD jobs in a large sample of cities mostly declined. US cities fell from 555 to 487 parking spaces per 1,000 CBD jobs, Canadian 390 to 319, Australian 367 to 298, and Singapore and Hong Kong declined too, from 136 to 121 parking spaces per 1,000 CBD jobs. In European cities, CBD parking rose a fraction from 224 to 241, but this was largely because of an unavoidable expansion of the definition of the CBD in Berlin due to German reunification, which increased the apparent CBD parking supply in that city (Kenworthy 2012).

11. Copenhagen has even introduced a new bike-sharing scheme featuring bikes with built-in tablet computers.

12. The driverless car from Google, which has already gained legislative approval to operate in test mode in five US states, may change this; Google is lobbying heavily in every state to alter road-safety legislation.

13. See: City of Melbourne, "Melbourne in Numbers" (Online), melbourne.vic.gov.au/AboutMelbourne/Statistics/Pages/MelbourneSnapshot.aspx (Accessed 28 Feb 2015); see also: Craig Butt and Christina Zhou, "Melbourne apartment development hits historic high," *Sydney Morning Herald* (Online), 7 Jul 2014, smh.com.au/business/property/melbourne-apartment-development-hits-historic-high-20140706-zsxyx.html (Accessed 28 Feb 2015).

14. Even our own city of Perth has been attracting residential development, with 2014 data showing around 27,000 people living in the city center (after only 700 were found when Jan Gehl began his studies in 1992), together with significant growth in jobs, numbers of people walking, and people attracted to activities (see: cityofperth.wa.gov.au). The city was once called "dullsville"—but no longer (Newman 2015).

Chapter 5 Notes

1. See: *Local Transport Today* 592, Mar 2014, p. 16–29.

2. See: awpr.co.uk/ (Accessed 5 Apr 2012).

3. See, for example: articles.latimes.com/1997-05-14/local/me-58478_1_freeways-capacity-traffic (Accessed 5 Apr 2012). See also: Siegel (2007).

4. See, for example: wired.com/2014/06/wuwt-traffic-induced-demand/ (Accessed 11 Nov 2014).

5. Personal communication with Rolf Monheim, July 1990.

6. See: strategy-business.com/article/li00064?pg=all (Accessed 19 Nov 2011).

7. See, for example, Kenworthy & Newman (1986a, 1986b) for a comprehensive historical assessment of this field, the fundamentals of which have not changed significantly
in 25 years.

8. See: *Local Transport Today* 592, transportxtra.com/magazines/local_transport_today
/news/?iid=467 (Accessed 11 Apr 2012).

9. See: theage.com.au/victoria/cars-out-in-latest-swanston-street-revamp-20110427
-1dwz1.html (Accessed 9 Feb 2015).

10. Sources for this list of examples include: Surface Transportation Policy Project, *Progress*,
March 1998; Seattle Urban Mobility Plan: Case Studies in Urban Freeway Removal (online),
cityofseattle.net/transportation/docs/ump/06%20SEATTLE%20Case%20studies
%20in%20urban%20freeway%20removal.pdf (Accessed 10 Apr 2012); Siegel (2007);
Trailer for *Seoul: The Stream of Consciousness* (online), pbs.org/e2/episodes/310_seoul
_the_stream_of_consciousness_trailer.html (Accessed 10 Apr 2014).

11. See, for example: Angie Schmitt, "Tear Down These 10 Freeways (And Then Tear Down
Some More), *Streetsblog USA* (online), usa.streetsblog.org/2014/02/13/tear-down-these
-10-freeways-and-then-tear-down-some-more/ (Accessed 24 Apr 2014).

12. Peter Newman was on the Advisory Council of Infrastructure Australia (IA) from
2010 to 2014, and in that time IA assessed road and rail projects together rather than
seeing them separately, as had been done before. The assessments did include WEBs
and avoidable costs, though they were rarely done very well as very few people knew
how to do these assessments. Rail projects invariably had better BCRs than road
projects. The overall outcome was that IA announced a lot more urban rail than
urban road projects.

13. Though Toronto was probably the first in North America (Newman & Kenworthy
1999a).

Chapter 6 Notes

1. *Density* refers to population and job density; both are measured by us and, as pointed
out in chapter 4, they are usually optimized together for achieving reductions in automobile dependence. Residential densities are usually the most contentious.

2. This is clear in, for example, Ho Chi Minh City, where despite having a density of
356 persons per hectare, making it the densest city in our Global Cities Database, the
city in 1995 had a tiny 10 vehicle-kilometers per person per annum of public transit
service, a figure that was about a third of a typical American city! This meant the city
had virtually no mass transit to speak of. As a result, it also had only 11 public transit
boardings per capita annually, an unspeakably low figure on a global scale. Even Phoenix and Houston had 15 and 21 boardings per person respectively, with urban densities of about 10 persons per hectare. The difference in Ho Chi Minh City is, of course,
that the city is so dense that walking, bicycles, and other mechanized, non-motorized
modes, as well as motorcycles, play a massive role in mobility.

3. Sadly, Paul Mees OAM passed away in 2013. Although in this section we take issue
with some of his assertions about automobile dependence being due mostly to transit
services, we mostly had a very strong working relationship, especially about ending
the fetish in transportation planning with freeway construction. Paul was a strong

leader of civil society NGOs seeking a different urban transportation future, especially in Melbourne.

4. See Gordon Price, *Price Tags* blog, pricetags.wordpress.com.

5. If it were 1.0 it would be a perfect correlation.

6. If it were 100 percent it would be the only factor needing to be included; virtually no social phenomenon can be explained by one factor alone.

7. A distinction needs to be made as well between overcrowding and density. *Overcrowding* is where there are too many people in one dwelling to maintain a reasonable standard of space and privacy. This is most common in lower-income situations and can have negative consequences, but it can also be moderated by cultural factors that are accepting of much lower space standards per person (e.g., in Japan and Hong Kong). *Density* is where there are a higher number of people living within a given urbanized territory. Urban density, of course, can be increased through overcrowding, but in the normal sense of the term, it results primarily from building dwellings at higher densities and having them inhabited by appropriate numbers of people for the internal space provided. Therefore, one needs to be careful to distinguish between studies that purport to show negative effects from *overcrowding* as opposed to *density*.

8. This is a term popularized by Edward O. Wilson in his book *Biophilia* (1984), in which he defines *biophilia* as the innate affinity that human beings have with other living things and with nature in general. He stresses that humans co-evolved with nature and so need it in their daily lives.

9. Singapore's biophilics can be seen in the film *Singapore: Biophilic City* by Peter Newman and Tim Beatley (youtube.com/watch?v=XMWOu9xIM_k, accessed 2 Mar 2015), as well as on the Tim Beatley biophilic urbanism website, *BiophilicCities* (biophiliccities .org/what-are-biophilic-cities/singapore/, accessed 2 Mar 2015).

10. There have been some interesting articles recently about the potential for the autonomous vehicle to cause sprawl (for example, see "The Self-Driving Tesla Might Make Us Love Urban Sprawl Again," wired.com/2014/10/tesla-self-driving-car-sprawl/, accessed 20 Nov 2014).

11. Filmmaker Linda Blagg has made films on the struggle for the city of Fremantle to reverse its economic decline after a heritage lobby prevented all development for 10 years until a sustainability-oriented mayor and council showed that green and pro-development was better than green and anti-development; see: vimeo.com/channels /lindablagg.

12. This was detailed in the blog *Josh's House*, joshshouse.com.au (Accessed 2 Mar 2015).

13. Tod Litman's Victoria Transport Policy Institute has released a new study, Analysis of Public Policies that Unintentionally Encourage and Subsidize Urban Sprawl, that shows sprawl is costing more than $1 million per year. Smart Growth America has a new tool to help local councils called The Fiscal Implications of Development Patterns.

14. Alternative funding applied to transit is mostly derived through land-value uplift-based mechanisms, rather than just consolidated revenue from government.

15. See papers from James McIntosh's PhD research: McIntosh et al. 2011, 2013, 2014a, and 2014b.

16. See also: mobility.tamu.edu/ums/congestion-data/ (Accessed 19 Jun 2014).

17. See: spitsvrij.nl/Upload/File/Bevindingen%20Spitsvrij.pdf (Accessed 23 Jun 2014).

18. This was true at least up until June 16, 2014, when Vancouver announced plans for comprehensive road pricing. Coyne (2014) states: "The plan? The mayors refer to it as 'comprehensive mobility pricing.' It's never quite spelled out what this means, but it's clear this would go far beyond putting tolls on the odd bridge or highway, of a kind the region's inhabitants have grown used to—a piecemeal approach that has simply shifted the burden of congestion, rather than reduced it. Instead, the mayors appear to favor a system that would see drivers pay to use the entire road network, much as they now pay to use their cell phones, with different charges applying on different roads at different times."

19. There have been other ambitious plans for systematic and even nationwide plans for road pricing. The Netherlands was aiming for such a system in the 1980s but it was ultimately defeated politically, with a lot of influence from the Dutch trucking industry, which is very powerful. Likewise in Hong Kong, where system-wide electronic road pricing had gone to the pilot phase, it was ultimately defeated politically on the grounds that such a scheme constituted an invasion of privacy. It remains to be seen whether Vancouver will be able to bring their ambitious road pricing plan to fruition.

Chapter 7 Notes

1. See: Sarah Gilbert, "Carscape: How the motor car reshaped England—in pictures," *Guardian* (Online), 12 Feb 2014, theguardian.com/artanddesign/gallery/2014/feb/12/carscape-how-the-motor-car-reshaped-england-in-pictures?index=1 (Accessed 27 Jun 2014).

2. The organization Carbon Tracker examines stranded assets due to the use of all fossil fuels. See: Carbon Tracker (Online), Carbon Tracker Initiative, 2014, carbontracker.org (Accessed 2 Mar 2015).

3. See: James Fishkin, Baogang He, Robert C. Luskin, and Alice Siu, "Notes and Comments—Deliberative Democracy in an Unlikely Place: Deliberative Polling in China," *British Journal of Political Science* 40 (2010): 435–48, chinesedemocratization.com/Baogang-English%20articles/6.BJPS-Deliberative%20Democracy%20in%20an%20Unlikely%20Place.pdf (Accessed 2 Mar 2015).

4. See: Michael Sivak, *Has Motorization in the U.S. Peaked?* Part 6: Relationship between Road Transportation and Economic Activity (online), University of Michigan Transportation Research Institute, Dec 2014, deepblue.lib.umich.edu/bitstream/handle/2027.42/110116/103145.pdf?sequence=1&isAllowed=y (Accessed 2 Mar 2015).

Chapter 8 Notes

1. See the blog *Josh's House*, joshshouse.com.au (Accessed 2 Mar 2015).

2. See: David R. Baker, "Here's how California lawmakers plan to cut greenhouse gases," *SFGate* (online), 11 Feb 2015, sfgate.com/business/article/Here-s-how-California-lawmakers-plan-to-cut-6073418.php (Accessed 2 Mar 2015).

3. See: Tom Randall, "Goldman: Here's Why Oil Crashed—and Why Lower Prices Are Here to Stay," *Bloomberg Business* (online), 11 Feb 2015, bloomberg.com/news/articles

/2015-02-11/goldman-here-s-why-oil-crashed-and-why-lower-prices-are-here-to -stay?hootPostID=3013e18458e6aedf15ba3a704124f25e (Accessed 2 Mar 2015).

4. See: ec.europe.eu/clima/policies/roadmap/index_en.htm (Accessed 19 Nov 2014).

5. See: "The future resident of Helsinki will not own a car," *Helsinki Times* (online), 4 Jul 2014,   helsinkitimes.fi/finland/finland-news/domestic/11062-the-future-resident-of -helsinki-will-not-own-a-car.html (Accessed 2 Mar 2015).

6. "Car Sharing in Bremen/Germany," Eltis: The Urban Mobility Observatory, eltis.org /index.php?id=13&study_id=2228 (Accessed 25 Jun 2014).

7. See: BusinessGreen, "China coal production falls for first time this century," *Guardian* (online), 27 Jan 2015, theguardian.com/environment/2015/jan/27/china-coal -production-falls-for-first-time-this-century?CMP=share_btn_fb (Accessed 2 Mar 2015).

8. A similar analysis of the potential for optimism in overcoming car dependency has been made by Embarq. See: sustainablecitiescollective.com/embarq/1016811/five -reasons-be-optimistic-about-sustainable-urban-mobility (Accessed 19 Nov 2014).

References

ANDERSON, W., KANAROGLOU, P. and MILLER, E. 1996. Urban form, energy, and environment: A review of the issues, evidence, and policy. *Urban Studies* 33 (1), p. 7–35.

ARRINGTON, G. B. and CERVERO, R. 2008. Effects of TOD on Housing, Parking, and Travel: Transit Cooperative Research Program (TCRP) Report 128. Washington, DC: Transportation Research Board (TRB).

ASHTON-GRAHAM, C. and JOHN, G. 2006. Travel Smart household program frequently asked questions in travel demand management and dialogue marketing. Perth, AUS: Government of Western Australia, Department of Transport.

ASHTON-GRAHAM, C. and NEWMAN, P. 2013. Case Study: Living Smart in Australian Households: Sustainability Coaching as an Effective Large-Scale Behavior Change Strategy. In: FUDGE, S. and PETERS, M. (eds.) *International Approaches to Behavior Change: The Global Challenge to Encouraging Sustainable Lifestyles.* London: Edward Elgar.

ATKINS, S. T. 1986. Transportation planning models—What the papers say. *Traffic Engineering and Control* 27 (9), p. 460–67.

ATLANTA BELTLINE INC. (ABI). 2014. How the Atlanta BeltLine is funded. [Online] Available from: beltline.org/about/the-atlanta-beltline-project/funding/ [Accessed 5 May 2014].

AUSTRALIAN BUREAU OF STATISTICS (ABS). 2001. 2001 Census. Canberra, AUS: ABS.

AUSTRALIAN BUREAU OF STATISTICS (ABS). 2011. 2011 Census. Canberra, AUS: ABS.

BACON, E. N. 1988. Planning and planners in the post-petroleum age: Fundamental issues facing metropolitan development and conservation. *Regional Development Dialogue* 9 (3), p. 1–6.

BAILLIEU KNIGHT FRANK (BKF). 1991. The wasting of the CBD: A paper on infrastructure use and employment in Melbourne. Melbourne: BKF Research.

BAKER, D. 2015. Here's how California's lawmakers plan to cut greenhouse gases. [Online] *SFGate.* 11 Feb. Available from: sfgate.com/business/article/Here-s-how-California-lawmakers -plan-to-cut-6073418.php [Accessed 2 Mar 2015].

BALDASSARE, M. 1979. Residential Crowding in Urban America. Berkeley, CA: University of California Press.

BANISTER, D. 2006. Transport, Urban Form, and Economic Growth. Paper presented at the 137th ECMT Regional Round Table. Berkeley, CA, Mar 28.

BANK OF CANADA. 2015. Monetary Policy Report. Ottawa. January.

BANSAL, R. and KIRK, S. 2015. Peak Carbon before Peak Oil. *Konzept*. Deutsche Bank.

BARTER, P. A. 1999. An International Comparative Perspective on Urban Transport and Urban Form in Pacific Asia: Responses to the Challenge of Motorization in Dense Cities: PhD Dissertation. Perth, AUS: Institute for Sustainability and Technology Policy (ISTP), Murdoch University.

BAY, J. H. 2011. Towards a fourth ecology: Social and environmental sustainability with architecture and urban design. *Journal of Green Buildings* 5 (4), p. 176–97.

BAYCAN, T., GIRARD, L. F. and NIJKAMP, P. 2012. Creative and Sustainable Cities: A New Perspective. In: BAYCAN, T., GIRARD, L. F. and NIJKAMP, P. (eds.) *Sustainable City and Creativity*. Surrey, UK: Ashgate.

BEATLEY, T. 2009. *Biophilic Cities: Integrating Nature into Urban Design and Planning*. Washington, DC: Island Press.

BEATLEY, T. and NEWMAN, P. 2009. *Green Urbanism Down Under: Learning from Sustainable Communities in Australia*. Washington, DC: Island Press.

BEATTIE, C. and NEWMAN, P. 2011. The Density Trade-off: Does High-Rise Construction Contribute More than Single Dwellings to Greenhouse-Gas Emissions? In: *Proceedings of 5th State of Australian Cities Conference*. Melbourne, Nov 29–Dec 2.

BEIJING TRANSPORT (BT). 2013. Beijing Transport Annual Report. Beijing, CHI: BT, Beijing Transport Development Research Centre.

BEILHARTZ, P. and HOGAN, T. (eds.) 2006. *Sociology: Place, Time, and Division*. Oxford, UK: Oxford University Press.

BENFIELD, K. 2013. New realtor's community preference poll: Americans want to have their cake and eat it, too. *Switchboard Blog*. [Online] Available from: switchboard.nrdc.org/blogs/kbenfield/new_realtors_community_prefere.html [Accessed 23 Apr 2014].

BLAGG, L. 2012. The sustainable revitalization of Fremantle. [Online] Vimeo. Available from: vimeo.com/51896517 [Accessed 5 May 2014].

BLAKE DAWSON. 2008. The new world of Value Transfer PPPs. Infrastructure: Policy, Finance and Investment. Newsletter of Blake Dawson, May, p. 12–13.

BOARNET, M. and CRANE, R. 2001. The influence of land use on travel behavior: Specification and estimation strategies. *Transportation Research Part A: Policy and Practice* 35, p. 823–45.

BOARNET, M. and SARMIENTO, S. 1998. Can land-use policy really affect travel behavior? A study of the link between non-work travel and land-use characteristics. *Urban Studies* 35 (7), p. 1155–69.

BODE, P. M., HAMBERGER, S. and ZÄNGL, W. 1986. Alptraum Auto / Grün kaputt / Sein oder Nichtsein: Alptraum Auto. Eine hundertährige Erfindung und ihre Folgen. Munich: Raben Verlag.

BOUANAH, B. J. and STEIN, M. M. 1978. Urban transportation models: A generalized process for international application. *Traffic Quarterly* 32, p. 449–70.

BRADLEY, M. and KENWORTHY, J. 2012. Congestion offsets: Transforming cities by letting buses compete. *World Transport Policy and Practice* 18 (4), p. 46–70.

BRASUELL, J. 2014. More criticism of transit record claims. *Planetizen News*. [Online] Available from: planetizen.com/node/67997 [Accessed 23 Apr 2014].

BREHENY, M. 1992. *Sustainable Development and Urban Form*. London: Pion.

BREHENY, M. 1995. The compact city and transport energy consumption. *Transactions of the Institute of British Geographers* 20, p. 81–101.

BROCK, W. A. and TAYLOR, M. S. 2005. Economic Growth and the Environment: A Review of Theory and Empirics. NBER Working Paper Series No. 10854. Cambridge, MA: National Bureau of Economic Research.

BROWN, H. J., GINN, J. R. and JAMES, F. J. 1972. Land-Use Transportation Planning Studies. In: BROWN, H. J., GINN, J. R., JAMES, F. J., KAIN, J. F. and STRAZSHEIM, M. R. (eds.) *Empirical Models of Urban Land Use: Suggestions on Research Objectives and Organization.* Washington, DC: National Bureau of Economic Research, p. 6–16.

BRUECKNER, J. K. 2000. Urban sprawl: Diagnosis and remedies. *International Regional Science Review* 23 (2), p. 160–71.

BRUUN, E. 2007. *Better Public Transit Systems: Analyzing Investments and Performance.* Washington, DC: APA Planners Press.

BUNNING, J., BEATTIE, C., RAULAND, V. and NEWMAN, P. 2013. Low-carbon sustainable precincts: An Australian perspective. *Sustainability* 5 (6), p. 2305–26.

BURCHELL, R. B., LOWENSTEIN, G., DOLPHIN, W. R., DOWNS, A., SESKIN, S., STILL, K. G. and MOORE, T. 2002. Transit Cooperative Research Program (TCIP): Costs of Sprawl—2000. TCIP Report 74. Washington, DC: National Academy Press.

BUREAU OF INFRASTRUCTURE, TRANSPORT, AND REGIONAL ECONOMICS (BITRE). 2013. Yearbook 2013. Australian Infrastructure Statistics: Statistical Report. Canberra, AUS: Australian Government, Department of Infrastructure and Regional Development.

BURRIENTOS, M. and SORIA, C. 2014. India crude oil production and consumption by year. *Indexmundi Data Portal.* [Online] Available from: indexmundi.com/energy.aspx?country=in [Accessed 6 Oct 2014].

BUSINESS GREEN. 2015. China coal production falls for first time this century. *Guardian.* [Online] 27 Jan. Available from: theguardian.com/environment/2015/jan/27/china-coal-production-falls-for-first-time-this-century?CMP=share_btn_fb [Accessed 2 Mar 2015].

BUTT, C. and ZHOU, C. 2014. Melbourne apartment development hits historic high. [Online] *Sydney Morning Herald,* 7 Jul 2014. Available from: smh.com.au/business/property/melbourne-apartment-development-hits-historic-high-20140706-zsxyx.html [Accessed 28 Feb 2015].

BYRNE, J. 2014. *Josh's House.* [Online] Available from: joshshouse.com.au/ [Accessed 5 May 2014].

CALTHORPE, P. 2010. *Urbanism in the Age of Climate Change.* Washington, DC: Island Press.

CAMPBELL, C. J. and LAHERRERE, J. H. 1995. The World's Oil Supply 1930–2050: Report. Geneva: Petroconsultants.

CARBON TRACKER. 2014. Carbon Tracker Initiative. [Online] Available from: carbontracker.org [Accessed 2 Mar 2015].

CENEX. 2008. Investigation into the Scope for the Transport Sector to Switch to Electric Vehicles and Plug-in Hybrid Vehicles: Report. London: Cenex.

CENTER FOR TRANSIT-ORIENTED DEVELOPMENT (CTOD). 2008. *Capturing the Value of Transit.* [Online] Available from: reconnectingamerica.org/public/display_)asset/ctodvalcapture 110508v2 [Accessed 5 May 2014].

CENTER FOR TRANSIT-ORIENTED DEVELOPMENT AND RECONNECTING AMERICA

(CTODRA). 2004. *Hidden in Plain Sight: Capturing the Demand for Housing Near Transit.* [Online] Available from: reconnectingamerica.org [Accessed 5 May 2014].

CERVERO, R. 1977. Transit-Induced Accessibility and Agglomeration Benefits: A Land Market Evaluation: Working Paper. Berkeley, CA: Institute of Urban and Regional Development, University of California.

CERVERO, R. 1984. Managing the traffic impacts of suburban office growth. *Transportation Quarterly* 38 (4), p. 533–50.

CERVERO, R. 1986. *Suburban Gridlock.* New Brunswick, NJ: Center for Urban Policy Research, Rutgers University.

CERVERO, R. 1998. *The Transit Metropolis: A Global Inquiry.* Washington, DC: Island Press.

CERVERO, R. 2004. Effects of light and commuter rail transit on land prices: Experiences in San Diego County. *Journal of the Transportation Research Forum* 43 (1), p. 121–38.

CERVERO, R. 2008. Transit-Oriented Development in America: Strategies, Issues, Policy Directions. In: HASS, T. (ed.) *New Urbanism and Beyond: Designing Cities for the Future.* New York: Rizzoli International Publications, p. 124–29.

CERVERO, R. and DUNCAN, M. 2002. Rail's added value. *Urban Land*, 61 (2), p. 77–84.

CERVERO, R. and EWING, R. 2010. Travel and the built environment: A meta-analysis. *Journal of the American Planning Association* 76 (3), p. 265–94.

CERVERO, R. and LANDIS, J. 1992. Suburbanization of jobs and the journey to work: A submarket analysis of commuting in the San Francisco Bay Area. *Journal of Advanced Transportation* 26 (3), p. 275–97.

CERVERO, R., MURPHY, S., FERRELL, C., GOGUTS, N., TSAI, Y. H., ARRINGTON, G. B., BOROSKI, J., SMITH-HEIMER, J., GOLEM, R., PENINGER, P., NAKAJIMA, E., CHUI, E., DUNPHY, R., MYERS, M., MCKAY, S. and WITENSTEIN, N. 2004. Transit-Oriented Development in America: Experiences, Challenges, and Prospects: Report. Washington, DC: Transportation Research Board, National Research Council.

CHATMAN, D. G. and NOLAND, R. B. 2014. Transit service, physical agglomeration and productivity in US metropolitan areas. *Urban Studies* 51 (5), p. 917–37.

CHEN, T. and ZHAO, J. 2012. Bidding to drive: Car license auction policy in Shanghai and its public acceptance. *Transport Policy* 27, p. 39–52.

CHINA AUTOMOTIVE INDUSTRY. 2012. *Annual Yearbook.* [Online] Available from: chinabook shop.net/china-automotive-industry-yearbook-2012-p-15535.html [Accessed 23 Apr 2014].

CHINESE BUREAU OF STATISTICS (CBS). 2014. *National Data.* [Online] Available from: data .stats.gov.cn/workspace/index?a=q&type=global&dbcode=hgnd&m=hgnd&dimension =zb&code=A070E06&region=000000&time=2013,2013 [Accessed 11 Nov 2014].

CHINESE BUREAU OF STATISTICS (CBS). 2013. Table 2.4. Indices of gross domestic product. *2013 Yearbook: Statistical Report.* [Online] Available from: stats.gov.cn/tjsj/ndsj/2013 /indexeh.htm [Accessed 6 Oct 2014].

CHINESE BUREAU OF STATISTICS (CBS). 2014. Table 8.2. Total consumption of energy and its composition. *2013 Yearbook: Statistical Report.* [Online] Available from stats.gov.cn/tjsj /ndsj/2013/indexeh.htm [Accessed 6 Oct 2014].

CITY OF KOGARAH. 2009. *Achieving sustainability—Kogarah Town Square development.* [Online] Available from: kogarah.nsw.gov.au/www/html/2075-achieving-sustainability-kogarah

-town-square-development.asp [Accessed 5 May 2014].

CITY OF MELBOURNE. 2014. Melbourne in Numbers. [Online] Available from: melbourne.vic.gov.au/AboutMelbourne/Statistics/Pages/MelbourneSnapshot.aspx [Accessed 28 Feb 2015].

CITY OF NEW YORK. 2011. Official Website of the City of New York. [Online] Available from: nyc.gov [Accessed 9 Feb 2011].

CITY OF SEATTLE. 2008. Case Studies in Urban Freeway Removal. In: *Seattle Urban Mobility Plan*. [Online] Available from: seattle.gov/transportation/docs/ump/06%20SEATTLE%20CASE%20studies%20in%20urban%20freeway%20removal.pdf [Accessed 10 Apr 2012].

COEVERING, P. V. D. and SCHWANEN, T. 2006. Re-evaluating the impact of urban form on travel patterns in Europe and North America. *Transport Policy* 13 (3), p. 229–39.

CONWAY, J. and ADAMS, B. 1977. The social effects of living off the ground. *Habitat International* 2, p. 595–614.

COYNE, A. 2014. Toll roads the only solution to traffic congestion. *National Post*. [Online] 16 Jun 2014. Available from: news.nationalpost.com/2014/06/16/andrew-coyne-vancouvers-road-pricing-proposal-a-revolutionary-fix-for-gridlock/#__federated=1 [Accessed 16 Feb 2015].

CURTIS, C., RENNE, J. L. and BERTOLINI, L. 2009. *Transit-Oriented Development: Making It Happen*. Surrey, UK: Ashgate.

CURTIS, C. and SCHEURER, J. 2010. Planning for sustainable accessibility: Development tools to aid discussion and decision-making. *Progress in Planning* 74, p. 53–106.

CZECH STATISTICAL OFFICE. 2013. *Statistical Yearbook of Prague*. [Online] Available from: czso.cz/csu/2013edicniplan.nsf/engp/101011-13 [Accessed 25 May 2014].

DALY, H. 1978. On thinking about energy in the future. *Natural Resources Forum* 3, p. 19–56.

DAVIS, M. 1990. *City of Quartz: Excavating the Future in Los Angeles*. London: Vintage.

DAVIS, B., DUTZIK, T. and BAXANDALL, P. 2012. Transportation and the New Generation: Why Young People Are Driving Less and What It Means for Transportation Policy: Report. San Francisco/Boston: Frontier Group and PIRG Education Fund.

DEBREZION, G., PELS, E. and RIETVELD, P. 2007. The impact of railway stations on residential and commercial property value: A meta-analysis. *Journal of Real Estate, Finance and Economics* 35 (2), p. 161–80.

DEPARTMENT FOR ENVIRONMENT FOOD AND RURAL AFFAIRS (DETR). 2000. General Guidelines on Environmental Reporting: Consultation Draft. London: Government of the United Kingdom, DETR.

DIAMOND, J. 2009. *Collapse: How Societies Choose to Fail or Succeed*. New York: Viking Books.

DITTMAR, H. and OHLAND, G. (eds.) 2004. *The New Transit Town*. Washington, DC: Island Press.

DODSON, J. and SIPE, N. 2006. "Unsettling Suburbia": The New Landscape of Oil and Mortgage Vulnerability in Australian Cities: Research Paper. Queensland, AUS: Griffith University, Urban Research Program.

DOWLING, J. and LUCAS, C. 2009. Suburban sprawl costs billions more. *The Age*. [Online] Available from: theage.com.au/national/suburban-sprawl-costs-billions-more-20090716-dmxj.html [Accessed 5 May 2014].

DRAKE, J. W. 1973. *The Administration of Transportation Modeling Projects*. Lexington, KY: D.C.

Heath and Company.

DUNCAN, M. 2010. The impact of transit-oriented development on housing prices in San Diego, CA. *Urban Studies* 48 (5), p. 101–27.

ECKERSLEY, R., DICKSON, J. and DOUGLAS, B. (eds.) 2005. *The Social Origins of Health and Well Being*. Cambridge, UK: Cambridge University Press.

ECOLA, L., WACHS, M. and THE RAND CORPORATION. 2012. Exploring the Relationship between Travel Demand and Economic Growth: Academic Paper. Washington, DC: Federal Highways Administration.

EDDINGTON, R. 2006. The Eddington Transport Study: Main Report—Transport's Role in Sustaining the UK's Productivity and Competitiveness. Norwich, UK: Government of the United Kingdom, Her Majesty's Stationery Office.

EDNER, S. M. and ARRINGTON, G. B. JR. 1985. Urban Decision Making for Transportation Investment: Portland's Light-Rail Transit Line: Report DOT-1-85-03. Washington, DC: US Department of Transportation.

ELTIS: THE URBAN MOBILITY OBSERVATORY. 2006. *Car sharing in Bremen/Germany.* [Online] Available from: eltis.org/index.php?id=13andstudy_id=2228 [Accessed 25 Jun 2014].

ENERGY INFORMATION ADMINISTRATION (EIA). 2013. Annual Energy Outlook: Report. Washington, DC: Government of the United States, Department of Energy, EIA.

ENO FOUNDATION. 1988. Report of the 20th Annual Joint Conference Eno Foundation Board of Directors and Board of Consultants. *Transportation Quarterly* 42 (1), p. 141–54.

EUROPEAN COMMISSION. 2014. *Roadmap for Moving to a Low-Carbon Economy in 2050.* [Online] European Commission Climate Action. Available from: ec.europa.eu/clima/policies/roadmap/index_en.htm [Accessed 19 Nov 2014].

EWING, R. H. 1994. Characteristics, causes, and effects of sprawl: A literature review. *Environmental and Urban Studies* 21 (2), p. 1–15.

EWING, R. and CERVERO, R. 2010. Travel and the built environment: A meta-analysis. *Journal of the American Planning Association* 76 (3), p. 265–94.

FALCONER, R. and NEWMAN, P. 2010. *Growing Up: Reforming Land Use and Transport in "Conventional" Car Dependent Cities*. Saarbruecken, GER: VDM.

FALCONER, R., NEWMAN, P. and GILES-CORTI, B. 2010. Is practice aligned with the principles? Implementing New Urbanism in Perth, Western Australia. *Transport Policy* 17 (5), p. 287–94.

FELS, M. and MUNSON, M. J. 1974. Energy Thrift in Urban Transportation: Options for the Future: Report. Cambridge, MA: Ford Foundation Energy Policy Project.

FETTING, T. 2007. *Seoul: The stream of consciousness.* [Online] Public Broadcasting Service (PBS). Available from: pbs.org/e2/episodes/310_seoul_the_stream_of_consciousness_trailer.html [Accessed 10 Apr 2014].

FISCHER, C. S. 1976. *The Urban Experience*. New York: Harcourt Brace Jovanovich.

FISHKIN, J., HE, B., LUSKIN, R. C. and SIU, A. 2010. Notes and comments—Deliberative democracy in an unlikely place: Deliberative polling in China. [Online] *British Journal of Political Science* 40, p. 435–48. Available from: chinesedemocratization.com/Baogang-English%20articles/6.BJPS-Deliberative%20Democracy%20in%20an%20Unlikely%20Place.pdf [Accessed 2 Mar 2015].

FLORIDA, R. 2005. *Cities and the Creative Class*. New York: Routledge.

FLORIDA, R. 2010. *The Great Reset: How New Ways of Living and Working Drive Post-Crash Prosperity*. New York: HarperCollins.

FLORIDA, R. 2012a. Cities with denser cores do better. *The Atlantic*. [Online] Available from: theatlanticcities.com/jobs-and-economy/2012/11/cities-denser-cores-do-better/3911/ [Accessed 15 Jun 2013].

FLORIDA, R. 2012b. *The Rise of the Creative Class: Revisited*. New York: Basic Books.

FLORIDA, R. 2012c. How and why American cities are coming back. *The Atlantic*. [Online] Available from: theatlanticcities.com/jobs-and-economy/2012/05/how-and-why-american-cities-are-coming-back/2015/ [Accessed 05 May 2014].

FRAKER, H. 2013. *The Hidden Potential of Sustainable Neighborhoods: Lessons from Low-Carbon Communities*. Washington, DC: Island Press.

FRANK, L. D. and PIVO, G. 1994. Impacts of mixed use and density on utilization of three modes of travel: Single-occupant vehicle, transit, and walking. *Transportation Research Record* 1466, p. 44–52.

FREEDMAN, J. L. 1975. *Crowding and Behaviour*. Oxford, UK: Freeman and Company.

FREEMAN, C. 1996. *The Longwave in the World Economy*. Aldershot, UK: International Library of Critical Writings.

FRIEDMAN, A. 2014. *Fundamentals of Sustainable Dwellings*. Washington, DC: Island Press.

FRUMKIN, H., FRANK, L. and JACKSON, R. J. 2004. *Urban Sprawl and Public Health*. Washington, DC: Island Press.

FUDGE, S., PETERS, M., HOFFMAN, S. M. and WEHRMEYER, W. (eds.) 2013. *The Global Challenge of Encouraging Sustainable Living*. London: Edward Elgar.

GAO, Y., KENWORTHY, J. and NEWMAN, P. 2014. Growth of a Giant: A Historical and Current Perspective on the Chinese Automobile Industry. Paper presented at the 42nd European Transport Conference. Frankfurt, Sep 29–Oct 1.

GARDNER, H. and NEWMAN, P. 2013. Reducing the Materials and Resource Intensity of the Built Form in the Perth and Peel Regions: Report. Perth, AUS: Australian Government, Department of Sustainability, Environment, Water, Population, and Communities.

GARGETT, D. 2012. Traffic growth: Modeling a global phenomenon. *World Transport Policy and Practice* 18 (4), p. 27–45.

GARREAU, J. 1991. *Edge City: Life on the New Frontier*. New York: Doubleday.

GEELS, F. W. 2011. Survey: The multi-level perspective on sustainability transitions: Responses to seven criticisms. *Environmental Innovation and Societal Transitions* 1, p. 24–40.

GEHL, J. 1987. *Life between Buildings: Using Public Space*. Washington, DC: Island Press.

GEHL, J. 2010. *Cities for People*. Washington, DC: Island Press.

GEHL, J. and GEMZØE, L. 2000. *New City Spaces*. Copenhagen: Danish Architectural Press.

GEHL, J. and GEMZOE, L. 2004. *Public Spaces, Public Life*. Copenhagen: Danish Architectural Press.

GEHL, J., MODIN, A., WITTENMARK, J., GRASSOW, L., MATAN, A., HAGSTRÖMER, E.,

BERNADO, L. and ENHÖRNING, J. 2009. Perth 2009: Public Spaces and Public Life: Study Report. Perth/Copenhagen: City of Perth/Gehl Architects.

GEHL, J., MORTENSEN, H., DUCOURTIAL, P., DUCKETT, I. S., NIELSEN, L. H., NIELSEN, J. M. R., ADAMS, R., RYMER, R., RAYMENT, J., MOORE, R. and CAMPBELL, A. 2004. Places for People: Study Report. Melbourne/Copenhagen: City of Melbourne/Gehl Architects.

GESSELLSCHAFT FÜR TECHNISCHE ZUSAMMENARBEIT (GTZ). 2004. *Sustainable Transport: A Sourcebook for Policy Makers in Developing Cities: Module 2a—Land-Use Planning and Urban Transport.* Frankfurt: GTZ, p. 10.

GILBERT, S. 2014. Carscape: How the motor car reshaped England—in pictures. *The Guardian.* [Online] 12 Feb. Available from: theguardian.com/artanddesign/gallery/2014/feb/12/carscape-how-the-motor-car-reshaped-england-in-pictures [Accessed 27 Jun 2014].

GILES-CORTI, B., RYAN, K. and FOSTER, S. 2012. Increasing Density in Australia—Maximizing the Health Benefits and Minimizing Harm: Report. Canberra, AUS: National Heart Foundation.

GIULIANO, G. and DARGAY, J. 2006. Car ownership, travel, and land use: A comparison of the US and Great Britain. *Transportation Research Part A: Policy and Practice* 40 (2), p. 106–24.

GLACKIN, S., TRUBKA, R., NEWMAN, P., NEWTON, P. and MOURITZ, M. 2013. Greening the Greyfields: Trials, Tools, and Tribulations of Redevelopment in the Middle Suburbs. Paper presented at the 2013 Annual Congress of the Planning Institute of Australia (PIA). Canberra, AUS, Mar 24–27.

GLADWELL, M. 2000. *The Tipping Point: How Little Things Can Make a Big Difference.* London: Little Brown.

GLAESER, E. 2011. *The Triumph of the City: How Our Greatest Invention Makes Us Richer, Smarter, Greener, Healthier, and Happier.* London: Penguin Press.

GLAESER, E. L. and GOTTLIEB, J. D. 2009. The wealth of cities: Agglomeration economics and spatial equilibrium in the United States. *Journal of Economic Literature* 47 (4), p. 983–1028.

GLAESER, E. L. and GYOURKO, J. 2002. The Impact of Zoning on Housing Affordability: Working Paper 8835. New York: National Bureau of Economic Research.

GLEESON, B. 2006. *Australian Heartlands: Making Space for Hope in the Suburbs.* Sydney: Allen and Unwin.

GLEICK, J. 1988. National gridlock: Scientists tackle the traffic jam. *New York Times Magazine.* 8 May.

GOLDBERG, J. 2012. The Brisconnections Airport Link: The Inevitable Collapse of a 5-Billion-Dollar Megaproject. Paper presented at the 35th Australasian Transport Research Forum. Perth, AUS, September 26–28.

GOODWIN, P. 1997. *Solving congestion (when we must not build roads, increase spending, lose votes, damage the economy, harm the environment and will never find equilibrium): Inaugural Lecture for the Professorship of Transport Policy.* [Online] London University College. Available from: discovery.ucl.ac.uk/1244/1/2004_22.pdf [Accessed 5 Apr 2012].

GOODWIN, P. and MELIA, S. 2011. Three views on "Peak Car." Special issue on "A future beyond the car." *World Transport Policy and Practice* 17, p. 3–6.

GOODWIN, P. and VAN DENDER, K. 2013. "Peak Car"—Themes and Issues. *Transport Reviews* 33, p. 243–54.

GORDON, P. and RICHARDSON, H. 1989. Gasoline consumption and cities—A reply. *Journal of American Planning Association* 55, p. 342–45.

GORE, A. 2008. *Moon Shot Speech.* [Online] NPR Radio. Available from: npr.org/templates/story /story.php?storyId=92638501 [Accessed 19 Nov 2014].

GOVERNMENT OF ABU DHABI. 2010. *Abu Dhabi Metro: World Class Transit.* [Online] Department of Transport. Available from: abu-dhabi-metro.com/tag/uae-rail-system [Accessed 21 Dec 2012].

GOVERNMENT OF HONG KONG. 1998. Appendix 17. *1998 Yearbook.* Central, HK: Hong Kong Monetary Authority.

GOVERNMENT OF NEW SOUTH WALES. 1974. Sydney Area Transportation Study (SATS) Report: Volume 2, Travel Model Development and Forecasts—Sydney. Sydney: SATS.

GOVERNMENT OF THE UNITED KINGDOM. 2008. *Making Personal Travel Planning Work: Practitioners Guide.* London: Department of Transport.

GOVERNMENT OF WESTERN AUSTRALIA. 2013. The Housing We'd Choose: A Study for Perth and Peel: Report, May 2013. Perth, AUS: Department of Housing and Department of Planning.

GRATZ, L. 1981. *The Vienna Underground Construction.* Vienna: Stadtbaudriektion.

GRATZ, R. B. 1989. *The Living City: How Urban Residents Are Revitalizing American Neighborhoods and Downtown Shopping Districts by Thinking Small in a Big Way*, 1st ed. New York: Simon and Schuster.

GREATER MANCHESTER COMBINED AUTHORITY (GMCA). 2012. *Greater Manchester City Deal: Report.* [Online] Available from: gov.uk/government/uploads/system/uploads/attachment _data/file/221014/Greater-Manchester-City-Deal-final_0.pdf [Accessed 5 May 2014].

GREEN, J. 2014. U.S. Public Transportation Use Hits Peak Not Seen Since the 1950s. *The Dirt Blog.* [Online] Available from: dirt.asla.org/2014/03/10/u-s-public-transportation-use-hits -peak-not-seen-since-the-1950s/ [Accessed 23 Apr 2014].

GROSSMAN, G. M. and KRUEGER, A. B. 1995. Economic growth and the environment. *Quarterly Journal of Economics* 110 (2), p. 353–77.

GROVE, A. and BURGELMAN, R. 2008. An electric plan for energy resilience. *McKinsey Quarterly—December.* [Online] Available from: emic-bg.org/files/9_An_electric_plan_for_energy _resilience.pdf [Accessed 5 May 2014].

GUANGZHOU TRANSPORT DEVELOPMENT (GTD). 2012. *Annual Report.* Guangzhou, CHI: GTD.

GUNNARSSON, O. and LELEUR, S. 1989. Trends in urban transport planning—The current shift in solving transport problems. *Prospect* 2, p. 2–6.

HAIGH, Y. 2006. Promoting Safer Communities through Physical Design, Social Inclusion and Crime Prevention through Environmental Design: A Developmental Study. Perth, AUS: Centre for Social and Community Research, Murdoch University.

HANES, S. 2015. The New Cool Cities. *Christian Science Monitor Weekly*, 2 Feb 2015, p. 27–32.

HARDESTY, L. 2013. Why innovation thrives in cities. *MIT News.* [Online] Available from: newsoffice.mit.edu/2013/why-innovation-thrives-in-cities-0604 [Accessed 23 Apr 2014].

HARGROVES, C. and SMITH, M. 2005. *The Natural Advantage of Nations.* London: Earthscan, p. 17.

HASS-KLAU, C., CRAMPTON, G. and BENJARI, R. 2004. Economic impact of light rail: The results of 15 urban areas in France, Germany, UK, and North America: Report. London: Brighton and Government of the United Kingdom, Environmental and Transport Planning.

HASS-KLAU, C., CRAMPTON, G., BIERETH, C. and DEUTSCH, V. 2003. Bus or light rail: Making the right choice—A financial, operational, and demand comparison of light rail, guided buses, busways, and bus lanes. London: Brighton and Government of the United Kingdom, Environmental and Transport Planning.

HELSINKI TIMES. 2014. The future resident of Helsinki will not own a car. [Online] 4 Jul. Available from: helsinkitimes.fi/finland/finland-news/domestic/11062-the-future-resident-of-helsinki-will-not-own-a-car.html [Accessed 2 Mar 2015].

HENDERSON, W. D. 1977. *The Unredeemed City: Reconstruction in Petersburg, Virginia—1865–1874.* Maryland, USA: University Press of America.

HENDRIGAN, C. and NEWMAN, P. 2012. A Three-Mode Plan for Perth: Connecting Heavy Rail, Light Rail and Bus with Urban Development to Achieve 21st-Century Goals: Report. Perth, AUS: Curtin University Sustainability Policy (CUSP) Institute.

HOWARD, J. 1988. Value capture and benefit sharing for public transit systems. In: ATTOE, W. (ed.) *Transit, Land Use, and Urban Form.* Austin, TX: Center for the Study of American Architecture, School of Architecture, University of Texas, p. 171–78.

INFRASTRUCTURE AUSTRALIA (IA). 2012. Infrastructure Financing and Funding Reform: Infrastructure Financing Working Group: Report. Canberra, AUS: IA.

INSTITUTE OF TRANSPORTATION ENGINEERING OF THE CITY OF PRAGUE. 2006. *The Yearbook of Transportation, Prague 2005.* [Online] Institute of Transportation Engineering of the City of Prague. Available from: tsk-praha.cz/static/udi-rocenka-2005-en.pdf [Accessed 25 May 2014].

INTERGOVERNMENTAL PANEL ON CLIMATE CHANGE (IPCC). 2013. Climate Change 2013: The Physical Science Basis—Contribution of Working Group 1 to Assessment Report 5. Geneva: IPCC.

INTERGOVERNMENTAL PANEL ON CLIMATE CHANGE (IPCC). 2014. Mitigation of Climate Change—Contribution of Working Group 3 to Assessment Report 5. Geneva: IPCC.

INTERNATIONAL MONETARY FUND (IMF). 2014. *Economic statistics: World economic outlook (WEO) data—GDP deflator.* [Online] Available from: econstats.com/weo/V005.htm [Accessed 23 Apr 2014].

JACKSON, T. 2009. *Prosperity without Growth: Economics for a Finite Planet.* London: Earthscan.

JACOBS, J. 1961. *The Death and Life of Great American Cities.* New York: Vintage.

JACOBS, J. 1970. *The Economy of Cities.* New York: Vintage.

JACOBS, J. 1985. *Cities and the Wealth of Nations: Principles of Economic Life.* New York: Vintage.

JAYARAM, R. 2012. Dedicated rail network plan for NCR on track. *Economic Times.* 16 May.

JEFFERSON, M. 1909. The Anthropography of some great cities: A study in distribution of population. *American Geographic Society* 41 (9), p. 537–66.

JOHNSON, C. and ROBINSON & COLE LLP. 2013. *Tax Increment Financing.* [Online] National Association of Realtors (NAR). Available from: archive.realtor.org/article/guide-tax-increment-financing [Accessed 8 Aug 2013].

KANE, M. 2010. The Knowledge Economy and Public Transport. In: NEWMAN, P. and SCHEURER, J. (eds.) *The Knowledge Arc Light Rail: A Concept for Delivering the Next Phase of Public*

Transport in Perth: Discussion Paper. Perth, AUS: Parsons-Brinkerhoff/Curtin University Sustainability Policy (CUSP) Institute.

KELLERT, S. R., HEERWAGEN, J. and MADOR, M. 2011. *Biophilic Design: The Theory, Science, and Practice of Bringing Buildings to Life.* Hoboken, NJ: John Wiley & Sons.

KELLY, J.-F., HUNTER, J., HARRISON, C. and DONEGAN, P. 2013. Renovating Housing Policy: Report. Melbourne: Grattan Institute.

KELLY, M. 2000. Inequality and Crime. *The Review of Economics and Statistics* 82 (4), p. 530–39.

KENWORTHY, J. 1991. From urban consolidation to urban villages. *Urban Policy and Research* 9 (1), p. 96–100.

KENWORTHY, J. 2008. An international review of the significance of rail in developing more sustainable urban transport systems in higher income cities. *World Transport Policy and Practice* 14 (2), p. 21–37.

KENWORTHY, J. 2011a. International Benchmarking and Best Practice in Adapting to a Future of Electric Mobility in Germany: Sustainable Transport or Just Electric Cars? Report to Hessen State Government. Frankfurt: University of Applied Sciences.

KENWORTHY, J. 2011b. *Update of the Millennium Cities Database for Sustainable Transportation,* Ongoing, Unpublished.

KENWORTHY, J. 2012. Don't shoot me, I'm only the transport planner (apologies to Sir Elton John). *World Transport Policy and Practice* 18 (4), p. 6–26.

KENWORTHY, J. 2013. Decoupling urban car use and metropolitan GDP growth. *World Transport Policy and Practice* 19 (4), p. 7–21.

KENWORTHY, J. 2014. Total daily mobility patterns and their implications for forty-three global cities in 1995 and 2005. *World Transport Policy and Practice* 20 (1), p. 41–55.

KENWORTHY, J. and LAUBE, F. 2001. *Millennium Cities Database for Sustainable Transport.* Brussels: International Association of Public Transport (UITP).

KENWORTHY, J. and LAUBE, F. with NEWMAN, P., BARTER, P., RAAD, T., POBOON, C. and GUIA, B. 1999. *An International Sourcebook of Automobile Dependence in Cities 1960–1990.* Boulder, CO: University Press of Colorado.

KENWORTHY, J. R. and NEWMAN, P. W. G. 1986a. The potential of ethanol as a transport fuel: A review based on technological, economic, and environmental criteria: Issues in Energy Policy in Western Australia, Discussion Paper 6/86. Perth, AUS: Department of Environmental Science, Murdoch University, p. 40.

KENWORTHY, J. R. and NEWMAN, P. W. G. 1986b. From hype to mothballs: An assessment of synthetic crude oil from shale coal and oil sands: Issues in Energy Policy in Western Australia, Discussion Paper 7/86. Perth, AUS: Department of Environmental Science, Murdoch University, p. 90.

KER, I. 2011. Too true to be good? A response to Morton and Mees (2010). *World Transport Policy and Practice* 17 (1), p. 14–26.

KILPATRICK, J., THROUPE, R., CARRUTHERS, J. and KRAUSE, A. 2007. The impact of transit corridors on residential property values. *Journal of Real Estate Research* 29 (3), p. 303–20.

KING, A. D. 1978. Exporting planning: The colonial and neo-colonial experience. *Urbanism Past and Present* 5, p. 12–22.

KINTNER-MEYER, M., SCHNEIDER, K. and PRATT, R. 2007. Impact Assessment of Plug-in Hybrid Vehicles on Electric Utilities and Regional U.S. Power Grids, Part 1: Technical Analysis Paper. Washington, DC: Pacific Northwest National Laboratory.

KIRWAN, R. J. 1992. Urban form, energy and transport: A note on the Newman-Kenworthy thesis. *Urban Policy and Research* 10 (1), p. 6–22.

KLAASSEN, L. H., BOURDREZ, J. A. and VOLMULLER, J. 1981. *Transport and Reurbanisation.* Surrey, UK: Gower.

KLEIN, J. and OLSEN, M. 1996. *Taken for a Ride.* [Online] American Documentary Inc., POV. Available from: pbs.org/pov/takenforaride/ [Accessed 23 Apr 2014].

KLINGER, T., KENWORTHY, J. and LANZENDORF, M. 2013. Dimensions of urban mobility cultures: A comparison of German cities. *Journal of Transport Geography* 31 (7), p. 18–29.

KNOX, P. 1982. Regional inequality and the welfare state: Convergence and divergence in levels of living in the United Kingdom, 1951–1971. *Social Indicators Research* 10 (3), p. 319–35.

KONIG, H. and HEIPP, G. 2012. The Modern Tram in Europe: Research Report. Munich: Municher Verkehrsgesellschaft GMBH (MVG).

KOOSHIAN, C. and WINKELMAN, S. 2011. *Recent trends in the travel intensity of the US economy.* [Online] Center for Clean Air Policy. Available from: cts.umn.edu/events /wstlur/symposium/2011/agenda/documents/presentations/2-kooshian.pdf [Accessed 7 Jul 2013].

KOSONEN, L. 2007. *Kuopio 2015: Jalankulku-, joukkoliikenne- ja autokaupunki* (English: *Kuopio 2015–A Walking, Transit, and Car City*). [Online] Suomen ympäristö 36/2007, Rakennettu ympäristö. Helsinki: Ympäristöministeriö. Available from: helda.helsinki.fi/bitstream /handle/10138/38432/SY_36_2007.pdf?sequence=5.

KOSONEN, L. 2014. The Three Fabrics Strategy in Finland. In: BARTON, H., THOMPSON, S., GRANT, M. and BURGESS, S. (eds.) *Planning for Health and Well-Being: Shaping a Sustainable and Healthy Future.* London: Routledge.

LANDRY, C. 2008. *The Creative City,* 2nd ed. London: Earthscan.

LARSON, T. D. 1988. Metropolitan congestion: Towards a tolerable accommodation. *Transportation Quarterly* 42 (4), p. 489–98.

LAVE, C. 1992. Cars and demographics. *Access* 1, p. 4–11.

LEINBERGER, C. B. 2007. *The Option of Urbanism: Investing in a New American Dream.* Washington, DC: Island Press.

LEINBERGER, C. B. 2011. The death of the fringe suburb. *New York Times.* 26 Nov.

LEINBERGER, C. B. and LYNCH, P. 2014. Foot Traffic Ahead: Ranking Walkable Urbanism in Americas Largest Metros: Report. Washington, DC: George Washington University, School of Business, Center for Real Estate and Urban Analysis.

LITMAN, T. A. 2004. *Rail Transit in America: A Comprehensive Evaluation of Benefits.* Melbourne: Victoria Transport Policy Institute.

LOHRY, G., YIU, A., YUANYUAN, T. and YUE, L. 2014. *Urban Mobility China.* [Online] Climate Environment Services Group (CESG). Available from: urbanmobilitychina.com/tag/metro/ [Accessed 6 Oct 2014].

LOMAX, T., SCHRANK, D. and ELSELE, B. 2014. *Congestion Data for Your City: Los Angeles.*

[Online] Texas A & M Transportation Institute. Available from: mobility.tamu.edu/ums/congestion-data/ [Accessed 19 Jun 2014].

LORENZ, K. 1966. *On Aggression*. York, UK: Methuen Publishing.

LOW, N., GLEESON, B., GREEN, R. and RADOVI, D. 2005. *The Green City: Sustainable Homes, Sustainable Suburbs*. Sydney: University of New South Wales Press.

LUKEZ, P. 2007. *Suburban Transformations*. Princeton, NJ: Princeton Architectural Press.

MÄNTYSALO, R. and KANNINEN, V. 2012. Trading between land use and transportation planning—The Kuopio Model. Helsinki: Tiede and Teknologia, Aalto University, Department of Real Estate, Planning, and Geoinformatics.

MARCHETTI, C. 1994. Anthropological invariants in travel behaviour. *Technical Forecasting and Social Change* 47 (1), p. 75–78.

MARMOT, M. and WILKINSON, R. G. 2006. *Social Determinants of Health*, vol. 1. Oxford, UK: Oxford University Press.

MATAN, A. 2011. Rediscovering Urban Design through Walkability: An Assessment of the Contribution of Jan Gehl: PhD Dissertation. Perth, AUS: Curtin University Sustainability Policy (CUSP) Institute.

MATAN, A. and NEWMAN, P. 2012. Jan Gehl and new visions for walkable Australian cities. *World Transport Policy and Practice* 17, p. 30–37.

MCDONALD, J. F. and MCMILLEN, D. P. 2007. *Urban Economics and Real Estate Theory and Policy*, 2nd ed. Hoboken, NJ: John Wiley & Sons.

MCGLADE, C. and EKINS, P. 2015. The geographical distribution of fossil fuels unused when limiting global warming to 2°C. *Nature* 517, p. 187–90. DOI: 10.1038/nature14016.

MCGRANAHAN, G., SONGSORE, J. and KJELLÉN, M. 1999. Sustainability, Poverty, and Urban Environmental Transitions. In: SATTERTHWAITE, D. (ed.) *The Earthscan Reader in Sustainable Cities*. London: Earthscan.

MCINTOSH, J., NEWMAN, P., CRANE, T. and MOURITZ, M. 2011. Alternative funding mechanisms for public transport in Perth: The potential role of value capture: Report. Perth, AUS: Committee for Perth.

MCINTOSH, J., NEWMAN, P. and GLAZEBROOK, G. 2013. Why fast trains work: An assessment of a fast regional rail system in Perth, Australia. *Journal of Transportation Technologies* 3 (2A), p. 37–47.

MCINTOSH, J., TRUBKA, R., KENWORTHY, J. and NEWMAN, P. 2014a. The role of urban form and transit in city car dependence: Analysis of 26 global cities from 1960 to 2000. *Transport Research Part D* 33, p. 95–110.

MCINTOSH, J., TRUBKA, R., KENWORTHY, J. and NEWMAN, P. 2014b. Framework for land value capture from the investment in transit in car-dependent cities. *Journal of Transport and Land Use* (In Press).

MCINTOSH, J., TRUBKA, R. and NEWMAN, P. 2013. Willingness to pay for access to rail transit: A quantitative case study into the potential for value capture in a car-dependent city: Report. Perth, AUS: Curtin University Sustainability Policy (CUSP) Institute.

MCINTOSH, J., TRUBKA, R. and NEWMAN, P. 2015. Tax Increment Financing framework for integrated transit and urban renewal projects in car-dependent cities. *Urban Policy and Research* 33 (1), p. 37–60.

MCWILLIAMS, E. 2015. Toronto skyline's "absolute transformation" captured by two photos taken 13 years apart. [Online] *National Post*, 17 Jan. Available from: news.national post.com/2015/01/17/toronto-skylines-absolute-transformation-captured-by-two-photos -taken-13-years-apart/ [Accessed 28 Feb 2015].

MEES, P. 2000. *A Very Public Solution: Transport in the Dispersed City*. Melbourne: Melbourne University Publishing.

MEES, P. 2009a. Density delusion? Urban form and transport in Australian, Canadian, and US cities. *World Transport Policy and Practice* 15 (2), p. 29–39.

MEES, P. 2009b. *Transport for Suburbia: Beyond the Automobile Age*. London: Routledge.

MERCER, D. 2015. Solar panels powering along. *West Australian*. 3 Feb. p. 23.

METZ, D. 2013. Peak car and beyond: The fourth era of travel. *Transport Reviews* 33, p. 255–70.

MILLARD-BALL, A. and SCHIPPER, L. 2010. Are we reaching peak travel? Trends in passenger transport in eight industrialized countries. *Transport Reviews* 31 (3), p. 1–22.

MINDALI, O., RAVEH, A. and SALOMON, I. 2004. Urban density and energy consumption: A new look at old statistics. *Transportation Research Part A: Policy and Practice* 38, p. 143–62.

MITCHELL, R. B. and RAPKIN, C. 1954. *Urban Traffic: A Function of Land Use*. New York: Columbia University Press.

MOKHTARIAN, P. L. and CHEN, C. 2004. TTB or not TTB, that is the question: A review and analysis of the empirical literature on travel time (and money) budgets. *Transportation Research Part A: Policy and Practice* 38, p. 643–75.

MONHEIM, R. 1988. Pedestrian Zones in West Germany: The Dynamic Development of an Effective Instrument to Enliven the City Center. In: HASS-KLAU, C. (ed.) *New Life for City Centers: Planning, Transport, and Conservation in British and German Cities*. London: Anglo German Foundation, p. 107–55.

MORRIS, D. 1968. *The Naked Ape*. New York: Dell.

MUMFORD, L. 1938. *The Culture of Cities*. London: Seeker and Warburg.

MUMFORD, L. 1961. *The City in History*. London: Penguin Press.

MYORS, P., O'LEARY, R. and HELSTROM, R. 2005. Multi-unit residential building energy and peak demand study. *Energy News* 23, p. 113–16.

NEFF, J. W. 1996. Substitution Rates between Transit and Car Travel. Paper presented at the 1996 Annual Meeting of the Association of American Geographers (AAG). North Carolina.

NETHERLANDS ENVIRONMENTAL ASSESSMENT AGENCY (MNP). 2007. Environmental Balance 2007: Report. Bilthoven, DEN: Statistics Netherlands (CBS) and Wageningen University and Research Centre (WUR).

NEWMAN, C. E. and NEWMAN, P. 2006. The Car and Culture. In: BEILHARTZ, P. and HOGAN, T. (eds.) *Sociology: Place, Time, and Division*. South Melbourne: Oxford University Press.

NEWMAN, P. 1986. Lessons from Liverpool. *Planning and Administration* 1, p. 32–42.

NEWMAN, P. 2005a. Pipe dreams and idealogues: Values and planning. *People and Place* 13 (3), p. 41–53.

NEWMAN, P. 2005b. The city and the bush—partnerships to reverse the population decline in Australia's Wheatbelt. *Australian Journal of Agricultural Research* 56, p. 527–35.

NEWMAN, P. 2006a. The environmental impact of cities. *Environment and Urbanization* 18 (2), p. 275–95.

NEWMAN, P. 2006b. Transport Greenhouse Gases and Australian Suburbs. *Australian Planner* 43 (2), p. 6–7.

NEWMAN, P. W. G. 2006c. Can the Magic of Sustainability Survive Professionalism? In: SHELDON, C. (ed.) *Environmental Professionalism and Sustainability: Too Important to Get Wrong.* London: Greenleaf Books.

NEWMAN, P. 2011. Sustaining Our Future: Resolving the Conflict over Population Models. In: *Proceedings of the 19th International Congress on Modeling and Simulation (MODSIM).* Perth, AUS, Dec 12–16.

NEWMAN, P. 2013. Imagining a Future without Oil in Car-Dependent Cities and Regions. In: RENNE, J. and FIELDS, B. (eds.) *Transport Beyond Oil.* Washington, DC: Island Press.

NEWMAN, P. 2014. Biophilic urbanism: A case study of Singapore. *Australian Planner* 51 (1), 47–65.

NEWMAN, P. 2014. Sustainability: Are We Winning? [Online] TED Talks. 27 Jan 2015. Available from: youtube.com/watch?v=6RFiyM89rbk [Accessed 28 Feb 2015].

NEWMAN, P. and BEATLEY, T. 2012. *Singapore: "Biophilic City."* [Online] Youtube. Available from: youtube.com/watch?v=XMWOu9xIM_k [Accessed 23 Apr 2014].

NEWMAN, P., BOYER, H. and BEATLEY, T. 2009. *Resilient Cities: Responding to Peak Oil and Climate Change.* Washington, DC: Island Press.

NEWMAN, P. and HOGAN, T. 1981. A review of urban density models: Towards a resolution of conflict between populace and planner. *Human Ecology* 9 (3), p. 269–303.

NEWMAN, P. and JENNINGS, I. 2008. *Cities and Sustainable Ecosystems: Principles and Practices.* Washington, DC: Island Press.

NEWMAN, P. W. G. and KENWORTHY, J. R. 1984. The use and abuse of driving cycle research: Clarifying the relationship between traffic congestion, energy, and emissions. *Transportation Quarterly* 38 (4), p. 615–35.

NEWMAN, P. W. G. and KENWORTHY, J. R. 1988a. Parking and City Center Vitality: An International Assessment. Paper presented at the 1st Australian Parking Convention. Perth, AUS, Oct 23–27.

NEWMAN, P. W. G. and KENWORTHY, J. R. 1988b. The transport energy trade-off: Fuel-efficient traffic versus fuel-efficient cities. *Transportation Research Part A: Policy and Practice* 22 (3), p. 163–74.

NEWMAN, P. W. G. and KENWORTHY, J. R. 1989a. Gasoline consumption and cities: A comparison of US cities with a global survey and its implications. *Journal of the American Planning Association* 55 (1), p. 24–30.

NEWMAN, P. W. G. and KENWORTHY, J. R. 1989b. *Cities and Automobile Dependence: An International Sourcebook.* Aldershot, UK: Gower.

NEWMAN, P. W. G. and KENWORTHY, J. R. 1991. Towards a More Sustainable Canberra: An Assessment of Canberra's Transport, Energy, and Land Use: Report. Perth, AUS: Institute for Science and Technology, Murdoch University, p. 157.

NEWMAN, P. W. G. and KENWORTHY, J. R. 1999a. *Sustainability and Cities: Overcoming Automobile Dependence*. Washington, DC: Island Press.

NEWMAN, P. W. G. and KENWORTHY, J. R. 1999b. "Relative Speed" Not "Time Savings": A New Indicator for Sustainable Transport. Paper presented at the 23rd Australasian Transport Research Forum (ATRF). Perth, AUS, Sep 29–Oct 1.

NEWMAN, P. W. G. and KENWORTHY, J. R. 2006. Urban design and automobile dependence: How much development will make urban centers viable? *Opolis* 2 (1), p. 35–52.

NEWMAN, P. and KENWORTHY, J. 2011a. Evaluating the Transport Sector's Contribution to Greenhouse-Gas Emissions and Energy Consumption. In: SALTER, R., DHAR, S. and NEWMAN, P. (eds.) *Technologies for Climate Change Mitigation Transport*. Copenhagen: UNEP Riso Centre for Energy, Climate, and Sustainable Development.

NEWMAN, P. and KENWORTHY, J. 2011b. Peak car use: Understanding the demise of automobile dependence. *World Transport Policy and Practice* 17 (2), p. 32–42.

NEWMAN, P. and KENWORTHY, J. 2011c. The density multiplier: A response to Mees. *World Transport Policy and Practice* 17 (3), p. 32–44.

NEWMAN, P., KENWORTHY, J. and GLAZEBROOK, G. 2008. How to create exponential decline in car use in Australian cities. *AdoptNet Policy Forum* 08-06-E-Ad.

NEWMAN, P., KENWORTHY, J. and GLAZEBROOK, G. 2013. Peak car and the rise of global rail: Why this is happening and what it means for large and small cities. *Journal of Transportation Technologies* 3 (4), p. 272–87.

NEWMAN, P., KOSONEN, L. and KENWORTHY, J. 2015. The theory of urban fabrics. *Town Planning Reviews* (In Press).

NEWMAN, P. W. G., KENWORTHY, J. R. and LYONS, T. J. 1988. Does free-flowing traffic save energy and lower emissions in cities? *Search* 19, p. 267–72.

NEWMAN, P. and MATAN, A. 2012a. *Green Urbanism in Asia*. Singapore: World Scientific Publishing Company.

NEWMAN, P. and MATAN, A. 2012b. Human health and human mobility. *Current Opinion in Environmental Sustainability* 4 (4), p. 420–26.

NEWMAN, P. and MATAN, A. 2013. *Stemming Car Dependency in Indian Cities*. Report to AusAID. [Online] CUSP, Curtin University. November. Available from: sustainability .curtin.edu.au.

NEWMAN, P., MATAN, A. and MCINTOSH, J. 2015. Urban Transport and Sustainable Development. In: REDCLIFT, M. and SPRINGETT, D. (eds.) *Routledge International Handbook of Sustainable Development*. London: Routledge.

NEWMAN, P. and WILLS, R. 2012. King Coal Dethroned. [Online] *The Conversation*. Available from: theconversation.com/king-coal-dethroned-6977 [Accessed 5 May 2014].

NEWTON, P., NEWMAN, P., GLACKIN S. and TRUBKA, R. 2012. Greening the greyfields: Unlocking the development potential of middle suburbs in Australian cities. *World Academy of Science, Engineering, and Technology* 71, p. 138–57.

NEWTON, P. and NEWMAN, P. 2013. The geography of solar PV and a new low-carbon urban transition theory. *Sustainability* 5 (6), p. 2537–56.

NEWTON, P. and TUCKER, S. N. 2011. Pathways to decarbonizing the housing sector: A scenario analysis. *Building Research and Information* 39 (1), p. 34–50.

NEW YORK CITY DEPARTMENT OF TRANSPORTATION (DOT). 2010. *New York City Department of Transportation*. [Online] Available from: nyc.gov/html/dot/html [Accessed 23 Nov 2010].

NICOLAISEN, M. S. and DRISCOLL, P. A. 2014. Ex-post evaluations of demand forecast accuracy: A literature review. *Transport Reviews* 34 (4), p. 540–57.

NILSSON, K., NIELSEN, T. S., AALBERS, C., BELL, S., BOITIER, B., CHERY, J. P., FERTNER, C., GROSCHOWSKI, M., HAASE, D., LOIBL, W., PAULEIT, S., PINTAR, M., PIORR, A., RAVETZ, J., RISTIMÄKI, M., ROUNSEVELL, M., TOSICS, I., WESTERINK, J. and ZASADA, I. 2014. Strategies for sustainable urban development and urban-rural linkages. *European Journal of Spatial Development*, March 2014 (4), p. 1–26.

ODGERS, J. and LOW, N. 2012. Rethinking the cost of traffic congestion: Lessons from Melbourne's City Link toll roads. *Urban Policy and Research* 30 (2), p. 189–205.

ORGANISATION FOR ECONOMIC CO-OPERATION AND DEVELOPMENT (OECD). 2011. Towards Green Growth: Strategic Report. Paris: OECD.

ORSKI, C. K. 1987. "Managing" suburban traffic congestion: A strategy for suburban mobility. *Transportation Quarterly* 41 (4), p. 457–76.

PANK, P. 2012. Welcome to the age of the bike: Cyclists "must be first" as car use passes its peak. (London) *Times*, 6 Nov 2012.

PEOPLE'S DAILY. 2012. High-speed rail construction not suspended. [Online] *People's Daily*. Available from: english.peopledaily.com.cn/90778/7754100.html [Accessed 18 Nov 2014].

PERKINS, A., HAMNETT, S., PULLEN, S., ZITO, R. and TREBILCOCK, D. 2009. Transport, housing, and urban form: The life cycle energy consumption and emissions of city centre apartments compared with suburban dwellings. *Urban Policy and Research* 27 (4), p. 377–96.

PHILLIPS, T. 2008. High above Sao Paulo's choked streets, the rich cruise a new highway. [Online] *Guardian*. 20 Jun. Available from: theguardian.com/world/2008/jun/20/brazil [Accessed 22 May 2013].

POOLE, R. W., JR. 1988. Resolving gridlock in Southern California. *Transportation Quarterly* 42 (4), p. 499–527.

PRATSCH, L. W. 1986. Reducing commuter traffic congestion. *Transportation Quarterly* 40 (4), p. 591–600.

PRIESTER, R., KENWORTHY, J. and WULFHORST, G. 2013. The Diversity of Megacities Worldwide: Challenges for the Future of Mobility. In: INSTITUTE FOR MOBILITY RESEARCH (ed.) *Megacity Mobility Culture: How Cities Move On in a Diverse World*. Munich: Springer, p. 23–54.

PUENTES, R. and TOMER, A. 2009. The Road Less Travelled: An Analysis of Vehicle Miles Traveled Trends in the U.S. Metropolitan Infrastructure Initiative Series. Washington, DC: Brookings Institute.

PUNTER, J. 2003. *The Vancouver Achievement: Urban Planning and Design*. Seattle: University of Washington Press.

PUSHKAREV, B. and ZUPAN, J. 1977. *Public Transportation and Land-Use Policy*. London: Indiana Press.

QIAO, H. 2013. China's high-speed programme back on track. [Online] *International Railway Journal (IRJ)*. Available from: railjournal.com/index.php/high-speed/chinas-high-speed-programme-back-on-track.html [Accessed 19 Nov 2014].

RANDALL, T. 2015. Goldman: Here's why oil crashed—and why lower prices are here to stay. *Bloomberg Business*, [Online] 11 Feb. Available from: bloomberg.com/news /articles/2015-02-11/goldman-here-s-why-oil-crashed-and-why-lower-prices-are-here-to -stay?hootPostID=3013e18458e6aedf15ba3a704124f25e [Accessed 2 Mar 2015].

RAULAND, V. and NEWMAN, P. 2011.Decarbonizing Australian Cities: A New Model for Creating Low-Carbon, Resilient Cities. In: *Proceedings of 19th International Congress on Modeling and Simulation (MODSIM)*. Perth, AUS, Dec 12–16.

RAULAND, V. and NEWMAN, P. 2015. *Decarbonising Cities: Mainstreaming Low-Carbon Urban Development*. London: Springer.

RECSEI, T. 2005. Pipe Dreams: The Shortcomings of Ideologically Based Planning. *People and Place* 13 (2), p. 68–81.

RILEY, R. Q. 2004. *Alternative Cars in the 21st Century: New Personal Transport Paradigm*. Warrendale, PA: SAE International.

RODRIGUE, J. P. 2013. *The Geography of Transport Systems*, 3rd ed. New York: Routledge.

ROMANOS, M. C. 1978. Energy price effects on metropolitan spatial structure and form. *Environment and Planning A* 10 (1), p. 93–104.

ROWLEY, S. and PHIBBS, P. 2012. Delivering Diverse and Affordable Housing on Infill Development Sites: Final Report. Melbourne: Australian Housing and Urban Research Institute (AHURI).

ROY, A. 2014. Territories of Poverty: Urban Informality in a Rearranged South-North World. Frankfurt: German Architecture Museum.

SACHS, J. D. 2015. *The Age of Sustainable Development*. New York: Columbia University Press.

SASSEN, S. 1994. *Cities in a World Economy*, 1st ed. New York: Sage.

SCHAFER, A. and VICTOR, D. G. 2000. The future mobility of the world population. *Transportation Research Part A: Policy and Practice* 34, p. 171–205.

SCHEURER, J., NEWMAN, P. and KENWORTHY, J. 1999. Can rail pay? Light rail transit and urban redevelopment with value capture funding and joint development mechanisms. Perth, AUS: Murdoch University, ISTP.

SCHILLER, P., BRUUN, E. and KENWORTHY, J. 2010. *An Introduction to Sustainable Transportation: Policy, Planning, and Implementation*. London: Earthscan.

SCHMIT, A. 2014. Tear down these 10 freeways (and then tear down some more). [Online] *Streetsblog USA*. [Accessed 24 Apr 2014].

SCHNEIDER, K. 1979. *On the Nature of Cities: Towards Creative and Enduring Human Environments*. San Francisco: Jossey-Bass.

SCHOETTLE, B. and SIVAK, M. 2015. Potential Impact of Self-Driving Vehicles on Household Vehicle Demand and Usage. Report No. UMTRI-2015-3. University of Michigan, Transportation Research Institute. February.

SCHULMAN, H., SÖDERSTRÖM, P., RISTIMÄKI, M., SALOMAA, K., JERIMA, M., NIELMELÄ, J., KOSONEN, P. and GRANQVIST, P. 2014. Nordic Capitals: Development of the Urban Form of Helsinki and Stockholm Metropolitan Areas: Research Report. Helsinki: University of Helsinki, Department of Geosciences and Georgraphy, and SYKE Finnish Environmental Institute.

SHEEHAN, P. 2014. Achieving Sustained Change in Energy Structure. In: *Proceedings of 1st Abrupt Change in China's Energy Path: Implications for China, Australia, and the Global Climate*. Melbourne, Jun 26.

SIEGEL, C. 2007. *Removing freeways, restoring cities: From induced demand to reduced demand.* [Online] Preservation Institute. Available from: preservenet.com/freeways/FreewaysInduced Reduced.html [Accessed 4 Apr 2012].

SIMPSON, A. 2009a. Environmental Attributes of Electric Vehicles in Australia: Discussion Paper. Perth, AUS: Curtin University Sustainability Policy (CUSP) Institute.

SIMPSON, A. 2009b. The electric revolution is on track. [Online] *Business Spectator.* Available from: businessspectator.com.au/article/2009/9/1/interest-rates/electric-revolution-track [Accessed 5 May 2014].

SIVAK, M. 2015. Has Motorization in the U.S. Peaked? Part 7 Update through 2013: University of Michigan Transportation Research Institute. Report no. UMTRI-2015-10. March. Available from: www.umich.edu/~umtriswt/PDF/UMTRI-2015-10_Abstract_English.pdf [Accessed 28 Mar 2015].

SMITH, M., HARGROVES, K. and DESHA, C. 2010. *Cents and Sustainability: Securing Our Common Future by Decoupling Economic Growth from Environmental Pressures: The Natural Edge Project.* London: Earthscan.

SOUTHWORTH, F. 1995. A Technical Review of Urban Land-Use-Transportation Models as Tools for Evaluating Vehicle Travel-Reduction Strategies: National Laboratory Report 6881. Oak Ridge, TN: Center for Transportation Analysis, Energy Division.

SPITSVRIJ. 2014. *Inspiratie voor de toekomst.* [Online] Spitsvrij. Utrecht, GER. Available from: spitsvrij.nl/Upload/File/Bevindingen%20Spitsvrij.pdf [Accessed 27 Jun 2014].

STANDING ADVISORY COMMITTEE FOR TRUNK ROAD ASSESSMENT (SACTRA). 1994. Trunk Roads and the Generation of Traffic: Report. London: Government of the United Kingdom, Department of Transport.

STANLEY, J. and BARRETT, S. 2010. Moving People—Solutions for a Growing Australia: Report. Canberra/Brussels: Australasian Railway Association / Bus Industry Confederation, International Association of Public Transport (UITP).

STOPHER, P. R. and MEYBURG, A. H. 1975. *Urban Transportation Modeling and Planning.* Lexington, MA: Lexington Books.

STORPER, M. and SCOTT, A. J. 2009. Rethinking human capital, creativity and urban growth. *Journal of Urban Geography* 9, p. 147–67.

SULLIVAN, G., JOHNSON, S. A. and SODEN, D. L. 2002. Tax Increment Financing (TIF) Best Practice Study: IPED Technical Reports, Paper 20. Austin, TX: University of Texas, Institute for Policy and Economic Development.

SUSTAINABLE CITIES COLLECTIVE. 2014. *Five Reasons to Be Optimistic about Sustainable Urban Mobility.* [Online] Sustainable Cities Collective. Available from: sustainablecitiescollective .com/embarq/1016811/five-reasons-be-optimistic-about-sustainable-urban-mobility [Accessed 19 Nov 2014].

SUZUKI, H., MURAKAMI, J., HONG, Y. and TAMAYOSE, B. 2015. *Financing Transit-Oriented Development with Land Values: Adapting Land Value Capture in Developing Countries.* Washington, DC: World Bank.

TADDEO, L. 2010. The brightest 16 geniuses who give us hope: Janette Sadik-Khan, urban reengineer. [Online] *Esquire*. Available from: esquire.com/freatures/brightest-2010/janette-sadik-khan-1210 [Accessed 5 May 2014].

THE FIFTH ESTATE. 2012. Cars are so yesterday: young and old leave guzzlers behind. [Online] *Fifth Estate*. Available from: thefifthestate.com.au/business/trends/cars-are-so-yesterday-young-and-rich-leave-guzzlers-behind/33691 [Accessed 18 Nov 2014].

THOMSON, J. M. 1977. *Great Cities and Their Traffic*. Middlesex, UK: Penguin Books.

THORMARK, C. 2002. A low-energy building in a life cycle: Its embodied energy, energy need for operation, and recycling potential. *Built Enviroment* 37, p. 429–35.

TRANSPORT AND ENVIRONMENT STUDIES (TEST). 1992. Trip Degeneration: A Literature Review: Report 99. London: TEST.

TRANSPORT SCOTLAND. 2012. *Aberdeen Western Peripheral Route / Balmedie to Tipperty*. [Online] Transport Scotland. Available from: apwr.co.uk/ [Accessed 5 Apr 2012].

TROY, P. 2004. *Saving Our Cities with Suburbs*. [Online] Griffith University. Available from: griffithreview.com/articles/saving-our-cities-with-suburbs/ [Accessed 23 Apr 2014].

TROY, P., HALLOWAY, D., PULLEN, S. and BUNKER, R. 2003. Embodied and operational energy consumption in the city. *Urban Policy and Research* 21 (1), p. 9–44.

TRUBKA, R. 2012. Agglomeration Economics in Australian Cities: PhD Dissertation. Curtin University, CUSP Institute: Perth, AUS.

TRUBKA, R., NEWMAN, P. and BILSBOROUGH, D. 2008. Assessing the Costs of Alternative Development Paths in Australian Cities: Report. Perth, AUS: CUSP Institute and Parsons Brinckerhoff Australia (PB).

TRUBKA, R., NEWMAN, P. and BILSBOROUGH, D. 2010a. Costs of urban sprawl (1): Infrastructure and transport. *Environment Design Guide* 83, p. 1–6.

TRUBKA, R., NEWMAN, P. and BILSBOROUGH, D. 2010b. Costs of urban sprawl (2): Greenhouse gases. *Environment Design Guide* 84, p. 1–16.

TRUBKA, R., NEWMAN, P. and BILSBOROUGH, D. 2010c. Costs of urban sprawl (3): Physical activity links to healthcare costs and productivity. *Environment Design Guide* 85, p. 1–13.

UMTRI. 2014. Sustainable Worldwide Transportation. [Online] University of Michigan Transport Research Institute. 13 Nov 2014. Available from: umich.edu/~umtriswt [Accessed 28 Feb 15].

UN ENVIRONMENT PROGRAMME (UNEP). 2011. *Decoupling Natural Resource Use and Environmental Impacts from Economic Growth*. Geneva: UNEP.

UNGER, J., CHAN, A. and CHUNG, H. 2014. Deliberative democracy at China's grassroots: Case studies of a hidden phenomenon. *Politics and Society* 42 (4), p. 513–35.

US ENERGY INFORMATION ADMINISTRATION (EIA). 2014. *County Analysis Brief Overview: India*. [Online] EIA. Available from: eia.gov/countries/country-data.cfm?fips=INandtrk=m#coal [Accessed 6 Oct 2014].

US ENVIRONMENTAL PROTECTION AGENCY (USEPA). 2013. *Infrastructure Financing Options for Transit-Orientated Development*. Washington, DC: USEPA.

US GOVERNMENT ACCOUNTABILITY OFFICE (US GAO). 2010. Public Transportation—Federal Role in Value Capture Strategies: Report. Washington, DC: US GAO.

URBAN LAND INSTITUTE. 2014. *Emerging Trends in Real Estate 2014*. Canada Edition. [Online]

Urban Land Institute. Available from: pwc.com/en_CA/ca/real-estate/publications/pwc-emerging-trends-in-real-estate-2014-en.pdf [Accessed 28 Feb 2015].

URRY, J. 2004. The system of automobility. *Theory, Culture, and Society* 21 (4/5), p. 25–39.

VAN WEE, B., RIETVELD, P. and MEURS, H. 2006. Is average daily travel-time expenditure constant? In search of explanations for an increase in average travel time. *Journal of Transport Geography* 14, p. 109–22.

VON WEIZSACKER, E., HARGROVES, K., SMITH, M., DESHA, C. and STASINOPOULOUS, P. 2009. *Factor Five*. London: Earthscan.

VUCHIC, V. R. 2005. *Urban Transit: Operations, Planning, and Economics*. Hoboken, NJ: John Wiley & Sons.

WAN, G. and KAHN, M. 2012. Green Urbanization in Asia. In: ADB (ed.) *Key Indicators for Asia and the Pacific 2012*. Mandaluyong City, PHI: Asian Development Bank (ADB).

WATT, K. E. F. and AYRES, C. 1974. Urban Land-Use Patterns and Transportation Energy Cost. Paper presented at the 140th Annual Meeting of the American Association for the Advancement of Science (AAAS). San Francisco, Feb 25.

WEBSTER, F. V., BLY, P. H. and PAULLEY, N. J. (eds.) 1988. Urban Land Use and Transport Interaction, Policies, and Models: Report. Avebury, UK: International Study Group on Land-Use /Transport Interaction.

WEINER, E. 1999. *Urban Transportation Planning in the United States: An Historical Overview*. Westport, CT: Praeger Publishers.

WENGER, J., OPIOLA, J. and IOANNIDIS, T. 2008. *The Intelligent Highway: A Smart Idea?* [Online] PwC Strategy& Inc. Available from: strategy-business.com/article/li00064?pg=all [Accessed 19 Nov 2014].

WENT, A., JAMES, W. and NEWMAN, P. 2008. Renewable Transport: Discussion Paper. Perth, AUS: Curtin University Sustainability Policy (CUSP) Institute.

WHITELEGG, J. 2011. Pay As You Go: Managing Traffic Impacts in a World-Class City: Report. Lancaster, UK: Eco-Logica Ltd.

WHITELEGG, J. 2012a. Editorial. *World Transport Policy and Practice* 18 (1).

WHITELEGG, J. 2012b. Editorial. *World Transport Policy and Practice* 18 (2).

WILLIAMS, R. 1985. *The Country and the City*. London: Hogarth Press.

WILSON, E. O. 1984. *Biophilia*. Cambridge, MA: Harvard University Press.

WILSON, P. 1976. *Public Housing for Australia*, UQ Press: Brisbane, AUS.

WILSON, A. and BOEHLAND, J. 2005. Small is beautiful—US house size, resource use, and the environment. *Journal of Industrial Ecology* 9 (1–2), p. 277–87.

WOODCOCK, I., DOVEY, K., WOLLAN, S. and ROBERTSON, I. 2011. Speculation and resistance: Constraints on compact city policy implementation in Melbourne. *Urban Policy and Research* 29 (4), p. 343–62.

WORLD BANK. 2014. *World Development Indicators: India*. [Online] World Bank. Available from: databank.worldbank.org/data/views/reports/tableview.aspx [Accessed 6 Oct 2014].

WORLD RESOURCES INSTITUTE (WRI). 2009. *Earth Trends—Environmental Information Portal: Database*. Washington, DC: WRI.

ZAHAVI, Y. and TALVITIE, A. 1980. Regularities in travel time and money expenditures. *Transportation Research Record* 750, p. 13–19.

ZEIBOTS, M. 2007. Space, Time, Economics, and Asphalt: PhD Dissertation. Sydney: University of Technology.

ZHAO, P., CHAPMAN, R., RANDAL, E. and HOWDEN-CHAPMAN, P. 2013. Understanding resilient urban futures: A systemic modeling approach. *Sustainability* 5, p. 3202–23.

ZHAO, J., CHEN, T., BLOCK-SCHACHTER, D. and WANG, S. 2014. Superficial Fairness of Beijing's Vehicle License Lottery Policy. Paper presented at the 93rd Annual Meeting of the Transportation Research Board, Washington, DC. Jan 12–16. [Online] Available from: trb.org/annualmeeting2014/annualmeeting2014.aspx.

ZHAO, Z. and LARSON, K. 2011. Special assessments as a value capture strategy for public transit finance. *Public Works Management Policy* 16 (4), p. 320–40.

ZHAO, Z., ZHAO, J. and SHEN, Q. 2013. Has Shanghai's transportation demand passed its peak growth period? *Transportation Research Record* 2394, p. 85–92.

ZHOU, W. 2012. In search of deliberative democracy in China. *Journal of Public Deliberation* 8 (1), Article 8. [Online] Available from: publicdeliberation.net/jpd/vol8/iss1/art8.

Index